Financial Planning Handbook for Physicians and Advisors

An Integrated Approach

David E. Marcinko, Editor

Chief Executive Officer and Provost
Institute of Medical Business Advisors, Inc.

JONES AND BARTLETT PUBLISHERS

Sudbury, Massachusetts

BOSTON   TORONTO   LONDON   SINGAPORE

World Headquarters

Jones and Bartlett Publishers	Jones and Bartlett Publishers	Jones and Bartlett Publishers
40 Tall Pine Drive	Canada	International
Sudbury, MA 01776	2406 Nikanna Road	Barb House, Barb Mews
978-443-5000	Mississauga, ON L5C 2W6	London W6 7PA
info@jbpub.com	CANADA	UK
www.jbpub.com		

Library of Congress Cataloging-in-Publication Data

Financial planning handbook for physicians and advisors / [edited by] David E. Marcinko.
    p. cm.
Includes bibliographical references and index.
  ISBN 0-7637-4579-0 (pbk.)
  1. Physicians--Finance, Personal--Handbooks, manuals, etc. I. Marcinko, David E. (David Edward)
  R728.5.F569 2004
  332.024'0088'61--dc22

                  2003026942

Production Credits
Executive Editor: Jack Bruggeman
Production Manager: Amy Rose
Editorial Assistant: Kaylah McNeil
Production Assistant: Tracey Chapman
Marketing Manager: Ed McKenna
Manufacturing Buyer: Therese Bräuer
Cover Design: Anne Spencer
Composition and Art: Bookwrights
Printing and Binding: Malloy, Inc.
Cover Printing: Malloy, Inc.

Printed in the United States of America
08 07 06 05 04   10 9 8 7 6 5 4 3 2 1

Table of Contents

DAVID EDWARD MARCINKO, HOPE RACHEL HETICO,
and RACHEL PENTIN-MAKI

Chapter 5   Medical Office Tax Reduction Strategies

THOMAS P. MCGUINNESS

David Edward Marcinko is a healthcare economist, and former private practitioner. He has edited three practice management textbooks and four personal financial planning books for physicians and healthcare professionals. His clinical publications are archived in the Library of Congress and the Library of Medicine at the National Institutes of Health. His economic thought leadership essays have been referenced by *Investment Advisor Magazine*, Medical Group Management Association (MGMA), American College of Medical Practice Executives (ACMPE), American College of Physician Executives (ACPE), JAMA.ama-assn.org, Healthcare Management Associates (HMA), CFP© Biz *(Journal of Financial Planning)*, Financial Planner's Library Online, the Business of Medical Practice, and others. A favorite on the lecture circuit, Dr. Marcinko speaks frequently to medical societies and financial institutions throughout the country.

Professor Marcinko received his undergraduate degree from Loyola College in Baltimore, his business degree from the Keller Graduate School of Management in Chicago, and his financial planning diploma from Oglethorpe University in Atlanta. He is a licensee of the Certified Financial Planner© Board of Standards in Denver, and holds the Certified Medical Planner© designation.

Professor Marcinko has earned a Series #7 (general securities), Series #63 (uniform securities state law), and Series #65 (investment advisory) license from the National Association of Securities Dealers (NASD), and a life, health, disability, variable annuity, and property–casualty license from the State of Georgia. He is also a board certified surgical fellow and a visiting scholar in healthcare economics at the Keller Graduate School of Management, and instructor in finance for the University of Phoenix, Graduate School of Business and Management.

Dr. Marcinko was the co-founder of an ambulatory surgery center that was sold to a publicly traded company and has been a Certified Professional in Healthcare Quality (CPHQ), an American Board of Quality Assurance and Utilization Review Physician (ABQAURP), a medical staff vice president of a general hospital, an assistant residency director, the founder of a computer-based testing firm for doctors, and the president of a regional physician practice management corporation in the midwest.

Currently, Dr. Marcinko is Chief Executive Officer of the Institute of Medical Business Advisors, Inc., a national resource center and referral alliance providing financial stability and managerial peace-of-mind to struggling physician clients.

Institute of Medical Business Advisors, Inc.
Peachtree Plantation - West
Suite # 5901 Wilbanks Drive
Norcross, GA 30092-1141
770-448-0769 (voice)
775-361-8831 (fax)
www.MedicalBusinessAdvisors.com
info@MedicalBusinessAdvisors.com
MarcinkoAdvisors@msn.com

Dedication

It is indeed a privilege to edit *Financial Planning Handbook for Physicians and Advisors: An Integrated Approach*. One of the most rewarding aspects of my career has been the personal and professional growth acquired from interacting with financial professionals of all designations, and medical professionals of all disciplines. I find that the mutual sharing and exchanging of ideas stimulates my mind and fosters personal advancement at many levels.

Creating *Financial Planning Handbook for Physicians and Advisors: An Integrated Approach* for physicians and advisors was a significant effort that involved all the members of our firm. Over the past year, we interfaced with outside private and public companies to discuss the series contents. Although impossible to list every person or company that played a role in its production, we wish to thank several people for their extraordinary assistance: Conrad S. Ciccotello, JD, PhD MBA, Associate Professor, Graduate Program in Personal Financial Planning, J. Mack Robinson School of Business, and the Academy of Financial Services; Peter R. Kongstvedt, MD, Partner-Health and Managed Care Consulting Division of Cap Gemini Ernst & Young, LLC; Robert J. Cimasi, ASA, CBA, CMP, AVA, FCBI, and Timothy Alexander, MLS of Health Capital Consultants, LLC; Dave Pickhardt, Vice President for Managed Healthcare at Aventis Pharmaceuticals,i Richard D. Helppie, Founder and CEO of the Superior Consultant Corporation (NASD-SUPC); Ahmad Hashem, MD, PhD, Global Healthcare Industry Manager, Microsoft Corporation; Daniel McGilvery, President of The Business Planning Institute; Marvin W. Tuttle, CAE, *Journal of Financial Planning*; and Jack Bruggeman, Executive Editor, and Tracey Chapman, Production Assistant, Jones and Bartlett Publishers.

Of course, this book would not have been possible without the support of my wife, Hope, and daughter, Mackenzie, whose love and support gave me the encouragement to pursue it to completion.

Above all, this book is dedicated to our contributing authors who crashed the development life cycle in order to produce time-sensitive material in an expedient manner. The knowledge I have gained, and the satisfaction I have enjoyed from working with them, is immeasurable.

> *Of making many books there is no end,*
> *and much study is a weariness of the flesh ...*
> Ecclesiastes 12-12

1. Aventis Pharmaceuticals is the underwriter of the Managed Care Digest Series™ which was developed and produced by Forte Information Resources, with data provided by the SMG Marketing Group, Inc. and the Medical Group Management Association (MGMA).

Financial Planning Handbook for Physicians and Advisors: An Integrated Approach is essentially a "how-to" book on finance and related economic topics for healthcare providers. Fortunately for patients, medicine requires a high degree of professional training, both in terms of science and technology. Unfortunately for providers, medical practice affords little time for acquiring comprehensive financial planning skills.

This is an unusual textbook on financial planning for two reasons. First, this book is a detailed guide for physicians seeking the road to success and profit in the complex and confusing healthcare economic arena. Rarely does one see such clarity of presentation— without the usual jargon that often discourages those trying to learn a foreign and for-bidding subject such as finance. Second, the subject matter is focused for medical providers who work in one of the fastest growing industries in the United States.

The contributing authors hope that by integrating financial planning disciplines, they will help foster affordable and profitable healthcare for our nation, which is so entre-preneurial, yet aging.

In my 35 years on Wall Street, I have observed that physicians are particularly disad-vantaged when it comes to anything regarding finance. Most medical professionals are too busy practicing their specialty and keeping up with healthcare technology and prac-tice trends, that planning for their financial future is often forgotten. Financial planning and sound investment practices for physicians require a solid background in how med-ical corporations work in the "real world," and an awareness of how they function within the economy. These economic essentials are vital to understanding business, so principles like budgeting, risk management, and rudimentary accounting are also pre-sented in this book. Furthermore, keeping up with state and federal insurance legisla-tion places a continual burden on the individual practitioner, group, or medical network seeking to stay abreast of current financial developments.

Most important, this book focuses on integrated financial planning and how the physician can increase his or her personal knowledge and skills. The book begins with a chapter on behavioral finance, life planning, and the psychological meaning of money. Next, the book moves on to microeconomic concepts ranging from time value of money calculations, cash flow budgeting, wedding planning, autos, and home mortgages to credit card principles, personal financial ratio analysis, bankruptcy, and debt. Sophisticated financial topics are then presented in detail including debt and equity investment vehicles, derivatives, mutual funds and hedge funds, portfolio management, and risk analysis, as well as the new tax laws of 2001 and 2003. There are also chapters on personal and corporate tax reduction strategies, and estate and retirement planning for doctors. The book rightly concludes with guidance on selecting financial advisors.

It seems to me that all physicians and their advisors would be well served by reading this book with its step-by-step process for financial success in a complicated business full of pitfalls and misinformation. Most useful will be the extremely detailed table of contents that allows the user to quickly pinpoint an area of interest and to get started solving a problem.

Simply put, my recommendation is to read *Financial Planning Handbook for Physicians and Advisors: An Integrated Approach,* and reap.

Frank A. Cappiello
President, McCullough, Andrews & Cappiello, Inc.
10751 Falls Road, Suite 250
Lutherville, MD 21093
Distinguished Visiting Professor of Finance
Loyola College, Maryland

Physicians have economic concerns that are different from most people's.

- First, they enter the workforce about a decade later than their non-medical contemporaries, leaving fewer productive years and beginning with enormous medical school debt levels.
- Second, they tend to marry and have children later in life, often postponing saving for their offspring's educational funding and their own retirement.
- Third, family members often erroneously think of them as affluent and seek financial assistance from them.
- Fourth, managed care has reduced remuneration just as governmental scrutiny and the Health Insurance Portability and Accountability Act (HIPAA) have burdened practices with costly IT and privacy regulations.
- Fifth, physicians lack managerial and financial expertise, especially after changes seen in the Economic Growth and Tax Relief Reconciliation Act (EGTRRA) of 2001 and the Jobs and Growth Tax Relief Reconciliation Act (JGTRRA) of 2003.

Therefore, informed advice from a medically focused Certified Financial Planner© and/or contemporaneous Certified Medical Planner© is vital. Construction of a comprehensive financial plan that acknowledges the impact of managed care is now almost an essential requirement for success.

Traditionally, a well-conceived financial plan consisted of tax reduction planning, various insurance matters, investing and portfolio management, and retirement and estate planning. For modern physicians, however, these disciplines and many more must be incorporated into the mix in a managerially and psychologically sound manner not counterproductive to individual components of the plan. As a sobering caveat, the integration of these protean disciplines is no longer an academic luxury, but a pragmatic survival imperative long recognized by iMBA, as the following two examples illustrate.

Recall the sad tale of Dr. Debasis Kanjilal, the pediatrician from New York who put more than $500,000 into the dot.com company, InfoSpace, upon the advice of Merrill Lynch's star analyst Henry Blodget. Is it any wonder that when the company crashed, the analyst was sued, banned for life from the securities industry, and Merrill settled out of court? Would passage of Senate bill HR 1000, also known as the Pension Security Act (PSA), which created the category of Fiduciary Advisor for qualified participants such as those with 401(k) plans, have prevented this mischief by adding stockbrokers to ERISA's (Employee Retirement Income Security Act) list of prudent experts?

Reflect a moment on medical colleagues willing to securitize their practices a few years ago and cash out to Wall Street servitude for riches not rightly deserved. Where are firms such as MedPartners, Phycor, FPA, Coastal Healthcare, and a host of others now? A recent survey of the Cain Brothers Physician Practice Management Corporation Index of publicly traded PPMCs revealed a market capital loss of more than 95% since inception. Would educated physician-executives with business, law, or economic degrees and certifications have been able to avoid this calamity?

Moreover, to restore physician and all investor confidence in the equity markets, New York Attorney General Elliot Spitzer is seeking Securities Exchange Commission (SEC) reform through the dormant Martin Act of 1921, while simultaneously battling corporate corruption on Wall Street through the Sarbanes-Oxley Act of 2002.

Of course, financial planning is always challenging because chaos is the constant element of life. It is even more so for physicians, who face the reality that medical care is a commodity in the United States. Even Dr. C. Everett Koop opined in 2002 that, although Americans have no constitutional right to health care, the perception of one is so strong that the country is likely to have a socialized system sometime in the near future. With our national agenda dominated by terrorism, the threat of biological and chemical warfare, bioengineering, and the ethical concerns of human cloning, it is unlikely that significant healthcare reform beneficial to physicians will take place anytime soon. In fact, many predict that over the next few years reimbursement rates set by the Center for Medicare Services (CMS) could further erode by 12–18%.

Individual provider and personal circumstances also change since the domestic healthcare milieu is in constant flux. Comprehensive financial planning is truly a journey and not a destiny. Progress toward personal and practice goals is the objective, not some composite index, annualized rate of return, or stock price.

Therefore, for physicians to survive financially in the new order, economic and financial competency is required. The requisite material has been codified for them and their advisors, in *Financial Planning Handbook for Physicians and Advisors: An Integrated Approach.*

David Edward Marcinko
Editor

Introduction for Condensed Reading and Review

Financial Planning Handbook for Physicians and Advisors: An Integrated Approach is written by, and for, doctors and those financial advisors with intimate knowledge of the healthcare financial complex. We use nontechnical jargon, without documenting every statement with a citation from the literature. This allows a large amount of information to be condensed into this single practical volume. It also allows the reader to comprehend an important concept in a single reading session, with a deliberate effort to include current information. The interested reader is then able to research selected topics. In this way, we have reduced the overlap of material, while reviewing important concepts for increased understanding.

The textbook is divided into 10 logically progressive yet stand-alone chapters by 15 contributors and integrated by our editorial staff.

Chapter 1 commences with the controversial topic of behavioral finance and life planning, the newest purported psychological machination in the financial planning armamentarium. Chapter 2 gives an overview of fundamental micro-economic and money management principals, as well as personal financial benchmarks for all medical professionals to consider. Chapter 3 reviews insurance strategies for doctors to protect their possessions and medical practices. Chapters 4 and 5 are conjoined: the personal tax reduction strategies outlined in chapter 4, are seamlessly carried over into the office practice environment in chapter 5. Similarly, the risks and benefits of basic and complex investment vehicles are described in Chapter 6. Chapter 7 integrates them into an strategic example of a psrofessionally managed portfolio of investments, using modern portfolio theory (MPT), along with the Capital Asset Pricing Model (CAPM) and the Arbitrage Pricing Theory (APT) of asset allocation. Chapter 8 initiates retirement planning and post-professional lifestyle, while chapter 9 represents the end of the financial planning continuum as estate planning is discussed. Chapter 10 naturally concludes the book with a discussion on choosing the financial consultant that represents the best fit for both the practice environment and physician personality.

In conclusion, as you read, study, and reflect on the topics of this challenging textbook, remember the guiding philosophy of Eric Hoffer: "In a time of drastic change; it is the learners who will inherit the future. The learned find themselves ill equipped to live in a world that no longer exits."

Hope Rachel Hetico
Rachel Pentin-Maki
Author's Editors

Contributing Authors

Charles Lynn Bucek, Jr., CPA, CVA
Null-Lairson, PC
11 Greenway Plaza
Suite # 1515
Houston, Texas 77046
713-621-1515 (voice)
713-621-1570 (fax)

Charles L. Bucek is a senior associate for Null-Lairson, PC, a certified public accounting firm in Houston. He is a member of the American Institute of Certified Public Accountants, the Texas Society of Certified Public Accountants, and the Houston Chapter of the Texas Society of Certified Public Accountants. Mr. Bucek is also a member of the National Association of Certified Valuation Analysts.

Gary A. Cook, MSFS, CFP©, CLU, ChFC, RHU, LUTCF, CMP©
Content Development Manager
COSS Development Corp.
13420 Reese Blvd, West
Huntersville, NC 28078
704-948-4103 (voice)
704-948-4612 (fax)

Gary A. Cook received a degree in mathematics from the Indiana University of Pennsylvania and his Master of Science degree in financial services from the American College in Bryn Mawr, Pennsylvania. As an accredited Estate Planner, he has taught courses in that discipline, as well as courses in insurance, business, and finance planning. Mr. Cook is past president of the Chester County Estate Planning Council. He is a professional author, sought after public speaker, and television guest for the Insurance Broadcast System, Inc. He is also a member of the Society of Financial Service Professionals, the Financial Planning Association, and the Association for Advanced Life Underwriting. Mr. Cook was formerly assistant Vice President, advanced market support, for AIG Life Insurance Companies (USA). At present, Mr. Cook is Content Manager for COSS Development Corporation.

Jeffrey S. Coons, Ph.D., CFA©
Manning & Napier Advisors, Inc.
1100 Chase Square
Rochester, New York 14604
585-325-6880 (voice)
585-325-9085 (fax)
jcoons@manning-napier.com
Dr. Jeffrey S. Coons is the Co-Director of Research at Manning & Napier Advisors, Inc., a Rochester, New York based investment advisory firm. He has primary responsibilities focusing on the measurement and management of portfolio risk and return relative to client objectives. This includes providing analysis across every aspect of the investment process from objectives setting and asset allocation to on-going monitoring of portfolio risk and return. Also, Dr. Coons is a member of the Investment Policy Group, which establishes and monitors secular investment trends, macroeconomic overviews, and the investment disciplines of the firm. Dr. Coons holds a doctoral degree in economics from Temple University, graduated with distinction from the University of Rochester with a B.A. in Economics, holds the designation of Chartered Financial Analyst, and is one of the employee-owners of Manning & Napier.

Christopher J. Cummings, CFA© , CFP©
Manning & Napier Advisors, Inc.
1100 Chase Square
Rochester, New York 14604
585-325-6880 (voice)
585-325-9085 (fax)
ccummings@manning-napier.com
Christopher J. Cummings is currently the Managing Director of Investment Risk at Manning & Napier, Rochester, New York based investment advisory firm. In this capacity, Mr. Cummings provides analysis across every aspect of the investment process from objectives setting and asset allocation to concurrent monitoring of portfolio risk and return. He received his undergraduate degree in accounting from the State University of New York at Geneseo. Mr. Cummings holds the Chartered Financial Analyst and Certified Financial Planner designations and is one of the employee-owners of Manning & Napier.

Robert J. Greenberg, CMP© , CFP©
Financial Network Investment Corporation
575 Anton Blvd. #300
Costa Mesa, CA 92626
714-432-6327 (voice)
714-432-6341 (fax)

rgreenberg@smarterdecisions.com

Robert J. Greenberg, CFP© has been widely quoted in national publications, such as *Financial Planning Magazine, Registered Representative,* and *Ticker,* and is listed in the *Who's Who Registry of Business Leaders* and *Who's Who in Finance and Industry.* He is active in healthcare issues as Chairman of the Board of Directors of the American Heart Association's Orange County Division and was past Vice President of the International Association of Financial Planners in Los Angeles. Mr. Greenberg is a Registered Principal for Financial Network Investment Corporation (FNIC), Member NASD/SIPC. FNIC is a registered investment advisory and brokerage firm headquartered in Torrance, CA.

Hope Rachel Hetico, RN, MHA

Institute of Medical Business Advisors, Inc.
Suite # 5901, Wilbanks Drive
Norcross, Georgia 30092
770-448-0769 (voice)
775-361-8831 (fax)
www.MedicalBusinessAdvisors.com

Hope Rachel Hetico received her nursing degree from Valpariso University and Master's Degree in Healthcare Administration from the College of St. Francis in Joliette, Illinois. She is author's editor of seven major textbooks and a nationally known expert in reimbursement, case management, utilization review, NACQA, HEDIS, and JCAHO rules and regulations. She is an instructor in healthcare administration at the University of Phoenix, Graduate School of Management, and a Certified Medical Planner© candidate. Prior to joining the Institute of Medical Business Advisors as President, she was a financial advisor, licensed insurance agent, and Certified Professional in Healthcare Quality (CPHQ).

Lawrence E. Howes, MBA, CMP©, CFP©

Sharkey, Howes and Javer, Inc.
720 S. Colorado Blvd.
Suite # 600 - South Tower
Denver, CO 80246-1919
303-639-5100 (voice)
303-759-2335 (fax)
larry@shwj.com

Lawrence E. Howes, a principal in Sharkey, Howes and Javer, Inc., in Denver, Colorado, received his undergraduate degree in management and an MBA from Regis University. He has served on the Institute of Certified Financial Planners National Committee on Communication, Government Affairs, and Education and drafted the legislative application for the first Investment Advisory Law in the State of Colorado. Currently, he is on the State Department of Treasury Investment

Advisory Committee and the Securities Commissioner's legislative subcommittee on financial planning and investment advisory regulation, for the same state. Mr. Howes writes for the *Journal of Financial Planning, Financial Advisory Practice*, and *Financial Planning Magazine*, among other consumer publications. He is a practice management consultant to investment advisory and legal firms across the United States and program leader for the Colorado and New Mexico Bar Associations.

Joel B. Javer, CLU, CMP©, CFP©
Sharkey, Howes, and Javer, Inc.
720 S. Colorado Blvd.
Suite #600 - South Tower
Denver, CO 80246-1919
303-639-5100 (v)
303-759-2335 (f)
joel@shwj.com
Joel B. Javer earned his undergraduate degree in industrial engineering from the University of Oklahoma and served as President and Chairman of the International Association for Financial Planning, Rocky Mountain chapter. He also served on the Charles Schwab Institutional Advisory Board and has been an expert witness for litigation support in areas of investment suitability, securities, malpractice, qualified plan, and small business valuations. He teaches the estate planning certification course at Metropolitan State College of Denver, and investment planning for the American Association of Retired Persons at the Colorado State University. He is also the weekly show host of It's Only Money for radio 1280 RALPH. Mr. Javer is a principal in the firm of Sharkey, Howes, and Javer, Inc.

Alexander M. Kimura, MBA, CMP©, CFP©
Financial Network Investment Corporation
1025 W. 190th Street
Suite # 120
Gardena, CA 90248
800-998-3642 (voice)
310-217-9274 (fax)
akimura@smarterdecisions.com
Alexander M. Kimura graduated with honors from Harvard University. He received an MBA from the Anderson School of Management at University of California at Los Angeles (UCLA), and began his Wall Street career at Morgan Stanley, one of the nation's pre-eminent investment banking firms. He is currently an adjunct faculty member at UCLA, teaching an extension course on Pensions and Other Retirement Benefit Plans. Mr. Kimura is a Senior Financial Advisor for the Financial Network Investment Corporation.

Thomas P. McGuinness, CPA, CVA
Null-Lairson, PC
11 Greenway Plaza
Suite # 1515
Houston, Texas 77046
713-621-1515 (voice)
713-621-1570 (fax)
ThomasMc@msn.com
Thomas P. McGuinness is a principal with Null-Lairson, PC, a certified public accounting firm in Houston. Earlier in his career, he was the emerging business services supervisor for Coopers & Lybrand and a senior accountant for Weinstein Spira & Company. Specializing in assisting medical professionals, Mr. McGuinness has served as a member of the Advisory Panel of the American Academy of Family Physicians, the American Academy of Family Practice, and the Medical Group Management Association. Mr. McGuinness is the current President of the National CPA Health Advisory Association. He is a nationally known author, frequent speaker at various healthcare seminars, and a Certified Valuation Analyst.

Daniel B. Moisand, CFP©
Spraker Fitzgerald Tamayo & Moisand, LLC
601 S Lake Destiny Road
Suite 165
Maitland, FL 32751
407-869-6228 (voice)
407-869-6558 (fax)
advisors@sprakerfitzgerald.com
www.SprakerFitzgerald.com
Daniel B. Moisand, Past Pesident and Chairman of the Central Florida Society of the Institute of Certified Financial Planners, served on the Institute's National Practice Standards Task Force. He has written for the *Wall Street Journal, Business Week, Forbes, Financial Planning Magazine, Smart Money, Bloomberg Personal Finance,* and TheStreet.com. Mr. Moisand teaches investment and business ethics courses at the Florida Institute of Technology and is a member of the CFP™ Board of Practice Standards. After founding the Optimum Financial Group, he joined Spraker-Fitzgerald, an independent Registered Investment Advisory firm that provides fee-only financial planning services to business owners, physicians, and executives. He also works with the disabled community, serving as Chairman of the Board for the Easter Seal Society of East Central Florida. Mr. Moisand is a member of the Board of Directors for the Brevard County Estate Planning Council.

Richard P. Moran, CMP©, CFP©
Financial Network Investment Corporation
1025 West 190th Street

Suite # 120
Gardena, CA 90248
800-998-3642 (voice)
310-217-9274 (fax)
RPMoran@SmarterDecisions.com
Richard P. Moran is a graduate of Purdue University with a degree in Economics.
Mr. Moran was named one of the 250 Best Financial Advisors in the country by the
editors of *Worth Magazine* in each of the past five years. He served on the CFP©
Board of Standards' Board of Practice Standards that developed mandatory
nationwide practice standards for the 36,000 CFP© licensees. Previously, Mr.
Moran was elected four times to the National Board of the International
Association for Financial Planning before it formed the Financial Planning
Association. Mr. Moran has been a member of the *Los Angeles Times* Investment
Strategies Conferences and is a founding member of Financial Network Investment
Corporation. He has held technical and managerial positions at three Fortune
500 companies.

Rachel Pentin-Maki, RN, MHA
Institute of Medical Business Advisors, Inc.
Peachtree Plantation – West
Suite # 5901 Wilbanks Drive
Norcross, Georgia 30092-1141
770-448-0769 (voicemail)
775-361-8831 (fax)
www.MedicalBusinessAdvisors.com
Rachel Pentin-Maki received her nursing degree from the Community College of
Springfield, Ohio, and her Master's Degree in Healthcare Administration from
Lewis University in Evanston, Illinois. She has helped edit several medical and
business textbooks and now is a nationally known expert in business staffing and
human resource management. Prior to joining the Institute of Medical Business
Advisors as Chief Operating Officer, she was the administrator and director of
human resources at the Finnish Retirement Hospital, Lantana, Florida. Currently,
she is on the Board of Directors at Finlandia University (Suomi College), in
Hancock, Michigan, and leads *i*MBA's European initiative in Helsinki.

Eugene Schmuckler, PhD, MBA, CTS
Consulting Psychologist
AVS Consulting, LLC
4015 S. Cobb Drive
Suite # 265
Smyrna, Georgia 30080
770-431-6858 (voicemail)
www.MedicalBusinessAdvisors.com

info@MedicalBusinessAdvisors.com
A licensed psychologist, Dr. Eugene Schmuckler was Coordinator of Behavioral Science at the Georgia Public Safety Training Center. He is on the board of directors of the Association of Traumatic Stress Specialists and is a certified trauma specialist. Dr. Schmuckler is an international speaker and author, with publications translated into Dutch and Russian. He is Director of Behavioral Finance for the Institute of Medical Business Advisors, Inc.

Dr. Kenneth Shubin-Stein, CFA©
Spencer Capital Management, LLC
10 East 53rd Street, 22nd Floor
New York, NY 1002
212-287-1569 (voicemail)
212-504-8172 (fax)
kss@spencercapital.com
Prior to joining Spencer Capital Management, Ken Shubin-Stein was a financial analyst at Promethean Capital Management in Manhattan and co-founder of Compo Asset Management, LLC, a United States based equity value investment partnership. Previously, he was a medical technology analyst for the Abernathy Group in New York, an investment management firm specializing in the medical and technology sectors. A graduate of the Albert Einstein College of Medicine, Dr. Shubin-Stein completed his surgical internship at the Mount Sinai Medical Center in New York. His undergraduate degree in dual concentrations is from Columbia College. He is a Chartered Financial Analyst©.

Richard B. Wagner, JD, CFP©
WorthLiving, LLC
240 St. Paul Street
Suite # 300
Denver, CO 80206
303-329-8309 (voice)
303-329-9429 (fax)
info@worthliving.com
www.WorthLiving.com
Richard B. Wagner received his undergraduate degree from the College of Wooster and his juris doctorate degree from the Lewis and Clark Law School. He served in Oregon's city government, was a Past President of the Institute of Certified Financial Planners, and is co-founder of The Nazrudin Project, a support group devoted to the spiritual dimensions of personal finance. He has also authored numerous articles, resolutions, and papers in the *Journal of Financial Planning*, the *Journal of Retirement Planning*, and others. Several years ago he wrote the book, *Prometheus' Children: Confronting Money Forces*. He is co-founder of WorthLiving, LLC, Denver, Colorado.

Disclaimer

The information presented in this handbook is not intended to constitute accounting, investing, insurance, legal, retirement, or financial planning advice. Prior to engaging in the type of activity described, you should receive independent counsel from a qualified professional. Examples are generally descriptive but do not purport to be accurate in every regard. The financial planning and healthcare industry is evolving rapidly, and all information should be considered time sensitive.

Chapter 1

Bridging Financial Planning and Human Psychology

Life Planning, Behavioral Economics, Trading Addiction, and the Art of Money

David Edward Marcinko
Eugene Schmuckler
Kenneth H. Shubin-Stein
Richard B. Wagner

There is another way of living with money, a way of both acknowledging money's useful roles, and also finding a way to connect with our most profound aspirations around money, our deepest ideals, our most difficult emotions, our darkest places, as well as our joys, putting it all together and understanding what all of our humanness has to do with our relationship to money.

Copyright George D. Kinder, CFP, Kinder Institute of Life Planning

In any modern text on financial planning, a chapter on behavioral finance or money psychology is typically placed at the end of the book, almost as an afterthought, if it is included at all. Moreover, the chapter is rarely written by an economist or reviewed by a psychologist, psychiatrist, or physician. It is most often written by laymen without original scientific research and included by fiat in guise of the popular sales rubric known as *life planning*. This current marketing theory *de rigueur*, also known as the *next big sales thing*, is akin to the variable annuity and limited partnership initiatives promoted by product mavens decades ago. However, we have elected to prominently place this topic at its rightful place as the premier chapter of our book.

We have placed this chapter first because the concept of life planning has emerged as a priority within the profession of financial planning from a dedicated core group of men and women of integrity, but using the more established academic discipline of behavioral finance as its pragmatic root core. Shifting the emphasis of the planning relationship to assisting clients in formulating their "life of choice" first, and related reasons for them, advisors then strategize the financial decisions that will support the unfolding goals and objectives of their life plan and its financial requirements.

Historical Review

Validating the emerging alliance between psychology (human behavior) and finance (economics) is the fact that two Americans won the 2002 Nobel Prize in Economic Science. Their research was an exceptional explanation of the idiosyncrasies incumbent in human financial decision-making outcomes.

Daniel Kahneman, PhD, professor of psychology at Princeton University, and Vernon L. Smith, PhD, professor of economics at George Mason University in Fairfax, Virginia, shared the prize for work that provided insight on everything from stock market bubbles to regulating utilities and countless other economic activities. In several cases, Kahneman and Smith tried to explain apparent financial paradoxes.

For example, Professor Kahneman made the economically puzzling discovery that most of his subjects would make a 20-minute trip to buy a calculator for $10 instead of $15, but would not make the same trip to buy a jacket for $120 instead of $125, saving the same $5.

In the 1960s, Smith initially set out to demonstrate how economic theory worked in the laboratory (*in vitro*), while Kahneman was more interested in the ways economic theory mispredicted people in real life (*in vivo*). He tested the limits of standard economic *choice theory* in predicting the actions of real people, and his work formalized laboratory techniques for studying economic decision making, with a focus on trading and bargaining.

Later, Smith and Kahneman together were among the first economists to make experimental data a cornerstone of academic output. Their studies included people playing games of cooperation and trust and simulating different types of markets in a laboratory setting. Their theories assumed that individuals make decisions systematically, based on preferences and available information, in a way that does not change over time or in different contexts. By the late 1970s, Richard H. Thaler, PhD, an economist at the University of Chicago, also began to perform behavioral experiments further suggesting irrational wrinkles in standard financial theory and behavior, enhancing the embryonic but increasingly popular theories of Kahneman and Smith.

Other economists' laboratory experiments tested ideas about competitive interactions pioneered by game theorists like John Forbes Nash, Jr., PhD, who shared the Nobel in 1994, as points of reference. But, Kahneman and Smith often concentrated on cases in which people's actions depart from the systematic, rational strategies that Nash envisioned. Psychologically, all this was a precursor to the informal concept of life planning.

Enter the Financial Planners

Of course, comprehensive financial planners have always consulted with their clients regarding their goals and objectives, hopes, and dreams, but typically from the point of view of money goals, rather than life ideals or business goals. The absence or presence of biological and/or psychological reasons for these goals was never discussed. However, quantifying future subjective and objective goals and analyzing technical factors such as risk tolerance, age, insurance, tax, investing, retirement, and estate planning needs have certainly been the norm, especially for Certified Financial Planners (CFPs).

Life planning and behavioral finance, as proposed for physicians and integrated by the Institute of Medical Business Advisors (*i*MBA), is somewhat similar. This uniqueness emanates from a holistic union of personal financial planning and medical practice management, solely for the healthcare field. Unlike pure life planning, pure financial planning, or pure management theory, life planning and behavioral finance are both a quantitative and qualitative "hard and soft" science. Life planning has an ambitious economic, psychological, and managerial niche value proposition never before proposed and *codified* and represents an evolving philosophy. Its zealous practitioners are called Certified Medical Planners (CMPs).

Financial Life Planning Defined

Life planning has many detractors and defenders. It had been defined formerly by Mitch Anthony, Gene R. Lawrence, AAMS, CFP, and Roy T. Diliberto, ChFC, CFP, of the Financial Life Institute, in the following *trinitarian* way.

> Financial Life Planning is an approach to financial planning that places the history, transitions, goals, and principles of the client at the center of the planning process. For the financial advisor or planner, the life of the client becomes the axis around which financial planning develops and evolves.

> Financial Life Planning is about coming to the right answers by asking the right questions. This involves broadening the conversation beyond investment selection and asset management to exploring life issues as they relate to money.

> Financial Life Planning is a process that helps advisors move their practice from financial transaction thinking, to life transition thinking. It is the first step aiming to help clients "see" the connection between their financial lives and the challenges and opportunities inherent in each life transition.

But informed physicians find the quasi-professional and informal approach of financial life planning inadequate for the largely separate disciplines of financial planning and medical practice management. Today's practice environment is incredibly complex; compressed economic stress from health maintenance organizations (HMOs), financial insecurity from Wall Street, liability fears from attorneys, criminal scrutiny from government agencies, information technology mischief from malicious hackers, economic benchmarking from hospitals, and lost confidence from patients all converge to require a robust new financial planning approach for medical professionals.

The *i*MBA approach to financial planning, as championed by the CMP, integrates the traditional concepts of financial life planning with the increasing complex business concepts of medical practice management. The former are presented in this textbook, the latter in its companion, *The Business of Medical Practice.* Others volumes on risk management and insurance; accounting, tax, and investing; retirement, practice succession, and estate planning are planned in our future *i*MBA Handbook series for physicians and their advisors.

For example, traditional views of medical practice, personal lifestyle, investing and retirement—both what they are now and how they may look in the future—are rapidly changing as the retail mentality of medicine is replaced in our book with a wholesale philosophy. We explain why views on maximizing current practice income might be more profitably sacrificed for the potential of greater wealth upon eventual practice sale and disposition. Physicians' ultimate fear is represented by Yale University economist Robert J. Shiller in *The New Financial Order: Risk in the 21st Century.* Dr. Shiller warns that choosing the wrong profession or specialty might render physicians obsolete by technological changes, managed care systems, or fiscally unsound demographics.

Yet, the opportunity to revise the future at any age through personal re-engineering exists for all of us and allows a joint exploration of the meaning and purpose in life. To allow this deeper and more realistic approach, the advisor and the physician must build relationships based on trust, greater self-knowledge, and true medical business and financial enhancement acumen.

[A] The *i*MBA Philosophy

As you read this book, you will embrace the opportunity to receive the focused and best thinking of some very smart people. Hopefully, along the way you will absorb concrete information that proves valuable in your own medical practice and personal money journey. Maybe you will even learn something that is so valuable and so powerful that future reflection will reveal it to be of critical importance to your life. The contributing authors certainly hope so.

At the Institute of Medical Business Advisors, we suggest that such an epiphany can be realized only if you have extraordinary clarity regarding your personal, economic, and practice goals, your money, and your relationship with it. Money is, after all, no more or less than what we make of it. Ultimately, your relationship with it, and with others, is the most important component of how well it will serve you.

This first chapter, then, is about the perspectives that are appropriate to attaining a solid and grounded relationship with money, medical practice, and life. Our goal is to facilitate balance and vision within that relationship.

Behavioral Finance Defined

Behavioral finance is an evolving area within the field of finance that incorporates economics, psychology, and neuro-physiology in an effort to explain human economic behavior and decision making. Even gender differences are studied. For example, as reported in *Research Magazine,* August 2003, men and women may invest differently:

Exhibit 1-1 *Breakdown of Investing Habits by Gender*

Self-Directed Brokerage Accounts Owned by:
Men: 45,000
Women: 14,000

Average Account Balance:
Men: $104,000
Women: $48,000
Trades per Quarter:
Men: 2.1
Women: 1.4

Equity Allocation:
Men 22%
Women: 17%

Mutual Fund Allocation:
Men: 44%
Women: 38%

Cash Allocation:
Men: 26%
Women: 40%

Data from Research Magazine, August 2003.

Traditional finance and economic theory is based on the notion that individuals will make decisions that are in their best economic interest and that are based on a rational analysis of available information. It has become apparent that these are flawed assumptions—not only will individuals often make irrational choices and cognitive errors, but these flaws in decision making are often predictable and will be repeated by the same individual even after the error has been recognized.

The field of behavioral finance has evolved to better understand how emotions affect decision making and why seemingly "hard-wired" mistakes in decision making are innate to human beings. As science advances, the field is drawing in economists, psychologists, and neuroscientists who are working together to explain how we make decisions and how our decision-making process changes over time due to experience.

Integrating Biology, Human Psychology, and Financial Planning

The human brain evolved to work optimally in a hunter-gatherer environment. At that time in human development, it was very important to recognize short-term patterns to find food and to have the ability to generate quick emotional and physiologic responses such as the fight-or-flight reflex in response to certain stimuli.

Those who were good at reacting quickly and running fast toward food or away from danger prospered. There was very little downside to overreacting, while there was a tremendous risk to being a contrarian and waiting to consider whether one was really in danger. So, hyper-reactive, crowd followers were fruitful and multiplied (thus passing on their genes), while analytical contrarians either starved or became lunch for one of the other members of the animal kingdom.

When humans advanced to having civilizations, evolution basically stopped for them. Long-term, independent thinkers did not reproduce at a higher rate than others, so there was no Darwinian pressure for their genes to become a predominant trait of our species.

Since successful decision making is predicated on the ability to rationally analyze data and make decisions that optimize the chance of having a desired outcome, it is important to understand the many ways that this process goes awry. Successful financial planning requires both the doctor-client and the consulting professional to set goals, develop a plan, and have a process to reach those goals. And, very importantly, success is predicated on having the discipline to stay with the plan even when there are predictable, but painful or exciting short-term stimuli (i.e., the stock market having a terrible or great year).

Psychological Biases Affecting Financial Planning and Investing

The following are some of the most common psychological biases of humans. Some are learned, while others are genetically determined (and often socially reinforced). While this chapter focuses on the financial implications of these biases, they are prevalent in most areas in life.

[A] Incentives

It is broadly accepted that incenting someone to do something is effective, whether it is paying office staff a commission to sell more nutriceutical products or giving bonuses to office employees when they work efficiently and see more HMO patients. What is not well understood is that the incentives cause a subconscious distortion of the decision-making ability in the incented person. This distortion causes the affected person to believe in a certain decision even if it is the wrong choice when viewed objectively. Service professionals, including financial advisors, physicians, and lawyers, are affected by this bias so that they honestly offer recommendations that may be inappropriate and that they would recognize as being inappropriate if they did not have this bias. It is important for each of us to examine our incentive biases and take extra care when advising physician clients or to make sure we are appropriately considering non-incented alternatives.

[B] Denial

Denial is a well known but underappreciated psychological force. Physicians, clients, and healthcare professionals (like everyone else) are prone to ignoring a painful reality, like putting off an unpleasant call (thus prolonging a problematic situation and potentially making it worse) or not opening account statements that may contain quantitative proof of losses. Denial also causes people to ignore evidence that a mistake has been made. If you think of yourself as a smart person (and what professional does not?), then evidence pointing to the conclusion that a mistake has been made will call into question that belief, causing a condition called cognitive dissonance. Our brains function to either avoid cognitive dissonance or to resolve it quickly, usually by discounting or rationalizing the disconfirming evidence.

[C] Consistency and Commitment Tendency

Human beings have evolved—probably both genetically and socially—to be consistent. It is easier and safer to deal with others if they honor their commitments and if they behave in a consistent and predictable manner. This consistency allows people to work together and build trust that is needed for repeated dealings and to accomplish complex tasks. In the jungle, this trust was necessary for humans to successfully work as a team to catch animals for dinner or to fight common threats. In business and life, it is preferable to work with others who exhibit these tendencies. Unfortunately, people may make errors in judgment because of the strong desire not to change or be different ("lemming effect" or "group-think"). So the result is that most people will seek out data that support a prior stated belief or decision and ignore negative data by not "thinking outside the box." Additionally, future decisions will be unduly influenced by the desire to appear consistent with prior decisions, thus decreasing the ability to be rational and objective. The more often people state their beliefs or decisions, the less likely they are to change even if it is evident that they should. This bias is a strong force in most people that causes them to avoid or quickly resolve the cognitive dissonance that occurs when faced with evidence that indicates that prior actions may have been a mistake. Therefore, it is particularly important for advisors to ensure that their prior communications with clients and the press do not restrict the advisor's ability to seek out and process information that may prove current beliefs incorrect. Since this is obviously irrational, an advisor must actively seek out negative information, be very careful about what is said and written, and be aware that "the more you shout it out, the more you pound it in."

[D] Pattern Recognition

On a biological level, the human brain has evolved to seek out patterns and to work out stimuli-response patterns, both native and learned. What this means is that we all react to a current situation based on prior experiences that may have shared characteristics. Many situations have so many possible inputs that our brains need to take mental short-cuts. Without pattern recognition, we would not gain the benefit from having faced a certain type of problem in the past. This often-helpful mechanism of decision making fails us when past correlations or patterns do not accurately represent the current reality, so that the mental shortcuts actually impair our ability to analyze a new situation. This biologic and social need to seek out patterns is especially harmful to rational decision making when the pattern is not a good predictor of the desired outcome (like short-term moves in the stock market not being predictive of long-term equity portfolio performance), or when past correlations do not apply anymore.

[E] Social Proof

It is a subtle but powerful reality that having others agree with a decision a person makes gives the person more conviction in the decision, while having others disagree decreases one's confidence in that decision. This bias is even more exaggerated when the other parties providing the validating/questioning opinions are perceived to be experts in a relevant field, or are authority figures, like people on television. In many ways, short-term moves in the stock market are the ultimate expression of social proof—the price of a stock one owns going up is proof that a lot of other people agree with the decision to buy, and a dropping stock price means a stock should be sold. When these stressors become extreme, it is of paramount importance that all participants in the financial planning process have a clear understanding of what the long-term goals are, and what processes are in place to monitor the progress toward these goals. Without these mechanisms, it is very hard to resist the enormous pressure to follow the crowd.

[F] Contrast

Sensation, emotion, and cognition work by contrast. Perception is not only on an absolute scale, but it also functions relative to prior stimuli. This is why room temperature water feels hot when experienced after being exposed to the cold. It is also why the cessation of negative emotions "feels" so good. Cognitive functioning also works on this principle. So one's ability to analyze information and draw conclusions is very much related to the context within which the analysis takes place and to what information was originally available. This is why it is so important to manage one's own expectations as well as those of clients. A client is much more likely to be satisfied with a 10% portfolio return if he or she was expecting 7% than if the client was hoping for 15%.

[G] Scarcity

Things that are scarce have more impact and perceived value than things present in abundance. Biologically, this bias is demonstrated by the decreasing response to constant stimuli (contrast bias), and socially it is widely believed that scarcity equals value. People who feel an opportunity may "pass them by," and thus be unavailable, are much more likely to make hasty, poorly reasoned decisions. Investment fads and rising security prices elicit this bias (along with social proof and others), and investors need to resist them. Understanding that analysis in the face of perceived scarcity is often inadequate and biased may help professionals make more rational choices and keep clients from chasing fads.

[H] Envy/Jealousy

This bias also relates to the contrast and social proof biases. Prudent financial and business planning and related decision making are based on real needs followed by desires. A person's happiness and satisfaction is often based more on the individual's position relative to perceived peers rather than an ability to meet absolute needs. The strong desire to "keep up with the Joneses" can lead people to risk what they have and need for what they want. These actions can have a disastrous impact on important long-term financial goals. Clear communication and vivid examples of risks are often needed to keep people focused on important financial goals rather than on spurious ones or on simply money alone for its own sake.

[I] Fear

Financial fear is probably the most common emotion among physicians and clients in general: the fear of being wrong, as well as the fear of being correct. This fear can be debilitating, as in the corollary expression of fear: the *paralysis of analysis.*

According to Paul Karasik, four common investor and physician fears can be addressed by financial advisors in the following manner:

- Fear of making the wrong decision: ameliorated by being a teacher and educator.
- Fear of change: ameliorated by providing an agenda, outline, and/or plan.
- Fear of giving up control: ameliorated by asking for permission and agreement.
- Fear of losing self-esteem: ameliorated by serving the client first and communicating that sentiment in a positive manner.

The Addictive Investing/Trading Personality

Dr. Dean J. Mondell, a pediatrician, is the type of individual who always needs to leave for the office 15 minutes ahead of schedule. The reason is that it takes that long to make the necessary number of trips to make certain that the door is truly locked.

Dr. Pamela A. Shaw, a general surgeon, is constantly rushing to a rest room so that she can wash her hands. As far as she is concerned, it is not possible to get her hands clean enough considering the recent Severe Acute Respiratory Syndrome (SARS) epidemics or the resurgence of Acquired Immune Deficiency Syndrome (AIDS) (as reported in the Fall of 2003, by Dr. Jim Curran, dean of Emory University's Rollins School of Public Health, in Atlanta, and a former AIDS director with the Centers for Disease Control and Prevention).

Although the behaviors displayed by these two doctors are different, they are consistent in that each, to some degree, displays behavior that might be called obsessive-compulsive.

[A] When Investing or Trading Is No Longer Fun

An *obsession* is a persistent, recurring preoccupation with an idea or thought. A *compulsion* is an impulse that is experienced as irresistible. *Obsessive-compulsive* individuals feel compelled to think thoughts that they say they do not want to think or to carry out actions that they say are against their will. These individuals usually realize that their behavior is irrational, but it is beyond their control to stop the action. In general, these individuals are preoccupied with orderliness, perfectionism, and mental and interpersonal control at the expense of flexibility, openness, and efficiency. Specifically, behaviors such as the following may be seen:

- Preoccupation with details;
- Perfectionism that interferes with task completion;
- Excessive devotion to work and office productivity;
- Scrupulousnous and inflexibility about morality (not accounted for by cultural or religious identification);
- Inability to discard worn-out or worthless objects without sentimental value;
- Reluctance to delegate tasks or to work with others;
- Adoption of a miserly spending style toward both self and others; and
- Demonstration of a rigid, inflexible, and stubborn nature.

Most people resort to some minor obsessive-compulsive patterns under severe pressure or when trying to achieve goals that they consider critically important. In fact, many individuals refer to this as *superstitious behavior.* The study habits required for medical students entail a good deal of compulsive behavior.

As the above examples suggest, a variety of addictions are possible. Recent news accounts have pointed out that even high-level governmental officials can experience *sex addiction.* The advent of the Internet has led to what is referred to as *Internet addiction* where an individual is transfixed, working on the computer for hours on end without a specific project in mind. The simple act of "surfing" offers the person afflicted with the addiction some degree of satisfaction.

Still another form of addictive behavior is that of the *compulsive gambler.* This individual is unable to resist the impulse to gamble. Many reasons have been posited for this type of behavior including the death instinct: a need to lose, a wish to repeat a big win, identification with adults the "gambler" knew as an adolescent, and a desire for action and excitement. There are other explanations offered for this form of compulsive behavior. The act of betting allows the individual to express an immature bravery, courage, manliness, and persistence against unfavorable odds. By actually using money to challenge reality, the gambler puts himself or herself into "action" and intense emotion. By gambling, the addicted individual pretends that he or she is favored by "lady luck," specially chosen, successful, able to beat the system, and escape from feelings of discontent.

Greed is another reason for lack of satisfaction. In fact, a 1987 poll conducted by the *Chicago Tribune* revealed that people who earned less than $30,000 a year said that $50,000 would fulfill their dreams, whereas those with yearly incomes of over $100,000 said they would need $250,000 to be satisfied. More recent studies confirm that goals keep getting pushed upward as soon as a lower level is reached.[1]

Question: So how much money is enough?

Answer: Just a little bit more.

Edward Looney, executive director of the Trenton, New Jersey-based Council on Compulsive Gambling (CCG), reports that the number of individuals calling with trading-associated problems is doubling annually. In the mid 1980s, when the council was formed, the number of people calling the council's hotline (1 – 800 Gambler) with stock-market gambling problems was approximately 1.5% of all calls received. In 1998 that number grew to 3%, and it is projected to rise to 7–8% by 2005. Dr. Robert Custer, an expert on compulsive gambling, reported that stock market gamblers represent over 20% of the gamblers that he has diagnosed. It is evident that on-line trading presents a tremendous risk to the speculator. The CCG describes some of the consequences:

- Dr. Fred B. is a 43-year-old Caucasian male physician with a salary above $100,000 who is in debt for more than $100,000. He is married with two children. He was a day trader.

- Michael Q. is a 28-year-old Caucasian male registered nurse. He is married and the father of one (7-month-old) child. He earns $65,000 and lost $40,000 savings in day trading and is in debt for $25,000. He has suicidal ideation.

[B] A Question of Suitability

Since on-line traders are in the business for many reasons, investment suitability rarely enters the picture, according to Stuart Kaswell, General Counsel, Securities Industry Association, in Washington, DC. The kind of question that has yet to be confronted by day or on-line trading firms is a statement such as: "Equities look good this year. We favor technology stocks. We have a research report on our Web page that looks at the semiconductor industry." This kind of report is seldom considered because it does not involve a specific recommendation of a specific stock. However, if a firm makes a specific recommendation to an investor, whether over the telephone, fax machine, face-to-face, or over the Internet, suitability rules should apply. Opining similarly on the "know your customer" requirements is Steven Caruso, of Maddox, Koeller, Harget & Caruso of New York City. "The on-line firms obviously claim that they do not have a suitability responsibility because they do not want the liability for making a mistake as far as determining whether the investor was suitable or buying any security. I think that ultimately more firms are going to be required to make a suitability determination on every trade."[2]

[C] On-line Traders and Stock Market Gamblers

Some of the preferred areas of stock market gambling that attract the interest of compulsive gamblers include options, commodities, penny stocks, index investing, new stock offerings, certain types of bonds, and contracts for government securities. These on-line traders and investment gamblers think of themselves as cautious long-term investors who prefer blue chip varieties. What they fail to take into consideration is that even seemingly blue chips can both rise and precipitously drop in value again, as seen in the summer of 2003. Regardless of investment choice, the compulsive investment gambler enjoys the anticipation of following the daily activity surrounding these investments. Newspapers, hourly radio and television reports, streaming computer banners, and hundreds of periodicals and magazines add excitement in seeking the investment edge. The name of the game is action. Investment goals are unclear, with many participating simply for the feeling it affords them as they experience the highs and lows and struggles surrounding the play. And, as documented by Bradley Skolnik, the North American Securities Administrators Association's president and Indiana Securities Commissioner, most day or on-line traders lose money. "On-line brokerage was new and cutting edge, and we enjoyed the best stock market in generations, until the crash. The message of most advertisements was "just do it," and you'll do well. The fact is, research and common sense suggest the more you trade, the less well you'll do."

Most day or on-line traders are young males, some who have quit their day jobs. Most of them start every day not owning any stock, then buy and sell all day long and end the trading day again without any stock—just a lot of cash. Dr. Patricia Farrell, a licensed clinical psychologist, states that day traders are especially susceptible to compulsive behaviors and addictive personalities. Mark Brando, registered principal for Milestone Financial, a day trading firm in Glendale, California, states, "People that get addicted to trading employ the same destructive habits as a gambler. Often, it's impossible to tell if a particular trade comes from a problem gambler or a legitimate trader."

Arthur Levitt, former Chairman of the Securities and Exchange Commission, asserts that the risks and misconceptions of investing are only amplified by on-line trading. In a speech before the National Press Club last year, he attempted to impress individuals as to the risks and difficulties involved with day trading. Levitt cited four common misconceptions that knowledgeable medical professionals and investors should know:

- Personal computers are not directly linked to the markets—Thanks to Level II computer software, day traders can have access to the same up-to-the-second information available to market makers on Wall Street. "Although the Internet makes it seem as if you have a direct connection to the securities market, you don't. Lines may clog; systems may break; orders may back-up."
- The virtue of *limit orders*—"Price quotes are only for a limited number of shares; so only the first few investors will receive the currently quoted price. By the time you get to the front of the line, the price of the stock could be very different."
- *Canceling an order*—"Another misconception is that an order is canceled when you hit 'cancel' on your computer. But, the fact is it's canceled only when the market gets the cancellation. You may receive an electronic confirmation, but that only means your request to cancel was received—not that your order was actually canceled."
- *Buying on margin*—"If you plan to borrow money to buy a stock, you also need to know the terms of the loan your broker gave you. This is margin. In volatile markets, investors who put up an initial margin payment for a stock may find themselves required to provide additional cash if the price of the stock falls."

How then can the medical professional tell if he or she is a compulsive gambler? A diagnostic may be obtained from Gamblers Anonymous. It is designed to screen for the identification of problem and compulsive gambling.

But it is also necessary for us to provide a tool to be used by on-line traders. This questionnaire is as follows:

1. Are you trading in the stock market with money you may need during the next year?
2. Are you risking more money than you intended to?
3. Have you ever lied to someone regarding your on-line trading?
4. Are you risking retirement savings to try to get back your losses?
5. Has anyone ever told you that you spend too much time on-line?
6. Is your investing affecting other life areas (relationships, vocational pursuits, etc.)?
7. If you lost money trading in the market, would it materially change your life?
8. Are you investing frequently for the excitement, and the way it makes you feel?
9. Have you become secretive about your on-line trading?
10. Do you feel sad or depressed when you are not trading in the market?

Note: If you answer yes to any of these questions, you may be moving from investing to gambling.

The cost of compulsive gambling and day trading is high for the individual medical or lay professional, family members, and society at large. Compulsive gamblers, in the desperation phase of their gambling, exhibit high suicide ideation, as in the case of Mark O. Bartons, the murderous day-trader in Atlanta. His idea actually became a final act of desperation.

Less dramatically for physicians is a marked increase in subtle illegal activity. These acts include fraud, embezzlement, CPT-upcoding, medical overutilization, excessive full risk HMO contracting, and other "white collar crimes." Higher healthcare and social costs in police, judiciary (civil and criminal), and corrections result because of compulsive gambling. The impact on family members is devastating. Compulsive gamblers cause havoc and pain to all family members, whose lives also go through progressive deterioration.

After this desperation phase, dysfunctional families are left with a legacy of anger, resentment, isolation, and, in many instances, outright *hate*.

[D] Day Trading Assessment

Internet day trading, like the Internet and telecommunications sectors, became something of a investment bubble a few years ago, suggesting that something lighter than air can pop and disappear in an instant. History is filled with examples from the tulip mania of 1630 in Holland and the British South Sea Bubble of the 1700s; to the Florida land boom of the Roaring Twenties and the Great Crash of 1929; and to $875-an-ounce gold in the 1980s and the collapse of Japan's stock and real estate market in the early 1990s. To this list, one might now add Internet day trading.

What Is Money?

So what is money? The concept of money is elusive. Money seems to demand so much from us. Not only does money seem utterly convoluted and alien, but it is also bafflingly personal. In between, we find complex monetary systems, multinational legalisms, a whole host of political and cultural mythologies, our most profound personal issues, and another zillion nuances that go into generating what we call "the money forces." Then, as if to heap insult upon injury, the art of handling money properly demands competency with your own personal intangibles.

Money has strong spiritual and religious components. Indeed, our relationship with money goes straight to our souls. Getting money, keeping it, and spending it all reflect our values, morals, and motivations precisely. Some believe money has its origins in religious rituals. Others believe that the love of money is "the root of all evil." Either way, it is no accident that the money issue is the second most frequently addressed topic in the Christian *Bible* and is clearly a part of most major religious traditions. Money has that kind of power in our lives.

What's more, money has much more in common with religion. Despite pretentious banalities decrying money as either a secular creed or an unworthy recipient of thoughtful attention by right thinking people, and in spite of trite condemnations of its hold on our value systems, money is a belief system with all the qualities and characteristics that generally attend belief systems. Money has only the values, functions, and meanings we collectively give it. No more. No less. It is myth at its best.

It also grounds humanity's best attempts to take care of its individuals while rationally allocating goods and services. Perfection? Hardly. However, money is still the best system we know for delivering life's necessities to the broadest possible group of living souls.

One may suggest the following to be financial axioms of our age:

- Money is the most powerful secular force on the planet.
- Money handling skills are quite literally 21st century survival skills.
- Money handling skills do not come with our DNA.

Therefore, these axioms may lead to multiple conclusions that directly affect core realities. If these observations are true and can be taken together as working presuppositions for life in the 21st century, well, you know, money is just plain powerful. Our lives will go better if we have a grip on it.

Money handling skills come in many forms and are much more than mere technical proficiencies. In fact, some money skills are simple coping mechanisms such as balancing creditors and cash flow, understanding insurance needs, or grasping the rudiments of our legal system.

Other money handling skills include an ability to deal with the array of money systems that have evolved in response to complex economies and relevant bureaucracies.

Also, an appreciation for history and social evolution is useful. At the very least, such an appreciation will enhance your coping skills. Much about our economic systems does not make much sense if taken in isolation.

The concept of money has been evolving for thousands of years. It has been an integral part of civilization. Money enables the marketplace. It is easy to become cynical about money, but without it, our systems grind to a halt. This includes our healthcare systems.

Money underscores the purpose of this chapter. Its work is grounded in these beliefs and the attendant exploration of their ramifications for individual lives. In doing this work, our discussion will range from the philosophical to the intensely personal. Be forewarned, this chapter will not teach you how to get rich but, hopefully, might help you live richly. To derive maximum benefit, you must bring a willingness to look into yourself as well as the world around you.

We are too easily daunted by money. Some of our fears are justified, but whole ranges of skill are resolved by simply understanding some basics. For all the mysteries and myths woven around money, truly crucial money skills are easily accessible to individuals. At the level required for 21st century survival, money skills are not particularly complex. If you do not have them, you can generally rent them or associate with them through a trusted financial advisor.

The simple fact is that if you read this whole book, you will be exposed to just about all there is to know about financial planning fundamentals and some practice management benchmarks. Really. If you do not find it between these covers, most of what is left to know is just a phone call or a couple of browser clicks away.

Don't misunderstand me. Certain financial and managerial issues are incredibly complex, require years of schooling, should only be used in the hands of the most skillful, and truly merit our awe and admiration. This is comparable to those times when a simple cough medicine is required. Sometimes it does the trick perfectly. So you don't need to do heart surgery to cure a cold, and you do not necessarily need complex solutions to your financial problems. Be careful out there.

This will undoubtedly get us into some philosophical trouble, but we ask you to understand the simple realities of the financial services and medical consulting industry. There are some great people in it. Nonetheless, in the wonderful world of personal finance and practice management, what others make complex often simply covers sales motives, crude politics, or some other form of pocketbook invasion. It may be an attempt to make someone appear sophisticated. It might possibly be simply an intellectual version of the old shell game, betting neither you nor a team of auditors could find the pea that has been so magnificently shuffled. Reducing gimmicks to essential components is a worthy skill. Never investing in something you do not understand is simply fundamental common sense. If you don't *"get it,"* accept the possibility that it may not be you. Hold off. Even if you *"get it,"* it is still a good idea to "get" the seller's motives. There is a difference between being paranoid and prudent, but even paranoid persons reduce their odds of getting mugged if their fear helps them stick to safer paths.

These and other basics are pure financial muscle. Whole industries are built around them and getting around them.

True sophistication comes with tailoring your money and practice to your particular needs. Imagine what you will know when you have completely absorbed the information contained here. *You will learn to build, staff, and plan for your medical business.* You might receive an overview of various taxation systems and miscellaneous methods for best working with their demands. Then you will be comfortably crunching numbers, multiplying, adding, subtracting, and dividing with the best of them. In the meantime, you have been exposed to investments, estate planning, insurance, "retirement" planning, and so forth. You will be absorbing details, possibilities, likelihoods, and the prospective repercussions for guessing wrong. Imagine.

And so what? At the end of the day, the real trick is to understand this information as it personally applies to you. Without knowledge of your own life dreams and goals, this knowledge is of dubious value.

Now step back a minute. How do these thoughts feel? Are you energized or daunted? Empowered or bewildered? Thrilled or bored? Be honest in your answers. Money has huge emotional and personal spiritual aspects. Overestimating either your aptitudes or your knowledge can be both expensive and time consuming. It can most certainly be intellectually daunting and spiritually depleting.

Money Handling Skills: Minutes to Learn. A Lifetime to Master

Assuming your goals ultimately have more to do with home, heart, health, patients, and happiness than logging larger numbers from your practice on your bank and brokerage statements, all of this ultimately needs to be about your perspective on money. It is about wisdom of the sort that will enable you to aspire realistically toward your visions while maintaining personal balance. Without these goals, money craft is fundamentally worthless.

In this book, we are trying to put money insights into context. We are looking at practicalities. We are also attempting to look at money from the standpoints of various modern social and economic systems. As we continue along this course, here are a few suggestions: you will be well-served by a sense of irony, a tolerance of paradox, and the well-founded belief that "everybody is weird about money."[3] Trust me. Everybody. You. Me. Everybody.

Allow us to suggest that financial health reflects attitudes more than aptitudes. The art of good money handling demands good judgment rather than gimmicks. Greed is not only one of the seven deadly sins; it is quite clearly dangerous to your wealth. So are the other six: pride, envy, gluttony, lust, anger, and sloth. An individual's fiscal health, as with his or her physical well-being, is more likely to respond favorably to good habits than great technical mastery.

There can be no doubt that financial and managerial issues can get complicated. It is equally obvious that money handling fundamentals are not so difficult to grasp that folks of reasonable intelligence should be intimidated. An abiding truth is that one need not be an "expert" to function effectively and efficiently around and within the money forces.

The relevant personal financial rules can be summarized in three rules of eight short words.

- Rule One: Save more.
- Rule Two: Spend less.
- Rule Three: Don't do anything stupid.

The relevant personal financial planning process corollaries can also be summarized briefly:

- Financial planning first, asset allocation second, your portfolio third.
- The financial planning process is insensitive to the economy and market outlook. For example, you do not buy equities because you think the market is going up.

You own them because their historical returns (absolute/compared to debt) are sufficient to meet the goals and objectives of your plan.

- Diversification at all times.
- A good long-term definition for the commodity money is purchasing power. The best test of income potential over time is total return, not current yield.
- Do not micromanage your plan, your portfolio, your advisors, or yourself.

That's it. Nothing daunting or inherently intimidating here. Just control your spending. At the very least, spend less than you make and do it for a long time. Save regularly. Your savings are raw power. They enable you to make choices that suit you. Understand your personal issues, particularly your vulnerabilities and most particularly the essentials of your obligations as a citizen of your family and your various communities. Then, make a plan, allocate your assets, get professional help to monitor your portfolio, and do not do anything stupid.

Other relevant fundamentals include living modestly and beneath your economic means. Stay married to your spouse. Grasp basic risk management (i.e., insurance and general prudence) and investment fundamentals, most particularly notions of cycles, greed, and time. Pay your taxes on time. Master medical records documentation and CPT billing codes. Adhere to the tenets of the Health Insurance Portability and Accountability Act, Occupational Safety and Health Administration, and Clinical Laboratory Improvement Amendments. Become skillful in financial ratio-analysis and business interpretation. Buy enough insurance to keep your promises and avoid catastrophe. Be skeptical of sales pitches yet generous with others. Save and invest for growth your entire life. Have faith in any god you wish. Worry less about your appearances than your realities. Be flexible and market responsive in your practice specialty and future life. Develop a hobby and plan a passionate retirement. Have faith in yourself and in your future. And, never, ever lose sight of the fact that, *above all else*, medical care should be delivered in a personal and humane manner, with patient interest, rather than self interest, as a guiding standard. *Omnia pro aegroto,* or "all for the patient." Finally, live your life with pride and joy but don't confuse good fortune with skill.

Adherence to these simple rules will generally ensure a rewarding relationship with money. Truly.

Our purpose here is not to denigrate technical financial knowledge as much as to suggest that attention to the technical, at the expense of one's human priorities and personal values, can lead to ruined lives. Which sort of misses the point of developing financial and business skills.

Assuming the above, there is substantial craft to technical financial proficiency. As with all crafts, genuine mastery requires time, experience, skill, knowledge, and discipline. The details may be easily accessible, but truly appropriate use of the details takes time and the sort of experience that comes with making mistakes or seeing them made by others. Even then, craft is of considerably less importance than understanding and judgment.

Money tends to reward those who treat it with respect and wisdom.

Full development of the money craft takes years of education and experience. Wisdom takes longer. Wisdom is not subject to rules and regulations. Wisdom requires the integration of financial issues with your own sense of life, its purpose, and its possibilities. Wisdom includes an ability to anticipate consequences of all sorts. The craftsman will help you to maximize your estates to benefit your family. A wise advisor will ask you if your family is emotionally or spiritually prepared for receiving money. If not, he or she will help you to avert a train wreck for those you love. Your practice may respond well to 80-hour work weeks. Will your mental and physical health? How about your soul? Will your marriage, friends, and relationships, as well? Or, your children? All are part of behavior finance and the art of money handling.

You may hate your current work environment because of HMOs and managed care. What are the possibilities for personal re-education and changing it? What is the cost of continued misery or a sense of meaninglessness? What are the intangibles for lives lived without inherent worth? Can you re-engineer and retool your life for a new career?

What may be obvious to many may be dead wrong for you. Do you want to allocate your precious life energies to "deals and heels"? You may choose not to play the maximization game. "Enough" may really be enough. You may make choices for reasons other than money. You can practice until you drop. You may choose to live simply. You can smell some roses. Truly, it is up to you.

Money is here to serve humans. Humans are not here to serve money. Humans are not money machines. More is not better. Enough *is* enough. Money is a terrific servant but a terrible master. Remember: You can't take it with you.

Is this heresy in a secular culture that allegedly reveres money at the expense of all else? Perhaps. Nonetheless, your relationship with money is uniquely yours. How you regard it, relate to it, use it, work with it, or play with it is entirely up to you. As ancient wisdom tells us, "Where your heart is, so shall your treasure be."[4] Your relationship with your money will reflect both your personality and your value systems. You are revealed through money more profoundly than through your handwriting. Neither your fingerprints nor your blood work are as individuated as your relationship with this ultimate intangible.

Money is inescapable. At base, we must understand that the money forces rage around us. We can no more escape money than we can escape water, nourishment, or oxygen. Money impacts everything about our lives every hour of every day. It is very strange, unique in its every aspect. It gets into the cracks of our personal, communal, regional, national, and international lives in a manner unlike any other part of human existence. And, we need money to survive.

So, what is money? First, as noted above, it is a belief system. Money only has the value that we impart to it. If humans ceased believing in money, money would immediately cease to be important.[5]

Second, it is a social lubricant and intellectual fertilizer. In the immortal words of Ben Franklin: "Money is like muck. Useless unless spread around." When money is used as nourishment, deserts bloom. When money serves as lubricant, our social machinery functions smoothly.

Using money, we build. Families. Communities. Schools. Hospitals. Libraries and cultural facilities. Stadiums. Highways. Utilities. Transportation systems.

We generate: Food. Clothing. Shelter. Books.

We create: Art. Literature. Science. Exploration.

We educate: We care. We tend.

We live.

Without money, we are simply an agglomeration of individuals. With it, we can be interdependent communities. Look at the poor economies of the world. Would you want to live in them? Imagine the prospect of feeding the planet's six billion souls without money. Not even close.

Third, money stores value. It enables trade and, in so doing, facilitates the development of resources and proficiencies with unparalleled efficiency. Imagine creating all that you consume. *Inconceivable.* Yet, through the miracle of money, much is enabled. The simplest act of consumption generally reflects the labors and/or mental genius of hundreds to thousands or millions, all performed in the name of money.

Fourth, money provides incentives and helps us keep score. Money frequently reflects excellence and reveals mediocrity. Successful medical practices serve humanity in miscellaneous ways and are rewarded with money. Unsuccessful practices move those associated with it to something more "productive." Money abuses tend to bring down the incompetent and the dishonest. Inefficiencies, dishonesty, and poor quality contain the seeds of their own destruction within themselves.

Similarly, money often serves as palpable recognition for discipline, thoughtfulness, creativity, deferred gratification, hard work, and/or vision. "Show me the money" has become a cultural icon for the very best of reasons.

It is obviously silly to accumulate money for its own sake, out of the context of your life requirements. You cannot eat it, wear it, or cure yourself with it. Without the hard work of others, there is no food, shelter, or, indeed, much else carrying with it even a scintilla of value. Money is certainly no substitute for love, self-esteem, prudence, knowledge, or professional integrity. The Disney character Scrooge McDuck may swim in it, but even such a nominal utility is denied the rest of us. For all the energy we throw at it, money is remarkably insubstantial.

Money has, in fact, become the most powerful secular force on earth. Nothing of consequence in our 21st century world takes place without money lurking somewhere nearby. Moreover, money is simply amazing in its ability to do "good," to spread power and counter brute force as a method of imposing will. It is my heartfelt belief that more acts of peace, love, and brotherhood occur in our daily pursuits of money than through any other aspect of our collective human existence. Nothing else induces enemies to cooperate with each other like the power of money. Lions lay down with lambs and swords are beat into plowshares in the contexts of markets and money forces. Nothing else can mobilize humans in their pursuit of knowledge, mutual benefit, and sharing. Imagine a healthcare system without money. This is highly unlikely.

The metaphors abound. Money is like water in the sense that it is the giver of life to healthy human enterprises. However, like water, money carries the taints and poisons of its origins. "Dirty money" is no joke. Stay away from it.

Money is like water in the sense that floods of it contain the power to destroy. A joke runs "Cocaine is God's way of telling you that you make too much money." One of many. Money without values is horrifying. Money destroys ecosystems and communities along with individuals, families, and businesses. Markets may be efficient, but they are not compassionate. Unfortunately, markets do not deal well with true off-balance sheet costs. Ostrich accounting often ignores the intangible or the immeasurable. However, these problems are not flaws in money handling as much as shortcomings in our methods of working with it.

Money issues find their way into our most intimate relationships. The family itself is a fundamental economic unit. Cities are strategically located to achieve certain economic advantages. Money issues lurk ominously around and about most forms of human conflict. These are just more good reasons for money's prominence within morality literature. Fairy tales, myths, and fables frequently focus on money and its ramifications.

Read the *Brothers Grimm,* the *Wizard of Oz,* or other world mythologies as money allegories. Fascinating. Indeed the book, *The Seven Stages of Money Maturity,*[6] finds parallels throughout history and the world's religions, literature, and wisdom (SevenStages.com). Authored by George D. Kinder, CFP, a Harvard graduate, Bronze Medal winner in the National Uniform Certified Public Accountant examination in Massachusetts, and Buddhist teacher, the seven stages as quoted from the book follow.

[A] Innocence

Innocence represents the beliefs, thoughts, stories, attitudes, and assumptions about money we hold onto for dear life no matter how fiercely the world works to remind us of their untruth. The process of entrapment in beliefs begins early in childhood, when parents pass on their own often-unstated attitudes about money. We seize upon these beliefs, sometimes burying them so deeply within that we don't even know they're there—yet they still influence every money decision we make. The desperate, often unconscious way we cling to our beliefs around money reflects the urgency of our basic needs.

[B] Pain

Where Innocence consists of our belief systems, thoughts, and stories, Pain represents the wild, unbearable, chaotic feelings hooked to these systems, thoughts, and stories— emotions such as envy, greed, desire, frustration, anger, despair, fear, humiliation, boredom, and sadness—the great mass of unpleasant feeling we would just as soon avoid. Attaching these feelings to stories gives us a way of tolerating and explaining them. Because we don't like these troubling emotions and try to push them away, they attach themselves, seemingly permanently and often unconsciously, to our belief systems, thoughts, and stories. Then we go round and round with them, inventing endless variations of the old themes as new money circumstances present themselves.

[C] Knowledge

The stage of Knowledge, while filled with practical things like budgets and taxes and investments, is actually rooted in virtue and integrity. Without integrity, economic systems and relationships fall apart. Our determination to act always with integrity in the day-to-day world forms the only healthy basis from which we can approach the universe of information and Knowledge about money.

[D] Understanding

Understanding is the most revolutionary teaching of all the Seven Stages. Because of its life-transforming nature, Understanding often takes us in directions and over distances we have never imagined possible. In Understanding we go back to the beginning, to contemplate Innocence and Pain again and resolve the cycle of suffering once and for all. Understanding stands at the center of the Seven Stages, the place where the transforming action of the heart takes hold. In Understanding we resolve the dilemma of childhood by unraveling the knot of suffering, letting stories and identifications go, turning suffering into wisdom and truth. Such transformation is possible because understanding gives us the capacity to enter, with grace and acceptance, the darkest areas of suffering.

[E] Vigor

Vigor centers on discovering purpose in life and putting one's energy into accomplishing that purpose. Vigor is centered in the throat, the place from which we speak with authority. Vigor concerns authority in the sense of "authoring" our own lives. In the world of money, Vigor represents the energy to accomplish financial goals and completes the work of adulthood on the path to Money Maturity.

[F] Vision

Vision is all about seeing. It entails coming to each moment of life with the focused awareness of someone who is vital and alive. Vision directs our sense of life purpose beyond ourselves, toward the health and welfare of communities. What propels us through life is no longer the deadening, blinding suffering caused by the dance of Pain and Innocence, but the full consciousness of every moment supported by the skills of adulthood and a calling toward what needs to be done.

[G] Aloha

The last stage is a place of wisdom and generosity. Given or received, Aloha is unmistakable. It is humility, kindness, and blessing that pass from one person to another.

Aloha lacks economic distinction. It can be given by a poor person to a rich one, as well as the other way around. Aloha arises from the interior place where we have emptied ourselves of attachments to objects and stories and can give ourselves spontaneously, genuinely, and lovingly to another.

We need these stages, or moral instructions, about money handling because it is so easy to get out of whack in our relationships with money. The consequences can be huge. Indeed, individual and collective failures to attain balance and vision in our personal money relationships lead to egregious consequences in virtually every area of our lives.

Which is to say that money is serious stuff. Which is *not* to say that life or medical practice is all about money or that you should sacrifice beyond measure to maximize either your competency with money handling, medical specialty, or your particular pile of money. It is just to say that money is serious stuff and that your life will be better if you understand it and your relationship with it.

Money impacts everybody and everybody has to come to terms with its role in our lives. Indeed, if you are having trouble in your own relationship with money, it might comfort you to know that you are in the best of company. Remember, "Everybody is weird about money."

Know Thyself

Money is personal and intimate. We are all uniquely wired in our relationship with it and our attitudes toward it. No one else is like you. You are like no one else. No one has your medical or secular experiences. No one else comes from your family, with your fears, with your traumas or joys. No one else has your prospects or your timetable.

Your own hard wiring may help or hurt you in achieving significant net worth, but without understanding yourself, achieving balance or vision in your personal relationship with money will be difficult for you. This is where the cold realities of financial health meet self-awareness and the mental health disciplines. No self-help book has the capacity to explain yourself to you, but your personal work toward self-understanding will go a long way toward easing the trials of your own money journey.

However, there is no substitute for working with mental health professionals and skilled financial advisors. The interface of money and mental health can pose tricky ethical and practical dilemmas. We recommend working with professional advisors who have both understanding of and respect for the skills of related professions.

The exercises that follow are designed to help with your self-awareness.

While these exercises can be useful by themselves, our experience is that humans have difficulty working with them in the depth necessary to receive full value. Also there may be other exercises or techniques that would be more particularly useful for you. Without a coach to monitor and mentor you, your progress and your responses, it would be hard to tell. Accordingly, we recommend working on these exercises in conjunction with a skilled advisor or advisory team. Licenses are not as important as skill sets. You want somebody who listens, understands what is going on, and has your best interests at heart and in mind. Financial planners, coaches, psychologists, psychiatrists, lawyers, accountants, or even Uncle Joe may all be excellent facilitators. Many with the same licenses will be terrible. Finding someone with whom you are comfortable, who understands money, who also has a minimal or nonexistent sales agenda is worth the effort.

Every aspect of your life will be improved when you have a healthy relationship to money. These additional exercises are designed to help you on your way. Working these problems will reward your efforts.

Exercise A: Money Autobiography Questionnaire

For understanding your relationship with money, these questions will help you be aware of yourself in the contexts of culture, family, value systems, and experience. This is a process of self-discovery. To fully benefit from this exploration, please address them in writing. You will simply not get the full value from the exercise if you just breeze through and give mental answers. While it is recommended that you first answer these questions by yourself, many people relate that they have enjoyed the experience of sharing them with others.

As you answer these questions, be conscious of your feelings, actually describing them in writing as part of your process.

1. Childhood
    a) What is your first memory of money?
    b) What was your happiest moment with money?
    c) Your unhappiest?
    d) Name the miscellaneous money messages you received as a child.
    e) How were you confronted with the knowledge of differing economic circumstances among people—that there were people "richer" than you and people "poorer" than you?

2. Cultural heritage
    a) What is your cultural heritage and how has your heritage traditionally interfaced with money?
    b) To the best of your knowledge, how has your heritage been impacted by the money forces? Be specific.
    c) To the best of your knowledge, does this circumstance of heritage or culture ave any motive related to money?
    d) Speculate about the manner in which your forebears' money handling decisions continue to affect you today.

3. Family
    a) How is/was the subject of money addressed by your church or the religious traditions of your forebears?
    b) What happened to your parents or grandparents during the Depression?

c) How did your family communicate about money? Be as specific as you can be, but remember that we are more concerned about impacts upon you than historical veracity.

d) When did your family emigrate to America (or its current location)?

What else do you know about your family's economic circumstances historically?

4. Your parents

   a) How did your mother address money?

   b) Your father?

   c) How did they differ in their attitudes toward money?

   d) How did they address money in their relationship?

   e) Did they argue or maintain strict silence?

   f) How do you feel about that today?

5. Please do your best to answer the same questions regarding your life or business partner(s) and their parents.

6. Childhood Revisited

   a) How did you relate to money as a child? Did you feel "poor" or "rich"? Relatively?

   b) Or completely?

      Why?

      Were you anxious about money?

   c) Did you receive an allowance? If so, describe amounts and responsibilities.

      (1) Did you have household responsibilities?

      (2) Did you get paid regardless of performance?

      (3) Did you work for money?

   d) If not, please describe your thoughts and feelings about that.

Same questions, as a teenager, young adult, and older adult.

7. Credit

   a) When did you first acquire something on credit?

   b) When did you first acquire a credit card?

   c) What did it represent to you when you first held the credit card?

   d) Describe your feelings about credit.

   e) Do you have trouble living within your means?

   f) Do you have debt?

8. Adulthood

   a) Have your attitudes shifted during your adult life?
      Describe.

   b) Why did you choose your personal path?

    c) Would you do it again?

    d) Describe your feelings about credit.

9. Adult attitudes

    a) Are you money motivated?

    b) If so, please explain why? If not, why not?

    c) How do you feel about your present financial situation?

    d) Are you financially fearful or resentful? How do you feel about that?

    e) Will you inherit money? How does that make you feel?

    f) If you feel well off today, how do you feel about the money situations of others?

    g) If you feel poor, same question.

    h) How do you feel about begging? Welfare?

    i) If you are well off today, why are you working?

    j) Do you worry about your financial future?

    k) Are you generous or stingy? Do you treat? Do you tip?

    l) Do you give more than you receive or the reverse? Would others agree?

    m) Could you ask a close relative for a business loan? For rent/grocery money?

    n) Could you subsidize a non-related friend? How would you feel if that friend bought something you deemed frivolous?

    o) Do you judge others by how you perceive them dealing with their money?

    p) Do you feel guilty about your prosperity?

    q) Are your siblings prosperous?

    r) What part does money play in your spiritual life?

    s) Do you "live" your money values?

There may be other questions that would be useful to answer. Others questions may occur to you as you progress in your life's journey. The point is to know your personal money issues and their ramifications for your life, work, and personal mission. This exercise will be a "work-in-progress" with answers both complex and incomplete. Don't worry. Just incorporate fine-tuning of your knowledge of money into your life's process.

Exercise B: Reality Check

This is where you match resources with goals. Does it work?

RESOURCES

Your so-called net worth statement does not accurately reflect the full extent of your financial resources. If your assets are those tangible and intangible pieces of your life that stand between you and financial disaster, you need to look at all aspects of your life. These include your earning power together with your knowledge and experience. Brains count. Medical acumen counts. Muscles count. Talents count. Write them down.

Resources also include your productive assets, like your medical practice, that may be worth much more to you than could conceivably be reflected on a balance sheet. Or not! Inheritances also count. While caution is appropriate against overreliance upon such anticipations, if you know that substantial resources are likely to come your way, this should be factored into your thinking. Finally, look at your family, community, patients, and other relationships that can provide trustworthy security in your various possibilities for personal disaster. They also do more for your quality of life than pieces of paper.

GOAL SETTING

Goals are the essence of financial planning. Why do you have money? Why do you want more? What do you expect it to do for you? What would you like it to do for you?

Genuine goal setting is among the most intimate and personal of undertakings. Going about it requires self-knowledge and self-honesty. There is insufficient space to enumerate all the possibilities for goal-setting tools. The following are the best we have encountered. Taken from the *Seven Stages of Money Maturity*,[7] they are reprinted with the permission of its author, George D. Kinder, CFP.

FIRST QUESTION:

This exercise is a set of three scenarios to be worked through in order. The first one, called "plenty of money," is playful and fun as well as revealing. Here's the question to consider: "You may not be as wealthy as Bill Gates or the Sultan of Brunei, but you do have all the money you need, now and in the future. What will you do with it? From this moment forward, how will you live your life?"

As you write your answer, let yourself dream. This part of the exercise has nothing to do with realism. Run loose, without tether or rein. Give yourself the right to have, do, or be anything that comes to mind. Only when you have completed this part of the exercise should you go on to part two.

SECOND QUESTION:

The second segment is called "just a few years left." You've just come back from a visit to a doctor who has discovered from your lab reports that you have only five to ten years to live. In a way, you're lucky. This particular disease has no manifestations, so you won't feel sick. The bad part is that you will have no warning about the moment of your death. It will simply come upon you in an unpredictable instant, sudden and final.

Let the emotional import of the situation sink in, then address yourself to this interwoven question: "Knowing death is waiting for you sooner than you expected, how will you change your life? And what will you do in the uncertain but substantial period you have remaining?" Again, spend time with this question and let the full answer emerge from you. And don't go to the next part until you've finished here.

THIRD QUESTION:

Now you are ready for the last step, named "Twenty-four hours to live." Again you've gone to the doctor, but this time you learn you'll be dead within twenty-four hours. The question isn't what you would to with the little time you have. Instead, ask yourself, "What feelings am I experiencing? What regrets, what longings, what deep and now-unfulfilled dreams? What do I wish I had completed, been, had, done in this life that is just about to end?" As with the other two parts of this exercise, write your answers with the greatest honesty and candor you can summon.

Goals can be defined linearly. Table 1-1 is a tool for putting goals into a chronological context. Practicalities demand that we make it small. Obviously, you can make it as big as you choose. Pretend each blank rectangle is its own legal pad if you choose. The point is to begin conceptualizing your most important goals in terms of the different, competing arenas of your life and then give each the perspective of time.

Table 1-1 *Goal Setting and the Perspective of Time*

	One Week	One Month	Six Months	One Year	Three Years	Five Years	Ten Years	Twenty Years	Life Time
Family									
Relationship									
Health									
Career									
Community									
Creativity									
Spirit									
Your category									
Your category									
Your category									
Your category									

Table 1-2 *Goal Setting Priorities*

	Got to	*Should*	*Like to*
Have			
Do			
Be			

The exercise shown in Table 1-2 involves a sort of "tic tac toe" chart.

The next step is to fill in the cells. Into the "got to" column, put all the things that, from the level of your heart or soul, you simply must do lest your life lack or lose meaning. "Have" refers to possessions, "do" covers accomplishments and activities, and "be" covers states of existence.

The same distinctions apply to the "should" column, which covers areas where you feel an obligation to do, have, or be. In the "like to" column, put the fluff and extras.

Now that you've completed the exercise, what does it reveal? Typically, issues of career, family, and home appear in the "got-to" column. Travel, special vacations, and second homes in resort locales usually occupy the "like-to" column. The "should" column fills up with practical issues as well as obligations, often toward parents and sometimes toward children. It is not unusual for many issues to appear in the "should" column.

Assessment

Just as life planning is a high visibility notion to financial planning practitioners, experimental methods have become hot topics for graduate and doctoral students in some of the top behavioral economics, statistics, and mathematics departments in the United States, Europe, Israel, and Japan.

Indeed, David I. Laibson, PhD, of Harvard University credits the rapidly rising interest in the *subject* of life planning to the strength of its science. Though the 2002 Nobel Prize in Economic Science given to Vernon L. Smith and Daniel Kahneman was the first Nobel Prize to reward such work, the Nobel committee has long shown an interest in the connection of economics and psychology. For example, Maurice Allais, PhD, who won the Nobel Prize in 1988, demonstrated how economic theory breaks down when used to predict people's choices between different sets of lotteries. Human beings' limited capacity to digest information needed to make complex decisions was a prime concern of Herbert A. Simon, PhD, an American who won the Nobel Prize in 1978.

Conclusion

The obsession to gain material wealth makes us sad. Mihaly Csikszentmihalyi, writing in the October 1999 edition of *The American Psychologist,* suggests that material advantages do not readily translate into emotional and social benefits.[8] He says that friendship, art, literature, natural beauty, religion, and philosophy become less and less interesting. The physician or advisor who responds only to material rewards becomes blind to any other kind and loses the ability to derive happiness from other sources.

If you are a medical professional or financial advisor, as you read the remaining chapters of this book, you will undoubtedly learn and reinforce information that will prove invaluable in your economic, personal, consulting, and practice life. More important, however, as you work with other professional advisors and physicians-clients, it will help define your relationship with them and assist in the never-ending balance between vision, finance, self-awareness, practice, risk, and reward.

Acknowledgment

To Hope Rachel Hetico, RN, MHA, for technical assistance in the compendium editing format of this chapter.

Endnotes

1. G. Easterbrook. *The Progress Paradox (How Life Gets Better While People Feel Worse).* New York: Random House, 2003.
2. www. investorprotection.com
3. Jacob Needleman, PhD, in an unpublished speech at the Naropa Institute, Spring 1999. Dr. Needleman is a professor of philosophy at San Francisco State University. www.JacobNeedleman.com
4. Matthew 6:21.
5. For what it is worth, we find this notion literally terrifying.
6. George Kinder, *The Seven Stages of Money Maturity,* New York: Delacorte Press, 1999. www.sevenstages.com
7. Delacorte Press, 1999.
8. Miska@ccp.uchicago.edu *www.APA.ORG*

Additional Readings and References

Altman, D. A., A Nobel that Bridges Economics and Psychology. *New York Times* (Oct. 10, 2002).
Karasik, P., The Four Fears. *On the Street* (August 2003). www.PaulKarasik.com

Marcinko, D. E., *The Business of Medical Practice (Advanced Profit Maximizing Skills for Savvy Doctors)*. 2nd ed., Springer Publishers, New York, 2004. (www.Springer-Pub.com)

Schmuckler, E., The Addictive Investing Personality, in D. E. Marcinko, *Financial Planning for Physicians and Healthcare Professionals*, Aspen Publishers, New York, 2001.

Shubin-Stein, K., Psychological Issues for Financial Advisors and Their Clients, in D. E. Marcinko. *Financial Planner's Library on CD-ROM*. Aspen Publishers, New York, 2003.

Wagner, R., The Art of Money, in D. E. Marcinko, *Financial Planning for Physicians and Healthcare Professionals,* Aspen Publishers, New York, 2003.

Chapter 2

The Economic Basis for Personal Financial Planning

Restraining Immediate Consumption . . . Promoting Delayed Gratification

David Edward Marcinko
Hope Rachel Hetico
Rachel Pentin-Maki

Consumerism is a pattern of behavior that helps to destroy our environment, personal financial health, the common good of individuals and human institutions.

www.verdant.net

B roadly speaking, Americans, particularly medical professionals, value their possessions. Mini-manses, sport utility vehicles, home surround-sound theaters, clothes, cars, computers, cell phones, personal digital assistants, and all sorts of new healthcare technology. Consumerism is the major variable dominant in our domestic marketplace that pushes the U.S. economy forward.

This became apparent to us while waiting in a physician's office one afternoon recently. The front office receptionist, who appeared to be about 21 years old, was breaking for lunch and her replacement appeared to be not much older. Realizing the possibility of a long wait, we were taken by the size of the waiting room and the number of patients coming in and out of the office. We realized that Americans consume health care, and a lot of it. There was another notable peculiarity. The sample prescription bags being carried out the door were no match for the bags under everyone's eyes, including the physician's. The office staff was probably working overtime, if not two jobs, and the physician was working harder and faster in a managed care system. Why? So they all could afford to buy more stuff and voraciously consume for their children and themselves. Americans indeed work longer hours than any other industrialized nation.

In fact, in a study by the Kaiser Permanente Foundation in California, physicians there chose to work four hours longer each week rather than take a 10% pay cut. These physician consumers clearly valued stuff over free time. Consumerism is what keeps economies alive and well. What a perfect way to describe medical professionals, sans most concepts of financial planning.

Basic Microeconomic Concepts

Let's begin by reviewing some of the important microeconomic concepts required for the personal financial planning process.

[A] Short-Term Assets

Short-term goals (less than 12 months) require liquidity or short-term assets. These assets include cash, checking and saving accounts, certificates of deposit, and money market accounts. These accounts have two things in common because the principal is guaranteed from risk of loss and the accounts pay a very low interest rate. As an investment, they are considered substandard, and one would keep only what is actually needed for liquidity purposes in these accounts.

[B] Long-Term Assets

Longer term assets (more than 12 months) include real estate, mutual funds, retirement plans, stocks, and life insurance cash value policies. Bonds may also be an appropriate long-term investment for a number of reasons, i.e., if one is seeking a regular and reliable stream of income or if one has no immediate need for the amount of the principal invested. Bonds also can be used to diversify one's portfolio and reduce the overall risk that is inherent in stock investments.

[C] Short-Term Liabilities

Short-term liabilities (less than 12 months) include credit card debt, utility bills, and auto loans or auto leasing. When a young physician leaves residency and starts practice, his or her foremost concern is repaying student debt. This is an unsecured debt that is not backed by any collateral except a promise to pay. There are recourses that an unsecured creditor can take to recoup the bad debt. Usually, if the unsecured creditor is successful obtaining a judgment, it can force wages to be garnished, and the Department of Education can withhold up to 10% of wages without first initiating a lawsuit, if in default.

It is also probable that young physicians have been using at least one credit card since their sophomore year in college. Credit card companies consider college students the most lucrative target market, and medical students use their first credit card for an average of 15 years. Several other types of other unsecured debt might include department store credit cards, professional fees, medical and dental bills, alimony, child support, rent, utility bills, personal loans from relatives, and health club dues.

[D] Long-Term Liabilities

A secured debt, on the other hand, is debt that is pledged for repayment of the loan by a specific property. This is a collateralized loan. Generally, the purchased item is pledged with the proceeds of the loan. This would include long-term liabilities (more than 12 months) such as a mortgage, home equity loan, or a car loan. Although the creditor has the ability to take possession of the property to recover a bad debt, repossession happens very rarely. A creditor is more interested in recovering money. Sometimes, a person borrowing money may be required to pledge assets that are owned prior to the loan.

Be aware that some assets and liabilities defy short-or long-term definition. When this happens, simply be consistent in your comparison of financial statements over time.

[E] Personal Net Worth Calculations

Once you know the value of all personal assets and liabilities, you can determine net worth with the following formula: *Net worth = assets minus liabilities.* Obviously, higher net worth is better.

In *The Millionaire Next Door*,[1] Thomas H. Stanley, PhD, and William H. Danko give the following benchmark for net worth accumulation. Although conservative for physicians of a past generation, this benchmark may be more applicable in the future because of the current managed care environment. Here is the guide: Multiply your age by your annual pre-tax income from all sources, except inheritances, and then divide by ten.

Example:

As an HMO pediatrician, Dr. Curtis earned $60,000 last year. If she is 35, her net worth should be at least $210,000.

How do you get to that point? In a word, consume less and save more. Stanley and Danko found that the typical millionaire set aside 15% of earned income annually and has enough invested to survive 10 years, at current income levels if he stopped working. If Dr. Curtis lost her job tomorrow, how long could she pay herself the same salary?

[F] Common Liability Management Mistakes

A common liability management mistake is not recognizing when one is heading for trouble. If one does not categorize one's debt, one could find oneself paying down non-priority debt while ignoring priority debt. A priority debt is one that is immediate or subject to serious consequences, if not paid. Examples include rent, mortgage payments, utility bills, child support, car payments, unpaid taxes, and other secured debt.

If in one month, a physician had to choose between paying his accounting bill or his rent, it would be essential to pay the rent. A physician cannot practice from the street.

Home Mortgages and Related Consumer Items

Before you apply for a home mortgage, review your credit history and then pre-qualify before you begin house hunting. A big car note, excessive credit card debt, and medical school or residency loan burdens are big obstacles to securing a favorable mortgage.[2] For buyers of moderately priced homes, Fannie Mae and Freddie Mac raised the conventional mortgage limit for single-family homes to $322,700 in 2003, allowing approximately 210,000 more families to take advantage of the program.

Jumbo mortgages above this amount can be privately arranged, but at a higher interest rate. A Web site such as *www.realtor.com* will assist one in finding a home since it claims to list more than 1.3 million homes for sale throughout the country.

Also, consider using a buyer's agent to find your dream home, since the agent probably will not cost you anything, except the agent may require a retainer for purchasing a very large home. A buyer's agent fee comes from splitting the commission with selling agents. However, unlike a seller's agent, a buyer's agent works for you and will not disclose any information that might help the seller.[3] Once you have found a home, the following types of mortgages should be considered.

An Adjustable-Rate Mortgage (ARM) is a long-term mortgage with short-term (usually annual) adjustments to the interest rate. It is common to start with an interest rate two percentage points below comparable fixed mortgage rates. If the prevailing rate on mortgages increases over time, so will the rate on the ARM. There is usually a high cap that the rate cannot exceed. An ARM is almost always cheaper than a fixed mortgage in the short run, such as the first five years. After that, the ARM will have to be re-evaluated to see if converting to a fixed mortgage is appropriate. If lower monthly housing costs are needed to make ends meet, an ARM may be the proper choice. Also, if one wants to live in the house only for the next five years or less, then an ARM is applicable. In some cases, the lender allows the ARM to be assumed by the new buyer.

If, on the other hand, you feel comfortable with the current mortgage rate and monthly payment, you may want to lock in the rate with a fixed rate mortgage. If the idea of increasing rates and payments is distasteful, a fixed rate mortgage might be appropriate. As your income rises, you can allocate more toward retirement and other goals or perhaps pay down the principal faster. There is a preferable way to accomplish this. Many physicians send to their lender an extra $100 or $200 each month in addition to the scheduled payment. In this case, the lender needs to recalculate your amortization schedule every time you make a payment. Some lenders are more equipped to do this than others. Others will only do this recalculation once each year on your anniversary date. You should never have to pay for such mortgage accelerator programs. A better way to keep track of your outstanding balance would be to pay down the exact principal amount due in the next or several monthly payments. You can do this easily by requesting an amortization schedule from the lender at the beginning of the process.

If you have a 30-year fixed mortgage, for example, you will have a schedule with payments numbered from 1 to 360. You could then submit your regular payment (number 1) and the principal amounts from payments numbers 2, 3, and 4. In this way, you will be advancing yourself in the amortization schedule, and you can figure out your outstanding balance, remaining term, and interest saved at any time. You will make it easier for the lender as well. A free mortgage calculator may be downloaded from www.money99.com, for more precise calculations and various "what if" scenarios. Another site for salary calculations is www.homefair.com/cal/salcalc_res.html.

Other types of mortgages are available. A hybrid mortgage starts out at a fixed rate for the first few years (from three to ten), then converts to an adjustable for the remaining term of the mortgage. In this way, you can start out with a lower rate than a normal fixed, and you can count on this payment staying the same for a period during which your income might be low. In later years, when your income rises, you can afford the mortgage rate to rise.

A two-step mortgage is similar to a hybrid, since it starts out as fixed rate, with a lower than market rate. Then, the two-step mortgage converts to a fixed with a higher than market rate. This would be advisable if you plan on moving before the conversion or if you will be able to refinance because of the improvement to your income.

A balloon mortgage starts off with a low fixed rate for an average of five years, and then the entire loan becomes due. Many large real estate deals are structured this way. If you are not able to pay the lump sum when due, you are expected to find another lender to refinance the loan.

An assumable mortgage can be taken over from the previous owner if the lender is willing to transfer the old loan to you at the same or a different interest rate. This may or may not be a bargain, depending on interest rates. Paperwork and closing costs are reduced, and closing time frames are usually shorter than with the other types of mortgages. Disadvantages include that the seller is usually liable for the note upon default, and therefore the seller is less willing to negotiate sale of the house for a lower price.

Remember, after you receive money from your mortgage lender, you will still need cash for various other negotiable items such as earnest money, closing costs, an application fee, title search and title insurance, attorney's fees, appraisal fees, points, and loan origination fees.

Other more sophisticated mortgage types include biweekly mortgages, growing equity mortgages, graduated payment mortgages, Federal Housing Authority and Veteran's loans. The following Web sites are helpful in this regard because they contain explanations of each type of loan, a real-time listing of rates and lenders, calculators, and other useful tools for traditional and sophisticated mortgages vehicles: www.hsh.com, www.homepath.com, www.bankrate.com, www.rate.net, www.iown.com, and www.kiplinger.com.

Generally, points and origination fees can be deducted in the first year on original mortgages, but not on refinancing loans. For refinancing, the deduction must be spread over the life of the mortgage. Real estate commissions on a home sale are not tax deductible.

Example: A 30-year, $100,000 refinancing loan with 1% origination fee and one point. Total points are the equivalent of 2%, or $2000. So, you may deduct $2000/30 years = $66.67 each year as pre-paid interest. Often, points and fees can be added to the loan, but if you refinance again, you may deduct rather than amortize the remainder of the points you paid on the refinancing. If you have refinanced twice, but did not deduct the points from the first refinancing, you may file an amended tax return to recapture the deduction.

Private mortgage insurance (PMI) premiums range from about 0.5% of a home mortgage to about 1%. PMI can be avoided with a down payment of at least 20%. The insurance protects the lender, not you, should a default occur. When rising home values boost your equity, PMI can be dropped upon request. Similarly, most mortgages can be prepaid without penalty. Any penalty can be treated as interest and may be deducted in the year paid.

[A] Mortgage Refinancing Considerations

Example: Now, let's assume that Dr. Jenninfer Sadowski, a poor credit risk, obtains a 30-year, $100,000 mortgage, at 10%, and her monthly mortgage payment is $878. She refinances the loan at 7.5% with a new monthly payment of $700. Her monthly savings is not $178, as one might initially assume, since no consideration has been made for after-tax consequences. In order to calculate this amount, she must multiply her tax bracket (28%) by the pre-tax savings amount of $178, and then subtract, to arrive at the accurate, tax adjusted amount:

$ 178
–50 ($178 x .28)
—————————
$128 less per month

[B] Mortgage Payback Ratio

Prepaying principal on your mortgage is not advisable unless you have an emergency fund available. Then it makes good sense to pay extra toward the principal on your mortgage. With the bull market of the past decade, some authorities opined that any extra funds might have earned a better rate of return if invested elsewhere. In light of the current bear market, however, was this a prudent philosophy?

Another rule of thumb is that you should spend only 28% of your gross monthly income on your mortgage payment, PMI, real estate, school tax, and homeowners insurance. Lenders use this test to determine how large a mortgage you would qualify for. A lender considers your other consumer debt payments such as your car, student loan, and credit card payments. Your total debt should not exceed 36% of your gross monthly income. This debt could be higher if you have an excellent credit history or you are making a large down payment. For peak financial health, we suggest that you only buy a home that you like and can comfortably afford. Also, stay away from mortgage insurance to cover the cost of your outstanding balance. It is too costly, and you can get a better deal using a term or universal life insurance policy.

Consider the following example if you want to refinance your existing mortgage.

Mortgage Refinancing: OK if the new rate is 1–2%, or less than the old rate
Payback Period (months): cost to refinance/savings per month
Cost of $1 deductible interest: $1 (1–Marginal Tax Bracket)

Current mortgage: $100,000 @ 10% for 30 Yrs = $877.57 / month
New mortgage: $100,000 @ 7% for 30 Yrs = $665.30 / month
Difference   **$212.27 / month**

[handwritten: Find spreadsheet on internet for this calculation]

Given:

1 point – origination fee = $1000
1 point – discount fee   = $1000
Title Insurance   =   500
Recording Fee   =   400
Total costs   **$3200 / $212.27 = 15 months**

Generally, a payback period of less than 24 months is recommended. In this case, if you stay in the house longer than 15 months, you would recoup the costs of refinancing and benefit from the lower rate.

Remember, that since it is not likely that your income will dramatically increase over time like physicians before managed care, a lender may not approve you for a larger mortgage than you can qualify for. Moreover, the more money you allocate toward housing, the less you are going to allocate toward other important goals like investing or retirement.

[C] Reverse Mortgages

A reverse mortgage gives medical professionals several options for withdrawing equity from their homes.

1. Line of credit option allows you to decide the timing and amount of withdrawals.
2. Tenure option involves equal monthly payments for as long as the home is occupied as a principal residence.
3. Modified tenure option is a mixture of loan payments and an available line of credit. Reverse mortgages may be ideal for medical professionals who own their own homes "free and clear," since payments are considered a "return of principle" and not taxable income. These mortgages can be prepaid at any time. Moreover, you do not give up any of the benefits or responsibilities of home ownership with a reverse mortgage, but upon your death, your heirs must pay the balance of the mortgage, normally with proceeds from sale of the house.

[D] Apartments and Renting

Most physicians should probably not spend more than 30% of take-home pay for rent on a personal apartment. Advantages of renting include: freedom and flexibility, more square footage for the money, less concern about property values, and more liquidity for other financial needs or desires.

According to *Career Magazine*, several Web sites link apartment rentals, real estate companies, and other resources (www.careermag.com/relocate/).[4] Another Web site amcic.com/relocation contains information on demographics, schools, crime reports, and realtors. Additionally, the firm 4Relo.com[5] compares Web sites, and the information the sites provide on renting and relocation home issues. Be sure to get replacement cost coverage renter's insurance, rather than the older cash value type insurance policy.

[E] Automobiles

Buying an expensive automobile has become a little less costly since 2001 because the luxury excise tax was reduced to 4% from 5%. Additionally, the threshold was raised to $38,000, from $36,000. Moreover, the tax was gradually phased out and continued to drop one percentage point through 2002, after which it expired on December 31, 2002. It is now 0%.

Regardless, physicians should try to avoid luxury cars and prudently not spend more than 10–15% of gross income on the cost of a car, including gas, insurance, and maintenance, regardless of whether it is new or pre-owned. Be aware that some new cars depreciate 10–20% the moment they are driven off the lot, so resist the urge to buy a new vehicle. Never finance for more than four years, sell your old car yourself, and make your car last at least seven years. Some insurance companies will give you a reduced rate for cars equipped with a driver side airbag or anti-lock brakes, as well as for physicians who live less than ten miles from the office.

Example: If Dr. Sue Kosmicky, a dermatologist, makes $80,000, her car allowance should not be more than $8,000, using the 10 percent gross income rule of thumb. So, if insurance is $1,200 annually, she can afford to make $6,800 in car payments per year. Adding $1,200 for gas and $800 for repairs reduces this amount to $4,800 per year, or $400 per month.

Leasing a car may have several advantages such as convenient maintenance, low down and monthly payments, no resale responsibility, and tax savings since you pay sales tax on the lease portion rather than the purchase price of the car.[6] Leasing might also be worthwhile if the after tax borrowing cost of a home equity loan is less than the lease-financing rate.

There are two types of leases: open and closed ended. In the former type, if the car is worth more than the set price upon expiration of the lease, you are responsible for the underage or coverage. In the more advantageous latter type, the responsibility for the value of the car is shifted to the leasing company. Other tips on car leasing include:

- Inform the lessor how you want the auto equipped; do not accept unwanted options.
- Obtain all delivery and other charges in advance, including down payment and security.
- Know deposit, registration fees, interest rates, residual value, rebates and all taxes (sales, personal property, use, and gross receipt).
- Know the capitalized cost (selling price) of the car.
- Know annual mileage limits, usually 15,000–18,000 miles, and all excess use charges.
- Avoid maintenance and service contracts and arrange for your own insurance.
- Understand that terms, such as money factor or interest factor, may be used instead of the term interest rate. In this case, simply multiply the rate by 24 for an estimate of the true interest rate involved.
- Read the contract and understand all penalties, especially for premature or late termination, purchase or return terms, and consequences of theft.
- Check the lease terms through an independent company such as First National Lease Systems.

A general rule of thumb for determining whether to buy or lease involves multiplying all the payments required by the number of months you will have to pay and adding the down payment to yield the total amount of the purchase. Then, multiply the lease payment by the number of months, and add required upfront costs, as well as residual value (end of lease buyout cost), to determine the total cost of leasing. Compare the two figures to determine the most economical deal. Typically, a cash deal is less expensive in the long run, providing that a higher after tax rate of return is not available as an alternate investment for the funds.

Perhaps the worst reason to lease a car is to drive one that you could not otherwise afford to drive. Most low monthly payments are composed of only two portions: interest on the note and the prorated cost of auto depreciation. No money is applied toward ownership of the vehicle. Finally, do not buy "gap" insurance to cover the difference between what your auto insurer would pay if your car was totaled and what you would owe the leasing firm. It is usually too expensive, and the risk is minimal.

Finally, according to the JD Powers and Associates 2002-03 Sales Satisfaction Index, you can expect expensive automobile models to show up on a list of top-rated used cars. But, affordable autos are on that list as well. The following 20 brands are listed in order of highest owner satisfaction ratings to lowest after five years of use:

1. Saturn	5. Jaguar	9. Mercury
2. Cadillac	6. Mercedes-Benz; Jaguar	10. Buick
3. Lincoln	7. Volvo	11. Infiniti
4. Lexus	8. Porsche	12. Oldsmobile

13. Saab	16. Land Rover	19. Chrysler
14. BMW	17. Ford	20. Audi
15. GMC	18. Chevrolet	

[F] Weddings

The average wedding costs about $20,500 in 2003, segmented in the following manner. Medical professionals often spend much more than average.

Reception:	$8,458	Flowers	856
Rings	4,060	Rehearsal dinner	798
Photography	1,311	Men's formalwear	649
Bride's Dress	896	Other	1,752
Music	830		
Bridesmaids' dresses	890	**Total:**	**$20,500**

However, if wedding spending is cut in half on the top three items, the $6,500 might be better invested for the future, and if it earns about 10%, at a 28% marginal tax bracket (MTB), the following will occur:

Year(s)	Balance	Return	Taxes	Year End Balance
1	$6,500	650	221	6,929
20	21,892	744	744	23,337
40	78,603	7,860	2,672	83,791

Therefore, do you want a big wedding party for your family and friends or an earlier retirement for yourself?[7]

[G] Personal Financial Ratios

The economic platitudes of the past, such as don't spend more than 15–20% of your net salary on food, or 5–10% on medical care, among others, have given rise to the more individualized personal financial ratio concept. Personal ratios, like business ratios, represent benchmarks to compare such parameters as debt, income growth, and net worth.

According to personal financial expert Edward McCarthy, MIB, CFP, the following represent useful modified ratios for the medical professional.

- Basic Liquidity Ratio = liquid assets / average monthly expenses. Should be 4–6 months, or even longer, in the case of a medical professional employed by a financially insecure health maintenance organization (HMO).

- Debt to Assets Ratio = total debt / total assets. A percentage that is high initially, and should decrease with age as the medical professional approaches a debt free existence.

- Debt to Gross Income Ratio = annual debt repayments/annual gross income. A percentage representing the adequacy of current income for existing debt repayments. Medical professionals should try to keep this below 25–30%.

- Debt Service Ratio = annual debt repayment/annual take-home pay. Medical professionals should try to keep this ratio below about 40%, or have difficulty paying down debt.

- Investment Assets to Net Worth Ratio = investment assets/net worth. This ratio should increase over time, as retirement for the medical professional approaches.

- Savings to Income Ratio = savings / annual income. This ratio should also increase over time, especially as major obligations are retired.

- Real Growth Ratio = (income this year –income last year) / (income last year – inflation rate). It is desirable for the medical professional to keep this ratio growing faster than the core rate of inflation.

- Growth of Net Worth Ratio = (net worth this year – net worth last year) / net worth last year – inflation rate. Again, this ratio should stay ahead of inflation.[8]

By calculating these ratios, perhaps on an annual basis, the physician can spot problems, correct them, and continue progressing toward stated financial goals.

[H] Current Rate of Return

Another important concept to understand is the current rate of return. According to this principle, the current rate of a taxable return must be evaluated in reference to a similar non-taxable rate of return. This allows you to focus on your portfolio's real (after-tax return), rather than its nominal, or stated, return. Since most physicians own a combination of both vehicles, it is important to calculate the average rate of return, as demonstrated in Exhibit 2–1. Usually, this will result in the assumption of more risk for the possibility of greater return.

Exhibit 2–1 *Current Rate of Return Matrix (Mtb = 28%)**

| (Not Currently Taxed) | | | | | |
Asset	Amount	Avg. Return	(X)	% Total	Weighted Est. ROR%
IRA	$8,200	9.0%		6.81	.61
IRA	$8,200	9.0%		6.81	.61
401k	$102,000	6.5%		84.70	5.51
Insurance	2,000	2.0%		1.66	.03
Cash Value					
Sub-Total	$120,400			100%	6.77%

(Currently Taxed) Asset	Amount	Avg. Return %	(X)	% Total	Weighted Est. ROR%
Checking	$9,500	3.0		31.32	.94
CD	10,000	8.		32.97	2.64
XYZ	8,406	5.0		27.71	1.39
Widget	2,425	3.2		8.00	.26
Sub-Total	30,331			100%	5.22
			times	(1-MTB)	x.72
				After Tax	3.76%

(Entire Portfolio)					
Not Currently Taxed	$120,400	6.77	X	79.87	5.408
Currently Taxed	30,331	3.76	X	20.13	.752
Total	$150,731				
				After Tax ROR	**6.16 %**

To compare after tax yields with taxable yields, use the following formulas:

Tax equivalent yield = yield / (1 – MTB), while taxable yield X (1 – tax rate) = tax exempt yield.

Example: If the yield on a tax exempt municipal bond was 6%, and you are in a 28% tax bracket, the equivalent taxable yield (ETY) is 8.3%, calculated in the following manner: 06 / 1.00 – .28 =.083, or 8.3% ETY. This means that you would need a taxable instrument paying almost 9% to equal the 6% tax exempt bond.

[I] Personal Budgeting Rules — ARTICLE

1. Set reasonable goals and estimate annual income. Do not keep large amounts of cash at home or in the office. Deposit cash in a money market account for safety and to earn interest.

2. Do not pay bills early, and do not have more taxes withheld from your salary than you owe. Develop spending estimates and budget fixed expenses first. Fixed expenses are usually contractual and may include housing, utilities, food, telephone, social security, medical, debt repayment, homeowner's or renter's insurance, auto, life and disability insurance, and maintenance.

3. Make variable expenses a priority. Variable expenses are not usually contractual and may include clothing, education, recreation, travel, vacation, gas, entertainment, gifts, furnishings, savings, and investments.

4. Trim variable expenses by 10–15% and fixed expenses when possible. Ultimately, all fixed expenses get paid and become variable in the long run.

5. Use carve-out or set-asides for big-ticket items and differentiate "wants from needs."

6. Know the difference between saving and investing. Savers tend to be risk adverse, and investors understand risk and takes steps to mitigate it.

7. Determine shortfalls or excesses within the budget period.

8. Track actual expenses.

9. Calculate both income and expenses as a percentage of the total, and determine if there is a better way to allocate resources. Then, review the budget on a monthly basis to determine if there is a variance. Determine if the variance was avoidable, unavoidable, or a result of inaccurate assumptions, and take needed corrective action.

[J] Zero-Based Budget

A zero-based budget means you start with the absolute essential expenses and then add expenses from there until you run out of money. This is an extremely effective, yet rigorous, exercise for most medical professionals that can be used personally or at the office. Guess what your first personal financial item should be? That's right, retirement plan contributions. Then your mortgage and other debt payments, and other required fixed expenses. From the office perspective, the first budget item should be salary expenses, both your own and your staff.

Operating assets and other big-ticket items come next, followed by the more significant items on your net income statement. Some physicians even review their income statements quarterly, line by line, in an effort to reduce expenses. Then add discretionary personal or business expenses that you have some control over. Do you run out of money before you reach the end of the month, quarter, or year? Then you had better cut back on entertainment at home or on that fancy new, but unproven piece of office or medical equipment. This sounds Draconian until you remind yourself that your choice is either a) entertainment now but no money later, or b) living a simpler lifestyle now as you invest so you're able to enjoy yourself at retirement. When you were a young physician, it may have been a difficult trade-off. But at mid-life, you're staring retirement in the face.

[K] Economic Impact of Children?

According to *Smart Money* magazine, the U.S. Department of Agriculture estimated that in 1995, over 18 years, a child cost approximately $145,320 in a middle-income family; a more realistic estimate, based on expenses from birth to college, might be closer to $400,000. The first year of a baby's life is just the beginning: The average family spends about $10,000 (including delivery, hospital stay, baby furniture, clothes, food, diapers, daycare, toys, books, well-baby visits, and immunizations) with some smart shopping, borrowing, and budgeting.

Since 1995, public university tuition has inflated at a rate of about 8%, while the tuition for independent private colleges has inflated about 6%. So, at a 4% general inflation rate, the new 21–22 year aggregate figure is closer to a whopping $575,000 per child, through college for 2004–05.

Use and Abuse of Credit

The horror stories involving credit card debt and credit reporting are well known. As of March 12, 2003, 46% of Americans were making only minimum or no payments on their credit card balances, according to the Cambridge Consumer Credit Index. In this age of managed care, understanding the rules of personal credit and credit card use is vital for all medical professionals.

[A] Medical Employers and Credit Reports

PULL FOR ALL CLIENTS?

What makes you qualify for credit? Certainly, medical professionals are no longer as desirable as creditors as they were only a decade ago, since all financial institutions now look at occupational growth potential. HMOs, hospitals, and other employers will also often run a credit report on prospective medical employees, since legal limits to the type of questions that can be asked have been strengthened. The credit report is a valuable tool since many believe that how you manage your personal finances may indicate your ability to handle job responsibilities.

For example, if you live a lifestyle you cannot afford, you may not be objective in a tough medical utilization review decision-making role. This may sound harsh, but financial personality profiling is on the rise. Thus, do not be surprised if your next job application contains an authorization for credit reports and a background check.

[B] Compiling Credit Reports

— ARTICLE HOW TO GET HOW TO BOOST WHY IMPORTANT

Your credit report is a data image of your payment history. It contains personal information, such as your social security number, date of birth, current and previous addresses, and financial payment information. Some credit reports also include your past or current employers.

Credit bureaus are information gatherers. Banks, mortgage lenders, credit card companies, and anyone else who is considering extending credit are information hunters. Credit reporting agencies sell credit reports. The three best known are Experion (formerly TRW Information Systems Inc.),[9] Trans Union Corporation,[10] and Equifax.[11] You may order a credit report from one of these agencies for about $10, while some states provide two free reports per year. If you live in Georgia, Maryland, Massachusetts, or Vermont, the reports are free. Be sure to indicate your desire for an individual or joint account report.

[C] Credit Ratings and Scoring *- part of article*

The category in which a credit agency classifies you is based upon payment history. Recently, credit reporting agencies have shifted away from ratings to a system known as credit scoring. Your score is determined by proprietary formulas that are based on your credit history, the higher the better. The practical benefits of this scoring system are numerous. First, medical professionals do not need to be experts at deciphering credit reports since the same scoring system is used by different companies. For example, Equifax sells a "Beacon Score," which is utilized in mortgage approvals. Fair Issacs is another company that offers a popular scoring system for the retail sector.

[D] Correcting Credit Report Errors *- part of article*

A credit bureau is not the place to have corrections made to your credit report. Instead, you must take the problem directly to the credit issuer. In any case, a late payment noted on a credit report by a durable medical equipment (DME) vendor, for example, has to be addressed directly with that merchant. The DME merchant then has 30 days to acknowledge your complaint and respond to you. In the meantime, you do not have to pay for the disputed items. Most credit errors cannot be reported or kept on your credit report for more than seven years. For legitimate late payments, you should contact the credit grantor and negotiate to take one of the following steps. Be tenacious, and either have the late payment removed or write a letter explaining that the problem has been resolved, and you now are a good credit risk again. This letter is a powerful tool and should be saved with other permanent financial records. The industry term for it is a letter of correction.

[E] Debt Ratios and Credit

The debt to income ratio is a formula used by most lenders and is represented as take home pay divided by your monthly debt. For example, let's say that ABC Bank has issued you a VISA card with a $1,500 limit. You use the card, and one day you receive a letter stating that your credit limit has been increased. The new higher limit is considered "available credit." Then XYZ bank sends you a MasterCard. Your credit limit is $2000, and all you have to do is call their toll free number to activate it. You wisely determine that you do not need the card and don't activate it. Unfortunately, the $2000 is still considered available credit and may be held against you. When you apply for a loan, the loan issuer will run a credit report on you. The credit report will add up your total credit card limits, whether they are active or not. This is your available credit. If your available credit is considered too high, you will not be approved for your loan, or approval will cost a higher interest rate. Taking the process one step further, the potential creditor will add your total available credit and figure out the minimum monthly payment. This number is used against you as follows.

Let's suppose that, as a new internist for an HMO, you are earning $8000 per month. You apply for an auto loan. A typical debt to income ratio is 35–40%. On the generous side, 40% of $8000 is $3200. In other words, your total monthly debt payment must be $3200 or less to have your loan approved. Unfortunately, your newly raised credit limit and nonused cards could cost you an additional $600 per month if they were maximized out. Your current monthly payments are $2600. Your new car payment is $450. The total is $3050. Your loan should be approved, but by including the extra $600, you realize that you could potentially be required to pay this money every month. Your monthly obligations are considered to be $3200. Add in a car payment of $450, and the total is $3650.

[F] Debit Cards

Unlike credit cards, debit cards deduct the amount of purchase directly from your checking or other account. There is no grace period or "float" on them, and the safeguards against loss or theft are not as strict as with conventional credit cards.

[G] Disposable Credit Cards

Disposable credit cards are the newest innovation to help reduce fraud and assumed identity scams on e-commerce based Web sites. As with traditional credit cards, these cards are numbered, but you use them only once. Then, they are erased electronically so that there is nothing left in the merchant's database for hackers to steal. Currently, disposable credit cards are available from American Express, Discover, and MBNA America (Wilmington, Delaware). Unfortunately, they can be inconvenient since use is not possible on one-click shopping sites like Amazon.com, where permanent card numbers must be stored.

[H] Reorganization and Bankruptcy

The medical professional should be familiar with the two kinds of bankruptcy. They are liquidation and re-organization. In the United States, the first bankruptcy laws date back to the early 1800s. Today's law is the Bankruptcy Act, which was enacted by Congress in 1978. Chapter 7 involves liquidation bankruptcy. Chapters 11 and 13 involve reorganizations, which require a repayment plan.

As a physician, if you file for a Chapter 7 bankruptcy, you are requesting that the court eliminate your debt. You must disclose all that you own and all the income you earn. The court then assigns a trustee. The trustee has the authority to take control of any non-exempt property you purchased prior to the filing. You keep control of property you claim to be exempt. What assets you claim to be exempt are scrutinized by the trustee. This is because the trustee has the ability to sell all non-exempt property to satisfy any unsecured creditors, either fully or partially. You can, however, keep any property you purchase after filing for bankruptcy. Examples of exempt property are clothing, personal effects, household goods, and some or all of the equity in your home or car.

When the bankruptcy case is closed, you are discharged of most or all of your debt. You can choose to have some debt non-canceled; in this case, you would keep the property and make payments under a new loan agreement.

Chapter 13 bankruptcy follows the same administrative procedure and paperwork. You still need to claim your assets, debts, and income. However, you also must provide a loan repayment plan that fits into your budget. You are allowed to pay your reasonable living and office expenses. If there is any surplus, that amount is surrendered to the trustee who in turn pays your creditors. If at the end of a three-year period, all debts are not fully repaid, they are usually forgiven. One type of debt that is usually not forgiven is federal income taxes. The Internal Revenue Service will, however, stop accruing interest on the outstanding balance. Also, Chapters 7 and 13 will not discharge alimony or child support payments, debts stemming from accidental infliction of personal injury or death, driving while intoxicated (DWI) related debt, and criminal fines.

There are a few differences between using a Consumer Credit Counseling Service (CCCS) and Chapter 13 bankruptcy. Under Chapter 13, there are filing and attorney fees. CCCS may have a small fee, which is sometimes waived. Creditors are stopped from proceeding with collection actions if you miss a monthly payment under Chapter 13. The CCCS plan does not provide this protection. After three years, your debts are wiped out under Chapter 13. The CCCS plan requires that your debts remain until paid in full.

Chapter 11 bankruptcy applies to healthcare professionals with unusually high debts. Typically businesses undergoing reorganization that want to remain in business would opt for Chapter 11. It is also available to individual physicians with debt in excess of Chapter 13 limits ($269,250 of unsecured debt and/or $807,750 of secured debt), or substantial non-exempt property such as real estate. The debtor would remain in control of the assets, so, in effect, the debtor becomes the trustee. Therefore, the debtor has the power to reject creditor claims with no penalty, extend the time for repayment, and even reduce the debt owed the creditor.

Chapter 11 may sound like a windfall for debtor physicians, but it does not come without great cost. It can take an extremely long time, averaging between several months and several years, to achieve Chapter 11 status. The filing fee is $830, and professional fees for a legal retainer generally start at $10,000 but can run to tens of thousands. Before the court confirms Chapter 11, the physician debtor must provide a Plan of Reorganization. This requires a tremendous effort in pre-bankruptcy planning. Many Chapter 11 physician bankruptcies turn into Chapter 7 bankruptcies.

Also, be aware that all bankruptcy options may be soon less inviting to debt-burdened physicians and consumers. A new U.S. Senate approved bill will push more people into debt repayment plans, rather than letting them erase their debts with the above machinations. As enacted, the bill would:

- Limit repeat bankruptcy filings;
- Require credit counseling before filing for bankruptcy with some exceptions;
- Place child support payments first in line, ahead of credit card debts and other obligations.

Basic Financial Planning Money Concepts

Most money principles of personal financial planning evolve from the following concepts.

[A] Marketability and Liquidity

Marketability and *liquidity* are two concepts that are interrelated but often confused by the medical professional. Marketability deals with the speed at which an asset can be turned into cash. Liquidity, on the other hand, deals with an asset that can be turned to cash without a significant loss of value. A physician's practice may be good investment, but it is not particularly marketable or liquid. A common stock traded on the New York Stock Exchange can be easily sold for its quoted fair market value.

[B] The Time Value of Money

To the young physician starting a career, the time value of money is not a primary concern. Time value involves spending dollars in the future compared with spending today. Paying off large student loans while earning a relatively low salary leaves barely enough for present personal consumption. In the past, the rationale to spend today, forsaking the future, was not only a function of necessity but stemmed from the probability that future income would grow appreciably higher. Today, this is no longer a given for medical professionals.

In the simplest terms, a dollar today is worth more than a dollar tomorrow. The supply and demand for a dollar today to be paid back in the future is what determines interest rates. This calls for an understanding of the concepts of present and future value.

Present value is what you have today. A dollar you have today is worth a dollar. Future value is what that dollar will grow to when compounded at a given interest rate. If you started with $100 and earned 10% income for five years, you would end up with $161. (See Exhibit 2-2.)

Exhibit 2-2 *Future Value Calculator (Dollars)*

Year	Paying Amount of	Interest Factor	Ending Amount	Interest (Annual)
1	$100	1.10	$110.00	$10.00
2	110	1.10	121.00	11.00
3	121	1.10	133.10	12.10
4	133.10	1.10	146.41	13.31
5	146.41	1.10	161.05	14.64
				$61.05

When you do not have a financial calculator such as a Hewlett-Packard 12-C, Texas Instruments BA III plus or computer spreadsheet handy, you can figure future value with this formula.

$$FV = PV (1 + i)^N$$

FV is future value, and PV is present value. The periodic interest rate is represented by the i. The number of periods being compounded is the n. The N means to the power of some number. In the example above, the equation would appear as follows:

$$FV = \$100(1+.1)^2$$
$$FV = \$100(1.21)$$
$$FV = \$121$$

Likewise, the formula for present value is: $PV = amount / (1 + i)^N$.

Other time value of money concepts, easily determined with a calculator or interest table (see Table 2-1 and Table 2-2), include the future value of multiple (equal) cash flows (ordinary annuity); conversion to an annuity due; the present value of multiple (equal) cash flows (ordinary annuity); and the conversion to an annuity due.[12]

[C] Personal Lifestyle

Additional risk determinations can be estimated from the following personal lifestyle matrix (Exhibit 2-3).

Exhibit 2-3 *Personal Life Cycle Matrix*

	Earnings	*Assets*	*Savings*	*Debt*
Accumulation Phase	rising	small	low	high
Preservation Phase	high	rising	increased	low
Dissipation Phase	lower	little	lower	none

[D] Preparing a Net Worth Statement

The key to starting the financial planning process is determining your current financial position. A statement of net worth includes all your assets and liabilities, at a specific time, whether you own them or provided by your practice. This is similar to a corporate balance sheet, except that a balance sheet shows assets at their original cost. Your net worth statement shows assets at their fair market value.[13]

Exhibit 2-4 provides a sample net worth statement for you to get started with your financial planning process. Because this part of the process is the basis of so many others, we separate the ownership of assets. This provides you with the backdrop for estate or retirement planning.

Table 2-1 *Lump Sum Interest Table*

(Future values of $1.00 lump sum invested at begnning of year one at various annual interest rates)

Year	5%	6%	7%	8%	9%	10%	11%	12%
1	1.05	1.06	1.07	1.08	1.09	1.10	1.11	1.12
2	1.10	1.12	1.14	1.17	1.19	1.21	1.23	1.25
3	1.16	1.19	1.23	1.26	1.30	1.33	1.37	1.40
4	1.22	1.26	1.31	1.36	1.41	1.46	1.52	1.57
5	1.28	1.34	1.40	1.47	1.54	1.61	1.69	1.76
6	1.34	1.42	1.50	1.59	1.68	1.77	1.87	1.97
7	1.41	1.50	1.61	1.71	1.83	1.95	2.08	2.21
8	1.48	1.59	1.72	1.85	1.99	2.14	2.30	2.48
9	1.55	1.69	1.84	2.00	2.17	2.36	2.56	2.77
10	1.63	1.79	1.97	2.16	2.37	2.59	2.84	3.11
11	1.71	1.90	2.10	2.33	2.58	2.85	3.15	3.48
12	1.80	2.01	2.25	2.52	2.81	3.14	3.50	3.90
13	1.89	2.13	2.41	2.72	3.07	3.45	3.88	4.36
14	1.98	2.26	2.58	2.94	3.34	3.80	4.31	4.89
15	2.08	2.40	2.76	3.17	3.64	4.18	4.78	5.47
16	2.18	2.54	2.95	3.43	3.97	4.59	5.31	6.13
17	2.29	2.69	3.16	3.70	4.33	5.05	5.90	6.87
18	2.41	2.85	3.38	4.00	4.72	5.56	6.54	7.69
19	2.53	3.03	3.62	4.32	5.14	6.12	7.26	8.61
20	2.65	3.21	3.87	4.66	5.60	6.73	8.06	9.65
21	2.79	3.40	4.14	5.03	6.11	7.40	8.95	10.80
22	2.93	3.60	4.43	5.44	6.66	8.14	9.93	12.10
23	3.07	3.82	4.74	5.87	7.26	8.95	11.03	13.55
24	3.23	4.05	5.07	6.34	7.91	9.85	12.24	15.18
25	3.39	4.29	5.43	6.85	8.62	10.83	13.59	17.00
30	4.32	5.74	7.61	10.06	13.27	17.45	22.89	29.96
35	5.52	7.69	10.68	14.97	20.41	28.10	38.57	52.80
40	7.04	10.29	14.97	21.72	31.41	45.26	65.00	93.05
45	8.99	13.76	21.00	31.92	48.33	72.89	109.53	163.99
50	11.47	18.42	29.46	46.90	74.36	117.39	184.56	289.00

Table 2-2 *Per Period Interest Table*

(Future values of $1.00 invested annually at begnning of each year at various annual interest rates)

Year	5%	6%	7%	8%	9%	10%	11%	12%
1	1.05	1.06	1.07	1.08	1.09	1.10	1.11	1.12
2	2.15	2.18	2.21	2.25	2.28	2.31	2.34	2.37
3	3.31	3.37	3.44	3.51	3.57	3.64	3.71	3.78
4	4.53	4.64	4.75	4.87	4.98	5.11	5.23	5.35
5	5.80	5.98	6.15	6.34	6.52	6.72	6.91	7.12
6	7.14	7.39	7.65	7.92	8.20	8.49	8.78	9.09
7	8.55	8.90	9.26	9.64	10.03	10.44	10.86	11.23
8	10.03	10.49	10.98	11.49	12.02	12.58	13.16	13.78
9	11.58	12.18	12.82	13.49	14.19	14.40	15.72	16.55
10	13.21	13.97	14.78	15.65	16.56	17.53	18.56	19.65
11	14.92	15.87	16.89	17.98	19.14	20.38	21.71	21.13
12	16.71	17.88	19.14	20.50	21.95	23.52	25.21	27.03
13	18.60	20.02	21.55	23.21	25.02	26.98	29.09	31.39
14	20.58	22.28	24.13	26.15	28.36	30.77	33.41	36.28
15	22.66	24.67	26.89	29.32	32.00	34.95	38.19	41.75
16	24.84	27.21	29.84	32.75	35.97	39.54	43.50	47.88
17	27.13	29.91	33.00	36.45	40.30	44.60	49.40	54.75
18	29.54	32.76	36.38	40.45	45.02	50.16	55.94	62.44
19	32.07	35.79	40.00	44.76	50.16	56.28	63.20	71.05
20	34.72	38.99	43.87	49.42	55.76	63.00	71.27	80.70
21	37.51	42.39	48.01	54.46	61.87	70.40	80.21	91.50
22	40.43	46.00	52.44	59.89	68.53	78.54	90.15	103.60
23	43.50	49.82	57.18	65.76	75.79	87.50	101.17	117.16
24	46.73	53.86	62.25	72.11	83.70	97.35	113.41	132.33
25	50.11	58.16	67.68	78.95	92.32	108.18	127.00	149.33
30	69.76	83.80	101.07	122.35	148.58	180.94	220.91	270.29
35	94.84	118.12	147.91	186.10	235.12	298.13	379.16	483.46
40	126.84	164.05	213.61	279.78	368.29	486.85	645.83	859.14
45	167.69	225.51	305.75	417.43	573.19	790.80	1095.17	1521.22
50	219.82	307.76	434.99	619.67	888.44	1280.30	1852.34	2688.02

Exhibit 2-4 *Net Worth Statement, Drs. David and Hope Smith, as of July 20, 2004*

Amount in Dollars Assets	Your Name	Spouse's Name	Joint Name
Bank Accounts:			
Checking			
Savings			
Savings Bonds			
Money Market Funds			
CDs			
Credit Union Account			
Stocks			
Bonds			
Mutual Funds			
Life Insurance (Cash Value)			
Residence (Current Value)			
Other Real Estate			
Practice Interest			
Other Business Interest			
Receivables			
Trusts			
Tax Shelters			
Personal Property:			
Jewelry			
Autos			
Furnishings			
Collectibles:			
Antiques			
Fine Art			
Precious Metals			
Retirement Plan Accounts:			
Pension/Profit Sharing Plan			
Annuities			
IRAs			
Stock Option Plans			
Saving & Incentive Plans			
401k Plans			
Deferred Compensation			
Total Assets	$_____	$_____	$_____
Liabilities			
Mortgages			
Notes			
Personal Loans			
Business Loans			
Credit Card Balances			
Auto Loans/Lease			
Total Liabilities	$_____	$_____	$_____
Net Worth (Assets Less Liabilities)	$_____	$_____	$_____

[E] Preparing a Net Income Statement (Personal Lifestyle Cash Flow Plan)

Preparing a net income statement (personal lifestyle cash flow plan) that covers a specific time period may be difficult to construct because many physicians perceive it to be a tool for setting up a budget. Most physicians do not live a disciplined spending lifestyle, and a budget is viewed as a possible compromise to their lifestyle. A cash flow plan is not designed to be a budgeting tool, although *it* certainly can be. A cash flow plan is designed to provide comfort when there is surplus income that can be diverted for other planning needs. If there is no surplus income, perhaps a budget is in order to generate the funds needed. For example, when retirement savings are treated as just another periodic bill, you are more likely to succeed.

A comprehensive cash flow statement, or lifestyle budget outline, begins with an analysis of your operating checkbook and a review of various source documents, such as your tax return, credit card statements, pay stubs, and insurance policies. A typical statement will show all cash transactions that occur within one year. It is helpful to establish a monthly equivalent to all items of income and expense. However, for the purposes of getting started, items of income and expense may be noted by the frequency you are accustomed to receiving or spending them.

Exhibit 2–5 *Net Income Statement (Cash Flow Plan) for Dr. David Smith, from 01/01/2004 to 12/31/2004*

Cash receipts or inflows	Monthly Amount	Quarterly Amount	Annual Amount
Income from practice	$_____	$_____	$_____
Income from employment			
Pensions/annuities			
Interest			
Dividends			
Net rentals			
Equipment leases			
Miscellaneous			
Total inflows	$_____	$_____	$_____
Cash Disbursements or Outflows			
Housing:			
Mortgage payment/rent	$_____	$_____	$_____
Real estate tax			
Home improvements			
Utilities			
Maintenance/repairs			
Home insurance			
Food (home)			
Lunches (away from home)			
Clothing			

(continued)

Exhibit 2-5 *Net Income Statement (Cash Flow Plan) for Dr. David Smith, from 01/01/2004 to 12/31/2004* (continued)

Cash receipts or inflows	Monthly Amount	Quarterly Amount	Annual Amount
Transportation:			
Finance/lease payment	_____	_____	_____
Gas/oil/maintenance	_____	_____	_____
Auto replacement fund	_____	_____	_____
License/registration	_____	_____	_____
Insurance	_____	_____	_____
Education	_____	_____	_____
Insurance:			
Disability	_____	_____	_____
Liability	_____	_____	_____
Malpractice	_____	_____	_____
Life	_____	_____	_____
Health	_____	_____	_____
Umbrella	_____	_____	_____
Long-term care	_____	_____	_____
Other	_____	_____	_____
Miscellaneous:			
Unreimbursed business expenses	_____	_____	_____
Medical expenses	_____	_____	_____
Alimony	_____	_____	_____
Child Support/maintenance	_____	_____	_____
Child care	_____	_____	_____
Parental support	_____	_____	_____
Discretionary:			
Charitable contributions	_____	_____	_____
Vacation & travel	_____	_____	_____
Vacation home expenses	_____	_____	_____
Club dues (golf, tennis, health)	_____	_____	_____
Restaurants	_____	_____	_____
Entertainment (guests)	_____	_____	_____
Entertainment (Self, theater, sports, movies)	_____	_____	_____
Babysitting	_____	_____	_____
Books, magazines, CDs	_____	_____	_____
Gifts (holidays, wedding, birthdays)	_____	_____	_____
Personal expenses (hair care, etc.)	_____	_____	_____
Dry cleaning	_____	_____	_____
Hobbies	_____	_____	_____
Family pets	_____	_____	_____
Liquor, cigarettes, cigars	_____	_____	_____
Other	_____	_____	_____
Wealth accumulation:			
SEP-IRA/ IRA contributions	_____	_____	_____

Cash receipts or inflows	Monthly Amount	Quarterly Amount	Annual Amount
Qualified plan contributions	_____	_____	_____
Salary deferrals	_____	_____	_____
Mutual Fund purchases	_____	_____	_____
Systematic savings	_____	_____	_____
Investment real estate	_____	_____	_____
Other investments	_____	_____	_____
Taxes:			
FICA/Medicare	_____	_____	_____
Federal	_____	_____	_____
State	_____	_____	_____
Miscellaneous			
Debt financing	_____	_____	_____
Student loans	_____	_____	_____
Practice development	_____	_____	_____
Practice buyout	_____	_____	_____
Other	_____	_____	_____
Total Disbursements	$_____	$_____	$_____
Surplus (Deficit)	$_____	$_____	$_____

[F] Common Cash Flow Mistakes

1. Preparing a cash flow budget is a planning tool, not a punishment. Keep the credit cards hidden until you've paid all prior credit card bills. Paying off debt may mean that you have to use some of your savings. It is better to save the 19% finance charge than to earn 5% on your savings.

2. Do not live beyond your means. If this translates to owning a late model American car instead of a new foreign sports car, your checkbook will thank you in the long run. But, do not deny your spouse an occasional luxury and negotiate on major purchases before making them.

3. Do not confuse your marginal tax rate with your average tax rate. The former is the highest tax rate on your last increment of income, while the latter is your total tax due, divided by your tax base. Obviously, your marginal rate is higher than your average rate.

4. Do not confuse a tax credit with a tax deduction. A credit is a dollar-for-dollar deduction from your income tax liability, while a deduction is only an equivalent of your MTB. For example, in a 28% MTB, a $1 credit still equals one dollar. But a one-dollar deduction only equals 28 cents, although the deduction can also reduce some state income taxes.

5. Refinancing consumer debt with a home equity loan will not only save you interest, but the refinancing will save you income taxes as well. Shop around for the lowest rate. Do not just use the bank you do business with.

6. Entertainment is a luxury, not a necessity. This is the first area to cut back on if you find yourself short at the end of a month.

7. Pay your estimated income taxes on time, and pay fourth quarter state estimated taxes by December 31st. There is nothing worse than having to come up with a huge lump sum for taxes at the same time you have to fund your practice retirement plan.

[G] What an Integrated Personal Financial Plan Includes

Financial planning can be accomplished on an integrated (insurance, tax, investing, retirement, and estate planning) or modular basis. As the name implies, modular planning means handling one issue at a time before moving to the next (asset protection and risk management, divorce and special situations, management, practice appraisals, and succession planning). Unfortunately, of all careers, medicine is probably one of the busiest, and little time is left over for comprehensive planning. Therefore, we suggest the assistance of a competent financial and/or medical planner. The time devoted to the planning task is well worth it and has a substantial long-term payoff.

Recall the story of the old man who spent a day watching his physician son treating HMO patients in the office. The physician had been working at his usual feverish pace all morning, and although he was working hard, bitterly complained to his dad that he was not making as much money as he used to. Finally, the old man interrupted him and said, "Son, why don't you just treat the sick patients?" The son looked annoyed at his father and responded, "Dad, can't you see, I don't have time to treat just the sick ones."

Remember to add a bit of life planning and behavioral finance into the mix as well.

Summary

Therefore, once you understand basics and have constructed your own cash flow and net worth statements, you are ready to draft your financial plan according to your own personal goals and objectives. The tools and templates in this book will help. Remember, true financial planning is a fluid journey and not a destiny. Progress toward economic, personal, and medical practice goals is the objective, not some composite index, annualized rate of return, or stock price.

Endnotes

1. T. Stanley, and W. Danko, *The Millionaire Next Door,* Atlanta: Longstreet Press, 1996.

2. *See* www.iown.com/

3. For more information, contact National Association of Exclusive Buyer's Agents, 800-986-2322, www.naeba.com; or American Homeowners Foundation, 800-489-7776, www.AmericanHomeowners.org

4. *Career Magazine,* 4775 Walnut Street, Suite 2-A, Boulder, CO 80301, or see: www.careermag.com

5. www.4relo.com/

6. IRC § 917.

7. The following Web sites will assist in providing information to make this decision: www.theknot.com, www.rachel.itgo.com, or www.weddingsabout.com/home/weddings/msub29.htm

8. E. McCarthy, *The Fast Forward MBA in Financial Planning,* New York: John Wiley & Son, 1999.

9. www.experion.com or 888.397.3742.

10. www.transunion.com or 800.916.8800.

11. www.equifax.com or 800. 685.1111.

12. Note that when a cash flow occurs at the beginning of a period, it is called an annuity due. A cash flow occurring at the end of a period is called an ordinary annuity.

13. "Getting Financially Organized" is a free booklet from Citibank (1-800-669-2635).

Chapter 3

Building a Solid Foundation with Insurance

Appreciating Odds and Statistics through the Law of Large Numbers

Gary A. Cook

Life insurance helps to ensure that your family and loved ones are protected against finan-cial difficulties in the event of a premature death. Combined with tax reduction strategies, investments, retirement and estate planning, life insurance is a fundamental part of any sound financial plan ... and even more so for today's medical professionals.

Consumer Information Center

Unless you are a financial planner or insurance agent advising physicians, you will have a strong tendency to skip this chapter. The word "insurance" seems to have that effect on many physicians. The physician is assured, however, that each topic, while important, will not be covered in laborious detail.

The basis for much of today's insurance evolved from the 17th century study of prob-abilities and what is called the Law of Large Numbers. Actually, it's the language of sci-ence—mathematics—and, more precisely, statistics. Statistically, whenever a potentially random event is to be predicted, the more events recorded or tested, the more likely the final outcome will match the predictions—the first concept of the Law of Large Num-bers. Actuaries believe this instinctively. It seems that the rest of us are always trying to beat the odds.

For example, looking at all the readers of this chapter as a sample set, and assuming that they are all licensed drivers, we could predict that the reader has been involved in a minor automobile accident at sometime in his or her lifetime. If only one person ever reads this section, the likelihood of this prediction being wrong is fairly high. The more people who read it, however, the more likely this prediction will be on target. Depending on the reader's age and sex, the number of miles driven in a year, his or her particular area of the country, and some other factors, the actuary can actually predict how often this will occur and, to an uncanny degree, even the extent of the damage. Accuracy of the predictions, then, leads to profits.

Expanding on this second concept within the Law of Large Numbers, the insurance company's marketing department is tasked with enticing enough drivers (readers), into the company's risk pool to ensure the frequency distribution (experience accuracy) of the actuarial predictions. Insurance coverage can generally be obtained for vehicle-related accidents, tornado damage, cancer expenses, theft losses, cost of repairing tooth decay, death caused by a falling space lab, or any other statistically predictable event. The potential of finding an insurance underwriter willing to predict the event and develop rates usually depends equally on finding enough willing buyers to make the predictions accurate. It is not personal; it is just business. The business of insurance is basically that simple.

General Types of Insurance Policies Covering Physicians

[A] Life Insurance Overview

Life insurance transfers the financial loss resulting from death. A myriad of different families of life insurance policies exist, but they basically have two main branches: term insurance and permanent insurance.

[B] Term Insurance

Term insurance is the simplest form of life insurance and is a sensible place to begin any discussion of life insurance. Term insurance is exactly what the name implies: It provides life insurance coverage for a specified period of time, i.e., the term. At the end of the term, the policy is either canceled or continued, typically by paying higher premiums.

[1] ANNUAL RENEWABLE TERM

The oldest form of term insurance is that of annual renewable term (ART). These policies have premiums that typically begin very low, but increase steadily each year. At the end of each year, the policy owner has the option to renew coverage at the higher premium or cancel the coverage. By the time an insured person reaches age 60, and the probability of dying becomes more pronounced, the premiums start to rise drastically. The increased premium is simply a reflection of the increased chance of dying combined with the obvious fact that there are fewer lives at that age to spread the risk over. ART insurance has lost much of its popularity recently since level-premium term products have captured more market share.

[2] LEVEL TERM INSURANCE

Level term policies offer a premium that remains level for a specified period of time, usually 5, 10, 15, 20, 25, or 30 years. The most popular products have premiums that are guaranteed to remain level for the prescribed period. Beware, however, in some policies the insurance company has the right to change the premiums during this period. Following the selected level-premium period, the term policy is typically canceled, although the owner may keep the policy in force by paying higher premiums. The premiums, however, may increase drastically, sometimes to an absurd amount.

The affordability (during the selected term period) and simplicity of these products have made them very popular. It is easy to see why a 40-year-old physician would be attracted to a term policy that guarantees its premium for 20 years. It is entirely reasonable for many to obtain affordable coverage that would end exactly when it is anticipated that it will no longer be needed—at retirement. This kind of coverage is seemingly a very nice fit, unless justification can be made for longer coverage, such as the potential for poor health and the need to renew the policy when needed most (noncancellable feature).

[3] DECREASING TERM INSURANCE

Decreasing (or reducing) term is another common style of term insurance that not only lasts for a specified period of time but also reduces in death benefit each year. These are often recommended by lenders to cover mortgages as the mortgage balance decreases each year. These policies have become very rare because level term insurance is so affordable that it makes little sense to buy decreasing coverage.

As currently marketed, term products generally have excellent premiums that allow a policy owner to purchase substantial coverage for an affordable price. But it is important to keep in mind why the premium is so affordable—the vast majority of term policies never pay a death benefit. The simple reason for this unexpected fact is that most people outlive the term period or their policies are not in force when they die.

[4] TRIPLE X

Regulation XXX, also referred to as Triple X, is a model regulation from the National Association of Insurance Commissioners that was implemented on January 1, 2000. This regulation has substantially changed the manner in which an insurance company must set aside reserves for any term policy with a premium guarantee longer than 15 years or a universal life policy with a secondary guarantee of more than five years (this will be covered soon). The resolution basically requires higher reserves for policies with longer guarantee periods. Higher reserves generally resulted in the insurance companies increasing their premiums. As a direct result, if the physician has a current policy with a premium or death benefit guarantee longer than five years, the policy probably should not be replaced or lapsed without some serious thought.

[C] Permanent Insurance

Permanent insurance differs from term insurance in two major ways. First, it is usually designed to last to age 95 or 100 (commonly referred to as the maturity date) without any future requirement to re-qualify for the coverage by providing proof of good health. Some newer contracts, in fact, have no maturity date at all and are being illustrated as lasting until age 115. Second, permanent policies have some form of cash value accumulation.

One permanent insurance policy can cover a single life, two lives, or an entire family. Policies covering two lives can provide a death benefit either on the first death or the last death.

Generally, permanent insurance has a predefined level-premium payable until a stated maturity, but the premium-paying period can potentially be shortened in a number of ways. Regardless, the predefined premium is substantially higher in a permanent policy than for a comparable face-amount term insurance policy. This higher premium results in the aforementioned aspect of an internal accumulation of cash value.

This accumulation was originally designed by actuaries to help level the premium over longer periods of time. It has since, however, been seen by many as a convenient method of accumulating funds in a tax-deferred manner.

[1] COMMON TYPES OF PERMANENT INSURANCE

Permanent insurance comes in four standard variations: whole life, variable life, universal life, and variable universal life. Do not be fooled by the title *permanent*, however. Today's life insurance products are very complex, and few policies are truly permanent. Events can occur that result in policies lapsing or paying reduced benefits even when specified premiums have been submitted in a timely manner. The word permanent simply reflects the fact that these policies are expected to last until the insured's death no matter when that may be.

[2] WHOLE LIFE

Whole life, also called straight life or ordinary life, is the oldest and the most classic type of permanent insurance. Whole life insurance typically has the highest required premium of the four standard variations, but it is also the least risky for the policy owner. Whole life remains in force until maturity and is guaranteed to pay the full death benefit if the required premiums have been paid in a timely manner. The whole life family of policies also includes those referred to as Life Paid-up at 65, 83, 85, 95, etc.

Whole life premiums are fixed, i.e., they cannot be arbitrarily changed from year to year, and they must be paid in a timely manner for the entire death benefit to be kept intact. Whole life is more rigid than universal life, but it offers the highest level of guarantees. Whole life, like all permanent policies, offers growing cash values that can be borrowed by the policy owner if needed.

Because whole life is considered expensive, companies have created ways, such as term riders, to reduce the premium to more affordable levels. However, the drawback of these term riders is that more risk falls upon the policy owner. When term riders are added to a whole life policy, the premium becomes cheaper, but the entire policy is no longer guaranteed to last to maturity and/or to pay full death benefits under some situations.

When purchasing a whole life contract, the death benefit is fully guaranteed, as long as the premium is paid on time every year. At the maturity date, the internal cash values (to be discussed later) will equal the amount of guaranteed death benefit: This is called Endowment.

If the insurance company offers a participating policy and has good experience with its business over the years, i.e., fewer people die than expected, the company may offer dividends through the policy.

Dividends, paid to participating policies, are considered a return of the policy owner's premium and, therefore, are not taxable income. A policy owner can generally take dividends in cash, use them to buy paid-up additions, use them to buy one-year term additions, or have them accumulate at interest, like an additional savings account. Using the dividend to buy paid-up additions or allowing them to accumulate at interest will provide the policy owner an additional source of future premiums.

At some point in the policy's life, these funds may be sufficient to allow the policy owner to cease paying premiums and direct the insurance company to take its annual premium from these excess values. This is sometimes called a "vanishing premium" or a "short pay" premium or a "premium offset." The premiums are still due and still paid each year, but instead come from the excess external policy values rather than the owner's pocket.

A life insurance agent, or Certified Financial Planner (CFP), may illustrate this discontinued premium flow as a benefit of the policy. Beware! This is a *projection*, meaning the company is not guaranteeing the ability to stop paying premiums. This may possibly occur if the company keeps doing well, but it is not guaranteed!

Many whole life policies were sold this way in the past, and while some policies actually did allow the owner to stop paying premiums, many policies did not. This surprised many policy owners who were expecting to cease paying their premiums. The medical professional or healthcare practitioner must make sure he or she understands what policy aspects are guaranteed and what are merely projections.

A well-informed physician, when purchasing a whole life policy, will ask his or her insurance agent to check both the Standard and Poor's (or Moody's) company rating and the *AM Best's Annual Historical Dividend Report*. The first source rates financial stability of the company, while the second reports how a company's actual dividends compared to their projections for each year. It is wise to be leery of illustrations from companies that consistently fail to meet their projections.

Before you purchase a whole life product, ask to see what happens to the death benefit and premiums if the company experiences a lower dividend scale (*worse* business conditions). This will allow the purchaser to see how sensitive the policy is to different business conditions. Beware of whole life policies that are very sensitive to reduced dividend scales.

[3] UNIVERSAL LIFE INSURANCE

Universal life was developed in the late 1970s and has become a very popular product in a very short time. Generally, in terms of price and risk to the policy owner, universal life falls between term and whole life.

Universal life is similar to a bank savings account that has automatic monthly withdrawals to pay for the death benefit. Each universal life premium goes into the policy and becomes part of the cash value just as a bank savings deposit becomes part of a savings account. Some policies have a premium expense charge that generally is designed to pay the individual state premium tax. The policy's cash value also has monthly debits to pay for the death benefit and/or any riders, and most policies also charge a monthly administrative fee. The resulting cash value of the policy earns a competitive money market-like interest rate. Finally, policy owners receive an annual report that itemizes all relevant costs, to the penny. Universal life has often been called "whole life unbundled" because of this feature.

Clearly, the cash value of the universal life policy will depend on whether the amount going into the policy (premiums and interest) or the amounts leaving the policy (the cost of the death benefit and the monthly administrative fees) is larger. Additionally, the charges for the death benefit will rise over time, as the insured physician gets older (just like ART rates).

Typically, in the early years of a policy, the amounts flowing into the policy are greater than the internal charges and the subsequent cash value increases. If, at some point, the outflows exceed the inflows, the cash value will cease growing and may even decline. If the cash value falls to zero, the policy generally lapses unless more premiums are paid.

The policy owner can periodically adjust the amount and timing of the universal life premiums and even skip premiums (without incurring a loan, which results with whole life). Any change in premium amount or mode of payment will also change the cash value projections on a policy illustration. Skipping premiums will cause a drop in cash values and possibly cause a policy to lapse. If ample cash value has accumulated in the contract, the ability to skip premium without adverse consequences becomes more probable. This flexibility is one of the reasons for the popularity of universal life policies.

Because universal life policies are very interest rate sensitive, a policy owner needs to keep track of the policy values each year to make sure the policy is performing as expected. When a policy owner receives his or her "Annual Report," it is a good idea to use this as a reminder to request (from the agent or the company) a reprojection of future amounts based on the then current assumptions. This is commonly called an in-force projection or mid-stream proposal.

Just as with "vanishing premium" whole life projections, there have also been problems with universal life. In the 1980s, interest rates were very high, and this appeared to make universal life policies appear very inexpensive, compared to whole life insurance. Unfortunately, interests rates have declined dramatically, and those policies have been credited with far less interest than originally illustrated. As a result, the cash values were lower than expected, and policy owners had to either increase their premiums or risk the policies lapsing.

If purchasing a universal life policy, the physician should definitely ask to see illustrations reflecting declining interest rates. Typically the illustrations do not have to be the guaranteed rate. Ask the agent, CFP, or broker for a history of the company's rates and gauge your request accordingly. If policy performance is drastically affected, commit to a higher premium so that coverage is not jeopardized in the event of falling interest rates.

Beside being interest rate sensitive, the insurance company can also change the internal cost of the death benefit on a universal life policy. Obviously, increasing these charges could cause the cash values to drop and the policy to lapse. Companies try to avoid doing this, but it can and does happen. A potential buyer should also inquire about the company's history of "mortality cost" increases before purchasing any universal life policy. Avoid companies that have a history of raising their insurance costs or that fail to provide this vital information.

[4] VARIABLE LIFE INSURANCE

Variable life is a type of permanent insurance that comes in the same two forms discussed above: universal life and whole life insurance.

The same general design of whole life and universal life, as described above, also applies to variable whole life and variable universal life insurance. The only real difference is the availability of investment choices for the cash value of the policy. With whole life and universal life, the insurance companies generally invest the money in fixed income investments like bonds and mortgages. The insurance company then declares the interest rate that gets credited to the company's policies except term, which has no cash value.

With variable policies, the company offers the policy owner a choice of investment options. These investment options are called separate accounts and resemble traditional mutual funds. Good variable life policies should offer a wide array of investment choices including money market funds, bond funds, balanced funds, stock funds, and international funds. It is not unusual to find policies offering in excess of 30 such separate accounts.

The policy owner then chooses the account, or accounts, that match the level of his or her investment risk. Most policy owners put a majority of their premium dollars into equity accounts because these accounts have provided historically better returns than most other investments. Of course, the higher the actual returns of the separate accounts, the more the cash value grows.

This higher growth results because the internal policy expense costs of a variable policy are typically higher than the internal costs of a fixed interest rate policy. Therefore, it takes a higher return inside of a variable life policy to offset the effect of these higher internal costs. Generally, one should not purchase a variable policy unless he or she expects the separate accounts to earn an average of at least 8.5% per year.

Variable life policies give the policy owner more control over how his or her premium dollars are invested. These policies allow greater potential returns, but at greater risk, which the policy owner assumes. Variable policies have become very popular over the last 10 to 15 years because of the current bull market. These products are most appropriate for policy owners with a moderate to high risk tolerance, who believe in the long-term superiority of high-risk equities as investments and who have a long-term time horizon.

The same principles that apply to investing in general also apply to variable policies. A wise variable policy owner will invest his or her premiums in several separate accounts in order to achieve diversification. Most variable policies will also allow dollar cost averaging and asset re-balancing.

[5] OTHER VARIETIES OF LIFE POLICIES

[a] Survivorship Life Insurance

Survivorship life is commonly referred to as Second-to-Die life insurance. Unlike the typical life insurance policy that has one primary insured person and pays a death benefit when that person dies, a survivorship life policy generally has two insured people and pays a death benefit only when both of the insureds are deceased.

Survivorship products have existed for about 30 years, but these policies became very popular after passage of the unlimited marital deduction in the Economic Recovery Tax Act of 1981. These policies are used almost exclusively in the estate planning realm where the husband and wife have a combined net worth of more than two times the current unified credit, i.e., $2 million in year 2003 and $3 million in year 2004. Wealthy couples, typically between the ages of 50 and 70, purchase survivorship insurance to assist in providing adequate liquidity for estate transfer and settlement costs routinely due at the death of the second insured person.

In 1996, a new feature, a secondary guarantee, was added in universal life policies and, in particular, survivorship universal life policies. The primary guarantees in these policies were a guaranteed minimum credited interest rate and a maximum amount of monthly charges, and specifically, a *maximum charge for mortality*. The earlier versions of these policies illustrated poorly with regard to guaranteed cash values unless a whole life-type premium was paid.

Secondary guarantees have also been called no-lapse guarantees. Basically, these policies are guaranteed to stay in force for a specified number of years as long as the policy owner pays a required cumulative premium before a particular date, even if the underlying primary guarantees would allow the policy to otherwise lapse. Most important, the new no-lapse premiums were still considerably lower than that of a whole life policy. Unfortunately, Triple X regulations have forced most insurance companies to remove these products from sale or substantially increase their premium requirements for this benefit.

[b] Joint First-to-Die Life Insurance

Just as with survivorship life insurance, a joint First-to-Die policy generally insures two people. Unlike survivorship insurance, however, a joint First-to-Die policy pays upon the death of the first insured.

Joint First-to-Die policies typically make sense in family insurance planning for households where both parents work, and occasionally these policies are used for mortgage (loan) protection. The vast majority of joint First-to-Die plans, however, are used in the business world. These policies are particularly well suited for multiple key-person or for stock redemption (entity) buy-sell plans.

It is important to remember that when the first insured dies under a joint First-to-Die policy, the death benefit is paid, and the policy is terminated; coverage no longer exists on the remaining insured(s). This problem can be solved by buying a guaranteed insurability option on the policy to allow the remaining insured immediately after the first death to purchase a new joint policy with no underwriting.

Another rider that should be considered when joint policies are purchased for business planning reasons is a substitute insured rider. This allows the policy owner to exchange an insured with a new insured. This rider comes in very handy if one of the insureds leaves the business and is replaced by someone else. Unfortunately many insurance companies have withdrawn this rider because of the difficulty in administering it.

[c] Interest Sensitive Whole Life

Interest sensitive whole life, also referred to as current assumption whole life, is a hybrid of whole life and universal life. Like whole life, the premiums are fixed. Some companies fix the premium for the life of the policy, but most fix the premium only for a specified period of time. Like universal life, the current internal mortality charges are lower than for a whole life policy, but the insurance company retains the right to raise them. Also like universal life, a competitive interest rate is credited to the policy cash values each month. These policies are currently not very common.

[d] Group Life

Group life insurance coverage is very common, and the vast majority of people have this form of coverage at work and/or have the opportunity to purchase more group life insurance coverage through their employer or other associations to which they belong. Most group life insurance policies are group term because term is affordable and easy to understand, but group universal life and group variable universal life policies exist as well.

Many employers, especially larger ones, typically offer a minimum of group life insurance as an automatic employee benefit. Since current tax code provisions allow up to $50,000 of group coverage as a totally tax-free benefit, this amount is often the initial coverage. Many employers also offer the employee the ability to purchase additional group life insurance with the premium being deducted from each paycheck. The main advantage of group life insurance is its convenience.

The major disadvantages of group life insurance concern the lack of flexibility. It may not be easy to change your coverage under a group life policy, and if you leave your company, it may not be possible to take the coverage with you. For this reason, most people prefer to purchase their own individual life insurance policy for the bulk of their life insurance protection.

[e] Single Premium Life

Single premium life is exactly as the name implies: The owner pays one premium for lifetime coverage. Clearly, the premium will be much larger than any other type of insurance for an equivalent death benefit.

These policies have become quite rare since the Modified Endowment Contract (MEC) rules were established to discourage large premiums early in the life of a policy (see "Taxation of Life Insurance" later in this chapter). Nonetheless, single premium life policies still have a limited number of uses. These policies may be appropriate if tax-deferred growth is desired and the money is not needed during the insured's lifetime.

[6] THE 5 - 100 RULE

With any universal life insurance policy (and certainly all variable life policies), fluctuating rates of return, the actual timing of the premium payments, and potential internal policy changes by the insurance company all contribute to results that will probably differ substantially from the original illustration. The 5 - 100 Rule states that, as a result of accounting for these elements, all initial projections of cash value beyond five years will necessarily be 100% incorrect when compared to actuality. A prudent policy owner should therefore keep on top of any changes and react accordingly. If a policy owner ignores his or her policy for even five years, any adverse changes could be so drastic that rectifying them is very costly.

[D] Death Benefit Settlement Options

Settlement options refer to the different ways a beneficiary can receive the death benefit payable upon the death of the insured. A beneficiary commonly receives the entire death benefit in a lump sum, but this is certainly not the only choice. Another possibility of a settlement option is the *interest only option* where the beneficiary leaves the death benefit with the insurer and receives the monthly interest. Another common option is the *lifetime annuity option* where the death benefit is paid out as a guaranteed lifetime income.

Settlement options can be left to the discretion of the beneficiary. In this way, the beneficiary can make an informed choice based on the individual's particular situation at the time. Alternatively, the policy owner can specify a particular settlement option. During the life of the insured, the policy owner can instruct the insurance company to pay the beneficiary according to a design the policy owner feels appropriate. It is the opinion of the author, however, that a better alternative would be to establish a trust for any beneficiary unable to manage his or her funds, rather than use a restrictive settlement option.

Taxation of Life Insurance

Life insurance has a number of tax advantages that can be potentially rewarding. However, there are also some pitfalls that should be avoided.

[A] Income Tax-Free Death Benefit

The simplest tax advantage of life insurance is that the death benefit is received as income tax free by the beneficiary. When the insured dies, the named beneficiary generally receives all death proceeds free of any income taxes. The word generally is used because there are situations that can cause the entire death benefit, or a large part of it, to become subject to income tax.

[B] Transfer for Value Problem

The Transfer for Value problem is a situation that can cause the death benefit of a life insurance policy to be income taxable. This can be a complicated topic, and the situation may arise unexpectedly, especially when life insurance is used for business purposes.

Generally, if an existing life insurance policy is transferred to a new owner for some type of consideration (money, exchange of property, or a *quid pro quo* arrangement), then the death benefit becomes taxable to the beneficiary to the extent the proceeds exceed the basis in the policy. *Basis* becomes the amount of consideration paid at the time of transfer and all future premiums following the transfer, paid by the new owner. There are five exceptions to this rule:

1. Transfers by any person or company of their ownership to the person insured by the policy;
2. Transfers by a business partner (in the strictest sense, i.e., not a co-shareholder) to another partner in the same business;
3. Transfers to a partnership by any of the partners;
4. Transfers to a corporation in which the insured is a stockholder or officer; and
5. Transfers between corporations (under certain conditions) in a tax-free reorganization.

If a transfer for value falls under one of these exceptions, then the policy retains its tax-free death benefit status.

[C] Tax-Deferred Growth

Another tax advantage of life insurance is its income tax-deferred cash value growth. As mentioned earlier in this section, life insurance products, other than term, have cash accumulation potential. The cash values will depend on the policy style, the amount of the premiums, and also the general economic environment. If there is growth in the cash value, the growth will be tax-deferred, under current tax laws.

[D] Withdrawals and Loans

Income taxes are generally not an issue unless cash values are removed from the policy while the insured is still alive. There are three methods of accessing a policy's cash value while the insured is living. The first choice is to surrender the policy. If the policy is surrendered and the cash value is greater than the total premiums paid, the difference is subject to ordinary income tax. A policy owner must carefully consider this option before surrendering the policy because the policy no longer exists after being surrendered.

What if you want to access a portion of the cash value but not lose the coverage? Two methods, withdrawals and loans, can accomplish this. A withdrawal, also called a partial surrender, does not cause the policy to terminate, but it does lower the death benefit of the policy by the amount of the withdrawal. If a withdrawal is requested, then under the current First In, First Out accounting rules, the total amount of premiums paid into the policy are removed first, and more important, without any income tax liability. Any withdrawals removed in excess of the gross premium paid would be taxable income.

Because withdrawals beyond a policy's basis are taxable, loans against the policy are often taken at this point, because policy loans are not taxable. If the insured dies while a loan is outstanding, the insurance company repays itself from the death proceeds, and the remaining death benefit goes to the named beneficiary. In other words, the death proceeds will decrease by an amount equal to each loan. Also, unless the interest charged on the loan balance is paid annually, the size of the loan will increase as the interest accrues to the loan. So when withdrawals and loans are combined, a significant portion of a policy's cash value can be accessed while the policy is still in force.

[E] Violating the Two out of Three Rule

Another common mistake involves an issue of gift taxation. Violating the "two out of three rule" can result in a policy owner unwittingly making a sizable gift of the entire death benefit and wasting a major portion of his or her unified credit as a consequence. The *three* refers to the parties to the policy: the insured, the policy owner, and the beneficiary. *Two* of these *three* parties should almost always be the same person.

[F] Policy Replacement–Section 1035 Exchanges

If a policy owner intends to replace an existing policy with a new policy, he or she has two choices. Once the new policy is issued, the policy owner can simply surrender the first policy and receive any applicable cash value. Income taxes will be due if there is a gain in the policy.

However, most policy owners would rather transfer the cash value from the old policy into the new policy, rather than actually receive it. If this is the case, the policy owner can take advantage of an Internal Revenue Code (IRC) Section 1035 exchange. This section of the tax code allows a policy owner to transfer cash value from one life insurance policy *directly* to a new policy. The main advantage of a Section 1035 exchange, unlike a regular surrender, is that the transfer is tax free, even if the first policy had a large gain.

Section 1035 exchanges have a definite procedure that requires the insurance companies to conduct the exchange of money, much as in the trustee-to-trustee transfer of qualified funds. Additionally, this procedure only permits the transfer of a life insurance policy to another life insurance policy or an annuity policy. That is, annuities can only be transferred to annuities.

Unfortunately, policy replacement is probably recommended more often than necessary. If replacement and a Section 1035 exchange are recommended, the medical professional or healthcare practitioner should carefully review the proposal. Ensure that the assumptions made for projecting the old policy into the future are consistent with those assumptions for the new policy. Also, if replacement is warranted, a policy owner should never cancel an existing policy until the new policy is in force. Replacement will be covered again later in this chapter.

[G] Modified Endowment Contracts

Modified Endowment Contracts (MEC) is the last tax issue to be addressed here in regard to life insurance policies. Because the *cash value* of a life insurance policy grows tax-deferred, many policy owners deposited large, single premiums into their policies. Unfortunately, this was perceived as abusive by Congress because people were buying life insurance primarily as a means of escaping income tax.

As a result, the laws were changed in 1984 to discourage putting very large amounts of money into life insurance contracts in the early years. Based on the age, sex, and size of the death benefit, an MEC premium (also referred to as the TAMRA seven-pay guideline) is established for each policy. For the first seven years of the policy, the policy owner cannot pay cumulative premiums greater than the cumulative MEC premium.

If a policy is classified as an MEC, then it is treated as an annuity contract and not as a life insurance policy for any and all lifetime withdrawals or loans. Taxable interest earnings are removed before basis is recovered, i.e., all funds removed from the policy in excess of basis will be immediately taxable. If the insured is under 59½, there will also be a 10% tax penalty. Thus, one of the basic tax benefits of life insurance is destroyed. Remember from our previous example that withdrawals of non-MEC policies are not taxable until the withdrawals exceed the cumulative premiums. Finally, once a MEC, always a MEC.

Annuity Overview

Annuity contracts transfer the financial risk of living too long, i.e., outliving one's savings to the issuing insurance company. Annuities are deferred or immediate, fixed or variable, and tax-qualified or non tax-qualified.

[A] Deferred Annuities

Some people find that the deferred annuity contract, like a permanent life insurance policy, is a convenient method of accumulating wealth. Funds can be placed in deferred annuities in a lump sum (Single Premium Deferred Annuities) or periodically over time (Flexible Premium Deferred Annuities). Either way, the funds placed in a deferred annuity grow without current taxation (tax-deferred).

[1] FIXED DEFERRED ANNUITY

Fixed deferred annuities provide a guaranteed minimum rate of return (usually around 3% per year) and typically credit a higher competitive rate based on current economic conditions. Fixed annuities are usually considered conservative investments.

[2] VARIABLE DEFERRED ANNUITY

Recently, variable deferred annuities have become popular. Like fixed annuities, variable deferred annuities offer tax-deferred growth. However, variable deferred annuities offer separate accounts (similar to mutual funds) that provide different investment opportunities. In addition, most of the separate accounts have stock market exposure, and, therefore, variable annuities do not offer a guaranteed rate of return. But the potential for financial gain is typically much greater for a variable deferred annuity than for a fixed annuity.

The value of a variable deferred annuity will fluctuate with the values of the investments within the chosen separate accounts. Although similar to mutual funds, here are some key differences:

- A variable annuity provides tax deferral whereas a regular mutual fund does not.
- If a variable annuity loses money because of poor separate account performance, and the owner dies, most annuities guarantee at least a return of principal to the heirs. It is important to note that this guarantee of principal applies only if the annuity owner dies. If the annuity value decreases below the amount paid in, and

the annuity is surrendered while the owner is alive, the actual cash value is all that is available.

- When money is eventually withdrawn from a deferred annuity, it is taxable at ordinary income tax rates. Taxable mutual funds can be liquidated and taxed at lower, capital gains rates.
- There is also a 10% penalty if the annuity owner is under 59½ when money is withdrawn. No such charge applies to withdrawals from a mutual fund.
- The fees charged inside of a variable annuity (called mortality and expense charges) are typically more than the fees charged by a regular mutual fund.

Variable deferred annuities are sensible for people who want stock market exposure while minimizing taxes. Most financial planners recommend regular mutual funds when the investment time horizon is under 10 years. But if the time horizon is more than 10 years, variable annuities may become more attractive because of the additional earnings from tax deferral.

Both types of deferred annuities are subject to surrender charges. Surrender charges are applied if the annuity owner surrenders the policy during the surrender period, which typically runs for five to ten years from the purchase date. The charge usually decreases each year until it reaches zero. The purpose of the charge is to discourage early surrender of the annuity.

[B] Immediate Annuities

Immediate annuities provide a guaranteed income stream. An immediate annuity can be purchased with a single deposit of funds, possibly from savings or a pension distribution, or it can be the end result of the deferred annuity, commonly referred to as annuitization. Just like deferred annuities, immediate annuities can also be fixed or variable.

Immediate annuities can be set up to provide periodic payments to the policy owner annually, semiannually, quarterly, or monthly. The annuity payments can be paid over life or for a finite number of years. They can also be paid over the life of a single individual or over two lives.

[1] IMMEDIATE FIXED ANNUITY

Immediate fixed annuities typically pay a specified amount of money for as long as the annuitant lives. They may also be arranged to pay only for a specified period of time, e.g., 20 years. Either way, they often contain a guaranteed payout period, so that, if the annuitant lives less than the guaranteed number of years, the heirs will receive the remainder of the guaranteed payments.

[2] IMMEDIATE VARIABLE ANNUITY

Immediate variable annuities provide income payments to the annuitant that fluctuate with the returns of the separate accounts chosen. The theory is that since the stock market has historically risen over time, the annuity payments will rise over time and keep pace with inflation. If the stock market rises, variable annuities are a good purchase, but this rise in value cannot be guaranteed. Some companies will, at a minimum, provide a guarantee of a low minimum monthly payment no matter how poorly the separate accounts perform.

[C] Qualified Annuities

The term qualified refers to those annuities that permit tax-deductible contributions under one of the IRC sections, i.e., § 408 Individual Retirement Accounts (IRA), § 403(b) Tax Sheltered Annuities, and § 401(k) Voluntary Profit Savings Plans. Qualified annuities can also result from a rollover from such a plan. Non-qualified annuities, then, do not permit deductible contributions.

There is much debate whether an annuity, which is tax-deferred by nature, should also be used as a funding vehicle within a tax-qualified plan, i.e., a tax shelter within a tax shelter. The investment options within the annuity are also generally available to the plan participant without the additional management expenses of the annuity policy. This could be a breach of fiduciary responsibility, and both the National Association of Securities Dealers and the Securities and Exchange Commission have gone on record as criticizing sales of qualified annuities.

Annuity Taxation

The tax treatment of annuities is extremely dependent on whether an annuity is a qualified or non-qualified annuity. Although both permit tax-deferred growth of the investment and both have penalties for early distributions, the two types of annuities are governed under different sections of the IRC. Since qualified annuities were just discussed, we will start with them.

[A] Qualified Annuity Taxation

Qualified annuities are treated no different from any other tax-qualified retirement investment. Growth of the investment, whether fixed interest or variable-based, escapes current taxation under one of the 400-series IRC sections. Additionally, if the funds are withdrawn prior to age 59½, there is a 10% penalty. As the money is withdrawn, every dollar is taxed as ordinary income. Finally, fund distributions must begin no later than April 1 of the calendar year following the year in which the owner turns age 70½.

[B] Non-Qualified Annuity Taxation

The taxation of nonqualified annuities is generally contained within IRC § 72. Again, the annuity has tax-deferred growth and a 10% penalty for early withdrawal.

The manner in which distributions are taken, however, will determine the method of taxation.

When non-annuitized funds are withdrawn, they are taxed under Last In, First Out accounting rules. Under these rules, the first funds withdrawn are considered the investment earnings, i.e., the last funds credited to the annuity. Ordinary income tax will be charged until all earnings are removed, and only the original principal remains. This principal, having already been taxed, can then be withdrawn without any further income taxation.

On the other hand, if the annuitization option is chosen, an exclusion ratio is developed by the insurance company using governmental tables. This permits a portion of each payment to be considered a return of principal and thus only a portion of each payment is taxable. This exclusion ratio remains in effect until the insurance company has returned all the original principal to the owner. After that, each payment received will be considered 100% earnings and totally subject to ordinary income taxation.

[C] Wealth Transfer Issues

Regardless of whether the physician has a qualified or non-qualified annuity, extreme care must be taken when specifying beneficiaries. Although these investments have great potential for appreciating sizable amounts of wealth during a lifetime, they are, unfortunately, very poor vehicles for the transfer of this wealth to successor generations after death.

Upon the death of an annuity owner, an annuity can be subject to both federal estate and federal income taxes. This double taxation often results in a 40 to 70% loss of annuity value before the heirs receive it. The retired physician should seek wealth transfer advice if he or she holds a large portion of his or her wealth in annuities or other qualified plans such as IRAs. One good strategy to consider is the Stretch IRA.

Health Insurance Overview

Health insurance transfers the potential financial hardship caused by severe or chronic health conditions resulting from accidents or illnesses (morbidity), whereas life insurance is concerned with death (mortality). Health insurance, like life insurance, also has families of policies. There are medical expense/hospital policies, disability income policies, and long-term care (LTC) policies. The medical expense/hospital family of policies will not be discussed here since the physician should already be familiar with them.

[A] Disability Income Insurance

Disability income insurance is designed to transfer the financial risk of lost wages due to an accident or illness to an insurance company. The actual benefits may be received for as short a period as six months in some short-term group policies, to age 65 in both group long-term and many individual policies, and possibly even to lifetime for some individual "professional" policies. The length of the benefit period is one of the main factors in determining the premium charged by the insurance company.

[1] DISABILITY DEFINED

Arguably, the most important issue when purchasing disability insurance is the definition of disability found within the policy. Disability insurance pays a monthly benefit to the insured if he or she satisfies this definition of disability. Unlike a life insurance policy death claim, a disability income claim can be a far more difficult issue. Different policies from the same insurance company can define disability differently, and a medical professional or healthcare practitioner must be comfortable with the definition found in policy.

The more liberal the definition of disability in any given policy, the easier it would be to meet that definition, and the more likely the insurance company would pay benefits. Consequently, these are also the most expensive policies. Many agents and financial planners recommend paying the extra premium so that you have a higher chance of receiving benefits. The last thing an insured wants to do after becoming seriously injured is have to fight an insurance carrier over benefits.

There are two common definitions of disability:

- The inability to perform the substantial and material duties of your occupation, and
- The inability to perform any gainful occupation for which you are reasonably trained.

Some aggressive insurance companies have even gone so far as to define the disability in terms of occupational and/or medical specialties. Regardless, the definition will almost always end with the words "and under a physician's care."

Some policies will pay benefits under the first definition for a couple of years and then use a second definition thereafter. This design permits the insured full monthly benefits immediately after a disability and then time to rehabilitate and establish a new career.

[2] PARTIAL DISABILITY

Some policies also allow fractional benefits for a partial, or residual, disability. Partial benefits can be available under two circumstances:

1. During a disability when the insured cannot perform some of the duties of his or her occupation, or
2. When the insured can still perform all the duties of his or her occupation, but only for a limited period of time during recuperation.

The physician should pay particular attention to the partial disability benefit language in his or her policy. Some companies require total disability prior to any partial claims payment. Other companies may have no such provision and, in fact, even pay a full benefit for the first three months of partial disability.

[3] ELIMINATION PERIOD

Another aspect used in the development of a disability income insurance premium is the waiting period, i.e., that period of time that elapses prior to the payment of any benefits during which the insured must generally be continuously disabled. This time period is also referred to as the *elimination period* and in individual contracts is usually specified as 30, 60, 90, 180, or 365 days.

The shorter the elimination period is, the higher the potential premium. In short-term group policies, the standard elimination period is the first day for accidents and the seventh day for sickness. Long-term group policies traditionally begin after six months. Medical professionals and healthcare practitioners with ample savings should consider a longer elimination period in order to save premium dollars, but those people with less savings should obviously choose a shorter elimination period.

[4] COORDINATION OF BENEFITS

Coordination between short-term group and both long-term group and individual contracts is often possible to complete an overall portfolio of coverage. Since most long-term group policies have a provision for coordination of benefits (insurance for "reduction of benefit payments") with individual coverage purchased subsequent to the group policy effective date, many financial service professionals will look for the opportunity to place substantial amounts of individual coverage prior to writing the group coverage.

[5] MONTHLY BENEFIT AMOUNT

Yet another aspect to be taken into consideration for developing the premium to be charged is the monthly benefit amount. The amount of coverage that can be initially purchased depends on the current level of pre-disability earnings. Insurance companies have usually been willing to insure 50% of current income (for the highest wage earners), to up to 70% of current income (for moderate to lower income workers).

[6] OCCUPATION

The hazard category of the insured's occupation is also important to develop an adequate premium. Obviously, bus drivers, fire fighters, cardiovascular surgeons, and financial service professionals face different risks during their typical day. The occupation classifications also take into account the claims experience related to that occupation. For example, dentists at one time were in the same top classification as physicians. However, because of poor claims experience, many companies have since lowered their classification, i.e., raised their premiums.

[7] INFLATION PROTECTION

When purchasing a disability income policy, it is strongly recommended that the policy include an inflation rider. In the event of disability, this rider will increase the benefit each year in an attempt to keep pace with inflation. Without this rider, if a young insured becomes totally disabled, his or her monthly benefit will certainly lose its purchasing power over the years. If the insured is young enough, a level benefit may become almost meaningless 20 to 30 years in the future. An inflation rider will cost extra, but it is money well spent.

[8] RENEWABILITY

The last major issue to be considered when purchasing a disability policy is the renewal feature of the policy. The typical renewal features are:

- Conditionally Renewable
- Guaranteed Renewable
- Noncancellable

Conditionally renewable policies allow the insurance company a limited ability to refuse to renew the policy at the end of a premium payment period. The insurance company may also increase the premium. Most policies sold to physicians will not contain this limitation.

Guaranteed renewable means the insurance company cannot cancel the policy, except for nonpayment of premium, but the insurance company can change the premium rates for an entire class of policies.

Noncancellable means the insurer cannot cancel the policy nor can it change the rates. This added level of security means noncancellable policies are more expensive than guaranteed renewable policies.

Although redundant, many disability income policies specify that they are both noncancellable and guaranteed renewable.

[B] Disability Income Taxation

The general rule for taxation of disability benefits is that if the policy owner pays the premiums from his or her own funds, then any benefits received as a result of the disability are income tax free. If the policy owner's employer pays the premiums as an employee benefit, then any benefits are taxable. Therefore, when choosing a monthly benefit amount, the physician should always factor his or her individual tax status of the benefits into the calculations.

[C] Disability Income Statistics

Risk of Disability:

- At age 30, long-term disability is 4.1 times more likely than death.

- At age 40, long-term disability is 2.9 times more likely than death.
- At age 50, long-term disability is 2.2 times more likely than death.

Risk of Disability Within Groups of People:

- At age 30, there is a 46.7% chance of any one person having a 90-day disability before age 65.
- At age 40, there is a 43% chance of any one person having a 90-day disability before age 65.
- At age 50, there is a 36% chance of any one person having a 90-day disability before age 65.

- At age 30, there is a 71.6% chance of any one person out of any two people having a 90-day disability before age 65.
- At age 40, there is a 67.5% chance of any one person out of any two people having a 90-day disability before age 65.
- At age 50, there is a 59% chance of any one person out of any two people having a 90-day disability before age 65.[1]

Long-Term Care Insurance

Long-term care (LTC) insurance is considered one of the newer forms of personal coverage insurance. LTC insurance is designed to transfer the financial risk associated with the inability to care for oneself because of a prolonged illness, disability, or the effects of old age. In particular, this insurance is designed to insure against the financial cost of an extended stay in a nursing home, assisted living facility, Adult Day Care Center, hospice, or home health care. It has been estimated that two out of every five Americans now over the age of 65 will spend time in a nursing home. As life expectancy increases, so does the potential need for LTC.

[A] Medicare

Currently, Medicare covers only skilled nursing care, and this care must be provided in a Medicare-certified skilled nursing facility. Custodial care is not covered. Most LTC policies have been designed with these types of coverage—or the lack thereof—in mind. To qualify for Medicare Skilled Nursing Care, an individual must meet the following conditions:

1. The individual must be hospitalized for at least three days within the 30 days preceding the nursing home admission;
2. The individual must be admitted for the same medical condition that required the hospitalization; and
3. The skilled nursing home care must be deemed rehabilitative.

After these requirements are met, Medicare will pay 100% of the costs for the first 20 days. Days 21 to 100 are covered by Medicare along with a daily co-payment, which is indexed annually. After the initial 100 days, there is no additional Medicare coverage.

Medicare Home Health Services cover part-time or intermittent skilled nursing care, physical therapy, medical supplies, and some rehabilitative equipment. These are generally paid for in full and do not require a hospital stay prior to home health service coverage.

[B] Critical LTC Policy Features

According to the U.S. Department of Health and Human Services and the Health Insurance Association of America, seven features should always be included in a good LTC policy.

1. Guaranteed renewable;
2. Covers all levels of nursing care (skilled, intermediate, and custodial care);
3. Premiums remain level (individual premiums cannot be raised due to health or age, but can be raised only if all other LTC policies as a group are increased);
4. Benefits never reduced;
5. Offers inflation protection;
6. Full coverage for Alzheimer's Disease; and
7. Waiver of premium (during a claim period, further premium payments will not be required).

In addition, another seven features are considered to be worthwhile and are included in the better LTC policies:

1. Home health care benefits;
2. Adult day care and hospice care;
3. Assisted living facility care;
4. No prior hospital stay required;
5. Optional elimination periods;
6. Premium discounts when both spouses are covered; and
7. Medicare approval not a prerequisite for coverage.

[C] ADLs

Most LTC policies provide benefits for covered insureds with a cognitive impairment or the inability to perform a specified number of Activities of Daily Living (ADLs). These ADLs generally include the inability to perform two of six of the following activities: bathing, dressing, toileting, transfering, eating, and continence in order to file a claim.

Another issue is whether the covered insured requires "hands-on" assistance or merely needs someone to "stand-by" in the event of difficulty. Obviously, policies that read the latter are more liberal and costly.

[D] Long-Term Care Taxation

Some LTC policies have been designed to meet the required provisions of the Kassenbaum-Kennedy health reform bill, passed in 1996, and subsequently are "Tax Qualified Policies." Insureds who own policies meeting the requirements are permitted to deduct from their taxes some of the policy's premium, based on the insured's age, income, and the amount of total itemized medical expenses. The major benefit of the tax-qualified LTC policy is that the benefit, when received, is not considered taxable income.

General Types of Insurance Policies Covering Possessions

Unlike those insurance policies covering people, where it is mostly a matter of personal choice, most coverages discussed are virtually required by law.

[A] Homeowners (and Renters) Insurance Overview

The basic model of the homeowners contract began in 1958 and contains three areas of coverage: property, theft, and liability. There are seven standard forms of homeowner contracts, and information about their coverage is contained in two sections.

Section I is for property and theft coverage and typically includes coverage for:

- The structure itself (commonly called the dwelling),
- Appurtenant structures (unattached buildings, fences, swimming pools, etc.),
- Unscheduled personal property (commonly just called contents within the structures and only those not itemized by endorsement), and
- Additional living expenses (the increased cost of living during the period after damage occurs while the structure is uninhabitable).

Contents coverage is typically 50% of the dwelling coverage for on premises losses. Off premises coverage is typically worldwide but limited to 10% of the limit for contents coverage. Typically, there are other restrictions, with some types of personal property totally excluded and other property with a dollar limitation applied against them.

It is important to have a basic inventory of your property in an off-site location, possibly a safe deposit box. This is often conveniently accomplished by periodically taking photos of each of the rooms in the house. If a fire damages one or more of these rooms, the photo may show property that was destroyed and for which you need to file a claim.

Section II is the liability protection section and covers personal liability for bodily injury to others or for damage to their property and includes reasonable medical payments for their injuries. Section II is identical in all seven forms. Liability protection often begins at $100,000 with medical payments at $1000 per person.

Briefly, the seven forms are as follows:

1. HO-1: The Basic form insures against fire, lightning, removal, vandalism or malicious mischief, glass breakage, and theft. It also provides Extended Coverage for damage from wind, civil commotion, smoke, hail, aircraft, vehicles, explosion, and riot. The dwelling protection is specified as a dollar amount, while the contents are covered at 50% of this amount, and the additional living expenses are covered at 10%.

2. HO-2: The Broad form gets its name from broadening the Extended Coverage perils of the HO-1. Coverage is now extended to include damage from falling objects; weight of ice, snow, or sleet; accidental damage to steam or hot water heating systems; accidental discharge of water or steam from those systems or domestic appliances; freezing of those systems or appliances; and electrical surge damage. Here again, the dwelling protection is specified, and the contents are covered at 50%. Additional living expenses are increased to 20% of the dwelling coverage amount.

3. HO-3: The Special form, also called the "all-risk" form, expands on the HO-2 by providing coverage for the dwelling, appurtenant structures, and additional living expenses on an all-risk basis. Rather than naming each peril to be covered, this form covers all perils not specifically named as an exception (flood, earthquake, war, and nuclear accidents). Coverage for the dwelling, contents, and additional living expenses is identical to the HO-2.

4. HO-4: The Tenants form is basically the same as the HO-2 and provides a named perils basis for the contents of renters. Additional living expenses are provided at 20% of the amount of coverage purchased for the contents.

5. HO-5: The Comprehensive Form is seldom seen now. This coverage is identical to that of HO-3 except contents are covered at 50% of the amount for the dwelling and provides this level for both on and off premises.

6. HO-6: The Unit Owners form is also referred to as the Condominium form. It is similar to the tenants form except additional living expenses are provided at 40% of the amount of coverage purchased for the contents. Other differences deal with (1) insuring additions and alterations by the unit owner and (2) the availability of optional coverage to protect against the exposure to losses from assessment by the condominium association for uninsured property damage or liability claims.

7. HO-8: The Modified Coverage form is designed specifically to provide coverage for older dwellings. Many older homes contain elaborate carvings and specialty features that would cause the replacement value to substantially exceed current market value. This form of coverage has no replacement cost provision but instead substitutes a "functional replacement" concept for any losses.

[B] Replacement Cost Versus Actual Cash Value

Actual cash value settlements provide payments for claims that generally start with the cost today to replace a lost, stolen, damaged, or destroyed item. However, these settlements take into account the length of time the item was owned or in service to develop a deduction for depreciation. Often, this depreciation amount is substantial and severe.

Under replacement cost coverage, insureds can collect for their losses without a deduction for appreciation up to the limits of the policy. This is an automatic but optional provision of all homeowner forms. To take advantage of this provision, the amount of insurance on the dwelling must be at least 80% of its replacement cost at time of claim.

[C] Inflation Protection

The easiest way for a homeowner to ensure replacement cost coverage is with the addition of a rider that automatically adjusts the value of the dwelling coverage by the inflation rate for their community as calculated by the insurance company. This coverage adjusts policy limits periodically to maintain appropriate levels of coverage.

[D] Other Homeowner Policy Endorsements

The homeowner is well advised to also consider a multitude of endorsements and/or potential increases in policy limits. Examples include:

- Scheduling personal property such as jewelry, furs, golf equipment, and computers, which have been exempted from coverage, or for which coverage has a severe dollar limitation.
- Increasing liability coverage to take advantage of the minimums needed for "Umbrella Liability."
- Theft extension endorsement to remove the exclusion for loss of unattended property from a motor vehicle, trailer, or watercraft.
- Earthquake and/or sinkhole collapse coverage.
- Increasing the deductible from the standard $250 to a convenient self-insurance amount.

[E] Title Insurance

As a routine part of any home purchase, a history of the title to the property, as well as any liens or conveyances, is completed. This history is referred to as title insurance and typically protects the mortgage lender from any title defects. If a title defect causes loss, the title insurance company will indemnify the lender, not the homebuyer, to the extent of the loan. These are single premium policies of indefinite duration, but they can be terminated when the loan is retired.

The physician should also inquire about the cost of personal title insurance policy. This second policy would protect the physician rather than the mortgage lender. Although it would undoubtedly add to the expense of closing, there is no harm in requesting that the seller be responsible for providing this protection to the purchaser as well.

[F] Boat Insurance Overview

Watercraft and small pleasure boats are usually covered within a homeowner policy, but generally for only $1000. More expensive boats are often insured either under a separate Inland Marine policy or as a Personal Articles Floater (attachment) to the homeowner's policy. The choice between these two alternatives usually involves the liability risk element. There is no provision in the Personal Article Floater for liability, and although liability could be increased on the homeowners policy, using a separate policy is usually preferable. Other items to consider are the size of the craft, maximum speed, engine horsepower, waters navigated, and special uses such as water skiing or racing.

Automobile Insurance Overview

With the possible exception of the handgun, the automobile represents the greatest single item of ownership that is capable of inflicting death, injury, and damage. America's fascination with the automobile has resulted in a marked increase in the power and potential speed of our vehicles. The recent popularity in the use of sports utility vehicles has caused a substantial increase in damage due to their higher ground clearance and heavier frames. The owners and operators of any vehicle must be financially able to respond to any resulting claims, or they need to transfer the risk through insurance. All states require some minimal coverage for personal vehicles.

The most frequently used policy to insure individual private passenger vehicle risks is the Family Automobile Policy (FAP). It provides two major types of coverage: liability and physical damage. Liability coverage includes both bodily injury and property damage. Physical damage, on the other hand, includes comprehensive and collision coverage.

[A] Liability Coverage

The liability section of the FAP is contained within most policies as Part A - Liability and Part B - Personal Injury Protection.

[1] BODILY INJURY

Bodily injury liability coverage generally includes sickness, disease, and death and is expressed in dual limits—per person and per occurrence. Nearly half of the states require minimums of $25,000 per person and $50,000 per occurrence. Higher limits of $100,000 per person and $300,000 per occurrence are often required for consideration of umbrella coverage.

[2] PROPERTY DAMAGE

Property damage liability is coverage for damage or destruction to the property of others and includes loss of use. Liability coverage limits usually include property damage limits as the third number, i.e., $100/300/25. The coverage here would be for $25,000 of property damage. As automobiles become more expensive, however, coverage to $50,000 is not considered excessive.

[3] PERSONAL INJURY

Personal injury coverage is provided for medical expenses, funeral expenses, and loss of earnings for anyone sustaining an injury while occupying your vehicle or from being struck by your vehicle while walking.

Liability insurance follows the vehicle, not the driver. Coverage is extended to the vehicle owner and any resident in the same household. It also covers anyone using the insured vehicle with the permission of the owner and within the scope of that permission.

Newly acquired vehicles are usually covered automatically for liability for 30 days after acquisition, but physical damage insurance must have been on all currently covered vehicles for the new vehicle to be included. Coverage is also typically extended to a temporary substitute automobile, but only if this vehicle is used in place of the covered automobile, because of its breakdown, repair, servicing, loss, or destruction.

[B] Physical Damage Coverage

[1] COMPREHENSIVE

Comprehensive physical damage includes coverage for theft, vandalism, broken windshields, falling objects, riot or civil commotion, and even damage from foreign substances, such as paint. Comprehensive is often described as coverage for all hazards other than collision.

[2] COLLISION

Collision involves the upset of the covered vehicle and collision with an object, usually another vehicle, and that has not been enumerated in the discussion of comprehensive. Colliding with a bird or animal is considered under the comprehensive coverage.

The distinction between comprehensive coverage and collision coverage is more than technical. The deductible provisions of the FAP often show a considerable difference in these areas, with the collision deductible typically being much greater.

Damage to tires can be covered by provisions in either comprehensive or collision. Exclusions typically include normal wear and tear, rough roads, hard driving, or hitting or scraping curbs.

[C] Repairs after the Accident

Following a collision, the insurance company will assign a claims adjuster to determine the extent of damage and the cost of repairs. If these repairs exceed the estimated value of the vehicle, it may be "totaled." Experience tells us that the value of the vehicle to the owner nearly always exceeds that estimated by the insurance company.

The physician is therefore strongly urged to consider purchasing replacement cost coverage rather than accepting actual cash value, which is the depreciated value of the vehicle. The cost may be higher for this coverage, but accepting a larger deductible will often make up the difference. Paying a little more toward the deductible could easily be worth it if the damage is extensive.

[D] Uninsured/Underinsured Motorists Coverage

Uninsured motorist coverage provides protection from the other driver who is operating his or her vehicle without insurance coverage. It covers expenses resulting from injury or death as well as property damage. There are currently a dozen states where it is estimated that over 20% of the vehicles on the highway are being operated without any insurance. A physician should not reject this coverage when buying automobile insurance.

Underinsured motorist coverage provides protection from the other driver who purchased only the state-mandated minimum liability insurance coverage. Again, this is coverage that the medical professional or healthcare practitioner should thoughtfully consider when buying automobile insurance.

Umbrella Liability Insurance Overview

Umbrella policies should be considered any time the physican has substantial current income or has accumulated a sizable estate and is concerned about asset protection from potential litigation. Umbrella policies vary greatly in structure so care should be taken to examine all the various aspects of the policy carefully. Not only do umbrella policies vary in structure, but they can also be arranged with many different endorsements to meet the specific needs of the physician. A few examples would be:

- The addition of personal injury coverage (to include libel, slander, and defamation of character),
- Incidental business pursuits (to include coverage to personal automobiles where the business activity was incidental and not the primary purpose of the use of the car), and

- The broadening of personal automobile coverage (to the insured regardless of whose vehicle he or she was driving and the coverage afforded that vehicle).

Needs Analysis Approach Toward Life Insurance

Needs analysis is a generic term used to help quantify the financial need for life insurance. And, whereas a broker or agent may use a simple needs analysis designed to pinpoint a certain life insurance amount, a CFP's model should include a more thorough review of insurance needs and a long- and short-term financial analysis. The CFP, or insurance agent assisting the physician, should request:

- An in-depth discussion of your goals, both financial and personal;
- A review of your current insurance (life, health, disability, property and casualty, etc.) and financial holdings, investment assets, and their projected growth potential;
- A review of your current estate plan, including any current wills and trusts;
- Any personally owned business information.

Keep in mind that there is a difference between using an agent or broker for this service and using a CFP. An agent or broker will not normally charge a fee for this service. A CFP will generally charge a set amount, depending on the size of the estate being analyzed. As your life and practice evolve, an in-depth re-analysis should periodically be performed. This will ensure an accurate, up-to-date plan for the future.

Business Uses of Life Insurance

[A] Key Person Insurance

Hospitals, a local family practice office, and a pharmaceutical company all likely have one thing in common. Somewhere within these companies or partnerships, there are key employees or profit makers. Due to their expertise, management skills, knowledge, or "history of why," they have become indispensable to their employers.

If this key employee were to die prematurely, what would potentially happen to the company? In many cases, especially in smaller companies, it would have a devastating effect on the bottom line or even precipitate a bankruptcy. In these circumstances, a form of business insurance, called key person coverage, is recommended in order to alleviate the potential financial problems resulting from the death of that employee.

The business could purchase and own a life insurance policy on the key person. Upon the death of the employee, the life insurance proceeds could be used to:

- Pay off bank loans,

- Replace the lost profits of the company, and
- Establish a reserve for the search, hiring, and training of a replacement.

[B] Business Continuation Funding

See the section on buy-sell agreements in the chapter on estate planning.

[C] Executive Bonus Plan

An executive bonus plan (or § 162 plan) is an effective way for a company to provide valued, select employees an additional employment benefit. One of the main advantages of an executive bonus plan, when compared to other benefits, is its simplicity. In a typical executive bonus plan, an agreement is made between the employer and employee, whereby the employer agrees to pay for the cost of a life insurance policy, in the form of a bonus, on the life of the employee.

The major benefits of such a plan to the employee include that he or she is the immediate owner of the cash values and the death benefit provided. The only cost to the employee is the payment of income tax on any bonus received. The employer receives a tax deduction for providing the benefit, improves the morale of its selected employees, and can use the plan as a tool to attract additional talent.

[D] Non-Qualified Salary Continuation

Commonly referred to as deferred compensation, non-qualified salary continuation is a legally binding promise by an employer to pay a salary continuation benefit at a specific point in the future in exchange for the current and continued performance of its employee. These plans are normally used to supplement existing retirement plans.

Although there are different variations of deferred compensation, in a typical deferred compensation agreement, the employer will purchase and own a life insurance policy on the life of the employee. The cash value of the policy grows tax deferred during the employee's working years. After retirement, these cash values can be withdrawn from the policy to reimburse the company for its after-tax retirement payments to the employee.

Upon the death of the employee, any remaining death benefit would likely be received income tax free by the employer. (Alternative Minimum Taxes could apply to any benefit received by certain larger C corporations). The death benefit could then be used to pay any required survivor benefits to the employee's spouse or to provide partial or total cost recovery to the employer.

In a typical plan, the terms of the agreement are negotiated: (1) the amount of benefit received by the employee, (2) when retirement benefits can begin, (3) how long retirement benefits will be paid, and (4) if benefits will be provided for death or disability. The business has established what is commonly referred to as "golden handcuffs" for the employee. As a result, the benefit will be received only if the employee continues to work for the company until retirement. If the employee is terminated or quits prior to retirement, the plan would end, and no benefits would be paid.

[E] Split-Dollar Plans

Split-dollar arrangements can be a complicated and confusing concept for even the most experienced insurance professional or financial advisor. This concept is, in its simplest terms, a way for a business to share the cost and benefit of a life insurance policy with a valued employee. In a normal split dollar arrangement, the employee will receive valuable life insurance coverage at little cost. The business pays the majority of the premium, but the business is usually able to recover the entire cost of providing this benefit.

Following the publication of Internal Revenue Service (IRS) Notices 2002-8 and 2002-59, there are currently two general approaches to the ownership of business split-dollar life insurance: Employer-owned or Employee-owned.

[1] EMPLOYER-OWNED METHOD

In the employer-owned method, the employer is the sole owner of the policy. A written split-dollar agreement usually permits the employee to name the beneficiary for most of the death proceeds. The employer owns all the cash value and has the unfettered right to borrow or withdraw it as necessary. At the end of the formal agreement, the business can generally (1) continue the policy as key person insurance, (2) transfer ownership to the insured and report the cash values as additional income to the insured, (3) sell the policy to the insured, or (4) use a combination of these methods. This is commonly referred to as "rollout."

Practitioners should be careful to not include rollout language in the split-dollar agreement. The rollout should not be included because if the parties formally agree that after a specified number of years—or following a specific event—related only to the circumstances surrounding the policy—the policy will be turned over to the insured, the IRS could declare that the entire transaction was a sham and that its sole purpose was to avoid taxation of the premiums to the employee. This would generate substantial interest and penalties in addition to the additional taxes due.

Death proceeds available to the insured employee's beneficiary are considered a current and reportable economic benefit (REB), and they are an annually taxable event to the employee. If an individual policy is involved, the REB is calculated by multiplying the face amount times the government's Table 2004 rates or the insurance company's alternative term rates, using the insured's age. If a second-to-die policy is involved, the government's PS38 rates or the company's alternative PS38 rates will be used. Any part of the premium actually paid by the employee is used to offset any REB dollar for dollar.

[2] EMPLOYEE-OWNED METHOD

With the employee-owned method, the insured employee is generally the applicant and owner of the policy. Any premiums paid by the business are deemed to be loans to the employee, and the employee reports as income an imputed interest rate on the cumulative amount of loan based on Code § 7872. A collateral assignment is made for the benefit of the business to cover the cumulative loan amount. In some cases, the assignment may allow the assignee to have access to the cash values of the policy by way of a policy loan. This method is unavailable for officers and executives of publicly held corporations because of the current restrictions on corporate loans (the Sarbanes-Oxley Act of 2002).

The employee-owned method is somewhat similar to the older collateral assignment form of split-dollar. The benefits for the employee are both the ability to control large amounts of death proceeds as well as developing equity in the policy. Whether or not this new method catches on will depend greatly on the imputed interest rate published by the IRS every July. If set low enough, this may be an excellent opportunity for the employee to use inexpensive business dollars to pay for life insurance. In July 2003, for example, the rate was 2.08%.

Other Business-Related Insurance

[A] Workers' Compensation

The purpose of Workers' Compensation insurance is not only to provide these benefits but also to reduce potential litigation. Employees accepting the benefit payments from a Workers' Compensation claim generally forgo the right to sue their employer. Workers' Compensation rates are established by job descriptions, and commercial rates for the medical professional's office are some of the lowest available. There are three methods of providing Workers' Compensation coverage:

1. Private commercial insurance,
2. Governmental insurance funds, and
3. Self-insurance.

There are, however, six "monopolistic" states—Nevada, North Dakota, Ohio, Washington, West Virginia, and Wyoming—that do not permit private commercial insurance.

Physicians may be inclined to use the third method, especially those with larger offices. Since the weekly benefits are typically below $500, this method would make sense. Since in larger groups, the officers and owners can elect not to be covered, it is usually more convenient for the medical professional to cover this risk with personal disability income insurance.

Larger offices or companies, which wish to take more direct control of costs and benefit management, should consider self-insuring only after receiving expert advice. This form of coverage truly requires a trusted, knowledgeable insurance advisor.

[B] Business-Owner Policy

Business-owner policies are offered on a simplified package basis. Similar to homeowner policies, these policies contain both property and liability coverage. Property coverage, available on either an actual value or replacement value basis, can be purchased for named-perils or on an all-risk basis.

Also like homeowner policies, physicians should compile a basic inventory of property to be covered. Medical records and important papers are typically covered for a flat amount. Do not forget to allow for supplies and leased equipment.

Liability coverage protects the business owner from claims arising from bodily injury or property damage when a person is injured on the premises. Liability insurance not only pays the damage awarded to the claimant but also the attorney fees and other costs associated with any defense of the suit.

Coverage under a business owner policy is typically very broad and can be tailored to fit almost any practice. Since coverage under this policy can often be coordinated with other business-related insurance, coverage should be handled by the same trusted insurance advisor.

Endnote

1. Cody, D. *National Underwriter Field Guide.* Erlanger, KY: 2003–2004.

Chapter 4

Deciphering Personal Income Tax Principles

Understanding the Intellectual and Ethical Pursuit of Tax Avoidance

Charles L. Bucek, Jr.
Thomas P. McGuinness

John Maynard Keynes felt that tax avoidance is the only intellectual pursuit that carries any reward. Oliver Wendell Holmes felt that taxes are what we pay for a civilized society. Thankfully, you don't have to finance 'civilized society' all by yourself. You're only obligated to pay your fair share, plain and simple. Well, sort of. Actually, the sum of your fair share will depend a great deal on what you do as you juggle the numbers. The fact is, you may be able to preserve more of your taxable income with a little tax planning, performed in a timely manner. With a few aptly applied tax strategies, you can get your taxes in good shape for Uncle Sam.

IHateFinancialPlanning.com

Virtually all investments have tax consequences that can reduce the amount of money left over to enjoy. However, the number of tax planning ideas is limited only by the imagination and unique circumstances of the healthcare professional.

Adjusted Gross Income Tax

The U.S. individual tax return is based around the concepts of adjusted gross income (AGI) and taxable income (TI). AGI is the amount that shows up at the bottom of page one of Form 1040, individual income tax return. The AGI is the sum of all of the taxpayer's income less certain allowed adjustments (alimony, one-half of self-employment taxes, a percentage of self-employed health insurance, retirement plan contributions and Individual Retirement Accounts (IRAs), moving expenses, early withdrawal penalties, and interest on student loans). This amount is important because it is used to calculate various limitations within the area of itemized deductions (e.g., medical deductions: 7.5% of AGI; miscellaneous itemized deductions: 2% of AGI). When a healthcare professional taxpayer hears the phrase "an above the line deduction," the line being referenced is the AGI line on the tax return. Generally, it is better for a deduction to be an above the line deduction, because that number helps a taxpayer in two ways. First, the deduction reduces AGI, and second, since it reduces AGI, it is also reducing the amounts of limitations placed on other deductions as noted above.

Obviously, if there is an above the line, there is also a "below the line" deduction. Below the line deductions are itemized deductions (or the standard deduction if itemizing is not used) plus any personal exemptions allowed. The AGI minus these deductions provides the TI on which income tax is actually calculated. All of that being said, it is better for a deduction to be an "above the line" deduction.

Although this is a bit dry, it helps to understand the concepts to know where items provide the most benefit to the medical professional taxpayer.

Exhibit 4–1 *Personal Taxation Calculations*

Gross Income (all income, from whatever source derived, including illegal activities, cash, indirect for the benefit of, debt forgiveness, barter, dividends, interest, rents, royalties, annuities, trusts, and alimony payments)

Less non-taxable exclusions (municipal bonds, scholarships, inheritance, insurance proceeds, social security and unemployment income [full or partial exclusion], etc.).

Total Income

Less Deductions for AGI (alimony, IRA and SEP contributions, 1/2 self-employed tax, moving expenses, self-employed health insurance, early withdrawal of savings penalty, student loan interest deduction, Archer MSA deduction and educator expenses).

Adjusted Gross Income (bottom Form 1040)

Less Itemized Deductions from AGI (medical, certain taxes paid, home mortgage interest, charitable contributions, casualty losses, involuntary conversions, theft, job and miscellaneous expenses, etc.), or

Less Standard Deduction (based on filing status)

Less Personal Exemptions (per dependents, subject to phaseouts)

Taxable Income

Calculate Regular Tax

    Plus Additional Taxes (alternative minimum tax, etc.)

    Minus Credits (child care, foreign tax credit, earned income housing, etc.)

    Plus Other Taxes

Total Tax Due

Filing Status and Tax Rate Brackets

One of the questions most frequently asked by physicians concerns the filing of a joint tax return versus the filing of a separate return. This question comes up because of the so-called marriage penalty that was built into the standard deduction and into the tax rates for married couples filing a joint return.

Fortunately, the 2001 tax bill has provisions that alleviate the concern. The basic standard deduction for married couples filing jointly will be increased to twice the amount for single taxpayers over a five-year period beginning in 2005. The 15% rate bracket for couples filing jointly will increase (phase in) to twice the singles bracket from 2005 to 2008.

Tax Planning Tip ■ The marriage penalty was eliminated for dual income married couples, effective January 1, 2003. The basic standard deduction amount is twice the standard deduction for single individuals in 2003 and 2004 and will be raised from the current $7,950 to $9,500. Those married couples who itemize their deductions on their income taxes will not see any effect, but the majority of couples who take the standard deduction will save $155.

But, for physicians living in either community property or common law states, extra care in the documentation of income and deductions ("ownership") is a must. In community property states, most items of both income and deduction will be split 50/50. However, each community property state has its own rules how income from separate property (property owned by one spouse or the other, not jointly, e.g., inherited property) is treated. For common law states, income is traced to ownership, and deductions claimed by one spouse must be paid from that spouse's separate funds.

Tax Brackets

There are currently six tax brackets: 10%, 15%, 27%, 30%, 35%, and 38.6%. The 35% rate applies to TI over $174,700 (joint), $143,500 (single), $159,100 (head of household), and $87,350 (married filing separately). The 38.6% rate results from a 10% surtax on TI over $311,950 ($155,975 for married persons filing separately and $9,350 for estates and trusts). The surtax does not apply to capital gains.

Exhibit 4–2   *Schedule X—Use If Your Filing Status Is Single*

If the amount on Form 1040, line 39, is: Over—	But not over— line 40	Enter on Form 1040,			of the amount over—
$0	$6,000	....		10%	$0
6,000	28,400	$600.00		15%	6,000
28,400	68,800	3,960.00	+	27%	28,400
68,800	143,500	14,868.00	+	30%	68,800
143,500	311,950	37,278.00	+	35%	143,500
311,950	....	96,235.50	+	38.6%	311,950

Exhibit 4–3   *Schedule Y-1—Use If Your Filing Status Is Married Filing Jointly or Qualifying Widow(er)*

If the amount on Form 1040, line 39, is: Over—	But not over— line 40	Enter on Form 1040,			of the amount over—
$0	$12,000	....		10%	$0
12,000	47,450	$1,200.00		15%	12,000
47,450	114,650	$6,517.50	+	27%	47,450
114,650	174,700	24,661.50	+	30%	114,650
174,700	311,950	42,676.50	+	35%	174,700
311,950	....	90,714.00	+	38.6%	311,950

Exhibit 4–4 *Schedule Y-2—Use If YourFiling Status Is Married Filing Separately*

If the amount on Form 1040, line 39, is: Over—	But not over— line 40	Enter on Form 1040,			of the amount over—
$0	$6,000	....		10%	$0
6,000	23,725	$600.00		15%	6,000
23,725	57,325	3,258.75	+	27%	23,725
57,325	87,350	12,330.75	+	30%	57,325
87,350	155,975	21,338.25	+	35%	87,350
155,975	....	45,357.00	+	38.6%	155,975

Exhibit 4–5 *Schedule Z—Use If Your Filing Status Is Head of Household*

If the amount on Form 1040, line 39, is: Over—	But not over— line 40	Enter on Form 1040,			of the amount over—
$0	$10,000	....		10%	$0
10,000	38,050	$1,000.00		15%	10,000
38,050	98,250	5,207.50	+	27%	38,050
98,250	159,100	21,461.50	+	30%	98,250
159,100	311,950	39,716.50	+	35%	159,100
311,950	....	93,214.00	+	38.6%	311,950

The limits for tax brackets have been increased for inflation. To stay informed of changes, visit the site www.irs.ustreas.gov for tax table updates.

Tax Planning Tip ■ According to the Jobs and Growth Tax Relief and Reconciliation Act (JGTRRA) of 2003, the regular income tax rates in excess of 15% are 25%, 28%, 33%, and 35%; the 38.6% bracket is eliminated. In 2011, the rates will revert to their previous levels, and the top tax rate will revert back to 39.6%.

For a couple with $70,000 in TI, the changes would reduce their tax bill from $12,606 to $11,120 this year, saving them $1,486. For a married physician couple with $400,000 in TI, the tax bill would drop from about $124,701 to $108,344, a savings of $16,357.

Marginal Tax Rates

Some medical professionals still do not appreciate the concept of marginal tax rates. When a nurse is in a 27% tax bracket, that means that his or her next dollar will be taxed at 27%, and a tax deduction will be worth 27 cents. A one-dollar tax credit however, is worth one dollar of tax, and this credit is a much better deal, if you can get it. This is not the nurse's true tax bracket, however, because of the many nuances and subtleties buried in the tax code. For example, a medical professional's itemized deductions are reduced for every dollar of income over $139,500 if "Married Filing Jointly," and, in effect, this is an extra income tax. Therefore, high-income taxpayers pay a much higher marginal tax rate.

Let's suppose that Dr. David Suppan's effective marginal federal tax rate is 41%, that he lives in a city where state and local income tax must be paid, and that his marginal rates for those two taxes are 8% and 4% respectively, for a total of 12%. However, he does receive a federal tax deduction for every dollar paid in state and local income tax. Now, perform the following mathematical calculations:

1. Multiply 41% times 12%, to get 4.92% or his effective tax savings.
2. Subtract 4.92% from 12% to get 7.08%, which is his effective additional cost for state and local taxes.
3. Add the 7.08% (state and local) to 41% (federal) to get his true effective tax bracket of about 48%.

The point of running the numbers is not precision, but simply the realization that with an effective tax bracket of almost 50%, the true economic benefit of every $1000 of annual investment interest or dividends is only about $500 after taxes.

Personal and Dependency Exemptions

Each personal or dependency exemption you claim reduces TI by $3050. For estates, simple trusts, and complex trusts, the exemptions are $600, $300, and $100 respectively. You can claim an exemption for yourself, your spouse, and each of your dependents. Higher earning medical professionals lose some, or all, exemptions according to a phase-out schedule where personal exemptions are reduced by 2% for each $2500 ($1250 for a married person filing separately) or fraction thereof by which AGI exceeds $209,250 for joint returns, $174,400 for heads of households, $139,500 for single taxpayers, and over $104,625 for married filing separately.

For example, Dr. Joe Miller, a DO surgeon and joint filer, with an AGI of more than $331,750 ($122,500 above the joint threshold) will lose 100% of the personal exemption.

[A] The Standard Deduction

For 2003, the standard deduction was as follows:

Married filing jointly and surviving spouses $7,950

Single taxpayers $4,750

Heads of households $7,000

Married filing separately $3,975

Dependents who file .... $ 750

These amounts are annually indexed for inflation.

Medical professionals who are blind or age 65 and over may obtain an additional standard deduction of $950 if married (whether filing jointly or separately), or $1150 if single or head of household. If a healthcare worker is both over 65 and blind, double these amounts.

Who Has to File

[A] The Standard Deduction

Married, filing jointly, both under 65 .... $14,050

Married, filing jointly, one spouse 65 or older $15,000

Married, filing jointly, both 65 or older $15,950

Married, filing separately $3050

Certain surviving spouses, under 65 .... $11,000

Certain surviving spouses, 65 or older $11,950

Head of household, under 65 .... $10,050

Head of household, 65 or older $11,200

Single taxpayers, under 65 .... $7800

Single taxpayers, 65 or older $8950

Remember, the above figures, as well as certain other thresholds and limits, are indexed for inflation each year. The above amounts relate to tax year 2003 filings.

The Taxpayer Relief Act of 1997

The current tax code includes more than 2.8 million words. The Taxpayer Relief Act of 1997 (The "Act") was 2 inches thick and added another 3000 pages of material to the subject of taxes. The following significant changes are highlighted below.

[A] Capital Gains and Losses

First, you must understand *tax basis*. When a physician reports capital gains, the taxable gain is the amount received minus the basis or cost for tax purposes. When cash has been received (constructive receipt), the gain is said to be *recognized*. Gain is said to be *realized* when a transaction has taken place, but cash has not yet been received. Gain is said to be *unrealized* when a transaction has not yet taken place—when the gain exists in an investment portfolio only on paper.

The Act created a great confusion regarding the holding period to be considered a long-term capital gain and the applicable capital gains tax rate. Much of this confusion is now gone since the transition period has passed. The rules are now much more clear-cut. When a taxpayer sells an asset held less than 12 months, the gain is short term and is taxed as ordinary income (the same rate the taxpayer would pay on wages or interest and dividends). Assets sold after being held more than 12 months will generate long-term capital gains (or losses). Long-term capital gains are taxed at 10% if the taxpayer is in the 15% bracket, and at 20% if the taxpayer is in any higher tax bracket. For real estate that has been depreciated, the tax rate on the gain up to the amount of depreciation taken is 25%, with the remainder taxed at 20%. Collectibles (art, coins, jewels, etc.) are yet a different story being taxed at 15% or 28% depending upon whether the taxpayer's tax bracket is 15% or higher.

There are now several strategies that can be adopted to utilize capital gains and losses. The obvious strategy is to periodically review any investment portfolio and cull the securities that are down in value without hope of a quick turnaround. These losses can be used to offset gains taken during the period. The main disadvantage to this strategy is that the taxpayer does not get the maximum bang for the deduction buck by eliminating a gain at 20% tax rate. The alternative is to plan to use capital losses to offset short-term capital gains and in years when there are no long-term capital gains. This strategy is fine, but remember, the maximum *net* capital loss deduction each year is limited to $3000, so this strategy has its limitations.

Tax Planning Tip ■ Effective May 6, 2003, the 10% and 20% tax rates on net capital gains was reduced to 5 and 15%, respectively. The 5% rate becomes zero in 2008. The change to the maximum tax terminates after 2008, and in 2009 the law reverts back to the maximum rate of 20%.

[B] Sale of a Personal Residence

For some medical professionals, a home is their largest asset. In addition, their home is their largest tax shelter as well. Certain costs of the purchase and ownership of the home are deductible expenses if the taxpayer itemizes (i.e., interest with total loan balance not to exceed one million dollars, interest on home equity loans up to $100,000, and property taxes). The law regarding the sale of a personal residence changed in mid-1997. This change in the tax law has been one of the most overlooked by all taxpayers. The new law states that the first $250,000 ($500,000 for married taxpayers filing jointly) of gain from the sale of a residence will be free of federal income tax. To qualify for this exclusion the medical professional taxpayer must have owned the residence and occupied it for at least two of the last five years prior to the sale. In addition, if the taxpayer does not meet the above requirement due to change in employment, health, or various other reasons, he or she may be able to obtain an exclusion for a portion of the above amount. An added bonus is that the taxpayer may take advantage of this same exclusion again after a two-year waiting period.

[C] Five-Year Holding Period Rule

Beginning after the year 2000, the maximum capital gain rates for qualifying assets held more than five years are lowered to 18% and 8% (rather than 20% and 10%). A special election became available in the year 2001 to medical professionals who want to restart their holding period on a pre-2001 asset by treating it as having been sold and repurchased for tax purposes at the asset's fair market value. The downside to this strategy is that the capital gain earned to the date of the election must be recognized in the current tax year.

[D] Small Business Stock

If you own a qualified small business stock (stock in a corporation capitalized with $1 million or less), you may exclude from income 50% of any capital gain realized from the sale or exchange of the stock provided you have held the shares for more than five years. The remaining gain is taxed at a top rate of 28%. You may also elect to roll over a gain from the sale or exchange of a small business held for more than six months by investing in other qualified small business stock within 60 days of the sale of the original stock.

[E] Estimated Tax Rules

The Internal Revenue Service (IRS) wants income taxes throughout the year. Most employees pay the required estimated income taxes throughout the year via withholding as wages are paid. Self-employed individuals or independent contractors are required to make estimated tax payments to the IRS each quarter. Otherwise, the IRS may assess a penalty for failure to make timely payments of taxes throughout the year.

The IRS looks at each quarter independently to determine whether a penalty applies. Hence, you cannot "catch up" in later quarters to avoid the penalty.

Penalties can be avoided by basing estimated tax payments on:

- 90% of the current's year's tax;
- 100% of the prior year's tax [(unless AGI is over $150,000 ($75,000 for married individuals filing separately)].

The safe harbor for AGI over $150,000 (or $75,000) will either be 90% of the current year's tax or:

If the preceding tax year begins in 2002 or thereafter, 110% of prior year's tax.

[F] Penalties

The following penalties apply to all U.S. taxpayers.

1. Failure to File Return: 5% per month (maximum 25%).
2. Accuracy Related Penalties:
   20% of underpayment attributable to the following:
   Negligence
   Substantial Understatement: Greater of 10% of tax or $5000
3. Civil Tax Fraud: 75% of underpayment with burden of proof on the IRS

[G] Deductions

Paying a deductible expense is less costly than paying a nondeductible expense since, in a 30% tax bracket, for example, a $1000 deductible expense will only cost the medical professional only $700.

Taxpayers with an AGI over $139,500 ($69,750 for married filing separately) must also reduce their itemized deductions by 3% of the excess over the threshold amount, up to a maximum of an 80% reduction. Deductions for medical expenses, investment interest, casualty, and similar items are exempt from the reduction.[1]

For example, Dr. Goodyear, a surgeon with AGI of $239,500 ($100,000 over the threshold) would have to reduce her itemized deductions by $3000, unless that amounts to more than an 80% reduction. These reductions have the practical effect of increasing the top tax rate for high-income taxpayers by several percentage points. The amounts are adjusted each year for inflation.

[H] Home Equity Loans

This vehicle allows the healthcare professional to take advantage of the equity in his or her home (personal or second residence) to obtain an interest deduction on items that may otherwise not be deductible. There are certain restrictions in general, such as the total amount of home equity debt cannot exceed $100,000 ($50,000 for married taxpayers filing separately) and not exceeding the FMV of the residences. However, especially for healthcare professionals, there are hidden traps to be considered. Since a personal residence is virtually creditor proof, it is one place that the healthcare professional can invest without the fear of losing the asset in a malpractice action. Utilizing the residence as collateral on another loan can place an unnecessary risk on one of the only safe harbors the healthcare professional has available. Use home equity loans with great care.

[I] Business Automobiles

A medical professional can claim deductions on business-related use of an automobile, using either the standard mileage rate methods or the actual expense method. The standard mileage rate for operating a passenger car was 36 cents per mile in 2003. If the standard mileage rate method is used, you may also deduct business parking fees and tolls, the business portion of state and local personal property taxes, and the business portion of auto loan interest.

If you own and operate only one business vehicle, you should choose the method that yields the greatest deduction. However, once you've claimed accelerated depreciation for a business car in prior years under the expense method, you cannot switch to the standard mileage rate method for that car in a subsequent year. The IRS now allows use of the standard mileage rate for a leased business automobile.

[J] Meals and Entertainment

The IRS allows only 50% of meals and entertainment expenses to be deducted for federal income tax purposes. The other 50% is considered a permanent difference that increases TI.

However, like most expenses if handled right, medical professionals can deduct part of their dining and entertainment costs. This can occur if bona fide business discussions occur directly preceding or following the dinner or entertainment. Be ready to justify the motivation that the entertainment was business in nature and not purely social.

For example, Dr. Simon Smith meets with several business associates during the day. In the evening, he entertains the physicians in his medical group and their spouses at a restaurant and then they attend a theater production. Even though the purpose of the entertainment is goodwill, the expenses are still partially deductible (50%). Further, the IRS concedes that it may be appropriate for a medical professional's spouse to assist in entertaining a business associate, accompanied by a spouse. Meals of the medical professional while entertaining away from home on a business trip would be deductible at 50%.

Whether you structure business trips around vacations or vacations around business trips, the IRS allows some deductions for some rest and relaxation. The total airfare to a business location outside of the United States is deductible if the entire trip took less than a week. A deduction is also allowed even if the trip lasts longer than a week provided less than 25% of the time was spent on personal activities. If you cannot comply with these regulations, then only a pro rata portion of the airfare is deductible. A few modifications to a planned business and vacation trip can qualify much of the expenses for a business deduction. Generally, any temporary overnight business trip made away from home, which is primarily for business purposes, entitles the medical professional for a full deduction of the transportation costs incurred, even if a portion of the trip involves leisure time activities. You must keep good records of the date, destination, purpose, and amounts spent on each trip.

Tax Planning Tip ■ Since medical professionals can benefit from the flexibility of deducting entertainment expenses, ensure that proper documentation is completed. Valid documentation should include the name(s) of person(s) entertained, amount, time, place, and business purpose involved. Expenses must be "directly related" or "associated with" the active conduct of the taxpayer's trade or business. In general "directly related" usually refers to the context of active business discussions, or a clear business setting for such discussions. On the other hand, "associated with" refers to expenses incurred for the purposes of building goodwill, following or preceding business meetings or discussions. In each case, only the portion of the expenses "directly related," or "associated with," the medical professional's trade or business is deductible. Strict scrutiny is exercised by the IRS where the medical professional exhibits a pattern of abusive or undocumented entertainment. Although you do not have to prove income or other benefit from the entertainment, it would help to substantiate the business purpose.

Caution! ■ The Internal Revenue Code states that where no distinction can be made between the commingling of expenses that are fully deductible with those that are only partially deductible, all expenses within that category will be considered only partially deductible. The bottom line here is that each deductible entity should segregate its meals and entertainment expenses from other expenses.

Tax Planning Tip ■ You do not have to save receipts or paid bills to substantiate travel expenses less than $75, unless the expenditure is for lodging. You must retain proper documentation of all your lodging expenditures, regardless of the amount.

[K] Simple Charitable Giving

For the healthcare professional wanting to include charitable giving in a tax strategy, the contribution of securities with large gains can generate a double benefit. By giving the security (i.e., stock, bond, etc.) directly to the charity, the healthcare taxpayer can obtain a tax deduction for the fair market value of the stock without having to list as income the capital gain.

Tax Planning Tip ■ If you are giving to a charity this year, but no cash is available at year-end, put the contribution on a credit card. A pledge is not enough to get a deduction but the credit card contribution will qualify for a current year gift, even though the credit card bill is paid in the next year.

[L] Complex Charitable Giving

Charitable remainder trusts and charitable lead trusts are two tools used in long-term planning strategies. With a charitable remainder trust, the donor gets the income from the economic value of the property given, and upon the donor's death, the remainder goes to the charity.

For example, Dr. Duke gives $100,000 in zero coupon bonds (these bonds pay no interest and are sold at a discount) to his favorite charity through a charitable remainder trust. He bought the bonds for $32,000 (a steep discount), and the bonds are now worth $150,000. The bonds are then sold inside the trust and reinvested in a stock portfolio paying a handsome dividend. Dr. Duke gets the income from this portfolio during his lifetime, along with a deduction for the present value of the remainder (the value of the trust at the end of the trust agreement with the charity), and the charity gets the assets upon the death of Dr. Duke.

A charitable lead trust works on the opposite concept of the charitable remainder trust. Using the example from above, the charity would get the trust's income; Dr. Duke would get a deduction for the present value of the trust's income; and Dr. Duke's heirs would get the remainder at the end of the term of the trust's agreement with the charity.

Many organized charities support charitable trusts with programs available to provide all the details necessary for setting up the trust.[2]

[M] Education and Related Expenses

Up to $2,500 of interest paid on a qualified higher education loan is potentially deductible, regardless of whether you itemize or use the standard deduction. However, phase-out income limits apply, beginning with AGI above $100,000 on a joint return and $50,000 on a return.

Prior to 2002, the deductible interest was limited to that amount that was paid within the first 60 months in which payments were required. This 60-month limitation has been repealed as of 2001.

A $3000 deduction for tuition and fees for qualified higher education is allowed for years 2002 through 2005. The taxpayer's AGI must be below $65,000 or $130,000 if married filing jointly. This above-the-line deduction must be coordinated with the education credits. The deduction and the credit cannot be taken in the same year for the same education expense paid.

[N] Employer-Paid Educational Assistance

Now is a good time for healthcare workers to take advantage of any educational assistance offered by a hospital, managed care organization, health maintenance organization, or other employer. If the person meets certain requirements, up to $5250 of employer-paid assistance can be excluded from taxable wages. This exclusion has been permanently extended and now includes expenses for graduate level courses.

[O] State and Local Taxes

When looking at your individual tax picture for the year, special consideration should be given to state and local taxes. A traditional strategy (if a taxpayer is itemizing deductions) would be to make sure all these taxes are paid by year end so that you can deduct them in the current year's federal income tax return. The alternative is to pay them early in the succeeding year and then wait another whole year before being able to take the deduction. If income is expected to go up significantly in the next year so that the taxpayer will be in a higher tax bracket, then he or she may want to hold off because that deduction will be worth more on the next year's tax return. Also, if the taxpayer is barely able to exceed the standard deduction in the current year, including the taxes, he or she should pay these taxes in the beginning of the year and pay next year's taxes before the end of next year. This "bunching" of deductions will allow for a higher amount of itemized deductions to be taken next year.

For the higher income medical professional, you must reduce your itemized deductions by 3% of the excess amount over a threshold. The threshold is inflation adjusted ($139,500 in 2003 for Married Filing Jointly; $69,750 for Married Filing Separately), and certain items are exempt from this limitation. These include medical expenses, investment interest expense, non-business casualty and theft losses, and wagering losses. You can't lose more than 80% of the affected deductions.

[P] Fringe Benefits

Most healthcare employers offer some sort of benefit package to their employees (and themselves). These benefits are among the best tax planning areas for an employed individual taxpayer. Many of these benefits (i.e., health insurance, group term life insurance up to $50,000, disability insurance, retirement plan contributions, etc.) create a tax deduction for the employer and are not included in the taxable income of the taxpayer. This is a win-win situation for both employer and employee, and is one of the few areas within the Internal Revenue Code where the taxpayer benefits without having to pick up income. Even when an employee contribution or salary reduction is required, such as is the case within a cafeteria plan or flexible spending account (FSA), it is typically made on a pretax basis (e.g., 401(k) contribution, dependent care, unreimbursed medical expenses, educational expenses). Therefore, these benefits should be maximized by the individual taxpayer wherever possible.

For example, Jane Thayer, a licensed practical nurse, has a child in daycare at a cost of $75 per week and estimates that she and her daughter will have a total of $600 of either uncovered or unreimbursed medical expenses during the year. Under her employer's cafeteria plan (a "menu" of employee benefits is available for participation on an individual choice basis via salary reduction), Jane elects to have a salary reduction of $4350. This amount will cover 50 weeks of daycare at $75/week and the $600 estimate of unreimbursed medical expenses. The amount is deducted evenly from her gross wages. When she incurs an expense for either daycare or out-of-pocket medical expenses, she turns the receipt in to her employer, and she is reimbursed for that expense. The effect is to pay for these benefits with pretax dollars. The benefit to the employee is that the amount of salary reduction is not included in taxable income; therefore, Jane saves the income tax on the $4350.

Caution! ■ Physicians should use care when estimating these costs since any amounts not used will be forfeited. Also, it is difficult to discontinue participation in the cafeteria plan during the year once you have elected it.

Tax Planning Tip ■ Estimate the amount to reduce salary by only those costs certain to be incurred. For instance, if Jane's child will be in daycare, these costs should be included. In addition, if the child has braces that will be on all year, including the monthly orthodontic fees would be reasonable. However, do not include laser vision correction costs that might happen at the end of the year. Include this procedure's cost when it becomes a certainty, rather than risking several thousand dollars in reductions on the possibility that it might get done this year.

For the small employer, the rule of thumb on providing a cafeteria plan or FSA is that the plan pays for itself at participation of about 10 employees. Before that amount of participation, the amount of employment tax savings will not cover the cost of annual administration and tax preparation costs.

Tax Planning Tip ■ In years of a large AGI, consider postponing itemized deductions that have a deductible limit, such as medical and miscellaneous expenses, until the next tax year. Likewise, a physician taxpayer can accelerate deductions and/or defer revenue-generating transactions (if the physician has such control) until early the following year to reduce the overall income tax impact.

[Q] Home Office

Recently, Congress eased the eligibility requirements for home office deductions to the delight of some medical professionals. Beginning in 2000, healthcare professionals who base their business at home but tend to perform their services away from home, like an anesthesiologist or independent certified registered nurse anesthetist, may no longer find it as difficult to qualify for home office deductions. These deductions include a portion of your utilities, security system, premiums for homeowner's insurance, and other upkeep expenses. Performing some fix-up work, inside, around, and outside the house may also yield extra home office deductions if physicians see patients at home. Deductions are generally limited to the amount of income from your business. Deductions for furniture and equipment purchases may also be limited by your income and other depreciation restrictions.

Tax Planning Tip ■ When a home office deduction is claimed on a pro-rated basis, it is important to make careful calculations and be prepared to back them up in the event of an IRS tax audit. Drawing up a floor plan that clearly documents the square footage used for personal and business purposes is a good idea. Alternatively, the number of rooms used for business divided by the total number of rooms in the house can be used to calculate the business use percentage. The taxpayer can choose the method that generates the largest business percentage. Then, apply office deductions based on the chosen percentage. Overstating the claim about which portions of the home you are using for business can get the physician into trouble with the IRS.

Therefore, do not claim deductions for shared spaces like bathrooms or kitchens. Taking several photographs of your file cabinets or the room strictly reserved for your business purposes will further support your case for the home office deductions.

Caution! ■ One reason the IRS has eased the standard deduction for business use of home is to turn an otherwise tax-free gain generated by the sale of a personal residence into a partially taxable transaction. The portion of a residence claimed as business property by the homeowner is viewed as business property by the IRS as well, rather than only a residence. The sale of the business property portion is a taxable transaction to the extent of the total depreciation deducted related to the property. Therefore, the question becomes, Is the annual office in home deduction worth more than the eventual TI generated from the sale of the "business" portion of the home?

[R] Computers

To qualify for a deduction when you purchase a computer to use for home business purposes, healthcare employees must pass a two-part test. First, the computer must be a "condition of employment," which means it must be essential to properly perform your job. Second, the computer must be for the convenience of the employer.

[S] Hobby Deductions

If you have a sideline business, such as selling vitamins, telecommunication cards, or magnets, you may need to take some year-end steps to ensure the IRS treats your sideline like a real business and not just a hobby. If the IRS deems it a hobby, you will be able to deduct expenses only to the extent of income from your sideline job. To write off more of your business expenses, you will need to demonstrate that your sideline is a profit-motivated enterprise and not just a pleasurable coincident to your health-care profession.

Tax Planning Tip ■ The best way to achieve this goal is to be profitable. The IRS will presume your sideline is a business, and not a hobby, if you show a profit in three of five consecutive years (two of seven for horse racing). If you cannot make a profit, you can still convince the IRS by offering evidence that you are operating the entity like a real business and attempting to make a profit.

Investment Taxation

[A] Capital Losses

Short- and long-term capital gains and losses must be offset against one another to produce a net short- or long-term figure. Net capital losses in excess of gains are fully deductible, dollar for dollar, against ordinary income up to a $3000 annual limitation. Any excess capital losses may be carried forward indefinitely.

Tax Planning Tip ■ Capital losses on securities can offset capital gains on other passive investments such as art or real estate. Capital gains and losses from all passive investments can be combined in figuring net capital gains and losses. Publicly traded securities are reported in the year the trade occurs, even if settled in the following year.

[B] Zero Coupon Bonds

Although no cash is received on zero coupon bonds, a portion of the original issue discount must be reported each year as taxable (phantom) interest. This accretion increases the medical professional's cost basis. Of course, no tax is due if the zero coupon bonds are held in a tax-deferred account.

[C] Tax-Exempt Bonds

A tax-exempt bond bought at a premium must be amortized over the life of the bond or to the earliest call date. The premium cannot be deducted because it is an expense of earning tax-exempt income. The basis of the tax-exempt bond is reduced by the amount of the premium attributable to the period for which the bond is held. If the bond is held to maturity, no capital loss results from the purchase of a tax-exempt bond at a premium.

[D] Stock Splits

A medical professional might receive additional shares or cash in lieu of those additional shares as the result of a stock split. The portion representing cash in lieu of the fractional shares is treated as if received from the sale of the fractional shares.

[E] Wash Sale Rule

The wash sale rule applies when one sells a security at a loss and repurchases securities substantially identical to those sold within 61 days, beginning 30 days before the sale and ending 30 days after the sale. A deduction is denied for losses realized under these circumstances. Instead, the disallowed loss is added to the basis of the substantially identical securities acquired. The holding period of the securities sold at a loss is added to the holding period of the newly acquired security.

A wash sale may be avoided by purchasing the replacement security outside of 30 days. Alternatively, the medical professional investor could reinvest in securities that are not substantially identical, such as those in another company in the same industry.

[F] Short Sales

The taxable event of a short sale (a sale of securities not currently owned by a taxpayer) occurs when the securities are delivered to the lender (brokerage firm) by the seller to close the short sale. Whether a capital gain or loss on a short sale is long-term or short-term depends on how long the seller held the stock that was used to close the short sale. These rules prevent the conversion of a short-term gain into a long-term gain or the conversion of a long-term loss into a short-term loss.

This "constructive sale rule" eliminates the deferral on the gain from "short sales against the box." Medical professionals must recognize the gain when they enter into a short sale. The immediate recognition of gain can be avoided if the following occurs:

- The medical professional remains at risk for the loss on the identical security (long position) for at least 60 days after closing the short position.
- Identical securities are purchased in the open market to close (cover) the short sale on or before the 30th day of the following year.

[G] Worthless Securities

To turn worthless securities into a tax write-off, you usually must sell or exchange the securities to establish a tax loss. However, you may be able to deduct the loss on worthless stocks or bonds without a sale if you can prove the securities became worthless during the taxable year. You can deduct the loss only in the year the security becomes completely worthless. Unfortunately, it is up to the medical professional to prove the securities have no value and became worthless in the year claimed.

[H] Vacation Homes

A vacation or second home can be a tax benefit if you are willing to rent it out. The tax benefit depends on how much you use the home personally. If rented for less than 15 days during the entire calendar year, then all rental income is tax-free. However, you are only allowed to deduct the real estate taxes, mortgage interest, and any casualty losses. If you rent the home for 15 or more days throughout the year, then the rent must be included in your income. The offsetting benefit is that you can deduct maintenance and repairs. This analysis assumes that you use the home for vacation for no more than 14 days a year, or 10% of the rental days. This assumption is not harsh when you consider that a fix-up day does not count toward the 14 days, even if the family comes along.

[I] Nanny Tax

Although not deductible for income tax purposes, the reporting of a nanny is required as part of the medical professional's individual tax return. The IRS has foreclosed all opportunity to call the nanny an independent contractor. If a nanny could be considered an independent contractor, then no payroll withholding taxes, in the form of social security, Medicare, or state and federal unemployment insurance premiums would be required. Thus, as an employee, the nanny's wages are subject to payroll withholding taxes and must be reported on Schedule H of an individual tax return.

However, one opportunity to save tax payments exists for the medical professional who employs a nanny—allocate some part of the nanny's day to helping at your office practice. For example, relaying business faxes or phone messages received at home is a justifiable expense. The business-related responsibilities of the nanny could then be deducted as a business expense.

[J] Investment Interest Expense

Investment interest expense deductions are limited to net investment income, which is investment income (interest, dividends, and short-term capital gains) minus investment expenses. An exception is that such net capital gains may be included in net investment income to the extent the medical professional elects to reduce the amount of net capital gains eligible for the 20% and 28% maximum capital gain tax rates. In the case of either a taxable or non-taxable bond, bought at a premium, the medical professional can either amortize or deduct the premium each year, with a corresponding reduction in cost basis, over the remaining life of the bond. Other complicated tax rules may also apply, depending on the specific year the bond was purchased.

Tax Planning Tip ■ Segregate consumer, business, and investment activities since, with the exception of home equity interest expense, the deductibility of interest depends on the use of the loan proceeds. For example, if securities are margined and the loan proceeds are used to purchase a new car, the margin interest is considered consumer interest and not investment interest. The IRS requires that the loan proceeds be traceable to the actual use of funds. Therefore, be sure to trace credit transactions so that they can be allocated to the proper activities.

[K] Municipal Bond Margin

Margin interest expense used to purchase municipal bonds or similar investments is not tax deductible. In addition, the IRS may infer a relationship between interest expense and the carrying of tax-exempt securities. A medical investor who borrows to finance a stock or bond portfolio while owning tax-exempt bonds may have an apportioned amount of the interest deduction disallowed. Similarly, interest expense is not deductible if loan proceeds are used to purchase or carry single premium insurance or annuity contracts. Interest expense incurred to purchase other life insurance contracts is considered consumer interest expense and is not deductible.

[L] Mutual Funds

The IRS allows four methods to determine cost, also known as the adjusted tax basis, for mutual funds:

1. FIFO (first in, first out): The holding period and cost for the first share sold is based on that of the first share purchased, and so on. The IRS uses this method, if one of the other three is not specified, because more tax is collected from this method.
2. LIFO (last in, first out): This is the opposite of FIFO and results in a lesser tax burden.
3. Specific Identification: The cost basis of each specific share is tracked and reported.
4. Average Cost Method: This is probably the most common method, as seen in Exhibit 4–6:

Exhibit 4–6 *Average Cost Method Calculations for Mutual Fund Shares*

(A medical investor makes three share purchases)

Transaction	Price	Shares	Total	Cumulative Cost	Avg. Cost
1/1/92 Purchase $ 2,000	$ 20	100	100	$ 2,000	$ 20.00
6/1/93 Purchase $ 5,000	$ 25	200	300	7,000	$ 23.33
2/1/00 Purchase $10,000	$ 50	200	500	17,000	$ 34.00

[M] Listed Stock Options

Writing stock options offers timing advantages for medical professionals because the premium becomes taxable only upon the close of the position by exercise or a closing transaction. The premium income is considered a short-term capital gain if the option expires unexercised.

[N] Broad-Based Index Options

Broad-based index options open at year-end must be marked to the market, and unrealized capital gains and losses are taxed as if the position had been closed at year-end. Under special rules, 60% of the capital gain or loss is treated as long term, and 40% is treated as short term, regardless of the actual holding period.

[O] Like-Kind Exchanges

An often ignored technique of decreasing TI is a like-kind exchange, which helps avoid paying taxes on appreciated business or investment property that would otherwise be sold to acquire new property. It is not available for securities or other types of assets.

[P] Real Estate

For medical professionals who *actively* managed rental real estate, there is an opportunity to deduct up to $25,000 in *passive losses* from that activity against other income.

Tax Credits

[A] Child Tax Credit

Healthcare workers can claim a $600 tax credit for each qualifying child, who is a son, daughter, stepson, or stepdaughter, or an eligible foster child who is a dependent, is a U.S. citizen, and under the age of 17. For joint filers with AGI from $110,000–121,001, $75,000–$86,001 for singles or heads of households, and over $55,000–66,001 for married filing separately, the credit is reduced by $50 for every $1000 or fraction thereof in excess of these limits. Low-income workers with three children may also qualify for a supplemental credit.

Tax Planning Tip ■ Under JGTRRA the child tax credit was increased from $600 to $1000. Parents who took the child tax credit on their 2002 returns received "advanced payment" checks in the summer of 2003 for up to $400 per child to reflect the new, higher credit. This functioned much like the advance payment rebate checks two years ago, when taxpayers received up to $300 each in the mail. The $1000 credit will last for two years before shrinking to $700 each year from 2005 through 2008. In 2009, the credit would rise again to $800 before returning to $1000 in 2010.

[B] Lifetime Learning Credit

As its name implies, this tax credit is not restricted to the first two years of postsecondary education for the healthcare professional. Undergraduate, graduate, and professional degree courses can qualify for this credit. The maximum credit is $1000 per taxpayer return (20% of expenses up to $5000), regardless of the number of students. Beginning in January 2003, up to $10,000 of tuition expenses, per taxpayer return, will be eligible for the credit for a maximum credit of $2000 per return (not individual).

If there is a choice between this credit, and a Hope credit, it is better to choose the more generous Hope credit. The Hope credit is equal to 100% of the first $1000 of tuition paid and 50% of the next $1000 of tuition paid for a total credit of $1500. It will not prevent you from also electing a lifetime learning credit for another eligible family member's expenses.

As an example, a married couple with a daughter who is a college freshman and a son who is a college senior can elect a Hope credit for their daughter and a lifetime learning credit for their son (assuming all other requirements are met).

[C] Child and Dependent Care Credit

For 2003, the child and dependent care credit increased to a maximum of 35% from 30%. The employment-related expense dollar limit is $3000 (up from $2400) for one individual and $6000 (up from $4800) for two or more individuals. The maximum 35% is allowed for taxpayers having AGI of $15,000 or less. This percentage decreases until it levels at 20% for taxpayers having AGI over $43,000.

The Alternative Minimum Tax

The aim of tax planning strategy for the healthcare professional is to generate the lowest possible tax within each taxpayer's unique set of circumstances. However, as noted earlier, Uncle Sam has a "safety net" to make sure that every taxpayer pays some tax and does not take advantage of the government by overutilizing the tax loopholes available. This IRS safety net is called the alternative minimum tax (AMT). This is a separate tax calculation based upon regular TI. The tax then adds back certain itemized deductions plus certain other tax deductions claimed in a year to calculate whether the taxpayer has received too much benefit from these items, which include tax exempt interest from private activity bonds, issued after August 7, 1986, bargain element in incentive stock options, and certain other accelerated depreciation items. No AMT deductions are available for personal exemptions, state and local income, personal property and real estate tax payments, medical expenses not exceeding 10% of AGI, and miscellaneous expenses subject to the 2% of AGI floor.

This calculation generates the amount of AMT income. This AMT income has its own tax rate and, if the tax derived from this calculation is higher than the regular tax calculation, the taxpayer pays according to the AMT calculation. The AMT tax rate is generally 26% (on the first $175,000 of AMT income and $87,500 for married filing separately) and goes up to 28% over that amount. AMT income consists of AGI, plus the preference income, minus certain itemized deductions and an exemption based on the filing status, as follows:

Married, filing jointly, surviving spouses:	$49,000
Single taxpayers, heads of household	$35,750
Married filing separately	$24,500
Trusts and estates	$22,500

The exemption amounts above are reduced 25 cents for every dollar by which the minimum tax base exceeds $150,000 for joint return filers, $112,500 for single tax payers and heads of households, and $75,000 for married professionals filing separately. The exemption is fully fulfilled at $346,000 for joint filers, $255,500 for single taxpayers and heads of households, $173,000 for married medical professionals filing separately, and $165,000 for trusts and estates.

Tax Planning Tip ■ The AMT is increasingly targeting medical professionals so that they should try to incur as much ordinary income as possible until they reach a crossover point where their regular tax liability equals their AMT liability. Each dollar subject to the AMT is taxed at either 26% or 28%, both of which are lower than the current top three regular tax rates (30%, 35%, and 38.6%).

Therefore, try to accelerate ordinary income by:

- Converting municipal bond (tax exempt) investments into taxable investments;
- Redeeming CDs, Treasury paper, Series E, or Series EE bonds, to generate interest income;
- Considering the withdrawal of money from IRAs, if not subject to a 10% or other penalties;
- Exercising nonqualified stock options, since their bargain element is taxed as ordinary income at the time of exercise; and
- Exercising incentive stock options and selling option stock in the same calendar year to recognize additional ordinary income and eliminate a like amount of tax preference.

Additionally, the medical professional should try to defer certain deductions that reduce regular taxes, but do not reduce the AMT. These tactics and tips include:

- Postponing miscellaneous deductions when possible to the following tax year; and
- Limiting estimated payment of state and/or local income taxes in the current year to an amount sufficient to avoid penalties.

Obviously, the object is to avoid the AMT, if possible. The additional tax from this calculation mitigates the work involved in planning for the lowest liability possible. This tax, calculated on Form 6251, is becoming much more common as the spread between regular tax rates and the AMT rates becomes less.

Medical professionals may take a credit against their regular tax for any AMT paid in prior years. This credit may not be used to reduce the AMT tax liability. The credit is limited to the portion of the AMT attributable to items that defer income, such as items of accelerated depreciation, rather than to items that cause a permanent exclusion of income.

Tax Planning Tip ■ Effective January 1, 2003, a significant increase was applied to the AMT exemption amounts for the years 2003 and 2004. After 2004, the exemption reverts to prior amounts.

The AMT, originally designed to ensure that wealthy physicians did not use loopholes to escape tax entirely, has snared more moderate-income physicians in recent years. The tax bill reduced that number by increasing the so-called AMT exemption to $58,000 for married couples filing jointly, up from the current $49,000. The AMT exemption for single filers will rise from $37,750 to $40,250.

Assessment

Much publicity has been given to the new, friendly IRS, which no longer places the burden of proof on the taxpayer. A nice sentiment, but in the future, because of sophisticated computerized data mining techniques, the IRS will eventually be able to detect both outright fraud and small-scale cheating. According to Paul Cosgrave, chief information officer of the IRS, in its customer friendly mode, small cheating is called "math errors."[3] But, when the IRS finds them, the taxpayer is still billed and, practically speaking, the IRS can easily shift the burden of proof back to the taxpayer.

Therefore, your only defense is proper documentation. An audit of your tax return is really an audit of your records. The benefit of the doubt will be given where information is well organized and easy to understand. All audits start with random verification of deductions. If the random testing raises suspicion, then full verification is inevitable. On the other hand, if the random test proves accurate, then a full verification is typically waived.

Another benefit to focusing on documentation is the risk of losing deductions. Many deductions are lost because of failure to remember the expenditures. For example, medical professionals can document and deduct all charitable contributions, even if receipts are not available, as illustrated in the scenarios below:

- Donations to a church during a visit;
- Mileage used during the year to transport Boy Scouts;
- The portion of a fund raising dinner's expense that benefits the charity; and
- Donations of personal property to charities.

Note that substantial documentation is typically required for contributions of $250 or more. Substantiation does not include a canceled check, but does include a receipt from the organization.

Also, do not forget such deductible items as state taxes, property taxes, business-related phone bills, medical expenses not reimbursed by insurance to the extent they exceed 7.5% of AGI, and other miscellaneous deductions such as professional association dues, subscription renewals to investment and trade publications, uniforms and laundry, and tax preparation related compute software. Unfortunately, healthcare employee business expenses may become harder to write off each year because these miscellaneous expenses are deductible only to the extent that they exceed 2% of AGI.

Finally, before you hunt for extra tax deductions, be sure your efforts will pay off. For example, if you are not able to itemize deductions on your 2003 tax return (i.e., you use the standard deduction), there is no use chasing the above list of potential deductions. Instead, consider waiting until after December 31 to pay expenses, in case you are able to itemize on your 2004 tax return.

Tax planning is a very personal task for the healthcare professional, and it is unique based upon the characteristics each one possesses. Do not be lulled into the follower syndrome. Just because a colleague in the lounge has used a tax planning strategy, do not assume that the same strategy will provide a similar benefit for you. A custom suit always provides a better fit than an off-the-shelf item, and the same goes with tax planning. Review the unique facts and circumstances surrounding the subject of the tax planning and find those deductions, credits, and strategies that best fit your individual circumstances.

Job Creation and Worker Assistance Act of 2002

The Job Creation and Worker Assistance Act of 2002 provides business tax breaks to help create jobs and boost the economy and individual tax breaks to help those affected by the economic downturn and the events of September 11, 2001. The legislation has a projected 10-year budgeted cost of $42 billion. A few of the highlights are discussed below. A financial or tax professional should be consulted to determine how this new tax act might affect you specifically.

[A] Net Operating Loss Carry-back Period

Net operating losses incurred in 2001 or 2002 can be carried back five years (compared to two years under prior law). The loss can reduce alternative minimum taxable income in full rather than the previous limit of 90% of alternative minimum taxable income.

[B] Depreciation

Depreciable assets with a class life of 20 years or less purchased after September 10, 2001, and before September 11, 2004, and placed in service before January 1, 2005, are allowed an additional 30% depreciation allowance in their first year of operation. This must be original use (new) property. Used property does not qualify for the additional allowance. This is in addition to any Section 179 expense elected, which is applied before the additional 30% allowance. The remaining depreciable basis then becomes the cost of the asset less Section 179 expense less the 30% allowance claimed. The 20-year life limit increases the importance of cost segregation between buildings you own, which have a 39-year recovery period and do not qualify for the 30% benefit, and building components or improvements to buildings you own.

[C] Luxury Vehicles

An additional $4600 is allowed for depreciation in the first year that the vehicle is placed in service. Coupled with the $3060 limit already in place, the total first year depreciation expense becomes $7660. This applies to vehicles acquired after September 10, 2001, and before January 1, 2005.

[D] New York City Tax Incentives

Several incentives are provided specifically to benefit businesses in the New York Liberty Zone. The specifics are beyond the scope of this chapter. A competent advisor should be consulted to discuss how these benefits might affect your business.

Synopsis of the Jobs and Growth Tax Relief and Reconciliation Act of 2003

The Jobs and Growth Tax Relief and Reconciliation Act (JGTRRA) of 2003 presents a significant opportunity for physicians and their financial advisors to rebalance an integrated personal financial plan. The typical taxpayer will save about $671, according to the U.S. Tax Policy Center. The most important provisions of the new law include the following.

[A] Reduction in Individual Capital Gains Rate

Effective May 6, 2003, the 10% and 20% tax rates on net capital gains have been reduced to 5 and 15%, respectively. The 5% rate becomes zero in 2008. The change to the maximum tax terminates after 2008, and in 2009 the law reverts back to the maximum rate of 20%.

[B] Dividend Tax Relief for Individuals

Retroactive to January 1, 2003, dividends received by an individual physician shareholder from domestic and qualified foreign corporations will be taxed at a maximum capital gains rate of 15% until 2009. A 5% rate applies to physicians in the 10% and 15% brackets (the 5% rate becomes zero in 2008). It applies to both regular income tax and AMT.

For example, a married couple with $50,000 a year in TI in 2002 would have paid $200 in capital gains taxes on a $1000 stock sale profit and another $270 on $1000 in dividend income. Under the new law, the tax on the dividend income would be $50. The tax on the gain would be $50, and the total tax, $100. The total tax savings would be $370.

[C] Increased AMT Exemptions

A significant increase applies to the AMT exemption amounts for 2003 and 2004. After 2004, the exemption reverts to prior amounts.

The AMT, originally designed to ensure that wealthy physicians did not use loopholes to escape tax entirely, has snared more moderate-income physicians in recent years. The tax bill reduced that number by increasing the so-called AMT exemption to $58,000 for married couples filing jointly, up from the current $49,000. The AMT exemption for a single person would rise from $37,750 to $40,250.

[D] Reduced Regular Income Tax Rates

Regular income tax rates in excess of 15% are 25%, 28%, 33%, and 35%; and the 38.6% bracket is eliminated. In 2011, the rates will revert to their previous levels, and the top tax rate will revert back to 39.6%.

For a couple with $70,000 in TI, the changes would knock their tax bill from $12,606 to $11,120 this year, saving them $1486. For a married physician couple with $400,000 in TI, the tax bill would drop from about $124,701 to $108,344, a savings of $16,357.

[E] Increased Section 179 Expensing

The amount a medical practice can claim as an expense under Section 179 has been increased to $100,000. This increase applies to property, equipment, and instruments placed in service in tax years 2003 through 2005. In addition, for the same periods, the $200,000 limitation on qualifying Section 179 property is increased to $400,000. For 2003, 2004, and 2005, physician taxpayers may make or revoke expensing elections on amended tax returns without IRS consent.

[F] Elimination of the Marriage Penalty

One of the questions most frequently asked by the medical professional in the past concerned the filing of a joint tax return versus the filing of a separate return. This question came up because of the so-called marriage penalty that was built into the standard deduction and also into the tax rates for married couples filing a joint return. Fortunately, the marriage penalty has been eliminated for dual income married couples. The basic standard deduction amount is twice the standard deduction for single individuals in 2003 and 2004 and will be raised from the current $7950 to $9500. Those who itemize their deductions on their income taxes won't see any effect, but the majority of couples who take the standard deduction will save $155.

Physicians living in either community property or common law states should take extra care in the documentation of income and deductions ("ownership"). In community property states, most items of both income and deduction will be split 50/50. However, each community property state has its own rules how income from separate property (property owned by one spouse or the other, not jointly, e.g., inherited property) is treated. For common law states, income is traced to ownership, and deductions claimed by one spouse must be paid from that spouse's separate funds.

[G] Special Depreciation Allowance for Certain Property

- Additional First Year Depreciation Deduction equals 59% of adjusted basis of qualified property;
- Property must be acquired after May 5, 2003 and before January 1, 2005, and be placed in service before January 1, 2005 (January 1, 2006 for certain other property); and
- The 50% added first year depreciation is coordinated with the 30% added first year depreciation allowed under the Jobs Creation Workers Assistance Act of 2002.

[H] Physician Residents and Young Children

The child tax credit was increased from $600 to $1000. Parents who took the child tax credit on their 2002 returns got "advanced payment" checks in the summer of 2003 for up to $400 per child to reflect the new, higher credit. This functioned much like the advance payment rebate checks two years ago when taxpayers received up to $300 each in the mail. The $1000 credit will last for two years before shrinking to $700 in 2005 through 2008. In 2009, the credit would rise to $800 before returning to $1000 in 2010.

Conclusion

Knowing the new rules of JGTRRA 2003 will benefit physicians and all taxpaying citizens. To stay informed, visit the site www.irs.ustreas.gov for tax tables and updates. To download a complete copy of the JGTRRA bill, visit www.taxplanet.com.

Acknowledgment

Dr. David Edward Marcinko, MBA, CFP, CMP for the JGTRRA 2003 material.

Endnotes

1. *See* the site www.ibert.org/tax.html for a listing of average deductions taken by individual taxpayers in prior years.
2. Vanguard Charitable Endowment Program (888-383-4483); Fidelity Investments Charitable Gift Fund (800-682-4438).
3. See www.fcw.com/fdw/articles/2001/0108/news-irs-01-08-01.asp, or www.uncle-fed.com/tax-news/1998/nr98-49.html.

Chapter 5

Medical Office Tax Reduction Strategies

Implementing Short- and Long-Term Techniques

Thomas P. McGuinness

Good Quote!

I live in Alexandria, Virginia. Near the Supreme Court Chambers is a toll bridge across the Potomac. When in a rush, I pay the dollar toll and get home early. However, I usually drive outside the downtown section of the city and cross the Potomac on a free bridge. This bridge was placed outside the downtown Washington, DC area to serve a useful social service, getting drivers to drive the extra mile and to help alleviate congestion during the rush hour. If I went over the toll bridge and through the barrier without paying the toll, I would be committing tax evasion. If, however, I drive the extra mile and drive outside the city of Washington to the free bridge, I am using a legitimate, logical, and suitable method of tax avoidance, and I am performing a useful social service by doing so. For my tax evasion, I should be punished. For my tax avoidance, I should be commended. The tragedy of life today is that so few people know that the free bridge even exists.

Justice Louis D. Brandeis, 1914

The objective of medical office tax planning is to arrive at the lowest overall amount of taxes on the activities performed. This means pushing as much income as possible beyond Uncle Sam and into personal or business accounts permanently. Some have stated that income tax planning is like playing a game and those who best know the rules of the game "win." This chapter will address items to be aware of and methods and strategies to use to reduce federal and state income taxes. "Winning" is a relative term when dealing with income taxes. A healthcare professional does not have to force fit every tax planning tool available in order to lower taxes (winning). Winning is achieved each time a tip or strategy is used to help reduce taxable income or to take a credit to reduce taxes to be paid.

Medical Corporation Tax Planning Process

Healthcare professionals have been taught to triage for their entire career. Deal with the "hottest fire" first and then move on. Although this thought process works well in your profession, it is detrimental in the tax planning mode and will lead to lost planning opportunities. It is too late to take advantage of most tax planning tips when sitting down to either prepare a tax return or assemble information for a tax preparer. Not planning ahead will always cost the physician money.

Tax Planning Tip ■ It is best to begin the tax planning process early in the year. This will allow sufficient time to review and take advantage of strategies that may take several months (or years) to fully implement. In addition, forethought will generate better financial results. For example, if contributing to a standard Individual Retirement Account (IRA) is in an individual's plans, making that contribution at the beginning of the tax year (early January) can put that money to work as much as 15½ months earlier than making the deposit in mid-April of the following year, when the individual's tax return is due. This hypothetical IRA contribution, at a 12% return (which would be an average return in the stock market over the past 15 years) would earn an additional $340 if contributed at the beginning of the tax year as in the above example. That is just for that one contribution over a 15½-month period. When this one change in thought process (or strategy) is evaluated over 20 years, the numbers become staggering.

Investing $2000 on January 1, 2000, and each year thereafter for 20 years, at the above 12% rate of return, generates $198,056 on December 31, 2020. Investing this same $2000 starting on April 15, 2001, and each year thereafter for 20 years at a 12% rate of return generates $169,762, or a difference of $28,294.

[handwritten margin note: Simple tip but still worth considering]

[A] Organization

Almost every person dreads the thought of going through all his or her records to segregate the information that is significant for preparing a tax return. This usually leads to procrastination and pushes the entire process back to a last minute task, well after the end of the year. In order for the tax planning process to be effective, this cycle must be broken. Instead of procrastinating, try an easy, more proactive approach.

/ MAKE UP FOR CLIENTS

Tax Planning Tip ■ Set up one file at the beginning of the tax year to store all potential tax information. During the year, as tax sensitive information is received from whatever source (i.e., receipts, paycheck stubs, charitable donation letters, stock purchase or sale information, etc.), put it in the "tax file." At year end, the tax gathering process is already done. More importantly, as potential opportunities arise during the year, all the pertinent tax information is already in one place for easy access and review of current tax status. This process can get much more detailed by segregating different types of tax information into separate files or setting up spreadsheets to track this information, but those additional processes are a matter of personal preference.

[B] A Quick Accounting Lesson

Although this may be boring, it is the one accounting lesson that will assist in making cash flow and tax planning decisions that can save untold dollars. There are two basic methods of accounting available to healthcare practice entities: the cash basis and the accrual basis of accounting.

[1] THE CASH BASIS OF ACCOUNTING

First, most healthcare practices utilize the cash basis (or cash method) of accounting. The cash basis of accounting recognizes revenue when cash is received and recognizes expenses when they are paid. This is the easiest concept to grasp because, with few exceptions, the income or loss for a particular period can be roughly estimated by looking at the change in the practice's bank account from the beginning to the end of that period. The exceptions, to name a few, would include asset purchases and loan principal payments that are not deductible for tax purposes (i.e., penalties and fines, one half of entertainment expense, or principal payments on loans) and those deductions that are not cash in nature (i.e., depreciation and amortization expenses).

The terms "tax basis" or "income tax basis" of accounting may also be heard. These are the same thing and are basically the same as the cash basis with modifications that are allowed by tax law. For example, various retirement plan contributions are deducted in the current year (typically at the entity's year end) and paid in the following tax year up to the due date of the entity's tax return plus any valid tax return extensions filed. The exception is that IRAs must be deposited by April 15th in order to be counted as a contribution for the prior year.

[a] Cash Basis Revenue Example

A physician sees a patient in the office on December 1st and the charge for the visit is $75. The patient makes a $10 co-payment, and two months later the patient's insurance carrier pays $40 of the accounts receivable balance and disallows the rest due to a contractual adjustment. The practice will recognize revenue of $50 (the $10 co-pay plus the $40 insurance payment), $10 in the current year, and $40 in the subsequent year.

[b] Cash Basis Expense Example

The telephone bill of $675 comes in on December 15th for this calendar year entity. If the bill is paid by December 31st, it is an expense for the current year. If it is paid on January 1st or any time thereafter, it will be an expense of the next year, and the entity will have to wait over a year to take advantage of that deduction for tax purposes.

[2] THE ACCRUAL BASIS OF ACCOUNTING

The accrual basis of accounting states that income goes on the books when it is *earned,* and expenses are booked when they are incurred.

[a] Accrual Basis Revenue Example

Using the same facts as in the above example, under the accrual method of accounting, the entire $75 is recognized as income at the point the physician has performed "substantially all functions necessary to earn the revenue." That is, after the physician has completed the examination of the patient.

This method is very unappealing for several reasons. First, most patients do not pay the entire bill at the time of the visit. Therefore, the majority of the charge ($65) goes into the accounts receivable subledger. Second, if this is an insurance charge, most insurance carriers pay the charge based upon their usual, customary, and "reasonable" fee schedule rather than the physician's fee schedule. For income tax purposes in this method, the entire $75 is considered revenue for the physician when he or she sees the patient. This creates a scenario where the physician is paying income tax on income that will never be realized.

Eventually, when the insurance carrier provides a correct explanation of benefits, the practice will be able to write off the remaining $25 ($75 charge minus the $10 co-pay and $40 insurance payment) as an adjustment against revenue. However, cash flow will have been used to pay income tax on "phantom" revenue. In the real world, there are always timing differences between the time a service is provided and when payment is received. When a year end falls in between the two events, the practice pays tax on the "paper income" represented in that timing difference.

[b] Accrual Basis Expense Example

The physician or office manager orders influenza vaccine from the office's typical supplier. When the vaccine is delivered to the office, the practice has incurred the expense of that vaccine.

This part of the accrual basis of accounting is more appealing, because it offsets to some degree the recognition of income per above. However, since most practices are "for profit" entities, it is hoped that there will be more revenue than expenses in the practice.

Under accrual basis accounting, most healthcare practices will typically pay more federal and state income taxes than when using the cash basis of accounting. In addition, the practice will probably pay somewhat more in accounting-related costs for keeping up with an accrual basis set of books. The accounts payable subledger, the year-end search for accrued expenses, and the potential of having to pay more for a staff person with a stronger accounting background are some of the factors that will generate the additional cost.

Tax Planning Tip ■ The accrual method of accounting is recommended for any proposed Independent Physicians Association or other practice entity contracting for capitation that it will either subcapitate or pay out for services not provided within its own entity. This advice is not the opposite of that previously stated. In a capitated arrangement, the entity receives funds each month in advance, at some predetermined (and hopefully negotiated) rate, to provide a menu of services to a defined population. This arrangement typically gives the appearance of large profits. However, the cost to this entity for providing such services is typically realized long before it receives payment. In fact, it could be many months later before all expenses have been paid. At year end using the cash basis method, the entity would have to pay tax on these capitation payment "profits," when, in fact, it will owe most or all of that cash flow to other practitioners (and facilities as well, if they are included in the contract) for services they have provided to the patient base during that period.

This exact scenario has played out many times: After taxes have been taken out, and all the actual costs have come in, there is not enough money in the accounts to pay for services rendered. Provider entities do not get paid and refuse to provide additional services because they fear they will not be paid. In a nutshell, this causes the collapse of the entity.

Tax Planning Tip ■ If the healthcare professional's core service entity is on the cash basis, and it is going into the type of capitation environment described in the prior tip, try this alternative. Set up a separate entity for this line of business and choose the accrual method of accounting for the new entity. Tax practitioners experienced in the healthcare industry have not been very successful in getting the Internal Revenue Service (IRS) to allow a change in accounting method from the cash basis to accrual basis for entities in the above situation. Although the accrual method most accurately reports income and expenses for healthcare entities (the IRS is supposed to use this criterion when considering a request for a change in an entity's method of accounting), the IRS has generally denied such applications.

[C] Practice Entities Utilized by Healthcare Professionals

Healthcare professionals practice within many different legal structures, and various differences in tax planning techniques depend upon the structure of the entity or entities you practice within. The various entities and types of returns that are filed for those entities are shown in Exhibit 5-1.

Exhibit 5-1 *Return Types for Various Practice Entities*

Entity	Type of Return
Sole proprietor	Schedule C, Form 1040
C Corporation (Inc., Corp., PA, or PC)	Form 1120
S Corporation (Inc., Corp., PA, or PC)	Form 1120S
Professional Corporation (PC)	Form 1120, or 1120S
Professional Association (PA)	Form 1120, or 1120S
Not for Profit Corporation	Form 1120
General Partnership	Form 1065
Limited Partnership	Form 1065
Limited Liability Partnership (LLP)	Form 1065
Limited Liability Company (LLC)	Form 1065, Form 1120 or 1120S
Foundation Model	Form 990
Tax Exempt, Not for Profit Corp.	Form 990

Each state is responsible for enacting its own legal statutes on the organization of physician corporations. Therefore, a corporate practice entity could be an Incorporation (Inc.), Corporation (Corp.), Professional Association (PA), or Professional Corporation (PC), depending on the state in which the practice entity is organized. In addition, almost every state has enacted legislation to create limited liability entities that provide the liability protection afforded a corporation while having the attributes of a partnership. These entities have become very popular with professional practices (physicians, lawyers, accountants, engineers, architects, etc.) because they allow more flexibility with regard to buy-ins and buyouts, and in the allocation of income and deductions. Since limited liability entities differ from state to state, the healthcare professional should seek out either an attorney or accountant familiar with the nuances of limited liability entities in their particular state. For federal income tax purposes, these entities are viewed as partnerships unless the entity elects to be treated as a corporation. The election is made on federal Form 8832 and is also known as a "check the box" election.

[1] CORPORATIONS

Within the C Corporation status, there is a distinction between entities providing personal services and those that provide goods and services not personal in nature. A physician corporation (C Corporation) is considered to be a "Personal Service Corporation" for federal income tax purposes. A personal service corporation pays federal income tax on every dollar of taxable income at a rate of 35%. All other C Corporations follow the progressive tax rate structure that taxes corporate income below $100,000 at lower tax rates (15% on the first $50,000, 25% on the next $25,000, and 34% on the following $25,000). The IRS believed that professionals could manipulate their year-end income and, therefore, the tax they paid. In 2003 the IRS asked Congress to close this loophole. Congress created the Personal Service Corporation designation to remove this tax planning opportunity. This is one of the disadvantages of a C Corporation for those providing personal services.

The difference between a C Corporation and an S Corporation is strictly a federal tax consideration. The S Corporation was created by Congress to allow small business corporations the flexibility of a partnership while retaining the limited liability advantages of the corporate structure. Therefore, for federal income tax purposes the S Corporation reports its income, deductions, expenses, and credits to its shareholders along the lines of a partnership. This is important since C Corporations are taxpaying entities, while all the other entities are generally considered to be tax reporting or passthrough entities. S Corporation status is achieved by filing Form 2553 with the IRS either within 75 days of when the practice is incorporated, when the business is actually started, or within 75 days of the beginning of a corporation's fiscal year. This election can be made even if an entity has been a C Corporation for many years; however, there are potential tax traps (known as the "built-in gains" tax) in a C Corporation conversion to an S Corporation for those unaware of the law. This is an area where the assistance of a qualified tax professional would be worthwhile since the tax cost of falling into the traps can be significant.

[2] PASSTHROUGH ENTITIES AND FAVORED TAX STATUS

Partnerships, S Corporations, and Limited Liability entities (LLPs or LLCs) are generally considered to be passthrough entities. The term "passthrough" entity is based upon the way in which the tax attributes of the entity (e.g., income, expenses, deductions, and credits) flow through to the owners and how the owners take them into account on their individual tax returns. This treatment allows the owner to avoid the potential for double taxation that exists in a C Corporation.

[3] SOLE PROPRIETORS

A sole proprietor is an individual business owner whose business is accounted for on a separate schedule of the owner's individual income tax return. Typically, owners filing their business returns via the use of Schedule C of Form 1040 have the lowest level of reporting requirements and also (in general) do the poorest job of keeping good records of business activity. There is only one level of tax for the sole proprietor. The net profit (or loss) from the Schedule C business is reported on page one of Form 1040 and is combined with all the other income items reported to arrive at gross income. Different from interest and dividend income, or investment income that is typically considered passive in nature, self-employment income is income generated by one's own actions. There is "Self Employment" tax to be paid on virtually all self-employment income reported in the tax return. Many sole proprietors get into trouble because they neglect to take this tax into account when estimating their tax liability for the year, and this tax is significant as noted below.

Self-employment tax is paid on 92.35% of all self-employment net profits. This tax is the equivalent of the combination of the employer's and employee's Social Security tax and Medicare tax. Social Security tax was 12.4% of the first $84,900 in 2003 in net income, and Medicare tax is paid 2.90% of net income without any upper income limit. The Social Security income limit is indexed and adjusted upward annually. The sole proprietor is allowed to deduct one half of the self-employment tax against income; however, this deduction is worth far less than the actual tax.

Example

Dr. Mary F. Soloman is a sole proprietor with a self-employment tax liability of $11,500. She deducts $5750 (50% of $11,500) against her income. She is in the 31% tax bracket; therefore, her deduction is worth $1782.50 in actual income tax dollars ($5750 × .31). The discrepancy between one half of the self-employment tax, $5750, and the self-employment tax deduction is $3967.50 in tax. Therefore, although Dr. Soloman received a 50% deduction for her self-employment tax, she actually pays $9717.50, or 84.5% of the self-employment tax.

This is not the bargain that the Congressional spin-doctors made it out to be when it was being sold to the general public. However, it is still better than paying the entire $11,500 in self-employment tax.

[D] General Tax Planning Issues

The following issues apply to all business entities. There may be minor differences in the section of the Internal Revenue Code (IRC) or nuances in the way that the Code section applies to the entity, but, in general, these areas are worthy issues not to be dismissed.

[1] PURCHASED ACCOUNTS RECEIVABLE

Several years ago, some physicians sold their practices to Public Practice Management Companies (PPMCs) or other buyers. However, many of those transactions soured since the PPMCs or other network models were not able to generate the earnings Wall Street or some other market force wanted. Many of these practices are now being repurchased by the same physicians who sold them several years earlier. If the physician is buying back an entity and relevant accounts receivable, the physician should be careful not to pick this item up as income twice. The costs can be immense to the practice or other business unit.

Example

Some physicians recently re-purchased their practice from a PPMC. Part of the mandatory purchase price, approximately $200,000 (the approximate net realizable value of the accounts receivable), was paid to the PPMC to buy back accounts receivable generated by the physicians buying back their practice. The office administrator unknowingly began recording the cash receipts specifically attributable to the purchased accounts receivable as patient fee income. If left uncorrected, this error could have incorrectly added $200,000 in income to this practice (a C Corporation) and cost it approximately $70,000 in additional income tax ($200,000 in fees × 35% tax rate).

The error in the above example is that the PPMC must record the portion of the purchase price it received for the accounts receivable as patient fee income. The buyer practice has merely traded one asset—cash—for another asset, the accounts receivable. When the practice collects these particular receivables, the credit is applied against the purchased accounts receivable (an asset), rather than to patient fees.

Tax Planning Tip ■ The above types of hidden costs lurk in many, if not all, business purchase and sale transactions of healthcare entities. The costs of incorrect accounting and tax treatment in such transactions can be very high, such as in the above actual example. Uncovering and removing this type of unnecessary transaction cost justifies hiring of competent tax counsel. In fact, the cost differential is usually the difference between a viable transaction and a bad deal.

[2] ORGANIZATION COSTS

When any entity is organized as other than a sole proprietorship, it will incur some costs associated with the startup of the business called organization costs. These costs typically include legal and or accounting fees to establish the entity. These costs are not deducted like regular expenses because they are considered to benefit not just the period in which they occurred, but all future periods in which the entity is open. Therefore (for income tax purposes), an election must be made, on the first tax return filed for the entity to capitalize these expenses. The amortization period, no matter what type of entity is involved, is 60 months starting from the date of registration with the state. Failure to make the election will technically disallow the deduction in the current or any future period. These costs become an asset that cannot be written off until the entity liquidates. Do not miss the opportunity to claim this deduction.

[3] ASSET EXPENSING ELECTION

Purchases of furniture, fixtures, machinery, equipment, and other personal property are typically not expensed when purchased. Rather, the entity is required to capitalize and depreciate these assets over their useful lives. The IRC of 1986 provides asset lives to be used for tax purposes. The listing in Exhibit 5–2 is not all-inclusive but is representative of the most often used Modified Accelerated Cost Recovery System (MACRS) asset class lives.

Exhibit 5–2 *Depreciation Allowances for Some Assets*

Type of Asset	*MACRS Depreciable Life in Years (in general)*
Computer software purchased	3
Computers and peripherals	5
Office machinery and equipment	5
Transportation equipment	5
Furniture and fixtures	7
Leasehold improvements	39
Real property, nonresidential	39

Tax Planning Tip ■ In the event that a practice is purchasing a building or making significant improvements to an existing structure, a "cost segregation" study should be considered. A cost segregation study is an analysis of the makeup of the improvements existing in or added to real property. To the extent improvements can be identified that are not "permanent" to the property, these items can be segregated from the remaining improvements and depreciated over a shorter timeframe than the standard 39 years as noted in Exhibit 5–2. These studies are typically performed by engineers or tax professionals specially trained in this discipline.

The cost segregation study entails a review of architectural plans to ascertain those items that are permanent (required by building code) versus those that are "excess." The cost savings via the use of this service can be significant. The biggest "bang for the buck" can be attained by having professionals such as engineers or tax professionals involved with the architect or draftsmen in the design/planning process. Minor modifications to plans can be the difference between a depreciation period of 39 years versus seven to ten years. The cost of this kind of study is economical ($5000 to $12,000) compared with the tax savings generated by the increased depreciation deductions and depends upon the size of the project. The fees for the study are also deductible.

Additional Depreciation

The Job Creation and Worker Assistance Act of 2002 signed into law on March 11, 2002, by President George W. Bush created significant additional depreciation deductions for assets purchased after September 10, 2001 ("The Act"). The Act, in general, allows for an *additional* first year depreciation allowance (deduction) equal to 30% of the adjusted basis of personal property with (or certain sale and leaseback, but not real property, i.e., buildings or land) *acquired or placed in service* after September 10, 2001. This additional first year allowance will continue for qualified property placed into service through September 11, 2004. The Act covers rebuilding or reconditioning of owned property; however, it does not include the purchase of used or reconditioned property. In addition, if a practice does not want to take advantage of this additional depreciation allowance, this election must be made.

The effects of the new Act, in conjunction with the cost segregation study concept, can provide for significant tax planning opportunities for most healthcare entities. However, the new Act, as with all other tax legislation, is very complex in nature, and the planning process should be undertaken with the assistance of competent tax counsel to take the maximum advantage of the benefits provided.

The above noted tax lives typically are not the same as the actual useful lives of the assets, but that should not be of any concern. There are also various methods of depreciating equipment, and these methods generate different amounts of expense. However, most healthcare entities wish to maximize the current deduction for depreciation. This strategy brings the entity closer to a pure cash in/cash out business.

IRC Section 179 allows an entity to expense a certain amount of asset purchases each year that would otherwise have to be depreciated over their tax lives. This deduction is available for tangible personal property only, not real estate or leasehold improvements, and is a big benefit to most businesses. This election is available for qualified asset acquisitions up to $200,000 during the year. This deduction is reduced dollar for dollar for each dollar of acquisitions in a year over the $200,000 threshold. Also, the depreciation expense created by this election cannot create or increase a tax loss for the practice. Any amount unable to be used in the current period can be carried forward to future periods to offset income in those periods.

The amount of the expense election is in the process of increasing up to a maximum of $25,000 in 2003. Table 5-1 provides the allowable deduction over the transitional period.

There are various tricks to use in choosing the equipment to elect for Section 179 depreciation. For instance, if the entity is adding assets in excess of the yearly limit, it would be wise to make the expensing election on those assets the entity fully intends to hold for that asset's entire tax life. Otherwise, the entity will have to recapture (pick up

Table 5–1 *IRC Section 179 Expense Deduction Table*

Year	Amount of Deduction
1999	$19,000
2000	$20,000
2001	$24,000
2002	$24,000
2003	$25,000

as income) the unused portion of the depreciation deduction that was taken early via the use of the election. Recapture can mitigate the tax benefit of this planning opportunity and should be avoided whenever possible.

Example

An obstetrics practice purchases four examination room set-ups for $20,000, along with an ultrasound machine for another $20,000. The practice makes the expense election on the ultrasound machine because it is easier to take the deduction on one asset. After being in practice one year, the physicians agree that they do not like their current ultrasound machine. They opt to sell it and buy another one they all prefer. In the year of sale, the practice must recapture 80% ($16,000) of the expense election they made when they purchased the first ultrasound machine. This adds $16,000 to their current year's taxable income. Had they used the expense election on the four exam room set-ups (that are not likely to be changed), they would be much better off for tax purposes.

Tax Planning Tip ■ If assets being purchased are in excess of $200,000, try to plan the asset purchases around a year end. This will allow you the ability to purchase up to $400,000 in assets and still use the Section 179 expense election to accelerate the deduction. In fact, this strategy will provide you the opportunity to use the expensing election twice and maximize the expense deduction.

Example

Dr. Jeffrey K. Adams is setting up a physical therapy clinic. The total acquisitions needed are $375,000. If all assets are purchased in December of the first year, Dr. Adams will have to depreciate 100% of the acquired assets based upon their useful lives and will not qualify for the expense election deduction at all. However, if he can put off the purchase of $175,001 of those assets until January of the second year, he can use the expense election to its maximum in both the first and second years. This technique can provide a significant additional depreciation deduction in each year for the practice.

The above tax planning tip works even better when a practice has only nominal purchase requirements. Straddling the purchases around a year end will have an even larger impact for a practice on a deduction to purchase percentage basis for the use of the expense election.

Example

Dr. Emily C. Swift set up a family practice office in 2003 requiring $40,000 in asset acquisitions. The entire $40,000 was expensed since the purchases are split between two years. In this case, a dollar for dollar deduction for out-of-pocket asset purchases can be achieved if the transactions can be planned around a year end to take advantage of two years' worth of expense elections. If this strategy cannot be fully achieved, any purchases that can be put off until the following year will help increase depreciation and reduce taxable income.

Tax Planning Tip ■ If the entity does not already have a policy, it should set a capitalization policy for purchases of assets. This policy should state that any purchase below a certain dollar value will be expensed and items over that threshold amount will be capitalized and depreciated. Even the IRS signs off on this one, because it views this policy on a cost/benefit basis. No purpose is served by creating additional accounting work capitalizing the cost of a trash can, calculator, or coffee maker when there is no significant accounting or tax difference between expensing and depreciating the item. To set this policy, review the types of purchases that are made within the entity. There is typically a breakoff point between office supply or temporary use items and larger more permanent items. In most healthcare related entities, this breakoff is between $100 and $250, but a higher number could be used if there is adequate reasoning to support a larger number. By setting this policy and following it consistently, the entity will reduce its chance of having the policy challenged in the case of an audit. The entity also reduces the number of "assets" the practice must track. The only caution here is not to get carried away with the threshold number. In a 2002 case (Alacare Healthcare), the IRS won a significant victory in making the taxpayer capitalize significant asset additions.

The taxpayer in this case appears to have "unbundled" many asset purchases on its books into component parts that did not exceed its stated capitalization policy ($500). Therefore, care should be taken in setting the entity's capitalization policy, and the practice should follow it without exception.

Tax Planning Tip ■ Due to the Jobs and Growth Tax Relief Reconciliation Act (JGTRRA) of 2003, the amount a medical practice can claim as an expense under Section 179 has been increased to $100,000. This increase applies to property, equipment, and instruments placed in service in tax years 2003 through 2005. In addition, for the same periods, the $200,000 limitation on qualifying Section 179 property is increased to $400,000. For 2003, 2004, and 2005, physician taxpayers may make or revoke expensing elections on amended tax returns without IRS consent.

[1] Purchase of an Entity

When a corporate entity is purchased, whether a physician's practice, an ancillary service provider, a durable medical equipment entity, or a hospital, it may be thought that the deal is done when agreement has been reached on the purchase price. However, for tax planning purposes, this is just the beginning of the exercise.

First, most buyers want to purchase assets because their investment in those assets can be recovered via depreciation or amortization over some period of time. The purchase of stock is considered a capital transaction and does not allow for the depreciation of the investment. Buyers of healthcare entities typically do not want to buy stock for another reason—namely, there is the potential acquisition of unknown and unwanted liabilities (e.g., legal problems including, product liability, malpractice lawsuits, other torts alleged under prior ownership).

Sellers, on the other hand, want to sell the stock of a corporation to obtain favorable capital gains tax treatment on the sale. Sellers do not like to sell assets of the corporate entity because the sales proceeds end up flowing into the corporation where they are either subject to double taxation or flow out to the shareholders in the form of salaries. Selling assets is very unappealing for tax purposes and creates a real problem that in many cases can be a deal breaker.

The IRC offers assistance in section 338. This code section allows the buyer the ability to elect asset purchase treatment for a stock purchase. This election has the effect of giving both the buyer and seller what they are seeking, and the IRS gets more revenue by having more deals take place. The attorneys can usually write enough indemnity language into the contract to protect the buyers against the potential of unknown liabilities. Sole proprietors and passthrough entities have a definite advantage here since, even in an asset sale, the tax attributes of sales proceeds (i.e., capital gains) are retained as the transaction flows through to the owner (or shareholder in the case of an S corporation).

Caution ■ This election is not a simple transaction to be crafted at home with a piece of do-it-yourself software. Instead, it is a complex area of the law, and competent legal and tax counsel should be engaged. The tax benefit in most cases will far outweigh the cost of hiring the experts. In addition, this type of transaction can wreak havoc at the state tax level if care is not taken to review all its ramifications.

Example

A recent third party billing company sale in Texas of approximately $9 million, handled in the above manner, saved the sellers a significant amount of dollars and avoided the ordinary tax treatment deal breaker. This transaction had a Texas State Franchise Tax consequence to the sellers of approximately $450,000. Even after the impact of the franchise tax, there was enough benefit for the buyers to consider the transaction a good deal. The bottom line is that this type of transaction has a place and can save many thousands of dollars, but just as with a patient, the healthcare professional wants to review all the information to "diagnose" whether this strategy could work in the entity's specific tax circumstances.

Caution ■ When an entity is being purchased or sold, one important detail is overlooked in many transactions. The purchaser needs to formally allocate the purchase price among the various classes of assets bought. This is a required function by both the purchaser and seller of a business for federal tax purposes. According to Internal Revenue regulations, this allocation must be documented in the tax returns of both purchasing and selling entities in the year of the transaction on Form 8594.[1] In addition, the allocation reported must be the same on both returns. Therefore, both parties must agree to the allocation.

Red Flag! ■ Missing this detail can be detrimental. The IRS has ways of identifying purchase and sale transactions that have taken place with an entity (like the filing of a final or initial return, seeing large increases in assets on the tax return balance sheet of an ongoing entity). If the entity does not spend the time to go through this exercise and allocate the price on its own behalf, or if the entity files the tax return without the proper disclosure, the IRS has the right to step in after the fact and reallocate the purchase price. The IRS allocation will be based upon what the IRS thinks the allocation should have been in the first place. This allocation will most assuredly be a favorable allocation to the IRS rather than the purchaser and seller.

---

[2] Amortization of Goodwill and Other Intangible Assets (IRC Section 197)

In many cases, the hard assets (furniture, fixtures, and equipment) you obtain in a purchase transaction make up only a small portion of the purchase price. At least part of the price will be allocated to "goodwill." Goodwill, or "blue sky" as it has also been called, is a premium paid for the reputation of the owner or the business, the company name, or other intangible assets identified within the entity. This goodwill, along with most other intangible assets, is amortizable over 15 years using the "straight line" method (IRC Section 197). The straight-line method is a ratable method calculated by dividing the asset's value by 180 months (15 years × 12 months). The importance of the asset allocation between asset classes (noted in the Caution above) becomes evident at this point since most other assets can be depreciated over much shorter periods of time, thus providing larger annual deductions to the business. It is preferred to allocate as much of the purchase price as reasonably possible to assets that can be depreciated over shorter periods of time. Earlier in this chapter, the repurchase of a practice from a PPMC was discussed. If any such repurchase agreement includes a Service Termination or similar document allowing for the separation from service, this allocated amount can be written off immediately rather than being amortized over 15 years as an IRC Section 197 intangible asset. The immediate writeoff rather than amortization has been agreed to in the Appeals Division of the IRS. The underlying reason is that there is, in fact, no *future* economic benefit to the agreement; therefore, it is not considered a long lived intangible asset requiring amortization in line with Section IRC 197.

Caution ■ An unreasonably high allocation of a purchase price to assets is likely to be challenged by the IRS. When making the allocation, be sure to document the reasoning behind the allocation. Keep any documentation or research that supports the allocation methodology. This documentation will be vital to upholding the healthcare entity's allocation if it has to be defended somewhere down the road. The IRS has three years from the date the return (including the allocation) is filed to challenge the allocation.

[3] Lease Versus Purchase of Assets

Looking back to the initial premise of tax planning, the idea is to put more net dollars into the entity's pocket. Leasing is a financing strategy that can have some advantages in healthcare practices. However, do not believe everything being stated about the tax advantages of leasing. If leasing entities were not making a lot of money leasing assets, there would be no such thing as a leasing industry. Typically, an entity will pay more to lease an asset over its useful life than it would have if it had purchased the asset outright. That being said, if the healthcare practice can tailor a lease to conform to its own needs, can pay only for the portion of the asset the entity uses, and can return the property without large penalties, there may be a place for leases within the entity's tax planning strategy.

For each buy versus lease decision, the healthcare professional should look at the total cost (including all potential fees and charges) for each option. Obtain answers to the following questions (in writing) and evaluate the additional cost each item adds to the property being considered before making a final decision.

1. What are the up front costs of each transaction (i.e., down payment, loan origination fees, first and last months rent, sales tax, documentation fees, or other deposit structures)?

2. What is the monthly lease payment vs monthly principal and interest payment on a loan?

3. Who is responsible for personal property tax payments on the asset while it is being leased?

4. What adjustments are made on the back end of a lease if the entity decides to return the leased property?

   • Make up payment to leasing company if actual residual value is less than estimate;

   • Cost for excess mileage above annual limits specified in the contract (for vehicles);

   • Cost of excess copies for a copy machine;

   • "Damage" estimates that can be assessed by the lessor on leased property that must be paid by lessee; and

- Shipping or delivery costs to put the leased assets in the location specified at the end of the lease.

5. What costs are incurred on the back end of a lease if you decide to keep the leased property (i.e., "purchase price" that can be anywhere from $1.00 to approximately 20% of the original cost of the leased property (or some other "residual value" as defined in the contract), potential sales tax on sale)?

Once all these questions have been answered, the healthcare professional can quantify the total cost of each alternative and can make an informed decision on which route is best for the healthcare entity.

Overriding factors may be involved in the decision-making process. These factors may include the entity's inability to find a lender that will loan funds to a healthcare entity. The inability to find a lender has been a very real problem for healthcare professionals in some parts of the country. In such cases, leasing may be the only viable alternative and the prudent healthcare professional would still go through the exercise to understand all costs involved. In addition, competition can be created by obtaining bids from various lessors for the property being leased. The end result, even in less than optimal circumstances, will be the best deal the healthcare entity can obtain on lease of property.

[4] Working Capital Loans

For those healthcare entities that have lenders willing to accommodate line of credit arrangements, the physician should take care to understand the underlying costs of borrowing. It is always a good idea to have a working capital credit line available in the event of collection slowdowns or necessary asset acquisitions. Some lending institutions charge what is called a loan commitment fee on the total working capital amount committed to the entity. This fee is obviously in addition to the interest cost that will be charged on any amounts borrowed against the credit line.

Example
Physicians who own a healthcare practice believe that the practice may need a $100,000 credit line to provide safe coverage for the operation of the business in the event of collection slowdowns. However, the bank offers the practice $250,000 because of its "good credit standing." The bank also charges a commitment fee in the amount of ½% of the committed funds, not the amount actually borrowed. Therefore, if the practice sticks to its plan of $100,000, the cost for the privilege will be $500 ($100,000 × .005). However, if the practice goes with the flattering bank proposal, the commitment cost will be $1250 ($250,000 × .005). In this instance, the bank may be padding its own bottom line at the expense of the healthcare entity's bottom line.

Be sure to shop around before even considering paying a commitment fee on a credit line. Not every lending institution charges such fees, and, although deductible, these fees reduce the entity's bottom line.

[5] Capital Contribution
Versus Loans to Your Entity

When starting or operating a healthcare entity, the need to capitalize the operation is always a concern to the owners. How should the owners put money into the entity? Most states require some minimum amount of cash or property contribution for an entity to be considered viable by statute. This amount is typically between $100 and $1000. However, beyond the minimum amount, there are planning opportunities available to business owners. By loaning additional cash flow requirements to the entity, the owners can be paid interest on any amounts loaned to the entity. This is a deduction to the entity when it is paid and is income to the owners when received. These payments avoid being considered compensation to the corporate shareholder or self-employment earnings for owners of unincorporated entities. The savings from using this strategy can be between 2.9% and 15.3% depending upon whether the individual owner has met the Social Security minimum for the year.

General Tax Planning Issues:
Income Statement Accounts

The prior section dealt with general tax planning issues that could appear on the balance sheets of most healthcare entities. This section will continue to review general tax planning issues available for virtually any entity; however, the items below will appear on the income statement. The following information provides insight to income and expenses that require better classification to take advantage of "special" tax rules. Segregating these items will give your entity the best chance to utilize the tax planning and saving opportunities that already exist.

[A] Interest Income

Most interest income earned within a business entity will be taxable. However, if the entity has excess cash in one or more accounts, it would be wise to consider investment of the excess funds in tax-exempt issues. Tax-exempt issues, in general, pay a lower rate of interest than do taxable issues because of the built-in tax advantage. In addition, the entity's tolerance for risk in the investment of these funds should be very low (the entity does not want to lose any part of this money); therefore it will not be looking for the highest return on these excess funds anyway. Interest from tax-exempt sources should be segregated into a separate account from otherwise taxable interest on the practice's books to highlight the tax advantage.

Tax Planning Tip ■ If not segregated, this tax advantage is easily forgotten and lost at year end. Tax-free income is often subjected to taxation along with the rest of the taxable interest income due to neglecting setting up a separate general ledger account to identify the tax advantaged income. Because this happens all too often, do not allow the healthcare entity to be a victim of this neglect.

Tax Planning Tip ■ If the healthcare entity is investing in tax-exempt securities, be sure to invest, whenever possible, in issues that are also exempt from state income tax. Ask the practice's investment advisor before the purchase, or, even better, set this double exemption as a prerequisite for the entity's investment in tax exempt issues. This research will save the entity from the unpleasant surprise of finding out that only half of the tax planning job was accomplished. Be careful to limit the tax-exempt income from "private activity" bonds. The interest on these bonds is subject to the Alternative Minimum Tax (AMT). As mentioned before, the AMT is a safety net for the IRS to make sure that every person or entity pays some tax on earned income. The AMT catches those who make too much use of certain deductions, credits, and tax exemptions to avoid paying tax.

[B] Paying Employee Bonuses without Withholding

It is easy to come up with an amount to give a person as a Christmas or merit bonus. However, many healthcare professionals feel that taking taxes out of this amount cheapens the thought. Although this may seem like a small issue to most, it is one of the areas that the IRS looks for in business returns. Healthcare professionals are susceptible to this trap.

Caution ■ In most states, the State Unemployment Agency is required to audit each business periodically. This may occur every three or four years. The auditor will request information on employee salaries. He or she will also look at several other accounts on the general ledger, if not the entire general ledger. This investigation usually uncovers compensation items such as the bonuses noted previously, and the auditor will assess the tax and penalties on any items considered to be compensation. In addition, all these state agencies share information with the IRS, so the additional wages will be reported to the IRS, and the employer will end up paying all taxes due on the bonus amounts, including the employee's portion. The IRS will also charge interest and penalties on these delinquent wages. The point of this caution is to always withhold taxes. Withholding in the beginning will save time, money, and a lot of problems in the long run.

[C] Penalties and Fines

Penalties and fines are usually assessed by a government agency (like the IRS) or municipality. These expenses are not deductible for income tax purposes. However, a common misnomer is that late payment "penalties" on invoices are penalties as well and are not deductible. These charges are more accurately considered to be interest or finance charges, and, therefore, they are deductible items and should not be overlooked. Therefore, before accepting a "penalty" at face value and chalking it up to a nondeductible expense, find out who issued the penalty or fine and then reclassify the item where appropriate to finance charges or an interest expense account.

[D] Disability Insurance

Some entities offer disability insurance to their employees on a group basis as part of an employee benefit program. The expense for this coverage is typically deducted as an ordinary and necessary expense by the employer entity. However, many entities also purchase additional disability insurance for the owners. This additional disability insurance expense should not be deducted on the entity's tax return for two reasons. First, it would probably be considered a discriminatory benefit to the owners, and, therefore, not allowed by the IRS as a deduction. Second, and more important, when a person becomes disabled and qualifies for disability benefits whose premiums have been deducted as a business expense by the entity, the disability insurance proceeds are considered taxable income to the person receiving them. This can be personally catastrophic since disability insurance covers only a portion (approximately 60%) of regular earnings. This coverage was designed to be paid on an after-tax basis. The benefits would be tax free to the beneficiary and would be close to the disabled person's net take home pay before being disabled (after consideration of federal and state tax deductions, Medicare, and Social Security taxes). This is one of those instances where the traditional tax planning thought process is overridden by a long term (potential) tax cost/benefit decision.

[E] Officers or Owners Life Insurance

Premium payments for life insurance on the owners of an entity are typically not deductible unless the owners are part of a group term life insurance policy covering all eligible employees of the entity, and then only up to a maximum of $50,000.[2] Any amount above $50,000 will generate fringe benefit income to the owner or other employee. Therefore, if the entity is paying large premiums for life insurance on the medical professional, be prepared for the taxable income that will show up at tax time, according to the table below:

Age*	Monthly cost per $1000 (in dollars)
Under 30	.08
30–34	.09

35–39	.11
40–44	.17
45–49	.29
50–54	.48
55–59	.75
60–64	1.17
65–69	2.10
70–	3.76

* Age determined on the last day of the taxable year

[F] Professional, Medical Union, and Trade Association Dues

Several years ago, the IRS required professional organizations, medical unions, and trade associations to disclose to their constituents the percentage of their dues that were being expended for political lobbying purposes. The portion of the dues payment associated with lobbying activities is not considered deductible for federal income tax purposes. This portion of dues should be segregated into a separate account along with dues to country clubs, hunting leases, and athletic facilities, since these dues are not allowed as deductible expenses to the taxpayer. Only the charges associated with direct entertainment are considered to be deductible and then only at the 50% amount mentioned earlier.

[G] Political Contributions

Political contributions are not deductible for income tax purposes, even though there might be the need from a business perspective to contribute to a specific candidate or Political Action Committee. These items should be segregated from other contributions being made by the entity to accurately identify the deductible versus nondeductible variety of contribution.

[H] Retirement Plans

Several tax planning strategies utilizing retirement plan vehicles can generate large tax deductions while providing continuing benefits to the healthcare entity and its employees. Retirement plan contributions can be accrued (even in a cash basis entity) and paid in the next year. This accrual can provide a large, one-time deferral that can have significant impact on the income of the entity. In addition, many of the plans currently available allow for flexible contributions, thus providing entities the ability to contribute based upon the availability of cash flow.

[1] 401(K) PLANS

Primary, and matching contributions, to a 401(k) plan, as well as its earnings, are tax deferred. The maximum annual employee contribution for a medical professional is increasing annually through 2006. The annual contribution limits are as follows:

Year	Amount
2001	$10,500
2002	$11,000
2003	$12,000
2004	$13,000
2005	$14,000
2006	$15,000

[2] 403(B) PLANS

Healthcare professionals employed by hospitals or other tax-exempt organizations may participate in their employer's 403(b) plan, also known as a tax-sheltered annuity. Both contribution limits and tax deferral status are similar to that of a 401(k) plan.

[3] SIMPLE PLANS

The Savings Incentive Match Plan (SIMPLE) is a retirement savings plan available to most small businesses including most healthcare practices. Employees who are eligible to participate can contribute up to a specified amount of pay per year on a pre-tax basis. Employers are required to contribute at least 3% of employee wages up to a maximum of $6000 per year. The employer matching percentage must be communicated to employees by November 1 of each year. The advantage of this type of plan is that there is no requirement to test for discrimination against the nonhighly compensated employees. The disadvantage is that the maximum contributions available on an annual basis are lower than for other qualified retirement plans. The maximum SIMPLE contributions are increasing annually through 2005 as follows:

Year	Amount
2001	$ 6,500
2002	$ 7,000
2003	$ 8,000
2004	$ 9,000
2005	$10,000

[4] TRADITIONAL IRAs

An individual may contribute up to $3000 of compensation to an IRA each year, and all investment earnings are tax deferred until withdrawal. If married, a couple may contribute up to $6000, if a joint return is filed, and together they have at least $6000 in earnings. This amount is fully deductible if the taxpayer and spouse are not participants in any other retirement plan. Income phase-out rules apply regarding full or partial deductibility if either the taxpayer or spouse (or both) participates in a qualified retirement plan.

For example, the income limit for traditional IRAs starts at $33,000 of adjusted gross income (AGI) for single filers and drops to zero at $43,000 of AGI in 2001. These limits are increasing annually through 2005 when the phaseout range is $50,000–$60,000. For joint filers, the limit starts at $53,000 and ends at $63,000 of AGI (in 2001). These limits are increasing annually through 2007 when the phaseout range will be $80,000–$100,000. If a medical professional is not an active participant in an employer-sponsored retirement plan, but his or her spouse is, the income limitation for deducting contributions starts at $150,000 combined AGI and phases out at $160,000.

Tax Planning Tip ■ Most retirement plans can be set up at any time during the year and can be retroactive to the beginning of the year for purposes of calculating the maximum contribution deduction available. The one exception is the Simplified Employee Pension, which can be set up at any time prior to the due date of the applicable tax return (including extensions).

Caution ■ The choice of the right retirement plan for a healthcare entity is a very important decision. Do not choose a particular plan just because of the current year tax benefit that can be obtained. Review each of the retirement plan alternatives for their respective benefits, responsibilities, and obligations. Once instituted, modification of these documents can be difficult without triggering unwanted results. This very complex area of law can generate very bad results when improperly applied. Seek the counsel of a competent tax or retirement plan specialist prior to committing to a specific plan. Many brokerage houses have prototype retirement plan documents available. Although this may be the most economical means of setting up a "boiler plate" retirement plan, the stockbroker may not have the knowledge to guide the healthcare professional to the right plan, much less through the elections to be made in a plan document.

[I] Property Taxes

Most healthcare practices will be subject to personal property taxes on fixed assets used in the business. These taxes are based upon the dollar value of personal property owned (and also those leased in some municipalities). The forms filed for the rendering of this tax segregate property by type and year of acquisition. The municipalities use the specific asset lives of the property and typically consider that each asset has some residual value (usually 10%). The assessed value is cost minus depreciation.

It is very important to review this report annually to make sure assets taken out of service during the previous year (i.e., broken, stolen, obsolete, sold, traded in) are removed from this listing. Failure to remove these items will subject the business to higher personal property tax expenses than necessary. Also, inquire what property (if any) is not required to be rendered. For example, in many municipalities software is not rendered for personal property tax purposes. Due diligence in this area can save hundreds of dollar each year.

Permanent Versus Timing Differences in Tax Returns

When reviewing income and expense items, it is important to understand whether the benefit being obtained is a temporary (a difference in the timing of the taxation of an item) or permanent tax benefit or cost. Obviously, tax benefits are much better than tax costs. Permanent differences are better than temporary differences when they are in your favor.

An example of a timing difference would be accelerated depreciation versus straight-line depreciation. Eventually the asset will be fully expensed under either method; the only difference revolves around when and how much of a deduction is available. Examples of permanent differences would be penalties and fines. Fines and penalties are paid out of business cash flow but are never deductible for income tax purposes.

[A] Tax Planning for C Medical Corporations

For those healthcare C corporations that are not considered personal service corporations, tax planning can be fairly easy. The progressive tax rate structure allows certain tax breaks for C corporations with less than $100,000 in taxable income. Exhibit 5–3 provides the tax brackets for corporate taxpaying entities.

Exhibit 5–3 *Tax Brackets for Corporate Taxpaying Entities*

Taxable Income is: (in dollars) Over	But not over	The Tax is: (in dollars)	Of Excess Over: (in dollars)
0	50,000	0 + 15%	0
50,000	75,000	7,500 + 25%	50,000
75,000	100,000	13,750 + 34%	75,000
100,000	335,000	22,250 + 39%	100,000
335,000	10,000,000	113,900 + 34%	335,000
10,000,000	15,000,000	3,400,000 + 35%	10,000,000
15,000,000	18,333,333	5,150,000 + 38%	15,000,000
18,333,333	——-	6,416,667 + 35%	18,333,333

Note: The above tax brackets do not take into account the potential effects of the alternative minimum tax, if applicable.

The use of bonuses, retirement plan contributions, and relevant combinations of the other items noted above can be used to reduce corporate tax liability into the preferred tax bracket. As mentioned earlier, the tax planning process requires action and some forethought on the part of the entity to position itself to optimize its tax situation.

Of course, with no tax planning at all, the corporation will still end up in one of the above tax brackets. The unpleasant part of this surprise is that the bracket will typically be higher, and the tax will definitely be more than it could have been.

In general, shareholders in a personal service corporation (C corporation) want to keep taxable income of the corporation as close to break-even as possible. Any income retained in the corporation will be taxed at 35% for federal income tax purposes as noted above plus any applicable state income taxes. Shareholders typically pay out the excess cash flow in the form of salaries or bonuses at year end to reduce taxable income and, therefore, the potential income tax. This is what is called "gutting" the income of the corporation. Although there is a tax advantage to gutting the entity on an annual basis, there are some very distinct disadvantages to this tax planning strategy.

Pulling out all the profit from the entity on an annual basis leaves no cash flow within the entity to carry on day-to-day operations of the business. Likewise, this strategy leaves no funds available for needed capital expenditures (updating or adding to facilities or systems). This deficit usually requires the shareholders to loan funds back into the entity to fund operations. In many cases, these funds are the same funds that were paid out as bonuses to remove profits. Does this sound familiar? It should be easy to see how the continued use of this strategy year after year will require larger annual loans to fund the deficits.

Many shareholders find the above strategy to be very frustrating and do not understand how they end up in the deficit position each year with only two alternatives seemingly available:

1. The continued funding of higher loan amounts, or
2. Payment of a large tax bill.

When unwanted tax surprises occur in a C corporation, it is usually due to nondeductible expenses (permanent differences) or limitations in otherwise deductible expenses reducing the offsets to current period income. In addition to the items listed above, one income exclusion item and several deduction limitations need to be considered in arriving at estimated taxable income.

[1] DIVIDEND INCOME

If a C corporation owns stock in a taxable domestic corporation, the corporation is entitled to a reduction in the amount of income to pick up on its tax return. The dividends received deduction (DRD) is an allowed exclusion from income and is a percentage of the dividends received. A base exclusion rate of 70% is allowed in most circumstances and, depending upon the type of corporation issuing the dividend, the exclusion can increase to 80% or even 100% of the dividends received. This exclusion is calculated on page two of Form 1120 and cannot exceed 70% of the receiving corporation's income (after certain adjustments including the DRD itself). Any DRD amount not used due to this limitation is lost, period. Dividends from mutual funds do not qualify for the DRD.

[2] CAPITAL GAINS AND LOSSES

Capital gains and losses are generated by the sale of capital assets. These assets include stocks, bonds, and other assets held for investment purposes, and real estate and personal property used in the business. The gain from the sale of such assets is treated the same way for all entities and is included in income in the year of the sale. However, capital losses are a different story. A capital loss in a C corporation is allowed only to the extent that it can offset a capital gain. Stated differently, a capital loss cannot be used to offset ordinary income. Unused capital losses can be carried back three years and carried forward five years to offset capital gains in those periods. Any unused capital losses remaining after the five-year carry-forward period expire and are lost.

Tax Planning Tip ■ A corporation considering the sale of a capital asset that will generate a capital loss should coordinate the sale of other assets generating capital gains to create an offset where available.

---

[3] CHARITABLE CONTRIBUTIONS

Many physicians contribute to charities through their corporations with the assumption that these contributions will reduce the taxable income of the corporation. However, the IRS places a limitation on the amount of deductible contributions a corporation may take in any year. The limitation is 10% of the corporation's taxable income before the charitable contribution deductions are taken into consideration.

Example

C Corporation has book income of $26,000 at year end. This income includes contributions of $4500 that C Corporation made during the year to various recognized charities. For federal and (most) state income tax purposes, taxable income would be as follows:

Book income	$26,000
Contributions	4,500
	30,500
Contribution limitation	10%
Allowable contributions	$ 3,050
Excess contributions disallowed	1,450
Book income	26,000
Taxable income	$27,450

The excess amount of contributions can be carried over to future periods to offset income. Any amount(s) carried over must be used to offset income within the next five years or they will expire and be lost forever. This becomes a trap for those who annually give through their corporation but also try to minimize their taxable income.

Tax Planning Tip ■ If your strategy is to reduce the corporation's tax liability to zero, do not make any charitable contributions through the corporation. Likewise, if the entity's income is close to zero on an annual basis, use up contribution carryovers before making additional contributions out of the C Corporation. This will minimize the potential of turning a timing difference into a permanent difference and losing a deduction forever.

There are several points to be noted from the above example. First, much of the standard tax planning that takes place to gut the corporation actually works against the deduction of charitable contributions. For that reason, the disallowance of charitable contributions in C Corporations is very common. Second, the contribution needs to be made to a "recognized" charity to be deductible. A recognized charity is one that has filed the necessary documents with the IRS so that contributions can be exempt from federal income taxes. Merely giving to a needy individual or organization is not enough to make the contribution deductible.

When all is said and done, the C Corporation is not the optimal entity to use for charitable giving, especially for small or personal service corporations.

Tax Planning Tip ■ The limitation for deductibility for (cash) charitable contributions at the individual taxpayer level is 50%. Therefore, it makes sense to generate charitable gifts at the individual, rather than the corporate, level. In most individual tax instances, the income limitation will not be an issue. In the event contributions have already been made during the current year, the corporation can reclassify those contributions to the owner employee as compensation, and the individual can take the entire deduction at the individual level.

---

[4] C CORPORATION SUMMARY

Several of the income statement items mentioned above generate tax benefits for the entity; however, most generate tax costs and provide unwanted income tax surprises at year end. It is important to keep all the above items and their respective amounts in mind as the year progresses because decision-making opportunities present themselves all during the year. The ability to identify an opportunity and act upon it in a timely manner will allow the healthcare professional to position the corporation for the best outcome available in its unique set of circumstances.

There is no "one size fits all" tax planning managerial strategy. The entity can remove the uses of corporate cash flow that do not generate a deductible expense for tax purposes. The entity can require the shareholders to fund annually the deficits caused by zeroing out income. The entity can adopt a strategy that requires the payment of some tax each year to reduce the constant escalation of year end borrowings needed to fund deficits that one day have to culminate in the corporation paying a lot of tax. The following Tax Planning Worksheet can be used to estimate the C Corporation's taxable income.

Exhibit 5–4 *Medical Corporation Tax Planning Worksheet*

	Gross Amt. (in dollars)	Percentage	Net Amount (in dollars)
Book income <loss> before taxes			
Less:			
Dividends received deduction			< >
Tax exempt interest			< >
Contribution carryover from prior period			< >
Section 179 depreciation			< >
Accrued retirement plan contribution			< >
Other			
Add Back:			
Capital losses			
Penalties & fines			
Excess charitable contributions			
Meals & entertainment		50%	
Nondeductible dues			
Political contributions			
Officers' life insurance			
Disability insurance			
Other			
Taxable income <loss>			

[B] Tax Planning/Awareness for Passthrough Entities and Their Owners

Passthrough entities report their income, deductions, expenses, and credits to their owner/shareholders via a form called a K-1. The K-1 is each owner/shareholder's pro rata share of items coming from Schedule K of the respective return (either Form 1065 or 1120S).

Various items of income and expense are reported as separate line items on Schedule K-1. The reason for this presentation is that these items flow into the owner/shareholder's individual tax return and are either subject to a limitation at that level or are used to calculate a limitation on the individual return. Examples of these amounts are Section 179 depreciation, charitable contributions, interest, dividend and royalty income, and capital gains and losses.

Not many tax planning opportunities are specifically available to taxpayers organized within these entities. Rather, a number of special rules affect the owner/shareholders of passthrough entities. Several of these rules will be discussed in the following paragraphs.

The Section 179 depreciation (expense election deduction) is limited for each individual to the same amount per year as noted above for corporations. Therefore, those individuals involved in many passthrough entities that are also able to exercise some level of control over the expensing election may have planning opportunities available.

Example 1

Dr. Simon G. James owns a medical practice as a sole proprietor and has $50,000 in asset purchases during the year 2000 (per the table above, $20,000 in Section 179 expense election is available). He is also a 50% owner (and an active participant) in an ambulatory surgical center (ASC) partnership with $200,000 in asset purchases and a 10% owner in five additional unrelated oil and gas partnerships that each utilized their $20,000 Section 179 deduction in the year 2000. Dr. James cannot do anything to influence the expense election in each of the five oil and gas partnerships. Therefore, he already has $10,000 in Section 179 deduction before taking into account the acquisitions in his practice and the ASC. Dr. James can maximize the expensing election in the ASC of $10,000 ($20,000 × 50% ownership) and have his practice depreciate the new assets over their useful lives. On the other hand, if all entities maximize the expensing election, Dr. James ends up with a Section 179 carryover of $20,000 ($20,000 × 100% ownership in his practice).

Example 2

Assume the same facts as above except that the practice purchases $220,000 in assets in the year 2000. Because the asset purchase limitation has been exceeded, Dr. James will not be able to deduct any Section 179 expenses in his practice. In addition, if any other entity has reported Section 179 depreciation to him, he will lose that deduction because his practice's purchases have made him ineligible to take any Section 179 deduction in the year 2000. Therefore, he loses the $10,000 deduction from the oil and gas partnerships and whatever the ASC elects in the year 2000.

Several problems occur when partners or shareholders are concerned because the partners also have opinions about whether to take such deductions, and their tax situations may all be different. This can create problems when planning for maximizing such deductions without generating unreasonable carryovers or losses. Although the Section 179 expense election carryover does not expire after some finite period of time, it is still not wise to generate large annual carryovers unless there is some assurance they will be used within the foreseeable future.

Charitable contributions flow through to the individual tax returns of the respective partners or shareholders. The limitation for the contribution deduction is applied to each individual at his or her individual level. Each individual's tax scenario is unique; therefore, the ability to deduct a contribution may differ from taxpayer to taxpayer.

Interest, dividends, annuities, and royalties are among the income items stated separately on the K-1. The reason these items flow through to the individual taxpayer is that investment income is the reference point for the limitation to the deduction of investment interest expense. If the passthrough entity has excess cash in an operating account, the movement of the excess above operational necessity could be invested to generate additional income to flow through to the owners and increase their individual ability to deduct investment interest.

Capital gains and losses flow through to the individual's return to allow for the calculation of the net capital loss limitation at the individual taxpayer level. This is an area where periodic updates by the passthrough entity can be beneficial to the individual owners in year end planning for capital gain and loss offsets.

Health insurance of the owner(s) of the passthrough entity is not a deductible expense at the passthrough level. Rather, it is reported as an "Other deduction" on the K-1 and flows through to the individual return. At the individual level, health insurance is only partially deductible as an adjustment to income. The remainder is included on Schedule A (itemized deductions) of the individual tax return as a medical deduction. To further complicate the issue, medical deductions are not deductible unless they exceed 7.5% of AGI. Unless there are unusually large medical deductions in the healthcare professional's family (i.e., for a chronically ill family member), it is difficult to eclipse the 7.5% limitation amount. Table 5–2 summarizes the amount of health insurance deduction allowed as a direct adjustment against income.

Table 5–2 *Health Insurance Premium Deductions*

Year	Deduction
2000	60%
2001	60%
2002	70%
2003 and beyond	100%

This is currently one of the disadvantages of organizing as a passthrough entity, although the disadvantage will disappear over the next four years.

Caution 1 ■ Cafeteria plans are another area that owners of passthrough entities need to be aware of when planning for deductions. The owners of these entities usually look to see the individual benefit available to them before agreeing to provide such a plan for the benefit of all employees. However, the rules associated with cafeteria plans apply "discrimination rules" to see whether the owners are receiving a disproportionately high amount of the cafeteria plan benefits. If this is the case, the ability for owners to participate will be limited.

Caution 2 ■ Retirement plans within passthrough entities also have certain limitations placed upon them that plans of C Corporations do not. Owners need to take care in the type of retirement plan being utilized since the participation of the owners is limited to a percentage of the participation of the nonowners. This is a simplified explanation but provides the notice that close review is required before choosing a retirement plan within a passthrough entity. In addition, owners are not allowed to make loans against retirement plan balances while nonowner employees are allowed to borrow from the plan, if this is provided for in the plan document.

[C] Medical Savings Accounts (MSAs)

Despite managed care, health insurance premiums soared up to 35% in some cases in 2003. This placed a significant burden on small medical practices. The Medical Savings Account (MSA), a separate account set up in conjunction with your practice's health insurance account, enables the physician–employer or employee to contribute money tax deferred into a savings account to be used at a later time for a variety of healthcare costs. The money in an MSA can be used to pay an employee's deductible and co-pays as well as a number of other health insurance costs not normally covered under traditional small practice heath insurance plans.

According to Roccy DeFrancesco, JD (www.wealthpreservation123.com), there are three main reasons to use an MSA. First, there is the possibility of lowering your health insurance premiums. Second, you can offer added benefits without any extra out-of-pocket costs. Third, if the money contributed to the MSA is not used during a calendar year, it not only rolls over for use during a later year, but at age 59½, the money can be used as a supplemental retirement benefit (similar, but more flexible than an IRA).

Today, most offices have health insurance deductibles between $250–$500 per person. That means the maximum exposure to the employee is that $250–$500 (plus any co-pays). Based on the health of your employees and the cost of the deductible, a health insurance company quotes your practice both a family and individual premium.

MSAs are based on the concept of high deductibles. Employee-only deductibles must be between $1600–$2400 a year and family deductibles are between $3200–$5250 indexed annually. The key is that, with the higher deductibles, the employee and family insurance premiums will be significantly lower.

The change to a high deductible plan is seen as having a negative impact by the employee and physician–employer. No one wants to be responsible for that extra high deductible. The key to success with a high-deductible plan is through incorporation of the MSA. A physician–employer or employee can fund the MSA to cover the extra cost of the deductible.

Why would anyone consider such a model? The simple answer is long-term savings and extra benefits. Now, once health insurance premiums are paid, the money will never come back to the employer–physician or employee. With an MSA, if the money is not used inside the MSA, the employee gets to keep the money for future personal medical expenses. Once enough money is deferred into the MSA to cover the deductible, an employer can choose to stop contributing to the MSA, thereby significantly decreasing the annual health insurance/MSA expenses. (See Exhibit 5–5.)

Exhibit 5–5 *Sample MSA Plan*

Example:

Assume with a small medical office health plan that the family premium is $600 a month with a $500 deductible. Also assume that a family premium with a $5000 deductible is $250 a month. Assume the family premium is for a doctor/owner of a medical practice.

Total premium for Doctor Smith for 1 year	$7200 for 1 year with a $500 deductible plan
	$3000 with a $5000 deductible plan
Total annual savings in premium for Dr. Smith	$4200

Note: Annual health insurance premiums were 60% deductible in 2001, 70% deductible in 2002, and 100% in 2003 for a physician/owner of a PC, LLC, or Sub S. Corporation. Employee premiums are 100% deductible to the corporation.

Dr. Smith's total contribution to a MSA for 1 year	$3600
Total out of pocket cost for Dr. Smith that includes the MSA contribution	$6600 ($3000 + $3600)
Dr. Smith tax deduction for normal $7200 premium/ $500 deductible plan	$7200 × 60% = $4320
Dr. Smith tax deduction for $3000 premium/ $5000 deductible plan	$3000 × 60% = $1800
Dr. Smith Tax deduction for MSA Contribution	$3600 × 100% = $3600

<u>Additional</u> tax savings by using the MSA in conjunction with a high deductible plan	$1080
Annual out of pocket savings using an MSA plus a high deductible plan over the $500 deductible plan	$7200 – $6600 = $600
<u>Total overall savings</u> for the physicians at the end of the year	$1680

Many physicians are unaware that they can deduct only 70% of their family health insurance that was paid for by the office. While the CPA, CFP, or CMP knows about this, the fact is often not communicated to the physician.

[1] MSA BENEFITS

In the above example, three good things happen. First, the total out-of-pocket expenses for the health insurance and the MSA costs are $600 lower than the traditional $500 deductible non-MSA plan. Second, the money contributed to the MSA is 100% deductible, thereby saving the physician an additional $1080 in taxes. Third, and just as important, is the fact that if the owner's family is relatively healthy and does not use all the money in the MSA, this money can be rolled over to the next year and cut the owner's next year's out-of-pocket costs. The owner could also continue to fund the MSA at $3600 a year to stockpile money in the MSA for other medical expenses (such as orthodontics) or for supplemental retirement benefits. However, MSAs are underutilized for three reasons.

First, many insurance agents despise the concept of MSAs. When an insurance agent lowers the premium for a physician–client, the agent takes a significant pay cut. The agent makes nothing on money contributed to the MSA.

Second, most employer–physicians do not have the courage to implement a plan that raises their employees' deductibles to $1600 a year. However, if the concept is fully explained to the employees, then the employees should jump at the chance to have an MSA implemented by their employer–physician. The employer is going to cover the difference between the old deductible and new deductible; and if at the end of the year the employee did not use the money in the MSA for deductibles, then that money becomes the employee's.

Third, offices with several sick employees (employees who always hit their deductible or more every year) will have a hard time making the MSA concept cost effective due to prohibitively high insurance premiums. Nevertheless, when appropriately used, MSAs can fill the special needs of many medical offices.

[D] Other Potential Deductions

The goal of paying less income tax requires some up front analysis to identify and capture all business expenses within the entity's accounting system. In addition to the typical business expenses deducted by the entity, physician owners should list all personally paid expenses that benefit the practice. The following is a partial list that might be appropriately allocated to the practice:

- Cellular phone: many medical professionals completely deduct the cost when the number is given to the answering service;
- Internet access: when time is spent communicating with the office, other medical professionals, or performing research;
- Home computer, telephone lines, periodicals, and books: to the extent used for the practice; and
- Automobile expenses: it is almost always more beneficial for an entity to own a vehicle and charge personal use back to an individual owner. The rules for this are complex and should be discussed with a tax advisor for specifics in each state. One disadvantage relates to the purchase of commercial auto insurance, which can be significantly more expensive than personal auto insurance. There are also liability issues to review. Therefore, care needs to be exercised before acting in this area.

The core deductions for passthrough entities are similar to the basic business deductions allowable for every entity. The rules noted above are different for passthroughs and, although not all-inclusive, the noted items cover the most common differences faced by healthcare professionals. Most of the tax planning issues with passthrough capability flow to the tax returns of the taxpayers they affect.

Acknowledgment

Dr. David Edward Marcinko, MBA, CMP, CFP for the JGTRRA 2003 information.

Endnotes

1. *See* www.irs.gov or Form 8594.
2. IRC § 79.

Chapter 6

Introduction to Investment Concepts

Analyzing Securities, Judging Risks . . . Achieving Returns

Jeffrey S. Coons
Christopher J. Cummings

If the forecasted cash flow from your equities don't change, a lower price implies a higher rate of return and a higher price implies a lower rate of return. Therefore, if several of your stock holdings have appreciated substantially, or even surpassed their fair value estimates, you might choose to take some profits and allocate money to your holdings that have greater potential upside.

Carl Sibilski, Securities Analyst

Introduction

The physician who wants to become a better investor has several options. A general understanding of different types of investments, coupled with a few basic investment planning rules-of-thumb, can help improve his or her goals and objectives. The physician can avoid most of the problems experienced by investors by keeping the following precepts in mind when making investment decisions:

- Understand and diversify risk to the extent possible;
- If it looks too good to be true, it probably is;
- Beware of projecting forward historical averages; and
- Understand the limitations of performance statistics.

This chapter introduces a wide range of investment planning concepts. The different types of investments, including stocks, bonds, derivative securities, and mutual funds, will be defined at the outset of the section. Although the fundamentals of investing were considered pedestrian a few years ago at the height of the stock market bubble, recent bearish events have refocused attention on them. This chapter will also review various portfolio management and security selection strategies. Finally, the usefulness and limitations of a variety of performance measurement statistics will be discussed.

When making investment decisions, it is always important to review the basic nature of the investment. In the most fundamental sense, investments are dollars reallocated today in exchange for the prospect of future dollars. An investment can take the form of real property such as art, real estate, baseball cards, etc., or "human capital" such as a college, business, or medical school education. The focus in this chapter is on investments in securities. Securities represent legal title to future dollars. Thus, the first question to ask when evaluating a security for investment is "what future cash flow will I be entitled to with this investment?"

Fixed Income Securities

If the investment is a fixed income security, then the cash flow an investor is entitled to receive is generally a combination of periodic coupon payments throughout the year plus the par value or face value of the security at its maturity date. The par value or face value of a fixed income security is the dollar amount promised on the date the security matures. The maturity date is the date on which the issuer is required to return an amount equal to the security's par value to the investor (i.e., the return of principal). The coupon or interest payment is the annual percentage of the par value to be paid in installments during the year, typically semi-annually.

A security that does not provide a coupon payment until it matures is typically referred to as a zero coupon bond. While zero coupon bonds do not actually make periodic interest payments, these bonds sell at a substantial discount to par value. Assuming that the investor holds the zero coupon bond until it matures, the interest received by the holder of a zero coupon bond is equal to the difference between what the investor paid for the bond and its par value.

Since a fixed income security represents a promise to pay dollars in the future, the investor should find out who is doing the promising, how many dollars, and on which dates. Key differences among fixed income or debt securities are based upon the following factors:

- The maturity date;
- The issuer (i.e., the original borrower);
- The coupon amount; and
- The underlying collateral used to secure the promised payments.

Fixed income securities with a maturity of less than one year are generally referred to as short-term debt securities. Common examples of short-term fixed income securities include Treasury bills (T-bills), commercial paper, and certificates of deposit. Intermediate-term fixed income securities generally have a stated maturity of 1–10 years and are often referred to as notes. Finally, long-term debt securities typically have a maturity of 10 years or greater and are commonly referred to as bonds.

Another key differentiating characteristic among fixed income securities is that the issuer of the security is the institution responsible for making the interest and principal payments over the life of the security. A government bond typically refers to a security issued by a federal government institution, including the U.S. Treasury or a specific U.S. governmental agency.

[A] Treasury Securities

Since the U.S. Treasury owns the printing press for the dollars it borrows, Treasury securities are considered the most creditworthy—the most likely to be paid back. In fact, the yield on a Treasury security is often referred to as the "risk-free" rate of return, since the probability of default is practically nonexistent. Treasury bills have a maturity of less than one year, and, like zero coupon bonds, are sold at a discount to par value in lieu of paying interest payments. Treasury notes have a maturity of 1 to 10 years, and Treasury bonds have a stated maturity in excess of 10 years.

[B] Agency Bonds

In contrast to Treasury bonds, agency bonds tend to be backed by loans or other revenue generating activities of that specific U.S. governmental agency. While agency bonds are typically backed by the "full faith and credit of the U.S. government," there is slightly less certainty regarding the coupon and principal payments. Examples of agencies issuing fixed income securities include Government National Mortgage Association, Federal National Mortgage Association, and Federal Home Loan Mortgage Corporation.

[C] Municipal Bonds

A municipal bond is a fixed income security issued by a state or local governmental institution. This kind of bond may represent a general obligation backed by the taxation powers of the municipality or a revenue bond backed by the revenue generated from a specific project. Examples of projects used to back revenue bonds include water and sewer maintenance, hospitals, housing, and airports. Since revenue bonds are typically backed only by one source of the municipality's total revenue, general obligation bonds tend to have stronger creditworthiness than revenue bonds. One characteristic of most municipal bonds is that their coupon payments are often exempt from federal income taxes, as well as state taxation for taxpayers in the state of issue, which is why these securities are also generally referred to as tax-exempt securities.

[D] Other Fixed Income Securities

In addition to the government and municipalities, corporations may issue fixed income securities. Corporate fixed income securities range from short-term borrowings, such as commercial paper to long-term bonds. Finally, financial institutions such as banks and insurance companies have developed fixed income securities such as certificates of deposit—typically a short-term zero coupon note of a savings institution—fixed annuities, a promised stream of coupon payments often with a zero par value.

[E] Credit Quality

Given that a fixed income security is nothing more than title to promised cash flows in the future, the ability of a borrower to pay is a key issue to consider when evaluating a fixed income security for investment. The credit quality of a fixed income security issuer is an assessment of the issuer's ability to pay the security's coupon and par value as promised. One source of credit quality opinions is a ratings agency such as Standard & Poor's, Moody's Investors Service, and Fitch Ratings Ltd. These firms have a grading scale to illustrate their view on an issuer's credit quality, typically distinguishing between investment grade issuers who are very likely to meet their obligations and those speculative grade or junk issuers whose ability to pay is less certain.

Standard & Poor's, Moody's, and Fitch's have the credit ratings scale shown in Exhibit 6–1.

Exhibit 6–1 *Fixed Income Securities Ratings*

	Standard & Poor's	*Moody's*	*Fitch's*
Investment Grade	AAA	Aaa	AAA
	AA	Aa	AA
	A	A	A
	BBB	Baa	BBB
Speculative Grade	BB	Ba	BB
	B	B	B
	CCC	Caa	CCC
	CC	Ca	CC
	C	C	C

There are two important issues to remember with respect to credit ratings. The first is that credit ratings are the opinion of the rating agency, reflecting the likelihood of an issuer meeting its obligations. Just as a speculative grade issue may meet its coupon and principal obligations in a timely manner, an investment grade security is not necessarily guaranteed to avoid a default. The second issue is that credit ratings agencies are generally making assessments based on data that are either already publicly available or are being made public in their report. Thus, it is often the case that both the basic credit rating and changes in credit ratings are already or very quickly reflected in the price of the security. Nevertheless, credit ratings are an important factor for understanding the risks associated with a particular fixed income investment.

How does a physician investor evaluate whether the risk associated with a particular credit rating is already in the price of a security? How does a physician investor compare securities from different issuers with different maturity dates and coupon rates? The best measure of the relative price of a fixed income security is its yield. The simplest way to calculate yield is the current yield, which is the coupon rate divided by the current price of a bond. For example, if a bond maturing in 10 years pays $45 a year in coupons for every $1000 in par value and has a current price of $900, the current yield is 45/900 = 5.0%. While this measure of yield is simple, it has its limitations including that it only takes into account the coupon interest earned on the bond [i.e., it ignores any capital gain (loss) that may occur if the bond is purchased at a discount (premium)]. A more dependable, albeit more difficult to calculate, measure of yield is yield-to-maturity. Yield-to-maturity represents the internal rate of return on the bond and is the average rate of return that will be earned if the bond is held to maturity, assuming that all coupon payments are reinvested at a rate of return equal to the bond's yield-to-maturity. Yield-to-maturity accounts for both coupon payments and differences between the current price and par value of the bond over the remaining maturity of the bond. For example, the yield-to-maturity of the 10-year bond above paying $45 per year in interest and trading at $900 is approximately 5.85%. The extra yield over and above the 5% current yield comes from the price appreciation from the current price of $900 to the par value of $1000 that will be paid when the bond matures.

Therefore, one way to value a fixed income security is to compare its yield to that of similar credit quality and similar maturity structure investments. Often these comparisons are provided in terms of credit spreads, which is calculated as the yield on the security less the yield on the "risk-free" asset (i.e., a Treasury security) with a similar maturity date. If one security has a larger, more favorable credit spread than another security of equal credit quality, then, everything else being equal, this security would generally be considered more attractive as an investment.

The graph of the yield on U.S. Treasury obligations across various maturity dates (i.e., short-term T-Bills through 30-Year Treasury bonds) is called the yield curve. The yield curve is typically sloped positively, as illustrated in Figure 6–1, with longer maturity securities having a higher yield than short-term investments. However, the yield curve may become inverted, with shorter-term yields exceeding long bond yields at times (e.g., prior to many recessions).

One way to look at a fixed income investment is as a promise of a periodic coupon payment until either its maturity date or call date. The call date represents a date when the issuer has the right to retire the security for a predetermined price prior to the maturity date. However, most of the portfolio construction methods discussed later in this chapter focus on total return including both income and capital appreciation. The income portion of the return is reflective of the yield on the security, while the capital

Figure 6-1 *U.S. Treasury Yield*

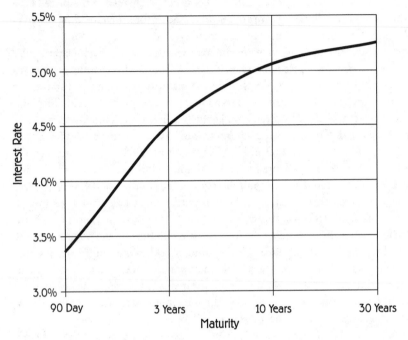

appreciation is a result of changes in the price that other investors are willing to pay for the same security.

Changes in the general level of interest rates (i.e., shifts in the yield curve) are the greatest influence on the price of most investment grade bonds. Let's say an investor purchased a 10-year Treasury bond paying a 6% coupon for par value of $1000, and the yield on 10-year Treasuries fell from 6% to 5%. Since the bond has a coupon greater than the current market yield, the price of the bond would adjust upward until its yield on that price was 5%. Bonds with coupon payments in excess of prevailing market yields tend to trade at a premium to par value, while bonds with coupon rates below current market yields tend to trade at a discount to par value.

Thus, a key point to understand about bonds is that there is an inverse relationship between movements in bond prices and interest rates. As interest rates decline, bond prices increase, and as interest rates rise, bond prices decline.

[F] Bond Duration

An interesting question arises from this illustration: how much will a bond's price change from a 1% change in interest rates? To answer this, consider the concept of duration. A bond's duration is the weighted average life of its cash flows. Thus, if your bond pays $60 per year in coupon payments for 10 years, and $1000 in par value at the end of the 10 years, the duration is the length of time that it takes for you to receive the present value of the coupon payments and par value. How does this help answer the original question? There is a handy rule-of-thumb that says the duration of a bond multiplied by the change in market interest rates is the approximate price change of the bond. Thus, the price of a 10-year Treasury bond with a duration of approximately 7.8 years will appreciate (decline) by about 7.8% with a drop (increase) in interest rates of 1%.

[G] Fixed Income Summary

In summary, fixed income securities are promises from an issuer to pay a combination of periodic coupon payments and/or par value at maturity. In the simplest sense, the issuer of a fixed income security is borrowing money from the holder of the fixed income security. Assuming that an issuer does not default on the coupon or principal payments and that the security is held to maturity, then a bondholder will receive a total return over the life of the investment equal to the market yield when the security was purchased. In the interim, however, the total return will fluctuate depending upon such factors as changes in the perceived credit quality of the issuer and changes in market interest rates.

Equity Securities

If a security represents legal title to a future stream of cash flows, then equity of a company designates ownership of earnings or profits after accounting for normal operating expenses, interest payments (e.g., coupon payments to bond holders), and taxes. In contrast to bondholders, holders of equity securities (i.e., shareholders) are considered owners of the company as opposed to creditors of the company. Typically, the primary benefit of being a shareholder in a company is that the investor benefits from the company's ability to generate profits. Thus, one way of analyzing the decision to acquire equity in a company is to ask: How much can the company earn above its fixed obligations? If an equity investment is considered instead on a termination value basis, then equity represents title to corporate assets after payment of all debts. The latter viewpoint offers almost a "worst case" evaluative question: If the company was to shut its doors and discontinue operations, what is the value of the assets minus liabilities?

When investors talk about equities, most of the time they are referring to common stocks, which represent title to income after all other obligations of the corporation have been satisfied (including interest payments to bondholders). Common stock is the least senior of all securities issued by a corporation—the obligations represented by all other securities and debts are expected to be paid before the common stock owner has a right to the assets or earnings. From a different perspective, a common stock holder has the ownership of all earnings after payment of expenses and taxes. Thus, if the company is extremely profitable, the common stock holder's upside is not limited by a fixed rate of return.

[A] Location of the Issuer

Key differentiating features of equity securities include the issuer's location, size, and industrial classification. Domestic stocks are simply equity securities issued by corporations based in the United States, while foreign stocks are equities issued by companies headquartered outside of the United States. Foreign stocks are typically further divided into developed and emerging markets, with developing markets generally representing countries with relatively well-developed economies, financial markets, and property rights. By contrast, emerging markets are characterized by smaller economies, with underdeveloped financial markets.

Investors based in the United States can acquire foreign stocks in several ways. First, certain foreign stocks are traded directly on U.S. stock exchanges or traded as American depository receipts (ADRs). An ADR is a security issued by a domestic financial institution, which is traded on a U.S. exchange, and represents a specified number of shares of a foreign stock held in trust at an affiliated financial institution abroad. Second, with accelerating globalization of financial markets and improved transactional efficiency of foreign stock exchanges, investors can often make direct foreign investments by actually investing in shares of companies that are traded on exchanges outside of the United States. While the separation between domestic and foreign stocks is generally thought of as a way to identify greater or lesser sensitivity to the U.S. economy, this idea fails to recognize that most corporations operate in an increasingly global economy. Many foreign and domestic multinational companies have as much exposure to foreign economies as the companies have to their home economy. On the other hand, the earnings of foreign corporations must be translated to U.S. dollars for a U.S. investor, so sensitivity to the currency of the foreign stock's home country remains. Thus, investors must consider the risk of unfavorable currency fluctuations (i.e., currency risk) when investing in foreign stocks.

[B] Size of the Issuer

Another differentiating feature among common stocks is the size of the company issuing the equity. Size is often measured by a stock's market capitalization, which is defined as the aggregate market value of the corporation's outstanding stock and calculated by multiplying outstanding shares by the current price per share. In general, companies are considered to be large capitalization stocks if their market capitalization exceeds $5.0 billion, while companies with a market capitalization of less than $1.5 billion are referred to as small cap stocks. Companies whose market capitalization falls between $1.5 billion and $5.0 billion are commonly referred to as mid-cap stocks. However, these thresholds should only be used as general guidelines since there are no universally accepted breakpoints used in the investment industry today.

Another classification that is related to size of a company is its seasoning, which is a concept related to the length of time over which a company has an operating history. The spectrum of seasoning runs from blue chip stocks to initial public offerings (IPOs). Blue chip stocks are the equities of high quality, large, established companies. Many of the stocks included in the Dow Jones Industrial Average are considered to be blue chip stocks. In contrast to large, well-established companies, IPOs are stocks of relatively new companies that generally lack a long-term corporate earnings track record. While blue chip stocks have historically been considered safe stocks due to their large size and strong position in their respective industries, it is important to remember that all investment decisions should be based on future expected returns. Because a company is large and well established does not guarantee that the company's stock will make a good investment. For example, in 2002 Bethlehem Steel, Enron, and WorldCom were considered high quality blue chip stocks that investors could not go wrong owning. However, as history has shown, once dominant stocks can fall on extremely hard times. Likewise, while the medical professional will often hear anecdotes of IPOs that turned out to be exceptional investments, many of these stocks may be considered speculative at best with significant risk of losing all their value. Thus, it is important for investors to remember that there may be changes in a stock's fundamentals, as well as the market and economic environment. This means that any equity investment, even in blue chip stocks, needs to be consistently evaluated and monitored. As an example, the strong stock market rally of the late 1990s was driven by a handful of large, well-established, blue chip and technology companies. Like the "Nifty Fifty" period of the mid-1970s, these stocks were hardest hit in the ensuing correction.

[C] Industrial Classification

The final classification of common stocks discussed here is the separation of companies by the industry or economic sector in which their primary business operates. In fact, there are 10 economic sector classifications and 122 industry subclassifications according to Standard & Poor's. Stocks in the same industry tend to move together, because the companies' revenue and earnings tend to be influenced by common industry-wide factors.

Just as the overall economy experiences periods of expansion and contraction (i.e., recession), specific industries experience periods of growth and decline that generally affect all companies in that industry. Likewise, some industries are more affected by economy-wide business cycles.

The distinction between cyclical stocks and defensive stocks lies in how closely related the stock's performance is to industry and economic cycles. Thus, stocks that operate in industries that are highly correlated to the strength of the domestic economy are considered to be cyclical stocks. For example, the construction and automobile industries are generally considered cyclical industries given that demand for their products is highly related to the current economic environment. In periods of weak or declining economic growth, demand for automobiles and new construction products decline, thus resulting in a decline in earnings for companies operating within those industries. Defensive stocks are viewed as being less susceptible to fluctuations in the overall economy. For example, since demand for food products is generally considered to be less dependent on the strength or weakness of the overall economy, food stocks are generally considered defensive stocks.

[D] Dividends

If the definition of a security is title to a stream of cash flows, then the dividends a company is expected to pay to equity shareholders on a periodic basis (e.g., quarterly) are a clear source of return for an investor. A dividend is simply a distribution of some portion of the company's earnings to equity shareholders. Like a bond yield, a stock's dividend yield can be used to measure the income return on the stock. To determine a stock's dividend yield, the trailing year's dividends per share paid are divided by the current stock price. However, a key difference between a dividend yield and a bond yield is the level of certainty that can be assumed regarding future payments, since a bond's coupon is generally predetermined and its payment is expected to be senior to the payment of dividends.

After a company has determined that it has earned a profit, management has to decide what to do with those profits. One choice is to distribute the earnings to shareholders in the form of dividends, while another option is to reinvest the profits in the company. A company's management may determine that the shareholders' interest is best served by using the earnings to pursue growth opportunities (e.g., capital expansion, research and development, etc.) at the corporate level. Thus, when management believes that its investment opportunities are likely to produce a higher return than what investors' could generate with their dividends or that reinvestment is needed to maintain its financial strength, the company will retain the earnings. As an example, as of September 2003, Dominion Resources, a large utility company, had a dividend yield of approximately 4.7% and Dell Computer, a technology company, had a dividend yield of 0%. The fact that Dominion Resources has a higher dividend yield than Dell does not mean that one stock is necessarily more attractive as an investment than the other.

Instead, it implies that Dell's management believes that investing its earnings in new technologies and research and development offers the potential for higher returns than distributing the earnings to shareholders in the form of dividends.

[E] Stock Valuation

If investments are the reallocation of today's dollars for expected dollars in the future, why would an investor buy a common stock that does not pay a dividend? The simple answer is that the investor expects to be able to sell the stock later at a higher price as a result of some combination of higher valuations on the company's existing earnings power and/or growth in future earnings. While the safety of knowing that a company has been paying a dividend is comforting, the lack of dividend does not necessarily mean that investors will not be rewarded for owning stocks with either low dividend yields or no dividend at all. An investor purchasing stocks is usually attempting to buy stocks that not only may pay dividends, but that will also increase in value over time.

Table 6–1 contains various statistics for a handful of stocks to illustrate that there can be dramatic differences in these statistics across different stocks. The primary statistic

Table 6–1 *Sample Stock Statistics*

Stock	Price-to-Earnings Ratio	Price-to-Book Ratio	Price-to-Sales Ratio	Dividend Yield	Consensus Earnings Growth Rate	Market Cap ($MM)
Dominion Resources	16.7	1.7	1.5	4.7%	6.0%	$16.9
Boeing	14.4	2.4	0.5	2.1%	12.8%	$26.4
General Motors	16.3	1.0	0.1	5.4%	6.4%	$20.7
Dell Computer	34.7	14.9	2.1	0.0%	14.9%	$69.0
McDonalds	12.8	1.9	1.3	1.5%	8.8%	$20.4
Microsoft	30.1	5.2	9.3	0.0%	13.6%	$276.4

Source: Factset as of December 31, 2002. Microsoft has a dividend yield of 0.3% with a dividend per share of 0.08, as of August 1, 2003.

used by investment professionals to measure a corporation's earnings power is known as earnings per share, which are simply the company's per-share profits distributable to the common stockholders (i.e., what is left over after accounting for expenses, including interest payments on debt obligations, taxes, and preferred stock dividends).

The three most common measures used to quantify a stock's valuation are the price-to-book ratio, price-to-earnings ratio, and price-to-sales ratio. A stock's book value is generally defined as the accounting value of the firm's assets less its liabilities. Thus the price-to-book ratio identifies how much investors are willing to pay per dollar of net assets. Similarly, the price-to-earnings ratio indicates how much investors are willing to pay for a dollar of earnings. Unfortunately, a corporation's earnings are very easily manipulated by adjusting certain accounting "assumptions." Therefore, some investors prefer to use price-to-sales as a measure of a firm's value since revenues or sales are generally subject to fewer accounting assumptions. However, it is important for medical professionals or those who advise them to remember that, because one stock may have a higher growth rate (or any other statistic) than another stock, it does not mean that the stock will produce necessarily a higher return.

[F] Stock Splits

Finally, medical professionals should understand the concept of stock splits. In a stock split, a corporation issues a set number of shares in exchange for each share held by shareholders. Typically, a stock split increases the number of shares owned by a shareholder. For example, XYZ Corporation may declare a 2-for-1 split, which means that shareholders will receive two shares for each share that they own. However, corporations can also declare a reverse stock split, such as a 1-for-2 split where shareholders would receive one share for every two shares that they own.

While stock splits can either increase or decrease the number of shares that a shareholder owns, the most important thing to understand about stock splits is that they have no impact on the aggregate value of the shareholder's position in the company. Using the XYZ Corporation example above, if the stock is trading at $10 per share, an investor owning 100 shares has a total position of $1000. After the 2-for-1 split occurs, the investor will now own 200 shares, but the value of the stock will adjust downward from $10 per share to $5 per share. Thus, the investor still owns $1000 of XYZ stock.

While stock splits are often interpreted as signals from management that conditions in the company are strong, there is no intrinsic reason that a stock split will result in subsequent stock appreciation.

[G] Common Compared to Preferred Stock

A common stock is the least senior of securities issued by a company. A preferred stock, in contrast, is slightly more senior to common stock, since dividends owed to the preferred stockholders should be paid before distributions are made to common stockholders. However, distributions to preferred stockholders are limited to the level outlined in the preferred stock agreement (i.e., the stated dividend payments). Like a fixed income security, preferred stocks have a specific periodic payment that is either a fixed dollar amount or an amount adjusted based upon short-term market interest rates. However, unlike fixed income securities, preferred stocks typically do not have a specific maturity date, and preferred stock dividend payments are made from the corporation's after tax income rather than its pre-tax income.

Likewise, dividends paid to preferred stockholders are considered income distributions to the company's equity owners rather than creditors, so the issuing corporation does not have the same requirement to make dividend distributions to preferred stockholders. Thus, preferred stock is generally referred to as a "hybrid" security, since it has elements similar to both fixed income securities (i.e., stated periodic payments) and equity securities (i.e., shareholders are considered owners of the issuing company rather than creditors).

Convertible preferred stocks (and convertible corporate bonds) are also considered hybrid securities since they have both equity and fixed income characteristics. A convertible security, whether a preferred stock or a corporate bond, generally includes provisions that allow the security to be exchanged for a given number of shares of common stock in the issuing corporation. The holder of a convertible security essentially owns both the preferred stock (or the corporate bond) and an option to exchange the preferred stock (or corporate bond) for shares of common stock in the company. Thus, at times the convertible security may behave more like the issuing company's common stock than it does the issuing company's preferred stock (or corporate bonds), depending upon how close the common stock's market price is to the designated conversion price of the convertible security.

[H] Equity Transactions

The purchase and sale of stocks typically takes place on one of the three major stock exchanges (i.e., The New York Stock Exchange (NYSE), The American Stock Exchange (AMEX), or the NASDAQ). The NYSE is the oldest of the three exchanges, dating back to 1817. As of July 2003, there were approximately 2800 stocks traded on the NYSE, with the majority of them categorized as domestic large capitalization stocks. In contrast, only approximately 800 stocks trade on the AMEX, and those stocks generally tend to have a smaller market capitalization than their NYSE brethren. Additionally, index shares and equity derivative products (e.g., options) are also frequently traded on the AMEX, and in early 2003, the approximately 120 largest NASDAQ stocks also started trading on the AMEX. Founded in 1971, the NASDAQ was the first electronic stock market. As of October 2003, approximately 5000 securities are traded on the NASDAQ, making it the largest of the three major stock exchanges. In addition to the NYSE, AMEX, and NASDAQ exchanges, there are several smaller regional exchanges including the Pacific Stock exchange, the Philadelphia Exchange, and the Midwest Stock Exchange.

While the actual sale of stocks generally takes place on an organized exchange, individual investors cannot access the exchanges directly. Thus, investors wishing to trade individual securities place their trades through a stockbroker. Typically investors place either a market order or a limit order to either purchase or sell a particular stock. By placing a market order, an investor is agreeing to buy or sell a security at the current market price, regardless of how much the stock's price moves between the placement of the order and the execution of the trade.

In contrast, a limit order establishes a set price that the stock will either be purchased (or sold) if the price falls below (or above) the limit price. A healthcare professional purchasing stocks will typically be quoted the ask price for a stock, which is the price that the stockbroker is willing to sell the stock. In contrast, an investor selling a stock will typically be quoted the bid price, or the price that the broker is willing to pay to buy the stock. The difference between the bid and ask price of a stock is referred to as the spread. For example, if the bid price for a stock is $31.50 and the ask price is 30.50, the spread is $1. In some cases, the stockbroker not only earns a commission for facilitating the execution of the investor's trade, but also benefits from the spread. Depending on the liquidity of the particular stock, the spread can represent a significant cost of investing. Highly liquid stocks tend to trade at smaller spreads, while less frequently traded securities may have much larger spreads.

Alternative Investments

Beyond stocks and bonds, several distinct types of investments may be referred to as alternative investments. Alternative investments to stocks and bonds include real estate, private equity/venture capital, derivative securities, commodities, and arts/collectibles.

While such investments often have features that differentiate them from the equity and fixed income securities that are central to most modern portfolio construction approaches, alternative investments can also be boiled down to their basic expected cash flows. As a result, the evaluation of alternative investments involves fundamentally similar concepts to the basics discussed for stocks and bonds earlier.

[A] Real Estate

The most common alternative investment and often single largest investment made by most individuals is real estate, since the family home is considered a key portion of wealth. Whether considering the family home, an office building, or a rental property, the evaluation of a real estate investment involves an assessment of the rents that may be received from those occupying the property.

Likewise, the value of real estate may be measured by the value of the property's assets minus its liabilities. Many real estate investors consider their real estate holdings to be similar to a fixed income security since the income from the investment tends to be relatively stable over time. However, the true nature of a real estate investment is more akin to equities. First, the income earned on a real estate investment must be considered on an after-expense basis, since the property owner is responsible for maintenance, property management, taxes, and debt servicing. Second, while long-term leases may dampen the uncertainty of the rents received by the property owner, both rental amounts and occupancy rates may be variable for a particular real estate investment. Occupancy rate can be thought of as either the number of units rented in a multiple unit property such as an apartment or office building or as the number of days/weeks of rental income achieved in a year for such property as vacation homes or hotels. Thus, like an equity security, the income from real estate is a net of expense number that may be quite variable, depending upon factors related to the demand for the property.

When considering real estate from an asset value basis, the similarity between real estate and equity investments becomes more apparent. Specifically, there is no preset par value or maturity date for a real estate investment anchoring its market value. Instead, the value of the real estate holding is driven by the supply and demand for land at a particular location, the building and other fixed property on the land, and the potential future cash flows achievable from the property minus all liabilities, including any potential environmental concerns. Thus, the value of a real estate holding may fluctuate with economic cycles, demographics, inflation/deflation cycles, local business conditions, and other causes.

[B] Real Estate Investment Trusts

In general, two characteristics of real estate as an alternative asset class include a basic lack of liquidity and a lack of direct comparability across properties. The lack of liquidity results because the real estate market is a negotiated market with individual transactions that typically occur infrequently. Real estate investment trusts (REITs) were developed in part to help offer greater liquidity to real estate investors. REITs are generally traded on organized stock exchanges, thus providing investors a mechanism for buying and selling real estate related investments in an efficient manner. Likewise, REITs generally allow investors to acquire diversified exposure to real estate securities, since REITs generally invest in multiple underlying properties. Finally, no two properties are identical, so it is difficult to generalize about the characteristics of real estate investments. Therefore, it is extremely difficult to compare one real estate investment to another.

[C] Private Equity/Venture Capital

Similar to the equity securities discussed earlier, private equity and venture capital investments typically involve ownership of shares in a company and represent title to a portion of the company's future earnings. However, private equity is an equity interest in a company or venture whose stock is not yet traded on a stock exchange. Venture capital is typically a special case of private equity in which the investment is in a company or venture that has little financial history or is embarking on a high risk/high potential reward business strategy.

Like real estate, private equity and venture capital investments generally share a general lack of liquidity and a lack of comparability across different individual investments. The lack of liquidity comes from the fact that private equity and venture capital investments are typically not tradable on a stock exchange until the company has an IPO. The lack of comparability is due to the fact that most private equity and venture capital investments are the result of direct negotiation between the investor/venture capitalist and the existing owners of the company/venture. With widely divergent terms and provisions across different investments, it is difficult to make general claims regarding the characteristics of private equity and venture capital investments.

[D] Derivatives

A derivative security is a security whose value is derived from one or more underlying securities. Derivatives can range from securities as simple as a stripped bond or pooled mortgage security to extremely complex securities customized for a particular investor's risk management needs. Even though derivative securities in some contexts can be a key source of volatility in the financial markets, these securities may be useful tools in the portfolio management process. Likewise, just as the basic asset classes discussed previously may be separated into a series of expected cash flows, any given derivative security may be understood as a series of date or event contingent cash flows.

Two basic derivative securities created from more traditional fixed income securities are pooled mortgage securities and strips. A stripped security represents either principal or interest payments from some underlying fixed income security. As an example, a principal-only Treasury strip represents the face value payment of a U.S. Treasury bond, while an income-only Treasury strip represents the right to the coupon payments of a particular U.S. Treasury bond. A pooled mortgage security is a derivative security that represents ownership in a collection of mortgages. An interesting feature of a pooled mortgage security is the principal paydown, with shares of the pooled mortgage security returned at face value as mortgages are refinanced and/or repaid.

Refinancing and prepayment of mortgages tend to happen when the original mortgage rate is above currently available mortgage rates, so pooled mortgages with higher coupon rates will tend to have the greatest prepayment risk. For example, the dramatic decline in mortgage rates during 2002 and into late 2003 led to a significant increase in refinancing activity, which in turn resulted in significant prepayment risk for many holders of pooled mortgage securities.

[1] PUTS AND CALLS

Two equity-related derivative securities are *puts* and *calls*. Puts and calls fall under the general category of options, because each offers the holder the right to sell or purchase a security at a predefined price over a predetermined period. A put represents the right to sell a security at a particular price within a specific period of time, while a call represents the right to buy at a particular price over a given time period. An *option* is exercised when an investor invokes his or her right to buy or sell as provided for with the option. A European option is an option that is exercisable only at its maturity date, while an American option may be exercised at or before its maturity date. If the price of a stock falls below (or rises above) the put (or call) price within the term of the option, then the option is said to be in the money, and the holder is likely to exercise the option and sell (or buy) the stock from the writer of the option at its strike price.

The primary use of options is to change the probability distribution of potential returns in either a single security or a portfolio, either to lower the downside risk of holding the underlying security or to take advantage of dramatic upward or downward movements in market prices. Several common strategies use put and call options either to hedge against volatility in an underlying security or to take advantage of that security's volatility. An example of the former is a *collar transaction,* which involves the sale of a covered call and a purchase of a protective put with the premium income received from selling the call. The collar essentially locks in the price of the underlying security between the put strike price and the call strike price. A price above the call price will mean that the shares of the security will be called away, while the security will be sold if it falls below the put strike price. If all the premium income is used to purchase the put, then the transaction is known as a zero cost collar, since the hedge of the underlying security for a price below the put exercise price costs no more than the lost opportunity for a price above the call price.

An options strategy that takes advantage of an underlying security's volatility is the straddle transaction. This strategy is based upon the purchase of both a put option and a call option at the same exercise price. If the security remains within a narrow range of the exercise price, then the investor will lose the premium paid for the options minus the gain on the particular option (i.e., either the put or call) that is in the money. However, if the security price deviates significantly either upward or downward from the strike price, then the value of either the call option or the put option will rise as well. Thus, the investor benefits from either a dramatic rise or fall in the underlying security price.

An option is considered out of the money if the stock rises above (or falls below) the put (or call) price. The price of an option is generally based on the option's strike price, the underlying security's price, the volatility of the underlying security, the time to expiration, and current interest rates. The first step in understanding how an option should be priced is to consider the idea of put-call parity. If an owner of a stock buys a put and sells a call with the same exercise price and expiration date, then the investor has locked in the strike price since either the put or call will be in the money whether the stock is below or above the strike price. To ensure that an arbitrage return (i.e., a riskless return above the risk free rate) is not possible, the relationship between the security price S, the put price P, and the call price C must be as follows:

$$C = S + P - \frac{E}{[1 + rt]}$$

In this formula, E is the exercise price, r is the risk free rate of return, and t is the contract period. In essence, the price of the call must reflect the current price of the security, and the price of the put option less the strike price discounted by the risk free rate of return.

While the put-call parity relationship defines the relative price of two options under a "no arbitrage profit" condition, the method of calculating an expected price of a call without the benefit of knowing the price of the put or vice versa is much more complicated. One of the best known attempts at establishing a pricing model for options is the Black-Scholes model. The Black-Scholes model calculates the price of an option based upon the current price of the security, the exercise price, the interest rate, the length of the contract, and the volatility of the security. While specific probability distributions are required for the Black-Scholes model, the price of an option in the model is essentially the current price of the security multiplied by a probability (i.e., from a cumulative normal distribution) minus the present value of the strike price times a probability. However, the actual price of an option traded on an organized exchange (e.g., AMEX, Philadelphia Stock Exchange, the Chicago Board of Trade, etc.) will be largely determined by supply and demand factors as well, so there are times when hedging strategies do not provide the expected protection. This is especially the case during extreme market movements, such as the market crashes of 1987 and 2001–2003. In fact, market observers have often commented that portfolio insurance strategies may have exacerbated the decline in stocks during that period as a result of forced sales from protected puts. While there is improved liquidity in the derivatives markets from that period, medical professionals should consider the implication of various derivatives strategies in the face of an imbalance between supply and demand before using such strategies for their investment portfolio.

While options can be useful risk management or speculative tools, the nature of these derivative securities should be understood by the medical professional before using them in an investment portfolio strategy. First, because options represent an agreed upon potential transaction between two parties, one key issue to consider with options is counterparty risk or the risk that the writer of the option is unable to deliver on the promised transaction. Also, it is important for an investor to understand that options tend to be extremely volatile relative to the underlying security, since small changes in price of the underlying security around the option's strike price may result in dramatic changes in the value of the option.

[2] FUTURES

One final derivative security type to be discussed in this section is a future. A future represents the purchase of a particular investment at a predetermined date. Futures are traded on a wide range of investments (e.g., baskets of stocks, interest rates, currencies, and commodities) and are useful tools for controlling the risk of cash flow timing for those who wish to lock in a particular price for a security. Likewise, they also provide some insight on the expected future price in the market of the security. The key difference between futures and options is that futures obligate both parties to make the agreed upon transaction, whereas options give the option holder the right, but not the requirement, to make the transaction.

Futures are typically traded on an organized exchange, such as the Chicago Board of Trade (e.g., interest rate and stock index futures) or the Chicago Mercantile Exchange (e.g., foreign exchange and stock futures). The design of the contract traded on an exchange typically includes a pre-defined contract size and delivery month. Also, futures transactions generally require maintaining a margin deposit (i.e., a fraction of the trade value held in reserve to help ensure the final settlement at the contract settlement date) and the recognition of gains and losses on a daily basis with movements in contract prices. The pricing of a futures contract is based upon the price of the underlying security (e.g., the S&P 500 Index price), the opportunity cost of cash (e.g., current borrowing rates), and any distributions expected from the security over the period (e.g., dividends). A "no arbitrage" pricing formula, in which an investor could not earn a risk-free profit from selling the security and buying the future or vice versa, is as follows:

$$F = S\left[1 + \frac{rt}{360}\right] - D_t$$

In this formula, F is the futures price, S is the current security price, r is the current interest rate for the period of the futures contract, t is the period of the contract, and D_t is the distributions over the period.

One of the key uses of futures contracts is to hedge an underlying exposure in a portfolio that may be a source of unwanted risk. For example, an investor may wish to own a particular foreign company's stock (e.g., a European stock), but avoid the risk of an adverse movement in the local currency of the stock (e.g., the Euro) compared with the dollar. By using a futures contract, the investor may be able to lock in a future exchange rate of the currency and limit the risk of a fall in the spot price of the currency adversely affecting the value of the investment. In our example, any gain in the futures transaction will offset the unrealized loss in the stock that relates to a drop in the Euro exchange rate. The price of a foreign exchange futures contract may be defined as follows:

$$F = \frac{S\left[1 + \frac{r_1 t}{360}\right]}{\left[1 + \frac{r_2 t}{360}\right]}$$

In this case, r_1 represents the domestic interest rate, and r_2 represents the foreign interest rate, while S is the spot price for the currency.

While the formula above represents the price expected under a "no arbitrage" condition in which there is "parity" between the spot price and the futures price, it is important to remember that futures are traded on exchanges. Therefore, futures are influenced by supply and demand factors that may impact their price over any period. That is, if there are not enough buyers to offset the supply created by sellers of a futures contract, then deviations from the "no arbitrage" price may be sustained. It is such dislocations caused by periods of low liquidity that can cause futures contract mispricing and imperfect hedges.

Therefore, most derivative securities may be best understood as a series of cash flows contingent upon the price of underlying assets at specific dates and/or events. While derivatives may be useful to satisfy a particular investor's needs, these securities often have clear risks that should be considered and understood by a prudent investor. Thus, derivatives may be an important tool to manage the risk of failing to achieve a specific goal for an investor, but derivatives are not typically considered a separate asset class having a central place in most approaches to modern portfolio construction.

[E] Commodities

A commodity is a standardized asset that is typically used as an input for production of one or more products. Almost any raw material or product that has very consistent characteristics irrespective of the producer (i.e., little to no differentiation between producers) may be considered a commodity. Examples of commodities that are traded broadly in the financial markets include food products, such as wheat and pork bellies, and metals, such as gold and aluminum. In most cases, the trading of commodities is done through futures.

Commodities do not have ongoing cash payments associated with them. Instead, a commodity's value is a result of supply and demand for the asset as a consumable or as an input for other goods. Thus, while some investors use commodity futures as a hedge to offset changes in the value of the commodity between now and the date the commodity is needed by the investor, others will make commodity investments based upon a belief that the supply/demand relationship will change in their favor. In the latter case, commodities represent a knowledge-based market in which an investor must believe that he or she has a better perspective on the future price of the commodity than other speculators. Consequently, if an investor does not have superior information regarding the future supply and demand for the commodity, then commodity investments become generally less attractive as compared to investments providing ongoing cash payments.

[F] Collectibles

So far, the focus of the discussion on investments has been on securities representing legal title to an underlying stream of cash payments. However, many medical professionals have a broad range of investments that typically do not include securities and rarely provide entitlement to specific cash flows.

One example is *collectibles*, which are durable real property expected to store value for the owner. The term collectible may represent such items as artwork, jewelry, sports memorabilia, stamps, and wine.

While a detailed discussion of the wide variety of collectibles markets is outside the scope of this chapter, there are common characteristics of collectibles as an investment. First, the value of a collectible generally rests entirely in the eye of the beholder. Since typically no cash flows are associated with a collectible unless the collector charges at the door for a look at the collection, the value of the collectible is only what another collector is willing to pay for that particular item. Also, while there are some collectibles that may be considered standardized across individual pieces in terms of quality and other defining characteristics, collectible investments are generally unique. As a result, there is typically not an active market with prices established on a regular basis for most collectibles in a manner similar to the stock and bond markets.

The lack of ongoing cash payments from a collectible, and the general noncomparability of items result in the collectibles market being more of a knowledge-based market than most of the investments discussed previously. Since the value of a collectible is limited to the amount that another collector is willing to pay for the item, a knowledgeable investor may be able to benefit from the lack of information of another investor. By the same token, if an investor does not have superior information regarding the value of a collectible, then the basic lack of economic fundamentals behind a return assumption for such investments makes collectibles generally less attractive as compared with investments providing ongoing cash payments.

Investment Vehicles

To illustrate this point, the chapter has covered fundamentally distinct asset classes or broad security types. In general, medical professionals are able to access these securities either directly with a brokerage account or through a separate account manager who buys securities for them on a discretionary basis. However, many investors who are building their own investment portfolio or are working with a Certified Financial Planner or other financial advisor will have a host of different investment vehicles (e.g., mutual funds or variable annuities) available that provide indirect exposure to the basic security types discussed above. When one of these investment vehicles is considered for investment, it is important for the medical professional to understand the characteristics of that vehicle, its cost structure, and the cash flows and valuations represented by the underlying investments of the vehicle.

[A] Separate Account Management

Separate account management offers physicians customized personal money management services. In the typical separate account structure, a money manager invests the individual's assets in stocks and bonds (as opposed to mutual funds providing exposure to specific asset classes) on a discretionary basis. For healthcare providers with significant investment assets (e.g., $100,000), a separately managed portfolio can be customized to reflect their tax situation, social investment guidelines, and cash flow needs. An additional benefit of the separate account management structure is that a client's portfolio may be positioned over time as opportunities arise, rather than forcing stocks into the portfolio without regard to current conditions. Although separate account management generally offers a higher degree of customization than mutual funds, fees for separate account management are generally consistent with mutual funds fees, especially considering that separate account managers may discount their fees for larger portfolios.

[B] Mutual Funds

Mutual funds are one of the most common investment vehicles available. A mutual fund is an investment company registered with the Securities and Exchange Commission (SEC) under the Investment Company Act of 1940. The mutual fund invests in securities in a manner consistent with the fund's prospectus on behalf of its shareholders. In other words, a mutual fund represents (equity) ownership of a company that is regulated by the SEC and makes investments based upon the terms outlined in its prospectus. Mutual funds generally provide investors diversified exposure to the securities markets at lower investment amounts than separate account management. In fact, the minimum investment in many mutual funds is as low as $2000. Thus, by pooling assets from multiple investors in an investment vehicle managed toward a broad goal such as capital growth (as opposed to a customized goal unique to each investor), mutual funds can offer investors access to areas of the financial markets that they would not otherwise be able to gain due to minimum investment restrictions.

The prospectus is a legal document describing the objectives, guidelines, restrictions, and disclosures of the investment company. A key reason why mutual fund advertisements end with a statement similar to "read the prospectus carefully before you invest" is that this document governs the management decisions made for shareholders. Typically, the prospectus will provide the investment manager of the mutual fund wide latitude in the types of securities that may be purchased in the mutual fund. A fund that focuses on domestic equity investments may have flexibility to allocate significant portions of assets to foreign stocks, bonds, derivatives, and other assets. Thus, while mutual funds are often separated in databases and by the media into categories reflecting the basic type of investments their managers may focus on, these broad categories may fail to capture the broad flexibility and wide array of investments in any one of the funds within a category.

Two basic types of mutual funds are open-end and closed-end. An open-end mutual fund is a mutual fund that accepts new investors and allows investors to sell the fund at a specific price determined by the investor's prorated share of the market value of the fund. That price, known as net asset value (NAV), represents the market value of the mutual fund's portfolio less any accrued liabilities (e.g., management fees). The NAV is calculated once a day and governs all transactions until the next closing price.

In contrast, a closed-end mutual fund is a mutual fund that is traded in the stock market in a similar manner as any other equity security with buy and sell prices established by supply and demand for the security. Thus, in contrast to an open-end fund, a closed-end fund might possibly trade at a substantial discount, which means at a price below its NAV, or even at a premium, which means a price above its NAV.

In the case of both closed-end and open-end funds, the cost structure of the mutual fund is defined by its expense ratio, which is calculated by dividing the costs of managing the investment company (i.e., including marketing, management fees, and other costs) by the net assets of the fund. Based upon data from the January 2003 Morningstar database, the average open-end fund expense ratio is 1.46% for a domestic stock fund, 1.83% for a foreign stock fund, and 1.10% for a bond fund.

On top of the expense ratio, an open-end mutual fund may have a sales charge or load, which is the percentage of an investor's assets that will be deducted to pay the advisor or broker selling the fund. Sales charges range anywhere from 0.00–8.00% and may be deducted as a front-end load upon original investment, a back-end load upon liquidation of the fund, or some combination of the two. A no-load fund is an open-end mutual fund that does not deduct sales charges from the balances of the investor. Additional fees may be paid to the distributor of the fund (i.e., the broker or advisor) in the form of marketing 12b-1 fees, which are charges already included in the expense ratio that represent payments for fund distribution. For closed-end funds, the average expense ratio is 1.42% for a domestic stock fund, 1.89% for a foreign stock fund, and 1.15% for a bond fund according to the January 2003 Morningstar Closed End Fund database. While sales charges do not apply to closed-end funds, transactions costs such as brokerage commissions apply to the purchase/sale of a closed-end fund.

[C] Exchange Traded Funds

Exchange traded funds (ETFs) or tracking stocks are essentially index funds that are traded on an organized stock exchange. ETFs provide investors with broad exposure to economic sectors, and market indices, including foreign stock markets. Examples of common ETFs include Spiders (SPY–tracking the S&P 500), Diamonds (DIA–tracking the Dow Jones Industrial Average), and Cubes (QQQ–tracking the NASDAQ 100). Beyond their diversification benefits, ETFs also allow investors the opportunity to take advantage of intra-day price fluctuation in various indices since the shares are traded just like individual stocks. In contrast, an open-end index mutual fund can be traded only at one price (i.e., NAV), determined at the end of the day. Furthermore, the fact that ETFs are traded on an organized exchange means that investors can short the shares (i.e., bet that the relevant index will go down), buy the securities on margin, and enter market, limit, and/or stop orders. ETFs typically have low expense ratios given the passive investment approach used in managing the underlying securities. However, recent entries to the ETF market have had annual expense ratios approaching 1.00% of net assets, so healthcare providers considering utilizing ETFs should monitor their costs, including trading costs (i.e., commissions) and annual expense ratios.

[D] Banks

A third provider of investment vehicles is a bank. While many banks have mutual funds registered with the SEC, a bank may also develop commingled funds under the banking regulations. The two most prevalent types of bank-maintained funds are the collective fund, which is a commingled fund for Internal Revenue Service qualified retirement plans, and the common fund, which is a pooled fund for nonqualified plans or individual investors.

In essence, bank-maintained commingled funds are trusts over which the sponsoring bank has discretionary management responsibility. Non-mutual fund pools sponsored by banks are generally passthrough entities in which the investor owns a prorated share of the underlying securities in the portfolio of the fund. In the case of collective funds, this passthrough feature has the added benefit of making the banking institution a fiduciary under the Employee Retirement Income Securities Act for the investment decisions being made on behalf of each individual plan. While a common or collective fund may have a standardized fee schedule deducted from the portfolio like an expense ratio, these funds often have individually negotiated fees on a client-by-client basis and should be evaluated on a case-by-case basis accordingly.

[E] Investment Trusts and Limited Partnerships

A final category of investment vehicles includes limited partnerships and investment trusts. These commingled funds are not considered mutual funds, insurance funds, or bank-maintained funds from a regulatory oversight point-of-view. Instead, these vehicles represent a specific contractual relationship between the investor and the management company. A unit investment trust (UIT) represents proportional ownership of a generally static portfolio of securities. The securities underlying the UIT are typically fixed income securities, with maturity of the securities resulting in liquidation of the trust and a return of principal to the investor. Generally, a management fee is deducted from the UIT on an annual basis.

In a limited partnership, the investor is a partner providing financial backing and having a liability equal to the original investment. In contrast, a general partner has responsibility for management of the entity and broader personal liability for the endeavor. Examples of limited partnerships as investment vehicles providing access to a pool of securities or property include oil and gas partnerships, real estate partnerships, and hedge funds.

[F] Hedge Funds

A hedge fund in the United States is generally a limited partnership providing a limited number of qualified investors with access to general partner investment decisions with little restriction in the type of investments or use of leverage. While the flexibility available to a hedge fund from a regulatory standpoint implies a high degree of potential risk, a wide range of investment philosophies, strategies, security types, and objectives are captured under the broad title of hedge fund. Thus, generalizations regarding the characteristics of hedge funds are even less appropriate than for mutual funds, and evaluation of the investment characteristics and merits of a hedge fund strategy must be on a case-by-case basis. Likewise, the cost structure of a hedge fund often includes a base management fee to the general partner plus a performance-based fee or percentage of the profits, and must be evaluated on a case-by-case basis.

Several different investment vehicles under the oversight of varying regulatory bodies provide access to an investment manager's discretionary decisions. While each approach generally represents ownership of an underlying pool of securities, the manager usually has a great deal of flexibility to deviate from a specific asset class or investment approach. Also, the fee structure of each vehicle can be quite large and vary greatly once distribution fees and sales charges are taken into account. Thus, it is important for a medical professional to remember the following:

- Evaluate the features and costs of an investment vehicle carefully;
- Consider the cash flows and valuations of the securities that the manager or management approach will focus on as if the investments were being made directly; and
- Above all, read the prospectus or agreement carefully before making an investment.

Chapter 7

Professional Portfolio Management

Identifying Appropriate Investments . . . Constructing a Proper Portfolio

Jeffrey S. Coons
Christopher J. Cummings

Modern portfolio theory is the philosophical opposite of traditional stock picking. It is the creation of economists, who try to understand the market as a whole, rather than business analysts, who look for what makes each investment opportunity unique. Investments are described statistically, in terms of their expected long-term return rate and their expected short-term volatility. The volatility is equated with "risk," measuring how much worse than average an investment's bad years are likely to be. The goal is to identify your acceptable level of risk tolerance, and then to find a portfolio with the maximum expected return for that level of risk.

MoneyChimp.com

Securities and investment vehicles are an important part of a successful investment program, just as pharmaceutical ingredients or medical devices are needed as part of a patient's treatment. However, the importance of securities and investment vehicles is their usefulness in the pursuit of an investor's financial needs and objectives. The process of identifying appropriate investments and constructing a portfolio consistent with an investor's goals is known as portfolio management. The asset allocation decision is generally the most important part of that process.

Setting Objectives

The portfolio management process begins with the medical professional's investment objectives for a given portfolio. In general, establishing reasonable investment objectives requires prioritization of various risk management goals, since there is often a trade-off between coverage of one investment risk and exposure to another. While most investors would like to have a portfolio that beats the stock market every year and never loses money over any single year, such investments simply do not exist (irrespective of any manager or fund's marketing material to the contrary). Therefore, when the medical professional sets the goals for a given portfolio, he or she should identify the basic need he or she has for these assets and the time horizon over which that need will be realized.

Example: Dr. Mary S. Wells expects to work for 25 years before she retires. She has a 401(k) plan that represents all her retirement savings. While one risk is lost capital over this full time period, her long-term time horizon makes such an event less likely. A more important risk management priority, on the other hand, is long-term growth of capital and avoiding opportunity cost. The priority for this investor would be a primary goal of long-term capital growth and a distant secondary goal of avoiding sustained losses over an intermediate-term time period.

Example: Dr. James K. Mattey is a retired physician who has donated a significant part of his assets to a charitable remainder trust from which he is receiving 8% of market value annually to meet his ongoing living needs. In this case, dampening volatility of returns is important since an 8% withdrawal after a significant drop in the portfolio's value may be difficult to overcome with future growth and may mean lower distributions to meet ongoing living expenses. Thus, while long-term growth above the withdrawal percentage is helpful to grow capital for the charity and future spending needs, the primary goal for this investor needs to be stability of total returns.

Asset Allocation

Once the risk management goals and objectives for the portfolio have been identified and prioritized, the next step is to build a mix of investments that will best balance any conflicting goals. Asset allocation is defined as the portfolio's mix between different types of investments such as stocks, bonds, and cash. The goal of any asset allocation should be to provide a level of diversification for the portfolio, while also balancing the goals of growth and preservation of capital required to meet the medical professional's objectives. Establishing the appropriate asset allocation for an investor's portfolio is widely considered the most important factor in determining whether or not he or she meets his or her investment objectives. For example, academic studies have determined that more than 90% of a portfolio's return can be attributed to the asset allocation decision.[1]

How do investors and their advisors typically make asset allocation decisions? One method is best characterized as a passive approach, in which a set mix of stocks, bonds, and cash is maintained based on their historical risk/return trade-off. The alternative is an active approach, in which the mix among various asset classes is established based upon the current and expected future market and economic environment.

In addition to pursuing a passive investment strategy such as indexing, medical professionals who support the notion that market prices accurately reflect all available information generally are not concerned with the timing of their investment decisions. The strategy most frequently used to avoid a market timing decision when establishing an initial allocation to stocks is referred to as dollar cost averaging. Dollar cost averaging entails investing the same amount of money at regular intervals. For example, an investor who wishes to dollar cost average may decide to invest 1/24 of the allocation on the first of each month for two years rather than investing the full amount immediately or trying to time buys when stocks are trading at a low point. Value-cost averaging does the same thing with the same number of shares, rather than the same dollar amount, for its regular intervals.

Modern Portfolio Theory

Modern portfolio theory (MPT) is the basic economic model that establishes a linear relationship between the return and risk of an investment. The tools of MPT are used as the basis for the passive asset mix, which involves setting a static mix of various types of investments or asset classes and rebalancing to that allocation target on a periodic basis.

According to MPT, when building a diversified investment portfolio, the goal should be to obtain the highest expected return for a given level of risk. A key assumption underlying modern portfolio theory is that higher risk generally translates to higher expected returns. From the perspective of MPT, risk is defined simply as the variability of an investment's returns. While MPT is based upon the idea that expected volatility of returns is used, risk is measured by standard deviation of historical returns in practice. Standard deviation is a measure of the dispersion of a security's returns, $X_1, ..., X_n$, around its mean (or average) return, $\overline{X}$, and is calculated as follows:

$$\sigma = \sqrt{\frac{\left(X_1 - \overline{X}\right)^2 + \left(X_2 - \overline{X}\right)^2 + ... + \left(X_n - \overline{X}\right)^2}{n-1}}$$

Standard deviation is often calculated using monthly or quarterly data points but is represented as an annualized number to correspond with annualized returns of various investments. The formula for annualized standard deviation of returns, $\sigma_{ann.}$, when there are n periods in a year, is as follows:

$$\sigma_{ann.} = \sqrt{\left[\sigma^2 + \left(1 + \overline{X}\right)^2\right]^n - \left(1 + \overline{X}\right)^{2n}}$$

Assume Stock A has a mean return of 10% and a standard deviation of 7.5%. Then, approximately 68% of Stock A's returns are within one standard deviation of the mean return, and 95% of Stock A's returns are within two standard deviations. In other words, 68% of Stock A's returns should be between 2.5% and 17.5%, and 95% of the returns for Stock A should be between negative 5% and 25%. However, a key assumption underlying this logic is that the returns for Stock A are normally distributed (i.e., including that the distribution curve of Stock A's returns is symmetrical around the mean). Unfortunately, in reality security returns may not be symmetrically distributed and, as we will discuss later, both the mean return and standard deviation of returns may shift dramatically over time.

There are many different sources of risk, but the two forms of risk hypothesized by Harry Markowitz, PhD, father of MPT, are systematic risk and unsystematic risk.[2] Systematic risk is sometimes referred to as nondiversifiable risk, since it affects the returns on all investments. In the capital asset pricing model (CAPM), systematic risk is defined as sensitivity to the overall market, while arbitrage pricing theory (APT) has several common macroeconomic and market factors that are considered sources of systematic risk. Investors are generally unable to diversify systematic risk, since they cannot reduce their portfolio's exposure to systematic risk by increasing the number of securities in their portfolio. In contrast, diversifying an investment portfolio can reduce unsystematic risk or the risk specific to a particular investment. Sources of unsystematic risk include a stock's company-specific risk and industry risk. For example, in addition to the risk of a falling stock market, investors in Merck also are exposed to risks unique to the pharmaceutical industry (e.g., healthcare reform), as well as the risks specific to Merck's business practices (e.g., success of research and development efforts, patent time frames). An investor can reduce unsystematic risk by building a portfolio of securities from numerous industries, countries, and classes of assets. Thus, portfolio risk in MPT refers to both systematic (nondiversifiable) and nonsystematic (diversifiable) risk, but a basic conclusion of MPT is that no investor would rationally take on nonsystematic risk since this risk could be diversified away.

Figure 7–1 illustrates that portfolio risk tends to be a function of the number of securities held in a portfolio.

Figure 7–2 provides a graphical representation of several hypothetical securities' expected returns and level of risk (as measured by standard deviation). Again, the theory is that higher returns correspond to higher risk and that investors typically desire to earn the highest return per a given level of risk. Using a trade-off between expected return and volatility of returns to make investment decisions is known as the mean-variance framework and is the central concept in many of today's passive asset allocation portfolio management principles.

The line connecting all points representing the highest return for each level of risk, or, its equivalent, the lowest risk for a given level of return on the mean-variance graph is called the efficient frontier. Thus, any portfolio with level of return below the efficient frontier would be considered inefficient, since an investor could earn a higher return without increasing his or her risk exposure by simply moving up to the point on the efficient frontier that corresponds to the given level of risk. An investor's tolerance for risk determines where on the efficient frontier he or she would find his or her optimal port-

Figure 7–1 *Portfolio Risk*

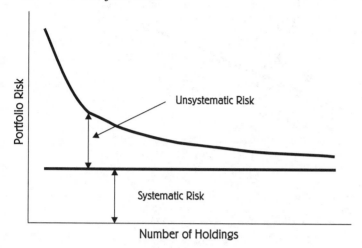

Figure 7–2 *Mean-Variance Framework*

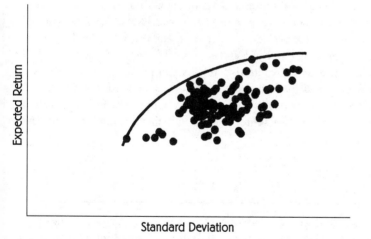

folio. An investor's optimal portfolio is the portfolio that is expected to provide the highest return per level of risk, up to the maximum amount of risk that the investor is willing to take.

While all investments entail risk, a key tenet in MPT is the existence of a risk-free rate of return. In practice, 30-day or 90-day U.S. Treasury Bills are often viewed as risk-free assets, since their return is guaranteed over the time period of the analysis (i.e., 30 or 90 days) and principal and interest payments are backed by the full faith and credit of the U.S. government. MPT holds that an investor's true efficient frontier is represented by the tangency line running from the risk-free rate of return through the optimal portfolio of risky assets. The best combination of return and risk lies on this tangency line,

Figure 7-3 *The CML Concept*

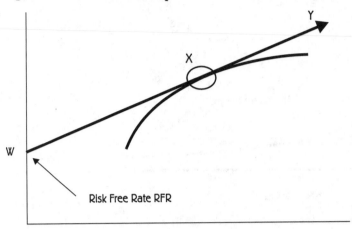

Risk Free Rate RFR

referred to as the capital market line (CML), which also represents the linear relationship between return and risk discussed earlier.

Figure 7-3 provides a graphical representation of the CML concept. According to MPT, an investor can maximize his or her return per a given level of risk by investing in various combinations of the risk-free asset (i.e., T-Bills) and the optimal risky portfolio (i.e., X). The investor can assume zero risk and earn the risk-free rate of return, or he or she can substitute the risky asset for the risk-free asset in pursuit of higher expected returns. Line WXY represents the best combination of risk and return available to an investor, although the part of the line to the right of the optimal portfolio (X) is attainable only by borrowing funds at the risk-free rate and investing the proceeds in the risky asset (i.e., the optimal portfolio).

Capital Asset Pricing Model

While Dr. Markowitz is credited with developing the framework for constructing investment portfolios based on the risk-return trade-off, William Sharpe,[3] John Lintner,[4] and Jan Mossin[5] are credited with developing the CAPM. CAPM is an economic model based upon the idea that there is a single portfolio representing all investments (i.e., the market portfolio) at the point of the optimal portfolio on the CML and a single source of systematic risk, beta, to that market portfolio. The conclusion is that investors should expect a "fair" return given the level of risk (beta) they are willing to assume. The CAPM equation is as follows:

$$E(R_j) = R_f + [E(R_m) - R_f] \, \beta_j$$

Thus, the excess return, or return above the risk-free rate, that may be expected from an asset is equal to the risk-free return plus the excess return of the market portfolio times the sensitivity of the asset's excess return to the market portfolio excess return. Beta, then, is a measure of the sensitivity of an asset's returns to the market as a whole. A particular security's beta depends on the volatility of the individual security's returns relative to the volatility of the market's returns, as well as the correlation between the security's returns and the market's returns. Thus, while a stock may have significantly greater volatility than the market, if that stock's returns are not highly correlated with the returns of the overall market (i.e., the stock's returns are independent of the overall market's returns), then the stock's beta would be relatively low. A beta in excess of 1.0 implies that the security is more exposed to systematic risk than the overall market portfolio, and likewise, a beta of less 1.0 means that the security has less exposure to systematic risk than the overall market.

The CAPM uses beta to determine the security market line (SML). The SML determines the required or expected rate of return given the security's exposure to systematic risk, the risk-free rate, and the expected return for the market as a whole. The SML is similar in concept to the CML, although there is a key difference. Both concepts capture the relationship between risk and expected returns. However, the measure of risk used in determining the CML is standard deviation, whereas the measure of risk used in determining the SML is beta. Thus, the CML estimates the potential return for a diversified portfolio relative to an aggregate measure of risk (i.e., standard deviation), while the SML estimates the return of a single security relative to its exposure to systematic risk. Figure 7–4 illustrates the SML and highlights the relationship between systematic risk and expected return.

There are several problems identified by academics regarding CAPM, not the least of which is the fact that a market portfolio of all assets is not measurable. A second shortcoming of CAPM is that it assumes systematic risk, as measured by beta, is the only factor determining an individual security's expected return. Thus, CAPM assumes that a particular security's volatility relative to the volatility of the overall market is the relevant

Figure 7–4 *Security Market Line*

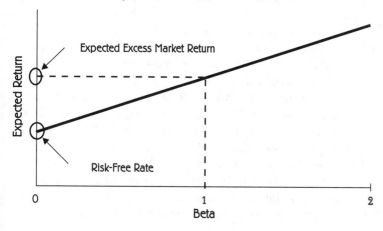

measure of systematic risk. In practice, many systematic factors beyond only market volatility influence a given security's returns. For example, inflation, interest rate changes, and gross national product (GNP) growth are systematic factors that impact all securities. However, the degree varies to which they impact different securities' returns.

Arbitrage Pricing Theory

Stephen Ross developed a more generalized MPT model called arbitrage pricing theory (APT):

$$E\left(R_i\right) - R_f = \left[\overline{\delta}_1 - R_f\right]b_{i1} + \ldots + \left[\overline{\delta}_k - R_f\right]b_{ik}$$

APT is based upon somewhat less restrictive assumptions than CAPM and results in the conclusion that there are multiple factors representing systematic risk. Thus, APT incorporates the fact that different securities react in varying degrees to unexpected changes in systematic factors other than just beta to the market portfolio. The risk-free return plus the expected return for exposure to each source of systematic risk times the beta coefficient to that risk is what determines the expected rate of return for a given security. An important point to keep in mind is that the APT focuses on unexpected changes for its systematic risk factors. The financial markets are viewed as a discounting mechanism with prices established for various securities reflecting investors' expectations about the future. Any excess return for an expected change will be arbitraged away (i.e., the price of that risk will be bid down to zero). For example, market prices already reflect investors' expectations about GNP growth, so prices of assets should only react to the extent that GNP growth either exceeds or falls short of expectations (i.e., an unexpected change in GNP growth).

Why do medical professionals and their advisors make mistakes in passive asset allocation decisions using MPT? The problem is less related to the limitations of CAPM or APT as theories, but more related to how they apply these theories in the real world. The basic premise behind the various MPT models is that both return and risk measures are the expectations assessed by the investor. Too often, however, decisions are made based on what investors see in their rear view mirror rather than what lies on the road ahead of them. In other words, while modern portfolio theory is geared toward assessing expected future returns and risk, investors and financial professionals all too often simply rely on historical data rather than on developing a forecast of expected future returns and risks. It is clearly difficult for investors to accurately forecast future returns or betas, whether they be for the market as a whole or an individual security. However, no reason supports the belief that simply using historical data will be more accurate. Thus, one major shortcoming of modern portfolio theory as commonly applied today is that historical relationships between different securities are unstable.

As an example, Table 7–1 uses Ibbotson data to show that the average returns and volatility for various asset classes, as well as the correlation between asset classes, may

Table 7-1 *20-Year Time Periods (1926 through 2002)*

	Low	*High*
• Annualized Returns		
• Stocks	2.19%	18.25%
• Bonds	0.69%	12.99%
• T-Bills	0.42%	7.73%
• Volatility (Annualized Standard Deviation of Quarterly Returns)		
• Stocks	14.02%	42.21%
• Bonds	3.86%	14.70%
• T-Bills	0.22%	1.55%
• Correlation		
• Stock/Bond	–0.18	0.49
• Stock/T-Bills	–0.42	0.18
• Bond/T-Bills	–0.28	0.28

fluctuate meaningfully over even long-term periods (i.e., 20 years). Thus, a physician or other healthcare provider should not rely on historical averages to establish a passive asset allocation.

The use of unstable historical returns in modern portfolio theories clearly violates the rule of thumb related to the dangers of projecting forward historical averages. However, MPT is an important concept for medical professionals to understand as a result of its frequent use by investment professionals. Further, MPT has helped focus investors on two extremely critical elements of successful investment strategies. First, MPT offers the first framework for investors to build a diversified portfolio. Furthermore, an important conclusion drawn from MPT is that diversification does help reduce portfolio risk. Thus, MPT approaches are generally consistent with the first investment rule of thumb, "understand and diversify risk to the extent possible." Additionally, the risk/return trade-off (i.e., higher returns are generally consistent with higher risk) central to MPT-based strategies has helped investors recognize that if it looks too good to be true, it probably is.

Active Asset Allocation

For healthcare providers and their advisors who believe that the financial markets misprice securities from time to time, especially for investors with different time horizons, an active investment selection strategy is likely to make sense. Investors who feel that the markets either overreact or underreact to a given piece of news related to a specific security are generally willing to commit their time and resources or to hire an investment manager who can find mispriced securities. For example, a medical professional with a long time horizon may feel that the financial markets are too focused on the near-term following a decline in a pharmaceutical company's stock from a disappointing Food and Drug Administration report. While the short-term disappointment associated with an unsuccessful research and development effort may be significant, long-term investors may believe that the company's product pipeline as a whole is strong and that the company's long-term future is still very bright. Thus, the healthcare provider may feel that the markets have overreacted to a short-term variable and lost sight of the long-term prospects for the particular investment. The investor may conclude that the financial markets have mispriced the security relative to his or her time horizon and expectations regarding the company's future.

If active asset allocation makes sense based upon the limitations of passive asset allocation in managing risk over even long periods of time, how do investors and their advisors make active asset allocation decisions? Two distinct active asset allocation approaches are used by financial professionals to build an investment portfolio. The top-down method and the bottom-up method differ based on how important economic and industry variables are to the decision-making process relative to individual security variables. The top-down approach establishes and adjusts asset allocation based primarily upon an overview of the overall economy and/or the industry in which the particular security operates. In contrast, bottom-up portfolio management approaches are geared toward identifying attractive investments on a security-by-security basis.

[A] Top-Down Approach

Advocates of the top-down approach generally begin their investment process by formulating an outlook for the domestic economy; and, in certain circumstances, the outlook is constructed for the global economy. This approach may be a direct result of a quantitative model using various market and economic data as input to reach a conclusion regarding the best asset mix on a tactical basis. On the other hand, it may be a more subjective process resulting from a qualitative assessment of the market and economic outlook. In developing an economic overview for qualitative top-down asset allocation decisions, the medical professional and/or his advisors typically consider factors such as monetary policy, fiscal policy, trade relations, and inflation. Clearly, macroeconomic factors such as those listed above are likely to have a significant impact on the performance of a wide range of investment alternatives. After a thorough analysis of the overall economy has been completed, top-down investors will either buy broad baskets of stocks representing an asset class or perform an analysis of industries that they believe will benefit from the economic overview that has been developed. Factors that may influence the attractiveness of particular industries include regulatory environment, supply and demand of resources, taxes, and import/export quotas. The top-down approach generally views the best company in a weak industry as being unlikely to provide satisfactory returns. The final step in the top-down process involves analyzing individual companies in industries that are expected to benefit from the forecasted economic environment.

[B] Bottom-Up Approach

In contrast, investors employing a bottom-up approach will focus their attention on identifying securities that are priced below the investor's estimate of their value. Investors using the bottom-up approach to asset allocation and portfolio construction will only purchase securities deemed attractive according to their basic pricing and security selection criteria, thus adjusting the overall mix of investments by the limit of securities considered attractive at current valuations. A truly bottom-up approach will consider economic and industry factors as clearly secondary in identifying investment opportunities. Investors using this approach will focus solely on company analysis. However, these investors must recognize that investment decisions cannot be made in a vacuum. Macroeconomic factors, as well as industry characteristics and traits, are likely to be key elements in identifying attractive investment opportunities even on a security-by-security basis.

The key to bottom-up asset allocation and portfolio management is to understand that the decision variables driving the basic mix of assets in the portfolio are more related to the availability of attractive individual investments than to a general top-down market or economic overview.

[C] Technical Analysis

There are two distinct forms of analysis often used by investors who desire to pursue an active investment strategy. The first strategy is referred to as technical analysis. Technical analysts, sometimes referred to as chartists, use historical price and transaction volume data to identify mispriced securities. A key belief shared by technical analysts is that stock prices follow recurring patterns. These analysts believe that once these historical patterns are identified, the patterns can be used to identify future security prices. The cornerstone of technical analysis is identifying significant shifts in the supply and demand factors for a particular investment. Skeptics of technical analysis generally subscribe to the notion that the markets efficiently and accurately price securities. In fact, the weak form of the efficient market hypothesis is based on the view that investors cannot consistently earn superior returns using historical data alone.

[D] Fundamental Analysis

In contrast to technical analysis, which relies on historical market return/transactions data, fundamental analysis focuses on the underlying company's earnings, risk, dividends, and economic factors to identify mispriced securities. The central theme behind fundamental analysis is the determination of a security's intrinsic value or the value that is justified by the security's earnings, assets, dividends, or other economic measures. While technical analysis focuses on market prices, a security's intrinsic value is determined independently of the security's market value. A medical professional utilizing fundamental analysis is attempting to find securities that are trading at market prices below their intrinsic value.

How do healthcare providers or their advisers determine a security's intrinsic value? The methods used to place a value on a stock are too numerous to list. The methods range from very simple methods (e.g., price-to-earnings multiplier) to much more complex methods (e.g., the dividend discount model).

The price-to-earnings multiplier method of determining a stock's fundamental value is appealing to certain investors because of its simplicity. Under the price-to-earnings multiplier method, a stock's intrinsic value is determined by multiplying the stock's expected earnings per share by the stock's expected price-to-earnings ratio. For example, if a physician feels that Stock Y will earn $2.00 per share and that a reasonable estimate for Stock Y's price-to-earnings ratio is 15, then Stock Y's intrinsic value as determined under the price-to-earnings multiplier method is $30. While the price-to-earnings multiplier method appears simple on the surface, an investor's success using this method lies not only in his or her ability to estimate a stock's earnings per share, but also the stock's price-to-earnings ratio. Unfortunately, it is often difficult to estimate the multiple to its earnings that a stock should trade. While an analysis of multiples of other stocks in the same industry may provide insight to what kind of earnings multiples could be reasonable, it is important for medical professionals to recognize that a stock's price-to-earnings ratio is determined by such factors as interest rates, stock market bullishness, and investor expectations regarding the company. Each of these variables can change dramatically in a short period of time.

The dividend discount model (DDM) is one of the most widely used valuation methods for estimating a stock's intrinsic value. As mentioned previously, a stock can be thought of as the right to receive future dividends. A stock's intrinsic value is defined as the present value of its dividends under the DDM. In its simplest form (i.e., zero-growth), the DDM determines a stock's value by dividing the stock's dividend by the investor's required rate of return. The investor's required rate of return should reflect current interest rates plus the risk associated with investing in the stock.

The rate of return determined under the CAPM is frequently used in the DDM. For example, assuming that ABC Corporation pays a $2.00 dividend per share and that an investor requires a 10% return for holding ABC stock, the stock's intrinsic value is $20 ($2 multiplied by 10%).

Shortcomings of the zero growth DDM include the following;

- The model assumes that the stock's dividends will remain constant over time;
- The model assumes that dividends are the only source of return available to stock investors and ignores the effect of reinvested earnings;
- The model can only be used to value stocks that pay dividends; and
- The model assumes that the company and the dividends will last forever.

Despite its shortcomings, the DDM highlights the point that the stock market is a discounting mechanism and that financial investments should be assessed in light of the future cash flows that they are expected to provide investors.

One variation on the DDM that may be appealing to healthcare professionals involves determining the present value of a stock's earnings rather than simply its dividends.

Theoretically, owning a stock entitles investors to a claim on the earnings of a company that are left after accounting for the company's costs (including interest costs). A model accounting for a stock's earnings rather than just its dividends may help account for the capital appreciation element of owning stocks. A corporation can either invest its earnings back into the company to pursue growth opportunities or distribute the earnings to shareholders in the form of dividends.

[E] Active Compared with Passive Asset Allocation

Can any single mix of stocks, bonds, and cash achieve the medical professional's needs across the various market environments that may arise over his or her investment time frame? If such a mix exists, then it is reasonable for a physician or other health care provider to maintain that particular passive (i.e., fixed) asset allocation. On the other hand, if no single mix exists that will certainly meet the portfolio's objectives over its time frame, then the investor must make some judgments regarding the best mix for the portfolio on a forward-looking basis. This case implies that some form of active decision making is required when determining a portfolio's asset allocation. To answer this question, let us consider the historical trade-off between the pursuit of growth and the need to preserve capital over various investment time frames.

Table 7–2 illustrates that a medical professional has to be willing to commit a majority of his or her assets to stocks to pursue capital growth. However, even an equity-oriented portfolio is not guaranteed to meet the medical professional's growth goals over a long-term time period. To provide a historical perspective using Ibbotson data, a mix of 50% stocks and 50% bonds provided an 8.4% annualized return from 1926 through 2002, but failed to surpass what many consider to be a modest return of 8% in approximately 45% of the rolling 10- and 20-year periods over this time. In fact, a portfolio of 100% stocks provided a 10.2% annualized return but failed to surpass 8% in almost one of every three 10-year periods and more than one of every four 20-year periods.

These data also reflect the difficulty throughout history of consistently achieving an 8% rate even with an aggressive mix of stocks and bonds. It is important to keep in mind

Table 7–2 *The Need for Growth*

U.S. Large Cap Stock/ Interm. Treasury Bond	20/80	40/60	50/50	60/40	80/20	100/0
Annualized Return (1926–2002):	6.8%	7.9%	8.4%	8.9%	9.7%	10.2%
% Periods with *Less* Than an 8% Return:						
Rolling 1-Year Periods	63.9%	46.9%	45.6%	44.3%	41.6%	40.7%
Rolling 3-Year Periods	69.0%	50.8%	46.8%	40.4%	35.0%	33.0%
Rolling 5-Year Periods	70.6%	56.1%	44.3%	41.9%	32.9%	29.4%
Rolling 10-Year Periods	70.6%	60.6%	46.5%	39.4%	33.1%	30.5%
Rolling 20-Year Periods	69.9%	67.7%	45.4%	31.0%	26.2%	24.9%

that taking more risk is no guarantee of higher returns. However, what is clear from these data is the importance of providing the flexibility to achieve meaningful exposure to stocks in attractive market environments to pursue the goal of long-term capital growth.

Of course, there is a clear risk of long-term declines in an equity-oriented investment approach, especially for a portfolio dealing with interim cash needs (e.g., ongoing withdrawal needs, required minimum distributions from qualified plans, etc.). An illustration of the sustained losses that might result from heavy allocations to stocks is the fact that one of every four one-year periods and one of every 10 five-year periods resulted in a loss for a portfolio of 100% stocks. Even the 50% stock and 50% bond portfolio had seen losses in almost one of every 5 one-year periods and more than one of every 25 five-year periods over the past 77 years of available Ibbotson data.

The data in Table 7–3 reflect the fact that no single mix of asset classes will satisfy an investor's conflicting goals of growth and preservation of capital in all market environments. Thus, a key factor influencing whether a health care provider should pursue a passive (or strategic) asset allocation approach or an active (or tactical) asset allocation approach is whether the investor believes that the financial markets generally offer returns commensurate with the risk entailed in the particular investment. To a large extent, this decision comes down to a conclusion of whether the medical professional believes the financial markets are efficient and that they accurately price securities based on the risk of owning those securities. The efficient market hypothesis (EMH) states that securities are fairly priced based on information regarding their underlying cash flows and that investors should not expect to consistently outperform the market over the long term.

There are three distinct forms of EMH that vary by the type of information that is reflected in a security's price:

Table 7–3 *The Need to Preserve Capital*

U.S. Large Cap Stock/ Interm. Treasury Bond	20/80	40/60	50/50	60/40	80/20	100/0
Annualized Return (1926–2002):	6.8%	7.9%	8.4%	8.9%	9.7%	10.2%
% Periods with Less Than a 0% Return:						
Rolling 1-Year Periods	11.2%	17.4%	20.3%	21.6%	24.9%	27.2%
Rolling 3-Year Periods	2.0%	4.0%	6.4%	9.1%	12.5%	14.8%
Rolling 5-Year Periods	0.0%	2.8%	4.2%	5.5%	8.3%	10.4%
Best/Worst Annualized Returns:						
Rolling 1-Year Periods	38.5%/ –17.0%	69.7%/ –32.6%	85.5%/ –39.7%	101.3%/ –46.2%	132.6%/ –57.7%	162.9% –67.6%
Rolling 3-Year Periods	20.1%/ –5.7%	23.1%/ –15.4%	26.5%/ –20.1%	29.5%/ –24.8%	36.3%/ –33.8%	43.0% –42.4%
Rolling 5-Year Periods	19.2%/ 0.1%	20.8%/ –-3.6%	21.9%/ –5.6%	24.6%/ –7.8%	30.0%/ –12.3%	34.8%/ –17.2%

- Weak Form

  Investors will not be able to use historical data to earn superior returns on a consistent basis. In other words, the financial markets price securities in a manner that fully reflects all information contained in past prices.

- Semi-Strong Form

  Security prices fully reflect all publicly available information. Therefore, investors cannot consistently earn above normal returns based solely on publicly available information such as earnings, dividend, and sales data.

- Strong Form

  The financial markets price securities so that all information (public and nonpublic) is fully reflected in the securities price; investors should not expect to earn superior returns on a consistent basis, no matter what insight or research they may bring to the table.

A rich literature has been established to test whether EMH actually applies in any of its three forms in real world markets. However, the most difficult evidence to overcome for backers of EMH is the vibrant money management and mutual fund industry charging value-added fees for its services. While there has been a growing move toward index funds as well, the strength of the money management industry may reflect investor concern with risk management and asset allocation as much as a view that a manager can "beat the market." Evidence of the view that active asset allocation is needed from a risk management perspective is reflected in Tables 7–4 and 7–5.

These tables (based on historical Ibbotson data) show the frequency of failing to achieve specific return goals is seen to increase when valuations in the market are relatively high, in this case when more than one dollar is paid for a dollar of corporate sales. Irrespective of whether an investor can "beat the market" through active management,

Table 7–4 *Failure Rates for Target Returns in Stock*

	One Year	Three Years	Five Years	Ten Years
5% target return	33%	18%	16%	11%
8% target return	39%	31%	26%	28%
10% target return	42%	42%	38%	40%

Table 7–5 *Failure Rates at High Valuations*

	One Year	Three Years	Five Years	Ten Years
5% target return	41%	33%	26%	41%
8% target return	46%	52%	48%	77%
10% target return	50%	62%	62%	97%

Note: Time Frame: 1955 through 2002. *Source:* Manning & Napier Advisors, Inc., 2003.

active asset allocation may be the effort to adjust the portfolio to changes in the risk/return trade-off among different types of investments.

The Impact of Taxes

The general goal of a medical professional's investment program should be to provide capital growth and control investment risk in line with his or her overall investment objectives. However, an important issue for medical professionals to keep in mind when evaluating their investment program is the tax implications of their investment decisions. Certain types of accounts, such as qualified retirement plans, Individual Retirement Accounts, and variable annuities, provide growth on a tax-deferred basis, so that income or capital gains earned within the account are not taxed until funds are withdrawn. As a result, investment decisions within these accounts may be made without concern for the interim tax implications of those decisions. In contrast, investors with nonqualified or taxable investment portfolios may incur taxes as the result of their investment decisions, and, therefore, they should understand the basic income tax implications of buying and selling securities.

[A] Capital Gains

The sale of a security typically results in either a capital gain, which results from shares being sold at a higher price than their original cost (after adjusting for splits and share spinoffs), or a capital loss, which results from shares sold at a price below their original cost. Capital gains and losses are categorized as either short-term or long-term depending on how the long the security was held. In order for a capital gain or loss to qualify as long-term, the underlying security being sold must have been held more than 12 months based upon the tax laws (as of this writing).

The Internal Revenue Code provides an incentive for investors to take a long-term view when making their investment decisions by taxing long-term capital gains at 20% (or 10% for taxpayers in the 15% or lower tax bracket), while short-term capital gains are taxed at the investor's marginal federal income tax rate, which can run as high as 38.6%. Thus, investors (especially those in high income tax rates) prefer long-term gains to short-term gains due to the tax rate differential (i.e., 20% versus 38.6%). As an additional incentive for investors to view their investments as long-term holdings, securities acquired after December 31, 2000, and held for more than five years will be subject to only an 18% capital gains rate.

Investors are generally allowed to reduce their capital gains by subtracting their capital losses, but long-term losses must be used to offset long-term gains before they can be used to offset short-term losses and vice versa. For example, an investor with $1000 in long-term losses, $500 in long-term gains, $500 in short-term losses, and $2000 in short-term gains must first net his or her long-term gains and losses (resulting in a $500 net long-term loss), followed by his or her short-term gains and losses (resulting in a net

$1500 short-term gain), and finally the $500 net long-term loss can be used to reduce the $1500 net short-term gain resulting in a $1000 overall short-term gain.

[1] THE JOBS AND GROWTH TAX RELIEF RECONCILIATION ACT OF 2003

However, since the Jobs and Growth Tax Relief Reconciliation Act of 2003, effective since May 6, 2003, the 10% and 20% tax rates on net capital gains have been reduced to 5 and 15%, respectively. The 5% rate becomes zero in 2008. The change to the maximum tax terminates after 2008, and in 2009 the law reverts back to the maximum rate of 20%.

Moreover, retroactive to January 1, 2003, dividends received by an individual physician shareholder from domestic and qualified foreign corporations will be taxed at a maximum capital gains rate of 15% until 2009. A 5% rate applies to physicians in the 10% and 15% brackets (the 5% rate becomes zero in 2008). This rate applies to both regular income tax and alternative minimum tax.

As an example, a married intern with $50,000 a year in taxable income in 2003 would have paid $200 in capital gains taxes on a $1000 stock sale profit and another $270 on $1000 in dividend income. Under the new law, the tax on the dividend income would be $50. The tax on the gain would be $50, and the total tax would be $100. The total tax savings is $370.

[B] Cost Basis

A key element in calculating capital gains is the concept of cost basis. To calculate the gain or loss on the sale of a particular security, the investor's cost basis, or the amount the investor originally paid to acquire the security adjusted for share splits, spinoffs, etc., is subtracted from the proceeds of the sale. Thus, a higher cost basis results in a lower capital gain, which in turn results in a lower capital gains tax liability.

The determination of cost basis is relatively straightforward in the case of a security that is purchased in one single transaction with no subsequent splits, with the security's cost basis equaling the total purchase price (including commissions and sales charges). However, there are several methods for determining the cost basis of a security that was acquired via multiple transactions, such as reinvested mutual fund dividends, systematic purchases (i.e., dollar cost averaging), or simply the purchase of multiple lots of the same stock at different points in time. The simplest method, which is available only for mutual fund investors, is referred to as the average cost method, where the security's cost basis is determined by calculating the weighted average purchase price. The last-in, first-out (LIFO) method assumes that the shares that were acquired most recently are the first shares sold, while the first-in, first-out (FIFO) method assumes that the shares that have been held the longest are the first shares sold. Finally, the specific shares method allows an investor to identify the specific shares that he or she sold. The following example illustrates these various methods of determining a security's cost basis:

Shares	Acquisition Date	Purchase Price
200	1/1/1997	$25.00
100	7/1/1998	$35.00

If the healthcare professional subsequently sells 150 shares of the security on December 31, 1999, what is his or her cost basis under the various methods?

Average Cost Method:	$28.33 [(200 × $25.00) + (100 × $35.00)]/300
LIFO Method:	$31.67 [(100 × $35.00) + (50 × $25.00)]/150
FIFO Method:	$25.00 (150 × $25.00)/150
Specific Shares Method:	$31.67 [(100 × $35.00) + (50 × $25.00)]/150

The specific shares calculation above assumes that the investor's goal is to minimize his or her capital gain by using the highest possible cost basis.

While medical professionals and their advisors should be aware of the tax implications of buying and selling securities in taxable investment portfolios, they must also not fall into the trap of letting the tax tail wag the investment management dog. While paying taxes is not an enjoyable experience for any investor, there is a clear trade-off between tax avoidance and risk management. Tax avoidance requires that the medical professional buy and hold securities in his or her taxable portfolio. Managing risk generally requires adjusting investments as market conditions and an investor's time horizon change. A buy and hold approach in the face of variable returns across the portfolio's securities is likely to lead to overweighted investments, usually at the time when those overweighted investments have the greatest price risk. Failing to properly diversify a portfolio as a result of avoiding capital gains increases the risk of the portfolio experiencing dramatic declines if the large, concentrated positions fall on hard times.

Thus, like risk, taxes should not necessarily be avoided, but rather managed. One step that a medical professional can take with his or her taxable assets is to consider tax-exempt (i.e., municipal) bonds in the place of the taxable government or corporate bond investments in the portfolio. While tax-exempt bonds generally have lower yields than taxable bonds of similar credit quality, investors with a high income tax bracket are often able to achieve a higher after-tax yield from tax-exempt bonds. Another step is to evaluate the investments in the taxable portfolio for potential tax loss candidates that may be sold to offset capital gains realized in the portfolio. While it is important to consider the opportunity cost of selling a security at a loss, a security below original cost with deteriorating fundamentals may provide a benefit of reducing a tax liability already incurred. Finally, mutual fund investors can take steps to limit their tax liability by avoiding the purchase of funds that already have significant unrealized capital gains in their portfolio (i.e., buying someone else's capital gains). All shareholders generally pay taxes on a fund's capital gains irrespective of when the gain was achieved. However, the recent bear market has greatly reduced unrealized capital gains within most mutual funds, and most funds have unrealized losses at this point. In fact, according to the December 2002 *Morningstar Principia Database,* the average potential capital gains exposure of the 10,000 equity funds included in the database is negative 44% of assets. Furthermore, less than 5% of the 10,000 plus equity funds included in the database have potential capital gains exposure of 10% or more of the fund's assets.

[C] Performance Measurement

If the healthcare professional holds securities in pharmaceuticals and medical devices, and if portfolio management and investment strategies are the treatments, then performance measurement is the checkup and physical examination that ensures the patient's health is on the right track. While many performance measurement statistics have been developed to assist in the evaluation of an investment program, the risk of misdiagnosis remains significant. In fact, the increase in computing power available to analyze investment performance has resulted in a proliferation of new statistical tools, but this improved capability to slice and dice performance has not necessarily coincided with improved understanding of the health of the investment program. Thus, it is important to understand the various performance measurement calculations and evaluate the results in the context of the market and economic environment.

[1] CALCULATING RETURNS

The first step in analyzing the results of an investment program is the calculation of total returns for the program. Total return represents the accumulated percentage increase in wealth from an investment and is measured by the sum of capital appreciation (i.e., realized and unrealized capital gains and losses) and income over the time period divided by the amount invested. For example, assume a portfolio starts the period with a market value of $100,000, earns $5000 in income over the period, and securities appreciate in value another $3000 to achieve an ending value of $108,000. The total return is $8000/$100,000 or 8% over the period.

In most situations, however, the total return calculation must be adjusted to deal with cash flow that may come in and out of a portfolio. The standard total return calculation for a portfolio in the investment industry to take into account cash flow is the time-weighted return. The time-weighted return is the compounded periodic return with each period's return calculated as follows:

$$R_t = \frac{EV - BV - CF}{BV + WCF} \qquad \text{for period } t$$

Where EV = Ending Market Value

BV = Beginning Market Value

CF = Cash Flow = Contributions – Withdrawals

$$WCF = \frac{[(Day\ of\ CF) - (Total\ Days\ in\ Period)] \times CF}{Total\ Days\ in\ Period}$$

The time-weighted return, R, over T periods is calculated as:

$$R = (1 + R_1) * (1 + R_2) * \ldots * (1 + R_T) - 1 \text{ for t} = 1, 2, \ldots, T$$

- **Example:** Dr. Michelle Hansen starts with $100,000 in a mutual fund on December 31 and buys $10,000 per month at the mid-month point for one year, with one $50,000 withdrawal at the end of June and with no fund dividends.

  Dr. Hansen started with $100,000 and added net cash flow over the full period of $70,000. The market value was $176,073 at the end of the year. The total investment gain was $6073. The return reported in the newspaper for the mutual fund would be 10% (i.e., $1.00/$10.00), which is also the time-weighted return achieved by Dr. Hansen (Table 7-6).

As is evident from Table 7-6, the time-weighted return calculation is intended to minimize the impact of cash flows and offers a performance number that can be used against other portfolios or investment vehicles. However, given a gain of only $6073 on a total net investment of $170,000, the time-weighted return calculation does not necessarily capture the rate of return achieved on each invested dollar. The calculation needed to measure the return on investment is called the internal rate of return or dollar-weighted return, which is defined as the percentage return needed to equate the initial market value plus a series of cash flows to the ending market value. The internal rate of return in our example is 4.5%.

The return calculations discussed so far measure the periodic return for an investment, which is then compounded to calculate the cumulative return. If the cumulative return covers a period of more than one year, the return is often annualized to reflect the rate of return on a yearly basis reflected in the cumulative return. To annualize a cumulative return R,

Table 7-6 *Time Weighted Returns*

Month Ending	NAV	Total Market Value	Contributions	Withdrawals	WCF	Monthly Time-Weighted Returns	Compound Time-Weighted Returns
Dec.	$10.00	$100,000	–	–	$5,000	–	–
Jan.	$11.00	$120,500	$10,000	–	$5,000	10.0%	10.0%
Feb.	$11.50	$136,205	$10,000	–	$5,000	4.5%	15.0%
March	$12.00	$152,344	$10,000	–	$5,000	4.3%	20.0%
April	$11.50	$155,788	$10,000	–	$5,000	-4.2%	15.0%
May	$11.75	$169,283	$10,000	–	$5,000	2.2%	12.5%
June	$10.50	$110,742	$10,000	$50,000	$5,000	-10.6%	5.0%
July	$11.00	$126,254	$10,000	–	$5,000	4.8%	10.0%
Aug.	$10.50	$130,288	$10,000	–	$5,000	-4.5%	5.0%
Sept.	$11.00	$146,730	$10,000	–	$5,000	4.8%	10.0%
Oct.	$11.25	$160,179	$10,000	–	$5,000	2.3%	12.5%
Nov.	$11.50	$173,849	$10,000	–	$5,000	2.2%	15.0%
Dec.	$11.00	$176,073	$10,000	–	$5,000	-4.3%	10.0%

$$R_{ann.} = (1 + R)^{(P/TP)} - 1$$

Where P = # of periods in a year

TP = total # of periods in the cumulative return

As an example, a cumulative return of 18.9% over a 2¼ year period is:

$$R_{ann.} = (1 + 0.189)^{(4/9)} - 1 = 8\%$$

While it is reasonable to annualize cumulative returns for periods greater than a year, it is generally inappropriate to annualize returns of less than a year. Why should an investor not annualize a partial year return? An annualized number is intended to bring a return achieved by a portfolio down to a rate experienced over a standardized time period, in this case, one year. However, when an investor or his or her advisor increases the period covered by the performance measurement to calculate an annualized return for a partial year period, the implication is that this rate would be achievable over a full year. Just as the stock market's +21.3% rise in the first quarter of 1987 should not be annualized to +116%, the –22.6% fourth quarter should not be annualized to –64%. Neither of these annualized numbers sheds any light on the actual 1987 calendar year return of +5.2% for the stock market.

[2] PERFORMANCE BENCHMARKS

Performance measurement has an important role in monitoring progress toward the portfolio's goals. The portfolio's objective may be to preserve the purchasing power of the assets by achieving returns above inflation or to have total returns adequate to satisfy an annual spending need without eroding original capital. Whatever the absolute goal, performance numbers need to be evaluated based on an understanding of the market environment over the period being measured.

One way to put a portfolio's time-weighted return in the context of the overall market environment is to compare the performance to relevant alternative investment vehicles. This can be done through comparisons to either market indices, which are board baskets of investable securities, or peer groups, which are collections of returns from managers or funds investing in a similar universe of securities with similar objectives. By evaluating the performance of alternatives that were available over the period, the investor and his or her advisor can gain insight to the general investment environment over the time period.

Market indices are frequently used to gain perspective on the market environment and to evaluate how well the portfolio performed relative to that environment. Market indices are typically segmented into different asset classes.

Common stock market indices include the following:

- Dow Jones Industrial Average—a price-weighted index of 30 large U.S. corporations.
- Standard & Poor's (S&P) 500 Index—a capitalization-weighted index of 500 large U.S. corporations.

- Value Line Index—an equally-weighted index of 1700 large U.S. corporations.
- Russell 2000—a capitalization-weighted index of smaller capitalization U.S. companies.
- Wilshire 5000—a cap weighted index of the 5000 largest U.S. corporations.
- Morgan Stanley Europe Australia, Far East Index—a capitalization-weighted index of the stocks traded in developed economies.

Common bond market indices include the following:

- Lehman Brothers Government Credit Index (LBGCI)—an index of investment grade domestic bonds excluding mortgages.
- Lehman Brothers Aggregate Index (LBAI)—the LBGCI plus investment grade mortgages.
- Solomon Brothers Bond Index—similar in construction to the LBAI.
- Merrill Lynch High Yield Index—an index of below investment grade bonds.
- JP Morgan Global Government Bond—an index of domestic and foreign government-issued fixed income securities.

The selection of an appropriate market index depends on the goals of the portfolio and the universe of securities from which the portfolio was selected. Just as a portfolio with a short-time horizon and a primary goal of capital preservation should not be expected to perform in line with the S&P 500, a portfolio with a long-term horizon and a primary goal of capital growth should not be evaluated by the return from Treasury Bills.

While the Dow Jones Industrial Average and S&P 500 are often quoted in the newspapers, broader market indices are available to describe the overall performance of the U.S. stock market. Likewise, indices like the S&P 500 and Wilshire 5000 are capitalization-weighted, so their returns are generally dominated by the largest 50 of their 500–5000 stocks. While this capitalization-bias does not typically affect long-term performance comparisons, there may be periods of time in which large cap stocks out- or under-perform mid-to-small cap stocks, thus creating a bias when cap-weighted indices are used versus what is usually non-cap weighted strategies of managers or mutual funds. Finally, the fixed income indices tend to have a bias toward intermediate-term securities versus longer-term bonds. Thus, an investor with a long-term time horizon, and therefore a potentially higher allocation to long-term bonds, should keep this bias in mind when evaluating performance.

Peer group comparisons tend to avoid the capitalization-bias of many market indices, although identifying an appropriate peer group is as difficult as identifying an appropriate market index. Furthermore, peer group universes will tend to have an additional problem of survivorship bias, which is the loss of (generally weaker) performance track records from the database. This is the greatest concern with databases used for marketing purposes by managers, since investment products in these generally self-disclosure databases will be added when a track record looks good and dropped when the product's returns falter. Whether mutual funds or managers, the potential or survivorship bias and inappropriate manager universes make it important to evaluate the details of how a database is constructed before using it for relative performance comparisons.

[3] STYLE-BASED PERFORMANCE EVALUATION

One relatively recent performance evaluation approach that was developed to help improve the relevance of comparisons is the separation of stock universes and managers by style. This classification method attempts to distinguish between stocks or manager philosophies based upon general financial characteristics of the investments. In very general terms, often a growth manager's investment approach focuses on stocks showing growth and momentum in its earnings and price. A value manager attempts to identify under-valued securities based upon fundamental analysis of the company. A stock may be considered either "growth" or "value" based on a given set of valuation measures such as price-to-earnings, price-to-book value, and dividend yield.

The goal of style-based performance comparisons is to take some of the biases of the market environment out of the comparison, since a portfolio's returns will ideally be evaluated compared to a universe of alternatives that represent similar investment characteristics facing the same basic market environment. Thus, if the environment is one in which investors in stocks with strong past earnings and price momentum have generally performed better than those using fundamental analysis to find undervalued stocks, comparing the growth/momentum portfolio to a growth index or universe should help eliminate the bias.

Style-based universes can help the medical professional better understand the basic environment captured over a given performance time period. However, there are significant limitations with the various approaches to constructing style-based stock and manager universes that should be understood in direct performance comparisons. Taking style-based stock universes separately from the style-based manager universe, one of the most significant issues regarding the categorization of stocks by "growth" and "value" styles is the lack of agreement in the specifications of what a growth stock is compared to a value stock. With some universes divided by price-to-book value, others by price-to-earnings and/or dividend yields, and some by combinations of similar variables, stocks are often classified very differently by two different stock universes. Furthermore, stocks move across a broad spectrum as their price and fundamentals change, resulting in stocks constantly moving between growth and value categories for any given universe. If there is ambiguity in the rating of a given stock, then the difficulty is only compounded when we attempt to boil what may be complex investment processes of an investment manager or mutual fund portfolio manager to a simple classification of growth or value. A beaten down cyclical stock that no self-respecting growth/momentum manager would purchase may be classified as "growth" because it has a high price-to-earnings ratio (i.e., from low earnings) or a high price-to-book value (i.e., from asset write-offs). Value managers are not the only ones to own low valuation stocks that have improving earnings.

The second problem with style categorization is that managers are often misclassified or they purposefully "game" the categorization of their own process to appear more competitive. For example, if a manager who typically looks for relatively strong earnings/price momentum is lagging in a period when "growth" managers are outperforming, the rank of the manager can be improved simply by claiming a "value" approach. Morningstar's "style box" classification of mutual funds by size and style of the current portfolio highlights this problem for any given fund by showing how its portfolio has changed its classification annually. This leads to an interesting question for the medical professional or his or her advisor: If a manager is still using the same basic investment philosophy and disciplines, but its "style" category has changed according to the ratings service, should you fire the manager? If the answer is "yes," then the burden of monitoring and the cost of manager turnover are an inevitable part of narrow style based performance comparisons. If your answer is "no," then it is easy to see the difficulty of fitting every management approach into a simple style box. The more reasonable alternative is to use style-based stock and manager universes as a tool for understanding the environment, rather than an absolute performance benchmark.

[4] TIME PERIODS FOR COMPARISON

What is the appropriate time period for comparison? Performance measurements over trailing calendar periods, such as the last one, three, and five years, are often used in the mutual fund and investment industry. While three to five years may seem like a long enough time for an investment strategy to show its value added, these time periods will often be dominated by either a bull or bear market environment and a large cap or small cap dominated environment.

One way to lessen the possibility of the market environment biasing a performance comparison is to focus on a time period that captures full range of market environments—a market cycle. The market cycle is defined as a market peak with high investor confidence and speculation through a market trough, in which investor bullishness and speculation subsides, to the next market peak. A bull market is a market environment of generally rising prices and investor optimism. While there have been several definitions of a bear market based upon market returns (e.g., a decline of 15% or more, two consecutive negative quarters, and others), the idea implied by its name is a period of high pessimism and sustained losses. Thus, one returns-based rule of thumb that can be used to identify a bear market is a negative return in the market that takes at least four quarters to overcome. By examining performance over a full market cycle, there is a greater likelihood that short-term market dislocations will not bias the performance comparison.

[5] RISK-ADJUSTED PERFORMANCE

Performance measurement, like an annual physical, is an important feedback loop to monitor progress toward the goals of the medical professional's investment program. Performance comparisons to market indices and/or peer groups are a useful part of this feedback loop, as long as they are considered in the context of the market environment and within the limitations of market index and manager database construction. Inherent to performance comparisons is the reality that portfolios taking greater risk will tend to outperform less risky investments during bullish phases of a market cycle, but these portfolios are also more likely to underperform during the bearish phase. The reason for focusing on performance comparisons over a full market cycle is that the phases biasing results in favor of higher risk approaches can be balanced with less favorable environments for aggressive approaches to lessen or eliminate those biases.

Can we eliminate the biases of the market environment by adjusting performance for the risk assumed by the portfolio? While several interesting calculations have been developed to measure risk-adjusted performance, unfortunately, the answer is that the biases of the market environment still tend to have an impact even after adjusting returns for various measures of risk. However, medical professionals and their advisors will have many different risk-adjusted return statistics presented to them. Therefore, understanding the Sharpe ratio, Treynor ratio, Jensen's alpha measure, Morningstar star ratings, and their limitations should help to improve the decisions made from the performance measurement feedback loop.

[a] The Treynor Ratio

The Treynor ratio, named after MPT researcher Jack Treynor,[6] identifies returns above or below the securities market line introduced in the Portfolio Management section. The Treynor ratio is calculated as:

$$T = \frac{R_p - R_f}{\beta_p}$$

Thus, the Treynor ratio measures the excess return achieved over the risk free return per unit of systematic risk as identified by beta to the market portfolio. In practice, the Treynor ratio is often calculated using the T-Bill return for the risk-free return and the S&P 500 for the market portfolio.

[b] The Sharpe Ratio

The Sharpe ratio, named after CAPM pioneer William F. Sharpe,[7] was originally formulated by substituting the standard deviation of portfolio returns (i.e., systematic plus unsystematic risk) in the place of beta of the Treynor ratio. Thus, a fully diversified portfolio with no unsystematic risk will have a Sharpe ratio equal to its Treynor ratio, while a less diversified portfolio may have significantly different Sharpe and Treynor ratios.

[c] Jensen Alpha Measure

The Jensen measure, named after CAPM researcher Michael C. Jensen,[8] takes advantage of the CAPM equation discussed in the Portfolio Management section to identify a statistically significant excess return or alpha of a portfolio. In an efficient market, the CAPM equation is as follows:

$$E(R_j) = R_f + [E(R_m) - R_f] \; \beta_j$$

However, if a portfolio has been able to consistently add value above the excess return expected as a result of its beta, then the alpha (α_p) of the equation below should be positive and (hopefully) statistically significant. Thus, the alpha term from a regression of the portfolio's returns compared to the market portfolio (i.e., typically the S&P 500 in practice) is a measure of risk-adjusted performance.

$$R_j - R_f = \alpha_j + [R_m - R_f]\,\beta_j + \varepsilon_j$$

While all these measures are interesting and compelling in theory, in practice their results tend to not be dependable on a consistent basis. In all cases, the market environment will tend to have a dramatic impact on the excess returns of various investments, so these measures will tend to be quite variable over time even with risk adjustment. For example, in Table 7–7 consider the following comparison of risk-adjusted return measures over two consecutive three-year time periods for the S&P 500 and the Russell 2000 (i.e., a broad index of small capitalization stocks). While the Russell 2000 is a well-diversified, passive stock index with seemingly stable characteristics, its risk-adjusted returns can vary greatly versus the S&P 500's statistics. Even risk adjustment cannot overcome the effects of the environment.

Although both the Treynor ratio and Jensen measure face the same criticism of CAPM (e.g., the lack of a testable market portfolio), an additional consideration for the Jensen measure is the difficulty of achieving statistical significance in the alpha measure. Given the variability of excess returns that results from changes in market environments, statistical significance is likely to be a difficult goal to achieve without decades of quarterly return observations. Likewise, just because a statistically significant alpha is achieved by a manager does not mean that such returns are repeatable in the future in a different environment.

[d] Database Ratings

The ratings given to mutual funds by databases, such as Morningstar, and various financial magazines are another attempt to develop risk-adjusted return measures. These ratings are generally based on a ranking system for funds calculated from return and risk

Table 7–7 *Measures of Performance*

	Russell 2000 %	S&P 500 %
1993–1995		
Sharpe Ratio	0.95	0.77
Treynor Ratio	0.10	0.07
Jensen Alpha	0.63	0.00
1996–1998		
Sharpe Ratio	0.14	1.27
Treynor Ratio	0.03	0.25
Jensen Alpha	−4.52	0.00

statistics. A popular example is Morningstar's star ratings, representing a weighting of 3-, 5-, and 10-year risk/return ratings. This measure uses a return score from cumulative excess monthly fund returns above T-Bills and a risk score derived from the cumulative monthly return below T-Bills, both of which are normalized by the average for the fund's Morningstar Category. These scores are then subtracted from each other, and funds in the asset class are ranked on the difference. The top 10% receive five stars, the next 22.5% get four stars, the subsequent 35% receive three stars, the next 22.5% receive two stars, and the remaining 10% get one star.

Unfortunately, these ratings systems tend to have the same problems of consistency and environmental bias seen in both non-risk adjusted comparisons over three-and five-year time periods and the other risk-adjusted return measures discussed above. For example, consider the ratings of the group of funds in Morningstar's October 1999 database with at least a five-year history and labeled as "Large Growth" compared with those labeled "Small Value." Of 200 "Large Growth" funds, 56 had a five star rating (28% of the total "Large Growth" group), 88 had a four star rating (44%), 39 were three stars (20%), and only 17 had a rating of less than three stars (8%). In contrast, "Small Value" had no four or five star funds, 12 three star funds (14% of the total "Small Value" group), and 71 funds below three stars (86%). Even with risk adjustment, the environment generally has a significant impact on performance measurement.

The bottom line on performance measurement is that medical professionals and their advisors should not take the easy way out and accept comparisons, no matter how sophisticated, at face value. Returning to our original rule of thumb, understanding the limitations of performance statistics is the key to using those statistics to monitor progress toward a medical professional's goals. This requires an understanding of performance numbers and comparisons in the context of the market environment and the composition/construction of the indices and peer group universes used as benchmarks. Another important rule of thumb is to avoid projecting forward historical average returns, especially when it comes to strong performance in a bull market environment. Much of an investment or manager's performance may be environment-driven, and environments can change dramatically.

Common Investing Mistakes

The sustained bear market environment over the last several years, which led to the largest decline in the domestic equity markets in 25 years, has taught many investors several difficult lessons. These lessons can be boiled down to a few basic investment mistakes that medical professionals and their advisors need to avoid. Here are some of the most common problems, along with suggested solutions.

1. Losing Sight of the Portfolio's Objectives

With the frenzy of the financial media and the anecdotes of either easy money or gloom and doom for the financial markets, at times medical professionals may forget that their portfolios are intended to serve a specific role (e.g., funding college expenses, retirement) in their broader financial plan.

Guideline ■ *Understand* **and diversify risk to the extent possible.** Investments should be selected with both risks and goals in mind. Time horizon, risk tolerance, and the investment environment are likely to change over time. A portfolio must be monitored to ensure that the underlying investments are consistent with the investor's goals.

---

2. Failing to Diversify

A single investment may become a large portion of a medical professional's portfolio as a result of market growth, a desire to avoid capital gains taxes, as a result of solid returns lulling an investor into a false sense of security, or some other reason.

Guideline ■ **Understand and *diversify* risk to the greatest extent possible.** Diversification is the only free lunch in investing. One key contribution of modern portfolio theories is that diversification can reduce portfolio risk, and the specific risk of a single stock may well overwhelm taxes or any other justification for failing to diversify.

---

3. Forgetting the Risk/Return Trade-Off

The healthcare provider can fall into a trap of chasing securities or mutual funds showing or promising the highest return without understanding the risk involved in the investment.

Guideline ■ **If it looks too good to be true, it probably is.** High returns are almost universally associated with exposure to some type of investment risk, so it is important to understand the risks embedded in the investment before a hidden risk becomes reality. The security with the highest potential return is not necessarily an appropriate investment, depending upon the objectives of the medical professional's portfolio.

---

4. Assuming that Stocks Always Provide 10% or Higher Annual Returns

Many investors and even some investment professionals make their investment decisions with the belief that stocks will consistently give them solid double-digit returns.

Guideline ■ **Beware of projecting forward historical averages.** Physicians and other healthcare providers should realize that the stock market is inherently volatile and that there are long periods of time when returns and risk deviate meaningfully from historical averages.

5. Confusing Investing with Trading or Speculation

During momentum-driven market periods, investors start to believe that profits are easy and that there is always a "greater fool" to buy at a higher price.

Guideline ■ **If it looks too good to be true, it probably is.** While the glitter of quick profits can be enticing, the healthcare professional would be well served to remember that investments should be made with a long-term frame of reference and in relation to the portfolio's goals. In contrast, trading and speculation are generally higher risk propositions that have more in common with gambling than investing.

6. Attempting to Time the Market

Some medical professionals or their advisors believe they are "smarter than the market" and can time when to jump in and buy stocks or sell everything and convert to cash.

Guideline ■ **If it looks too good to be true, it probably is.** While jumping into the market at its low times and selling exactly at the high times is appealing in theory, medical professionals should recognize the difficulties and potential opportunity and trading costs associated with trying to time the stock market in practice. In general, healthcare providers might be best served by matching their investments with their time horizon and looking past the peaks and valleys along the way.

7. Confusing a Bull Market for Investment Savvy

A strong bull market environment like the one experienced in the late 1990s often produces favorable investment results for even questionable investment strategies.

Guideline ■ **Understand the limitations of performance statistics.** Healthcare providers would be wise to distinguish between sound investment strategies and those that are clinging to the coattails of a bull market. Examine results over bear market periods as well as the good times to understand better the potential risk of a strategy.

8. Buying High, Selling Low

The desire to sell yesterday's losers and buy yesterday's winners often results in a poor performing investment program, because environments change, and the relative returns of different types of investments also change.

Guideline ■ **Understand the limitations of performance statistics.** Avoid reacting to the market by buying yesterday's winners, whether they take the form of "hot" stocks or mutual funds. Generally, investors should avoid switching from underperforming, but otherwise sound, investment strategies to strategies more in favor in the current environment.

9. Accepting Performance Statistics as Gospel

The easiest decision is to sell a fund, fire a manager, or bow out of a security as a result of unfavorable performance statistics and lagging returns. However, this might not be the decision in the best interest of the medical professional.

Guideline ■ **Understand the limitations of performance statistics.** All investors would like their investments to provide strong returns every year. Unfortunately, investment returns are volatile by nature, and typically the market environment heavily influences measures of investment performance. Therefore, the medical professional should not let performance considerations be the sole factor governing investment decisions.

10. Failing to Recognize the Impact of Fees and Expenses

An attractive investment and a slick sales pitch can often hide the underlying costs of the investment, leading some medical professionals to give up a significant portion of the long-term growth of their assets.

Guideline ■ **If it looks too good to be true, it probably is.** Fees and expenses can have significant impact on the success or failure of a particular investment program or strategy. Monitor the costs of an investment program to ensure that fees and expenses are reasonable for the services provided and are not consuming a disproportionate amount of the investment returns.

Web Sites of Interest

Investment Theory Sites
    www.stanford.edu/~wfsharpe/
    www.efficientfrontier.com
Investment Research Sites
    www.hoovers.com
    www.sec.gov
    www.morningstar.com
    www.marketguide.com
    www.yardeni.com
    www.aima.org
Investment News Sites
    www.bloomberg.com
    www.businessweek.com
    www.thestreet.com
    www.finance.yahoo.com
    www.wsj.com

Endnotes

1. Beebouer, Gilbert L., "Determinants of Portfolio Performance II, an Update," *Financial Analysts Journal* (May/June 1991).

2. "Portfolio Selection," *Journal of Finance,* 1952, 7(1), 77–91.

3. Sharpe, William F. "Capital Asset Prices. A Theory of Market Equilibrium Under Conditions of Risk," *Journal of Finance* (September 1964), 425–442.

4. Linnter, John, "Security Prices, Risks, and Maximal Gains from Diversification; *Journal of Finance* (December 1965), 587–616.

5. Mossin, Jan, "Security Pricing and Investment Criteria in Competitive Markets," *American Economic Review* (December 1969), 749–756.

6. Traynor, Jack L., "How to Rate Management Investment Funds," *Harvard Business Review* (January/February 1966), 63–74.

7. Sharpe, William F., "Mutual Fund Performance," *Journal of Business* (January 1966), 1119–1138.

8. Jensen, Michael C., "The Performance of Mutual Funds in the Period 1945–1964," *Journal of Finance* (May 1968), 389–416.

Chapter 8

Milestones in Retirement Planning

Getting Off the Practice Treadmill . . . Achieving Inner Peace

Alexander M. Kimura
Robert J. Greenberg
Richard P. Moran

Other than facing up to the thought of never writing another prescription or studying another X-ray, perhaps the greatest challenge for a physician approaching retirement is making reliable assumptions about the future. Since the quality of life in retirement will be determined by the quality of a long-term financial plan, it is imperative to make prudent and conservative investment choices. Just like preparing for a complex medical procedure, even a slight miscalculation in planning could cause a wide margin miss to your desired result.

Robert B. Wolf, CFP

Many physicians feel that practicing medicine today just is not as much fun or rewarding as it used to be. With managed care, your income may be lower while your efforts have increased substantially—have you wondered how you can get off the treadmill? This chapter is designed to provide concrete steps you can take to make practice optional. Imagine being able to work because you want to, not because you must! The information is organized to provide answers sequentially to nine important questions:

1. How you can have enough money for retirement;
2. How you can determine what lifestyle you want during retirement;
3. How you can stay on track;
4. How you can maximize the benefits of a qualified retirement plan like a 401(k) during your working and retirement years;

5. How you can maximize the benefits of your qualified retirement plan;

6. How you should invest money that is not in your qualified retirement plan;

7. Why your retirement planning should determine your investment approach, not your risk tolerance;

8. What role should Social Security play in retirement planning; and

9. Why estate and retirement planning are two sides of the same coin, and how to integrate them.

How Much Money Is Enough?

One of the most critical steps for the medical professional's future is to create a personal retirement cash flow plan to help him or her know how much he or she needs and how to get that amount. The cash flow planning process determines whether what the healthcare professional is currently doing will be adequate, helps make informed decisions, points out areas that need improvement, and then tests those decisions to see if the plan is likely to work. While no one knows the future, a plan that is monitored and adjusted as time passes is the single most important step a medical professional can take if he or she is in mid or late career.

[A] Planning Issues–Early Career

Doing long-term projections early in the medical professional's career will have the highest degree of inaccuracy, since many unknown factors need to be considered. Projecting income increases, retirement expenses, savings, and other critical items would be very difficult without any historical base. The most important steps for the medical professional to take are:

1. Live beneath your means. This is the primary reason *The Millionaire Next Door* has accumulated wealth, according to Tom Stanley's popular book. The real cost of an expensive lifestyle is the lost opportunity for your money to compound. For example, having a car payment of $250 per month instead of $500 per month means an extra $500,000 of retirement age savings over 30 years, assuming 10% annual returns.

2. Be an informed and prudent investor since the compounding of your money over time accelerates the benefits of higher rates of return. In the example above, having a 7% return instead of a 10% return would cost you over $200,000!

3. Save as much as possible in your 401(k) or other plan. Maximizing this benefit can literally create millions in retirement savings and is critical for a comfortable retirement. For example, saving $2000 per year from age 22 to age 29 (eight years) and making no additional contributions, you would have over $399,000 at age 60 (assuming 10% growth.) If you wait until age 30, then contribute $2000 every year until age 60 (30 years), you would have only $328,000! If you save $3000 per year from age 22 through age 60, you would have over $1,000,000!

4. Plan early for your children's college expenses, setting aside money in tax-efficient investments for their future. This prevents having to choose between retirement for you and college education for your children.

[B] Planning Issues—Mid-Career

The medical professional should

1. Begin planning in earnest. Do an in-depth retirement cash flow plan now, so you can make informed choices about your finances. **Note:** For a "snapshot" view of your retirement progress, consider doing a simple exercise. You might multiply all nonbusiness expenses per year times 20, which gives you an idea of the total investment assets you should have accumulated. Remember, this is not a substitute for planning, since it ignores many other important factors.

2. Look at your savings and investments more critically, since the development of an investment strategy becomes more important as you accumulate wealth. In particular, you need to have effective planning strategies for maximizing the after-tax returns on the investments outside of a retirement plan.

3. Implement your plan. Doing the analysis without taking action is like diagnosing cancer without treating it.

[C] Planning Issues—Late Career

1. If you have not already done so, it's critically important to do your retirement cash flow planning now. Without planning, you are making decisions in a vacuum that may mean a severely restricted lifestyle later.

2. This is also the time to plan for the sale or succession of your practice. There are steps to be taken that can significantly enhance your benefits, but planning for this often takes a few years to provide meaningful results.

3. This may be the time to consider long-term care insurance, depending on your financial situation. A good financial planner can guide you on the appropriateness of this insurance for your needs.

4. Integrate both your estate and retirement planning, since the steps you take for one dramatically affect the other. For example, making gifts to your children may be prudent estate planning but terrible retirement advice, depending on your particular situation.

What Is a Retirement Cash Flow Plan?

A retirement cash flow plan is a year-by-year analysis of how all your likely decisions will impact your finances. The result of this planning is that you know whether what you are doing will work, and how much money you should have accumulated at any time.

[A] What the Medical Professional Needs to Consider in a Retirement Cash Flow Plan

[1] INCOME SOURCES

1. Your current balances in retirement accounts such as Individual Retirement Accounts (IRAs) or 401(k) plans, and the contributions you are making to your retirement and nonretirement accounts each year, with inflation increases as appropriate.
2. Savings and investments outside your retirement plans, if this will be available for your retirement.
3. Income during retirement from part-time work or consulting, with any increases for inflation.
4. Other sources of retirement income, such as pensions or social security.
5. Installment payments from the sale of your practice, if any.
6. Rental property income, if you plan on keeping the property. Will there be annual increases?
7. Income from a reverse mortgage, if appropriate.
8. Any deferred compensation payments.

[2] ONE-TIME WINDFALLS

1. Expected proceeds from the sale of your home, less the cost of your new home and any taxes due. Will you pay cash or finance this home?
2. Any inheritances you expect.
3. After-tax cash from the sale of rental property.
4. After-tax cash from the sale of your practice.

[3] FIXED PERIODIC EXPENSES

1. Mortgage expenses until the debt is paid off. If you have refinanced every few years in the past, extending your mortgage term, will this continue?
2. Car payments, if any, including replacements as appropriate.

[4] VARIABLE PERIODIC EXPENSES

1. Expected taxes when withdrawing money from your retirement accounts.
2. Likely cost of living, based on the retirement lifestyle you want, not on some "rule of thumb."
3. The cost of supporting a parent or disabled child, if likely.

[5] SIGNIFICANT ONE-TIME EXPENSES

1. The payment of major debts, such as your mortgage.
2. The costs of educating your children, since this may occur at the same time as you begin retirement.
3. Other lump sum expenses, such as for weddings or a second home.

[6] PLANNING ASSUMPTIONS

1. Your life expectancy and that of your spouse (if appropriate). If your family has consistently lived to be 100, do not make your plans based on living only to 78.
2. The overall inflation rate you expect, and an often lower rate for social security increases.
3. The expected long-term return on your retirement portfolio, and the after-tax return of your other accounts. Realistic projections have to be based on long-term history, which shows stock market returns of around 10% and bonds at approximately 5%. These returns might be modified if academic research indicates lower returns are likely.
4. The rate of withdrawal from your portfolio in retirement.

[7] ESTATE PLANNING

1. How much you want to leave to your heirs or other beneficiaries can affect your required rate of return. Over many years, the compounding of even a 1% difference in return can make a huge difference.
2. The cost of making gifts to your children and grandchildren.
3. The cost of funding life insurance policies for your heirs.

Determining Retirement Lifestyle

Many physicians do not plan for . . . the transition from work to retirement. Your work has been an important part of your life. That is why the emotional adjustment to retirement may be one of the most difficult in your life. Recent studies indicate there are three phases in retirement, each with a different spending pattern. The three phases are:

1. **The Early Retirement Years.** There is a pent-up demand to take advantage of all the free time retirement affords. You can travel to exotic places, buy an RV, and explore 49 states, or go on month-long sailing vacations. It is possible during these initial years that after-tax expenses increase, especially if your mortgage has not been paid off yet. Usually this period lasts about 10 years until most retirees are in their 70s.

2. **Middle Years.** Medical professionals decide to slow down on the explorations and start simplifying their life. They may sell their house and downsize to a condo or townhouse. They may relocate to an area they discovered during their travels or to an area close to family and friends, to an area with a warm climate, or to an area with low or no state taxes. People also do their most important estate planning during these years. They are concerned about leaving a financial legacy, taking care of their children and grandchildren, and fulfilling charitable intent. This is a time when people spend more time in the local area. They may start taking extension or college classes. They spend more time volunteering at various non-profits and helping out older and less healthy retirees. People often spend less during these years. This period starts when a retiree is in his or her mid- to late-70s and can last up to 20 years, usually to mid- to late-80s.

3. **Late Years.** This is when you may need assistance in your daily activities. You may receive care at home, in a nursing home, or an assisted care facility. Most of the care options are very expensive. It is possible that these years might be more expensive than your pre-retirement expenses. This is especially true if both spouses need some sort of assisted care. This period usually starts when the retiree is in his or her 80s; however, this period could start in the mid- to late-70s.

[A] Planning Issues—Early Career

Most retirement lifestyle issues do not have to be addressed at this point. Keeping a healthy, balanced lifestyle will help to ensure a more productive retirement. This is the time to focus on the financial aspects of retirement planning.

[B] Planning Issues—Mid-Career

If early retirement is a major objective, start thinking about activities that will fill up your time during retirement. Maintaining your health is more critical at this time, since your health habits will often dictate how healthy you will be in retirement.

[C] Planning Issues—Late Career

Three to five years before you retire, start making the transition from work to retirement.

- Try out different hobbies;
- Find activities that will give you a purpose in retirement;
- Establish friendships outside the office or hospital; and
- Discuss retirement plans with your spouse, if any.

Staying on the Retirement Track

To most physicians, needing millions of dollars in the future seems overwhelming, so breaking up your goals into small steps will make the task easier.

[A] Planning Issues—Early Career

1. Use annual targets as a guide to your final objective at retirement;
2. Rebalance your portfolio whenever percentages drift significantly from your initial plan; and
3. Revise and refine your analysis every few years as your objectives change.

[B] Planning Issues—Mid-Career

1. Continue following the steps in early career;
2. Understand your assumptions more clearly; and
3. Start to integrate your estate and charitable goals with your retirement plan.

[C] Planning Issues—Late Career

1. You should be very comfortable with your retirement assumptions; and
2. Understand how your estate and charitable intent influences your withdrawal rate. Decide on a withdrawal rate that you are comfortable with and that incorporates your other sources of income.

[D] Monitoring Your Progress

[1] WHAT IF YOU'RE BEHIND YOUR TARGET FOR THE YEAR?

If none of your assumptions have changed, and you feel that you can make up the difference in the next year, you probably can use the same retirement cash flow plan for that year. As a rule of thumb, if you are less than 10% off your goal, you may not need to do anything. If you fall so far behind that each year's target seems unachievable, you will probably need to make some changes. However, before you change your planning, you need to see why you are behind.

If you have not saved as much as you expected, take a look at your expenses to see where you can cut down. Remember, you need to pay yourself first before you spend on luxuries. Contribute as much as possible to your qualified retirement plan at work.

Next, you need to look at your investment returns. For the past three years the stock market has been undergoing one of its inevitable "corrections," which can significantly impact your balances. Remember, your return assumptions are based on averages that should include the bad and good years. If you are close to retirement and have a large shortfall, then you may need to increase the risk in your investment portfolio to meet your goals. If the market falls more or stays down for some time, increasing risk by buying more stocks forces you to "buy low," and that should pay off over time.

[2] WHAT IF YOU'RE AHEAD OF YOUR ANNUAL GOAL?

Again, if the difference may be eliminated the next year, you probably should not make any changes.

If you are more than 20% ahead of your goal, you can either decrease the risk in your portfolio or change your planning. For example, you might decide to retire earlier, increase your retirement income, or contribute less to your retirement portfolio. Since it is more difficult to catch up when you are behind, it may be worthwhile not making any changes until you are fairly close to retirement; then you can adjust your assumptions.

If you are significantly ahead because of much better than expected investment returns, and you feel the stock market is overvalued, reducing your investment risk when you are above your target is a reasonable step—why not take some profits while you are ahead? Be sure to consider the tax consequences of any changes to see if they would be worthwhile.

Planning Note ■ If you are working with a financial advisor, your advisor may want to link your annual objective to the volatility of the portfolio developed for you, using standard deviation as the measure of volatility. The advisor might suggest alternative actions if your results varied by more than two standard deviations. This deviation indicates that you are probably outside of the expected range of results for your long-term plan.

---

[3] HOW SHOULD I BE MONITORING MY INVESTMENTS?

In addition to tracking whether you are close to your annual goal, you will want to make sure that your asset allocation percentages remain close to your plan. Whenever the percentages are significantly different from your plan, you will want to rebalance your portfolio—buy or sell your investments to bring them more in line.

If your investments are in a taxable account, you can use new purchases to buy those areas that are under-represented, rather than incurring taxes by selling the investments that represent too high a percentage of your portfolio.

[4] WHAT IS A SAFE WITHDRAWAL RATE FROM RETIREMENT ASSETS?

An additional variable in staying on track after retirement is your withdrawal rate or the amount you take out of your accounts each year. Most people want to have a steady income, similar to the paycheck they received while working.

Most retirement analyses assume a certain inflation rate and assume your accounts go up a fixed percentage each year. Unfortunsately, the stock market and inflation differ from year to year. Therefore, high withdrawal rates can reduce your retirement assets and eat into your principal when the market is down, requiring you to decrease your spending. You have two choices in selecting a safe withdrawal rate. You can choose from the following:

1. Decide to maximize the amount of withdrawal while maintaining a high probability of not running out of money. You will invest for total return and may spend some of the principal; or

2. Decide to live on only the income generated from the portfolio. The focus is on investment yield and not on total return.

Based on recent studies, it is suggested that, if you want to have a steady inflation-adjusted income despite market fluctuations, a safe withdrawal rate is 4% of your retirement assets. This assumes that you withdraw 4% from the initial portfolio value and change that amount by an inflation (or deflation) adjustment each year. At this withdrawal rate, you have very little chance of running out of money in most stock market scenarios. The studies determining this withdrawal rate assume that you invest at least half your money in stocks and the rest of your money in bonds. They also assume that you will live another 30 years in retirement. This withdrawal rate may seem like a very low percentage, since Treasury Bills pay more than 4%. However, at this withdrawal rate, your income will keep up with inflation, tripling your income over 30 years.

Another factor in determining your withdrawal rate is the amount you want to leave for your children, grandchildren, and your favorite charity. The amount you want to leave your beneficiaries and charities will be major determinants influencing the rate of return that you will need to achieve all your goals.

Ask your advisor: To reduce your concern over yearly fluctuations, you may want to reserve one year's expenses in a money market account and replenish the cash with the dividends from the retirement assets. Another way to reduce concern over portfolio fluctuations is to have enough bonds to cover your fixed expenses and rely on your stock portfolio to fund your variable expenses.

Maximizing Qualified Retirement Plan Benefits While Still Practicing

When you work for a hospital, health maintenance organization, or health system, your employer selects the type of retirement plan that will be available for the employees.

The first step as an employee is to understand the type of plan that is available and all its features. The best way to obtain a list of all the features is to look at the summary plan description that is provided by your company. The summary plan description should be updated annually. If the summary plan description has not been updated for a while and is not comprehensive enough to answer your questions, look at the plan document. Your human resource manager will be able to provide a copy of both the summary plan description and plan document.

Second, find out whether the employee can make salary deferrals into the plan or whether the plan is funded entirely by the employer.

Third, determine whether investing decisions are made by the employer or the employee.

If the employer is responsible for all the funding and the investment decisions, your responsibility is to understand how the benefits are determined, what is normal retirement age, and what happens if you leave your employer before normal retirement age.

If you are responsible for either the investment or funding decisions, you have more influence over your retirement future, and you should do the following:

1. Perform a retirement analysis;
2. Include the employer contribution in the analysis and understand the impact of changing jobs or vesting;
3. Determine the savings rate and investment return needed to retire comfortably at the desired retirement age;
4. Develop an investment strategy to generate the desired investment return;
5. Understand the various investment options within the qualified plan and implement the investment strategy; and
6. Monitor performance to make sure the plan is on target.

[A] How Can I Benefit from an Employer-Sponsored Plan?

Often, your employer-sponsored retirement plan is the single most important and effective savings method for retirement planning. If you participate in your employer's plan, or set one up, you receive the following benefits:

1. **Reduce your income taxes.** If you contribute to your employer's retirement plan, these contributions are deducted from your income, so you can reduce your income taxes.
2. **Employer gets a deduction.** If the employer contributes to the plan, the employer can deduct those contributions as an expense.
3. **Defer taxes on your investment earnings.** When you make money on your investments, you usually have to pay taxes for that year. Within a retirement plan, you do not have to pay taxes on these earnings until you take the money out, which is usually after you turn 59½ years old. This is true for your salary deferrals and employer contributions.
4. **Employer gives you free money.** Often employers contribute to the retirement plans—either matching a portion of the employee's salary deferral or funding the entire employee benefit.
5. **Tax breaks on your retirement distribution.** If you decide to take a lump sum distribution (distribution of your entire balance), and you were born before January 1, 1936, you are allowed to pay taxes as if you had received the money over 10 years.
6. **Your plan is portable: have plan will travel.** If you leave your employer, you are often allowed to leave your money in the qualified retirement plan until retirement

age. However, you can also roll over your balance into an IRA or another qualified retirement plan without paying taxes.

7. **Your spouse can continue tax deferral.** If you pass away, your spouse is allowed to roll over the account into his or her own IRA. The spouse is also allowed to keep the account in your name.

8. **Extra-strength creditor protection for qualified retirement plans.** In 1994, the U.S. Supreme Court held that a participant's interest in a qualified retirement plan was exempt from the claims of creditors in a bankruptcy proceeding.

[B] What Are the Most Important Features in My Employer's Retirement Plan?

[1] WHO IS ELIGIBLE TO PARTICIPATE?

When can you start participating in the employer's retirement plan? Generally, qualified retirement plans must include all employees who are 21 years of age and who have been employed for more than one year. The one-year employment requirement may be increased to two years (for plans other than 401(k)s and Savings Incentive Match (SIMPLE) if the plan offers immediate vesting.

[2] WHAT IS VESTING AND HOW DOES IT AFFECT ME?

Vesting defines how much you own of your employer's contribution. Employers have vesting schedules so that there is an incentive for an employee to stay at the company. If you are 100% vested, that means you own 100% of the employer contribution. Of course, you own 100% of the money you put into the plan.

There are two types of vesting schedules. First, if the plan has a gradual vesting schedule, you own an increasing portion of the employer's contribution every year you stay with the employer. The gradual vesting schedule cannot exceed seven years (six years if the plan has matching contributions). Second, if the plan has a cliff vesting schedule, you do not own any of the employer contribution until you stay with the employer for a certain period of time. The period of time cannot exceed five years (three years if the plan has matching contributions).

[3] ARE LOANS AVAILABLE?

Many employers offer loans because employees often will not contribute without this feature. However, loans are not a requirement. The plan must specifically allow for loans.

Loans are permitted for all qualified retirement or Section 403(b) plans. However, many defined benefit plans do not allow for them, because loans create difficult administrative issues for these types of plans.

Let's say you borrow money from your plan. In reality, you are borrowing money from yourself. The interest that you pay for the loan goes back into your account. However, you cannot decide which interest rate you pay yourself. The plan administrator decides the interest rate, which is the current market rate or usually one or two percentage points above the prime rate, or what the banks are currently charging their best customers. The borrowed money is withdrawn from your balance, and the return you receive on that borrowed money is based on the interest rate charged for the loan. However, if the stock market has tremendous returns, you will lose out on those returns.

If your plan offers loans, you can take out a loan for:

(1)   Up to $50,000 or

(2)   The greater of

    (a) one-half the vested balance, or

    (b) $10,000

You must pay back the loan within five years unless you use the money to purchase your primary residence; in either case, the loan must provide for a fully amortized schedule of payments. You will usually repay the loan through payroll deductions.

If you leave your employment before paying off the loan, in most cases, you have to pay it back immediately. If you do not, the loan is considered a premature withdrawal, and you will have to pay income taxes on the outstanding balance and a 10% early withdrawal penalty if you are under age 59½.

[4] WITHDRAWALS WHILE STILL WORKING FOR THE SAME EMPLOYER

What happens if you have an emergency and you absolutely need to take money out of your retirement plan?

This is known as an in-service distribution or withdrawal while you are still working for the employer who sponsored your retirement plan.

However, not all employer-sponsored retirement plans allow you to have in-service distributions. Defined benefit plans and defined contribution plans that work like pensions (such as money purchase plans and target benefit plans) do not allow in-service distributions unless you have reached normal retirement age or early retirement age.

Profit-sharing plans usually allow in-service distributions but most require a hardship as defined by the plan. Most employers are liberal about defining a hardship. There are limits to the amount that can be withdrawn from profit-sharing plans. The amount cannot exceed the vested account balance, and the vested balance must have been in the plan for at least two years.

401(k)s have very strict hardship withdrawal guidelines that must be satisfied before in-service distributions are allowed. According to the Internal Revenue Service (IRS), a qualifying hardship is a situation where the need is immediate and will incur a heavy burden and the participant does not have other resources easily accessible to satisfy the need. Some of the hardships allowed are:

- Medical expenses;
- Purchase of a principal residence;
- Payment for education expenses for participant, spouse, or dependent; and
- Payment to prevent eviction or foreclosure on your home.

Hardship withdrawals come with a hefty price. You will owe income taxes on the withdrawal amount and also a 10% early withdrawal penalty if you are under age 59½. If you are in the 28% federal income tax bracket and include state income taxes, you may lose up to 40% of the withdrawal to taxes and penalties.

[C] What If I'm the Owner?
Should I Sponsor a Retirement Plan?

You should sponsor an employer-sponsored plan only if it is the best way to achieve your goals. Here are some of the major reasons why you may want to set up a retirement plan:

1. You are losing a lot of money through taxes, and you want to contribute and deduct as much as possible each year;
2. You have partners or important employees who have the same problem, and you want to help them so they will stay with you;
3. You would like to provide an incentive to all your employees so they do not leave because your competition has a plan and you do not;
4. You need a retirement plan to successfully recruit new employees, since everyone wants a retirement plan at work.
5. You overspent for years and did not save much. Now you are taking retirement planning seriously, but you need to put away a lot of money each year.

[D] What Is the Best Plan for You? If You Already
Have a Plan, Do You Need to Make Any Changes?

There are four major issues you need to consider:

1. Your objectives: what combination of the five major reasons discussed in the previous question motivated you to set up the retirement plan?
2. Census information: who are all your employees, what are their ages, full- or part-time status, salaries, and length of service?
3. Employee funding capabilities: what will employees contribute?
4. How much you want to contribute: what does the owner want to contribute to the plan?

What are the most common issues for an employer at each stage of his or her career? Each of the plan types is described in more detail in the next section.

[1] PLANNING ISSUES–EARLY CAREER

1. Try to save early, and let compound interest work in your favor. Save between 10–15% of your income at the minimum.
2. There will be additional cash needs at the start of your practice.
3. Start with a SIMPLE IRA or Simplified Employee Pension (SEP) Plan IRA. If you are a business owner without employees and would like to contribute a larger amount, you may want to consider an individual 401(k).

[2] PLANNING ISSUES–MID-CAREER

1. You may want to consider a 401(k) plan for employee contributions and for profit sharing; and
2. With these additions, you may be able to save as much as $40,000 per year. If you are at least 50 years old, the limits increase to those shown in Table 8–1.

[3] PLANNING ISSUES–LATE CAREER

1. If you are just starting to save money for retirement, you will need to save a large amount quickly.
2. You may want to consider a defined benefit plan, where you may be able to save significantly above the levels shown in Table 8–1.

[E] What Are the Different Types of Employer-Sponsored Retirement Plans?

[1] WHAT IS A QUALIFIED RETIREMENT PLAN?

There are two parts to the qualified retirement plan. First, it is a retirement plan that the employer or the employee's organization (such as a union) sets up to provide retirement income for the employee. In addition, this retirement plan can allow the employees to defer income into the plan. Second, this retirement plan qualifies for special tax treatment from the IRS. In order to qualify for the special tax treatment, the retirement plan must meet all the Internal Revenue Code requirements.

Table 8–1 *Retirement Contribution Limits For Those Age 50*

Year	Limit
2002	41,000
2003	42,000
2004	43,000
2005	44,000
2006 and after	45,000

[2] WHAT ARE THE TYPES OF QUALIFIED RETIREMENT PLANS?

There are two major types of qualified retirement plans. Defined benefit plans provide a specified benefit to the participant. Defined contribution plans specify the contribution amount allowed by the employer and employee. These two major types of plans also differ in how the benefit is allocated to the participant. The participant in a defined contribution plan receives the accumulated account balance, whereas the participant in a defined benefit plan receives a monthly check or lump sum based on a formula established for the plan.

[a] Defined Benefit Plans

The defined benefit plan is what most people consider a pension plan. The employer contributes all the money, which is pooled into one account, so there are no individual accounts for each participant. The employee has little or no choice in how the plan operates. This plan promises to provide a monthly pension to the participant when he retires. Usually this benefit depends on three factors:

1. The age of the participant at retirement;
2. The number of years of service or how long the participant has worked at the company; and
3. Salary at retirement, usually based on compensation over a number of years.

The employee's benefits manual will provide more details regarding how the monthly pension is calculated. If you need additional information, ask your human resources manager for a summary plan description or a copy of the actual plan document.

Planning Note ■ One caution with defined benefit plans is that you should understand the "penalty" for retiring before the normal retirement age. There can be a significant difference in payment amounts if you delay retiring for just two to three years. To prevent missing any opportunities, you should request and review projections from your human resources department regarding retiring at different ages.

Most defined benefit plans require vesting before you are eligible to receive the benefit. Vesting can vary from immediate, to gradual, to full vesting in the future (known as "cliff" vesting).

One variation of the defined benefit plan is the cash balance pension plan. This plan is a cross between a money purchase plan and a defined benefit plan. Like a money purchase plan, the contribution rate is a percentage of salary; however, unlike a money purchase plan, the actual contribution percentage is actuarially defined. The contribution rate is based on the expected benefit for the employee. An employer-guaranteed earnings rate is pre-determined. However, since the interest crediting rate is never exactly the same as the investment return, the sum of all the account balances will not equal the total asset value of the plan. A defined contribution plan always has the sum of all the account balances equal to the total plan assets. The plan assets of a cash balance account plan will have either a surplus or deficit and, therefore, cannot be a defined contribution plan. If the actual plan earnings are below the interest crediting rate, the employer makes up the difference.

Another variation of the defined benefit plan is the Insured Defined Benefit Plan or 412(i) Plan. This plan usually allows for larger contributions and simpler administration because the assets are invested in either annuity or life insurance contracts that guarantee the payments to plan participants. These plans are most commonly used when there are very few employees and a desire to maximize the amount that can be contributed by the employer for the benefit of the employees. Of course, these are guaranteed investments, and their rate of return may be lower than other more aggressive options.

[b] Defined Contribution Plans

The defined contribution plan provides individual accounts for each participant. The participant's retirement benefit is dependent on the value of the participant's account at retirement. All allocations, investment returns, and forfeitures from participants who terminated before vesting will contribute to each participant's account value. The 401(k) is an example of a defined contribution plan. Other common types of defined contribution plans are:

1. **Profit Sharing Plans.** The company makes discretionary contributions each year. The contribution limit is 25% of the total payroll of covered employees. These contributions are allocated among the participants based on a predetermined formula.

Planning Note ■ Often the profit sharing plan will be considered when you are in mid-career. Profit-sharing plans allow you to save the full contribution while maintaining flexibility.

2. **Money Purchase Plans.** The company makes the contribution and the contribution is fixed and determined ahead of time: for example, the company will contribute 5% of each employee's compensation each year. The company's contribution rate can vary from 0 to 25%. This contribution rate can only change if there is a formal amendment to the plan.

3. **Target Benefit Plans.** This is a money purchase plan that is age-weighted. It has features of a money purchase plan and defined benefit plan. The plan starts with a defined benefit formula that provides a target annual retirement benefit for each participant. The company's contribution percentages are determined actuarially so that each participant will receive the targeted benefit. The contribution percentage is determined for each employee when he or she enters the plan and the percentage does not change. Therefore, there are no periodic actuarial valuations. Individual accounts are maintained, and the participant's benefit is dependent solely on the participant's account balance at retirement or termination. The same as the money purchase plan, the employer deduction limit is 25% of total payroll of all covered employees.

Planning Note ■ Target Benefit Plans may be appropriate for those physicians in the late career stage. This plan provides a means to contribute a higher rate for the older employees than the younger employees.

---

4. **401(k) or Cash or Deferred Arrangement Plan.** This plan comes from a section of the IRS Tax Code § 401, paragraph (k). A 401(k) is a type of profit sharing plan in which the employees are allowed to contribute their own money on a pre-tax basis. The maximum amount the employee could contribute is $11,000 in 2002 ($12,000 in 2003, $13,000 in 2004, $14,000 in 2005, and $15,000 in 2006 and thereafter). If you are over the age of 50, the limit in 2002 was $12,000 ($14,000 in 2003, $16,000 in 2004, $18,000 in 2005, and $20,000 in 2006 and thereafter). Usually most 401(k)s limit employee deductions to 15% of compensation. The employer has the option of matching the employee's contribution. Instead of providing a match for every employee contribution, or in addition to a matching contribution, the employer has the option of providing a discretionary profit sharing based on the employee's salary.

401(k)s are popular because the employee can take more control of his retirement. Generally, if the employee leaves the company before he retires, he can take his 401(k) with him. More employers are offering 401(k)s because they want to attract and retain good employees.

Planning Note ■ This plan is a good option for those medical professionals in mid-career.

Individual 401(k). This type of 401(k) may enable medical professionals to contribute a larger amount. This type of plan can be used by the business owner, his or her spouse (if working at the business), and any partners in the business and their spouses (if working at the business). If any other employees are added, the plan becomes much more complicated and mandatory contributions to the new employees will likely come into play. In 2002, the total individual contribution limit, including employer profit-sharing and/or matching contributions, was the lesser of $40,000 or 100% of income. Previously, it was the lesser of $30,000 or 25% of income. In terms of employer contributions only, the limit is 25% of total payroll. Employee contributions are not counted against this percentage. Annual contributions are not required. In addition, eligible participants can make the age-50 catch-up contributions to increase funding.

As an example, a sole owner of a C Corporation who earns $50,000 could defer $12,000 in 2003. In addition, the owner could contribute 25% as an employer contribution or $12,500. The total contribution could be $24,500, even though the owner's income is $50,000. If the owner is 50 years old or older, the owner can contribute an additional $1000.

Cross-Tested Safe Harbor 401(k) (3% Contribution) Profit Sharing Plan Example:

Sometimes a highly qualified pension administrator can get very creative within the limits of the law. Table 8–2 shows an example that combines a traditional corporate profit sharing plan, a 401(k) plan, and a 3% Safe Harbor contribution. Three pools of money are being administered together.

Under the revised Cross Testing regulations, we must use an allocation rate for the non-highly compensated employee that is no less than one-third the rate of the highest compensated employee contribution rate.

Table 8–2 *Combination Retirement Plan*

	Compensation	Age	Safe Harbor Contribution	Profit Sharing Contribution	401(k) Deferral	Totals	Pct of Pay
Owner	200,000	55	6,000	23,000	12,000	41,000	20.5%
Employee	30,000	30	900	550	0	1,450	4.8%
Total	230,000		6,900	23,550	12,000	42,450	18.5%

5. **SIMPLE 401(k) Plan or IRA Plan.** Both plans are for employers with 100 or fewer employees. The SIMPLE 401(k) is a qualified plan, while the SIMPLE IRA is not. In both plans, the maximum amount an employee can defer is $7000 in 2002 ($8000 in 2003, $9000 in 2004, $10,000 in 2005 and after). If an employee is over the age of 50, an employee can defer $7500 in 2002 ($9000 in 2003, $10,500 in 2004, $12,000 in 2005, $12,500 in 2006, and thereafter). The employer must provide contributions in the form of a match or as a contribution to all employees who qualify for the plan. In a SIMPLE 401(k), the contributions are made to a trust, while in a SIMPLE IRA, the contributions are made to individual IRAs in the name of each participant. Employer contributions are always fully vested in both plans.

SIMPLE IRAs must include all employees who made at least $5000 in the two preceding years and who are expected to earn at least $5000 in the current year.

Planning Note ■ This is a good plan for medical professionals during their career. If creditor protection is important to you, consider the SIMPLE 401(k).

---

6. **Simplified Employee Pension Plans.** A SEP is not a qualified plan, so the qualified plan rules do not apply. It appears to the participant as a qualified plan and may be a good option for smaller employers. Contributions are made by the employer and are made into individual IRAs for the benefit of the participant. All contributions are fully vested. The employer can contribute up to 25% of compensation or $40,000, whichever is lower. The rules for SEPs are in code section 408(k):

1) Must cover an employee who has been employed less than three years, provided the employee is at least 21 years of age. Part-time employment counts toward years of service.

2) Contributions do not need to be made to employees who made less than $450 in 2003 (indexed for inflation).

3) The plan can exclude employees who are covered under a collective bargaining agreement or are non-resident aliens.

Planning Note ■ This is a good plan for medical professionals during the early stages of their careers.

Now that you have maximized your savings and made best use of your employer-sponsored retirement plans, you need to decide how to take the money out when you retire.

Maximizing Qualified Plan Benefits in Retirement

So, you were successful with your retirement planning, and you are ready to retire. A large portion of your retirement assets may be in a qualified retirement plan your employer provided. What is the best way to handle the assets in the plan?

[A] What If Your Plan Is a Traditional Pension or Defined Benefit Plan?

You will either receive a monthly check or have an option to receive a lump sum. If you select the monthly check, you have a short time after retirement to decide whether to take a check over your lifetime (known as the single-life option) or a smaller check over your and your spouse's lifetime (known as the joint and survivor option). Often, you are provided several alternatives of joint and survivor options:

1. Giving your spouse an equivalent monthly check if something should happen to you (known as 100% joint and survivor); or

2. Giving your spouse a reduced monthly check if something should happen to you (for example, 50% joint and survivor).

The single-life option provides the largest check. If your spouse is much younger than you are, the check for both of your lives could be significantly less. Most people choose the 100% joint and survivor option because it is difficult to tell your spouse that everything will be fine while you are alive, but he or she will suffer if you die.

Another alternative instead of taking the 100% joint and survivor option is a technique called pension maximization. This technique may be used if the spouse is in poor health and would be likely to die before the participant. If you selected the 100% joint and survivor option, and your spouse predeceased you, you will continue to receive the lower monthly check based on both lives. Therefore, to receive the higher income based on one life and still make sure your spouse receives a similar benefit if you should predecease him or her, use the pension maximization technique as follows:

1. Take the monthly benefit based solely on your own life;

2. Purchase life insurance on your life with a part of the increased monthly benefit. For this technique to work, the insurance death benefit should be large enough to provide your spouse the equivalent monthly income, assuming a reasonable investment return. Your spouse will probably not receive an equivalent income if he or she selects a risk-free investment, so this option will be more risky for him or her; and

3. If your spouse predeceases you, cancel the insurance.

Before selecting the single-life option, make sure you are insurable (have the policy in your hands before making the selection). The payout selection is irrevocable, so be careful.

Planning Note ■ You may want to consider pension maximization if your spouse is much younger than you are. In this case, your 100% joint and survivor option may result in much lower monthly payments than a single-life option.

[B] What If Your Plan Is Like a 401(k) or Is Another Type of Defined Contribution Plan?

You have several alternatives:

1. You can leave the money in your defined contribution plan. Each employer has rules for the qualified plan that dictate how long you can stay in the plan once you retire.

2. You can roll over the money to an IRA.

3. You can take all the money out of the qualified plan, which is called a lump sum distribution. You may receive special tax treatment if you take this option.

4. If you are younger than age 55, and you are ready to retire, you can take money out of the plan in substantially equal payments over your life expectancy. You must continue to take these payments at least five years or to age 59½, whichever is longer. In addition, you must separate from service before starting the payments.

Planning Note ■ You can also take substantially equal payments from an IRA if you are under age 59½. With an IRA, there is no requirement to separate from service.

---

[1] LEAVE THE MONEY IN THE QUALIFIED PLAN

The major benefit in staying in your employer's qualified plan is increased creditor protection. In addition, your spouse may have rights to an annuity income that he or she would give up if you move the money to an IRA. Your spouse also has these same rights to your pension or defined benefit plan, so consider that when taking the lump sum option instead of the monthly benefit.

If you are the employer, you may want to keep the money in the qualified plan. However, qualified plans must have a legitimate business entity to sponsor a plan. Usually, when healthcare professionals retire, the business entity disappears. Therefore, you should see a pension attorney if you want to keep your money in the qualified plan after retirement.

[2] ROLL OVER THE MONEY TO AN IRA

Many healthcare professionals move their funds from the qualified retirement plan to an IRA and continue to defer taxes. Some of the benefits of the IRA are portability (you can move it to any custodian you want), control over the investment options, and possible tax advantages through greater control over beneficiary designations and minimum distribution elections.

Another advantage of an IRA is the ability to convert to a Roth IRA. You cannot convert directly from an employer-sponsored retirement plan to a Roth IRA. You will need to first move the money from an employer-sponsored plan to an IRA. Then you can convert from an IRA to a Roth IRA.

If you decide to move money from a qualified plan to an IRA, you will want to elect a direct rollover. A direct rollover moves the funds directly from the qualified plan to the IRA custodian and is a trustee-to-trustee rollover. Money is never in your name (if the money is sent to you, it will be made out to the custodian for your benefit). If you do not select a direct rollover and decide to receive the money in your name, the qualified plan trustee will withhold 20% to make sure that taxes are covered. When you put the money in an IRA, you have to deposit the missing 20%, or you'll be fined 10% if you are under age 59½ and taxed as if it were a distribution.

Planning Note ■ You can roll over after-tax money that you contributed. However, you will need to keep track of the accounting on your own or you may have to pay tax on the money again because it will be considered pre-tax. If you elect to take out the after-tax money, you will receive a check for the after-tax amount, and the earning on that money will be rolled over.

[3] TAKE A LUMP-SUM DISTRIBUTION

Instead of moving money to an IRA, you can also take a lump sum and pay taxes. If you qualify, you can elect to receive special tax treatment, called forward averaging. Five-year forward averaging allows you to pay taxes as if you had received the money over five years, even though you must pay all the taxes in the year you take the distribution.

Ten-year forward averaging is available only to people who were born on or before January 1, 1936, and allows you to pay taxes as if you received the money over 10 years. There is a catch, though. You must pay taxes at the 1986 tax rates, which were significantly higher than today. Also, you must pay all the taxes in the year you take the distribution.

Planning Note ■ If your employer provided company stock to you in your qualified plan, you may receive some tax benefits. If you take a lump sum of your company stock, you will only have to pay tax on the amount your employer paid for the stock (or for non-deductible contributions you made, the amount you paid for the stock). All the gain accumulated in the plan is called net unrealized appreciation and is not taxed until you sell the securities. When you sell, the net unrealized appreciation will probably be taxed at capital gains rates, which are often much lower than ordinary income tax rates. You may want to consider this option before you decide to roll over your money to an IRA. This option is available only if you take the securities out of a qualified retirement plan. If you first move the securities to an IRA, you will lose the benefit of this tax-favored option.

The major disadvantage to this option is that you will need to pay tax even though you have not sold the employer stock. If you combine this strategy with a charitable remainder trust, you can significantly reduce that tax liability. This combination might result in more income for you and more money for your favorite charity. You'll want to talk with your financial advisor to evaluate either of these alternatives.

[4] YOU ARE RETIRING BEFORE AGE 55 AND NEED THE MONEY FROM THE QUALIFIED PLAN

If you want to take the payments from your qualified plan, you need to make sure that your plan allows this option. You have to leave the company where you have the plan before you can start taking distributions.

If your plan does not allow substantially equal payments over your life, you can roll over the money to an IRA and then take the payments. Furthermore, if you already have enough money in an IRA, you can take the payments from the IRA, and you are not required to leave the company.

If you are interested in this option, there are several ways to calculate how much you can take out each year. Once you select a method, you cannot change it. See a financial advisor before electing one of the options.

Planning Note ■ Some advisors believe you need to aggregate all your IRAs when taking substantially equal payments. However, based on IRS private letter rulings, other advisors believe you can take your substantially equal payments from one IRA, and you do not need to combine all your IRAs. This second approach will allow you a lot more flexibility. However, the IRS forbids you to base your payments only on a portion of a single IRA. Once the substantially equal payments start from an IRA, you cannot transfer additional money in or out of that IRA during the payments. Talk to your financial advisor before electing your options.

[C] Planning Issues—Early Career

It is still early, so most of these issues do not apply to you. If you expect to retire at an early age, estimate how much of your money will be in qualified plans or IRAs at retirement. Then estimate how much you can withdraw each year. If this amount is not enough to support your lifestyle, you will want to save money outside of the retirement plans, so you can live comfortably before you reach age 55.

[D] Planning Issues—Mid-Career

Again, it is a little too early to worry about how you are going to take your money out of your retirement plans unless you are planning to retire soon.

[E] Planning Issues—Late Career

This is the time to start thinking about all your alternatives. Healthcare professionals need to integrate retirement plan distributions with tax planning. Depending on your age and on the type of plan that you have, you have some decisions to make before you retire. These decisions can get quite complicated, so it is wise to seek the advice of a Certified Financial Planner.

Nonqualified Retirement Plan Investing

Tax qualified employer-based retirement plans may be the best way to save for retirement, but they are likely to fall short of providing enough income to support your lifestyle. While many Baby Boomer physicians expect to work in retirement, making work optional will most likely require additional investments, over and above contributing the maximum to your 401(k) or 403(b) plan.

Assuming you have set aside enough money for emergencies (three to six months' expenses), you should evaluate other personal plans. Let's cover these now.

[A] Non-Employer Plans (Personal Plans)

The primary focus of these plans is for you to have complete control of your savings and investments. It is important to mentally segregate your investments based on their purpose, since near-term needs are best satisfied with more conservative approaches. You might think of this money as being in different "buckets," one for an emergency reserve, one for a home purchase, one for retirement, and so forth.

[B] Tax Diversification

Since no one knows what our tax system will look like years from now, it is just as important to diversify by the tax treatment of your investments as it is to diversify the types of investments you use. Having "buckets" using tax deductible contributions, tax free income, tax efficiency, and tax deferral can have a huge impact on your retirement security.

[C] Retirement Assessment

The healthcare professional and his or her advisor will want to measure the effectiveness of the different tax strategies as they apply to your unique situations. For example, a strategy that appears best using 9% earning rates may not be best using 11% or 7% earning rates. Also different time periods could result in different strategies appearing better.

Some tax strategies lend themselves to estate planning flexibility and others do not. Strategy 1 generally requires that the accumulated assets be taxable in your estate for federal estate tax purposes. The other strategies do not. You may choose to use Strategy 1 only in conjunction with other strategies.

Most importantly, make your economic assumptions as consistent as possible when comparing different strategies.

[D] How Can You Achieve Tax Deferred or Even Tax-Free Growth?

[1] IRA ACCOUNTS

First, and perhaps most complex, are various types of IRA accounts. There are five primary IRA types: traditional deductible and nondeductible IRAs, conduit (or rollover) IRAs, contributory Roth IRAs, and conversion Roth IRAs. Each of these provides tax deferral but has different tax treatments, advantages, and disadvantages. For your reference, we have placed a chart in the appendix to this book with more information on each of these options.

Planning Tips ■ There are many considerations in deciding on an IRA strategy. Here are some general rules to use, all subject to the particulars of your situation:

---

1. **Contributing to an IRA.** You should contribute to a Roth IRA if you cannot qualify for a deductible traditional IRA. This provides tax-free income in retirement instead of taxable income. In addition, you are never forced to take distributions from the account, so there may be estate planning and income tax benefits.

   If your joint modified adjusted gross income is above $160,000, you cannot contribute to a Roth IRA. Your only IRA option is the traditional nondeductible IRA, if you do not qualify for a deductible IRA.

2. **Roth Conversion IRA.** You might consider converting existing IRA accounts to a Roth IRA if you can qualify: (have a modified adjusted gross income of less than $100,000) other money to use in paying for the taxes due, and many years before retirement. Converting triggers current taxes on your account balance, but

the tax-free income could more than offset the loss. Do not convert without calculating the likely results and talking to your advisors.

3. **Conduit IRA.** When you leave an employer, you should evaluate whether to leave the money in your old employer's plan or to roll over your money, either to your new employer's plan (if allowed) or to a conduit IRA. A 401(k) plan has certain advantages over an IRA, such as better creditor protection and could provide the ability to borrow from the plan. In addition, other distribution benefits might result from these plans. The disadvantage of these plans is that your investments are limited to those offered by the plan; however, with an IRA, the choice is virtually unlimited. You need to consider the investment options in the new plan to see if you are sacrificing performance.

What other tax-deferred choices do you have?

[2] VARIABLE ANNUITIES

Variable annuities are described in the insurance chapter, but there is a controversy surrounding them.

The benefits of a variable annuity usually cost around 1.4% of your balance each year, plus money management averaging around 0.60%. If you invest in the average mutual fund at 1.4% per year, you would save 0.60% per year.[1] You need to decide whether 0.60% provides enough benefits to be worth the cost.

Most analyses compare tax deferral to mutual fund investing, not on the other features of these plans. This has become more of an issue with the reduction in capital gains rates to a maximum of 15% compared to the ordinary income from the annuity. Unfortunately, an analysis is subject to the variability of mutual fund taxation from fund to fund, as well as how long the individual holds the fund without selling it. One often ignored advantage of variable annuities is the ability to make changes in your investments without incurring any additional tax.

According to a Morningstar Study of January 2001, the average domestic equity mutual fund lost 21% of its return to taxes over the prior 15 years.

Using this example, $10,000 growing for 20 years in a taxable mutual fund at 10% (7.9% net) would be worth $45,754, while the annuity would be worth $60,304 (9.4% net). In five years, the taxable fund would be worth $14,625 compared to the annuity at $15,670.

No matter how you analyze this example, here are some general rules:

1. Consider variable annuities after you have completely funded your qualified plan and IRA options;

2. Look for contracts with minimal surrender periods, i.e., you can take your money out without penalty in a short time; and

3. Consider the value of the additional features, and buy only those you feel are worthwhile. As in all investments, watch your expenses.

[3] MODIFIED ENDOWMENT CONTRACT

The newest modified endowment contracts are structured to use the joint lives of both you and your spouse, which can dramatically reduce your insurance costs. It is important to be clear on your goals and the costs inherent in the specific contract you are evaluating to see if this contract is suitable to your situation.

[4] UNIVERSAL LIFE INSURANCE

Universal life insurance has also come under fire recently, mainly for the agent's lack of disclosure that people were actually buying life insurance. This type of life insurance should primarily be bought for the protection of your loved ones (or business) in the event of your death. Two basic types of policies should be considered, as described in the chapter on insurance: (1) traditional universal life and (2) variable universal life.

Planning Hints ■

1. In general, this approach works best if you need life insurance, have reasonably stable income, have discretionary money to invest after funding your qualified retirement plan, and can plan on keeping the contract for many years. If you are likely to need to stop making premium payments or to cancel the contract prematurely, this is not the right approach for you.

2. To maximize your benefits, plan on maximizing the funding of this contract while maintaining its life insurance status.

3. Do not be a conservative investor in this situation. To overcome the costs and grow your money over time, invest your money in the more aggressive options. If you are using this approach, you have many years to ride through the ups and downs of more aggressive investments.

[5] MUTUAL FUNDS

Mutual funds, often used inside of IRAs and other retirement accounts, take on the tax characteristics of those accounts. The taxation of funds outside of these accounts and how to use funds most effectively to supplement qualified retirement plans is the subject of this section.

Healthcare professionals should understand how to manage their portfolios for maximum after-tax returns with whatever asset allocation mix they are using.

First, here is an explanation of how funds are taxed. Generally, you pay taxes on funds four ways: stock or bond dividends; tax free dividends; capital gains from the sale of securities by the fund each year; and capital gains from the sale of your share in the fund. Since mutual funds are jointly managed for many shareholders, the taxes generated by the fund are shared proportionately by the percentage of the fund assets you own.

Let's look at bonds for a moment. Most of your return in a bond fund is from the dividends paid by the bonds in the fund, although some funds have also generated capital gains through the active buying and selling of their holdings. The dividends paid on most bond funds are taxed as ordinary income, at a maximum tax rate today of 39.6%. Municipal bond funds invest in tax-free bonds, meaning the income is not subject to federal and (sometimes) state income tax (but may be a preference item for alternative minimum tax calculations). This income is usually at a lower rate than similar quality taxable bonds.

Which is better? The healthcare professional's goal should be to get the highest after-tax return, not the lowest tax. The easiest way to decide whether tax-free or taxable bonds are better is to determine the "tax equivalent yield," which compares taxable and tax free income. Divide the tax-free rate by the inverse of your maximum tax bracket, and you can compare the two options. For example, if the tax-free rate is 4.5%, and your bracket is 35%, the formula is:

$$4.5\%/(1 - 0.35) = 4.5\%/0.65 = 6.92\% \text{ tax equivalent yield}$$

At this point, simply choose the higher of the tax equivalent or taxable bond yield and you are (almost) home free. Be sure to consult your tax advisor before you act because the alternative minimum tax calculation might change your results.

What about stock fund taxation? First, many companies pay out part of their profits to shareholders in the form of dividends, which are taxed as ordinary income. Since these are taxed at higher rates than capital gains, your goal might be to choose funds that minimize dividends, although over the last 70 years, about half of the return of the S&P 500 has been through dividends.[2]

Next is the issue of capital gains taxation, triggered by the selling of stocks within the fund at a profit. Since these are paid out by most funds on an annual basis, it is important to realize you may get a tax bill for gains that other people received. Be careful when investing in a fund near year end, since these distributions are usually paid in November or December. It is not unusual for an investor to be losing money and still have to pay taxes on gains.

Lastly, and, easiest to control, are capital gains triggered by selling your shares in a fund. Any gains over your original investment, plus the value of all reinvested dividends and capital gains, are taxed at capital gains rates (if you have held the fund for at least 12 months); otherwise, this is a short-term gain taxed at the same rates as ordinary income).

Planning Hints   ■   Here are ways to minimize taxes on a fund portfolio:

1. Do not reinvest dividends so that this money can be used when you rebalance your portfolio. This simplifies your recordkeeping and provides money to "buy low" without having to sell some of the better performing portions of your portfolio,

which may trigger taxes. Do not forget to reinvest, though, since the loss of compounding this money can be significant.

2. Use funds that have been tax efficient in the past, although past performance is not necessarily an indicator of future tax efficiency. Generally, lower turnover funds have been more tax efficient, the same as those with lower dividend yields.

3. Another approach is to use index funds, which have been relatively tax efficient. One concern may be the large capital gains already trapped inside some index funds, which might be paid out to you if the market drops and shareholders cash out.

4. If you can realize a loss, sell funds that have performed poorly each year before they pay out their capital gains distributions. This can be used to offset gains in other parts of portfolio for tax purposes. You might buy a similar fund to maintain your asset allocation mix or buy the same fund back after waiting 31 days or more. Remember, a fund with poor performance may not be a bad fund; it may be investing in part of the market that is not doing well. In a well diversified portfolio, you almost always will have at least one asset class doing poorly, which is no reflection on the manager.

In the last few years, a category of mutual fund called "tax managed" funds has appeared, with a certainty of more choices in the future. These funds are specifically managed to defer or minimize taxes on investments, which can create significant advantages for you. First, these funds attempt to provide higher after-tax returns, and second, they provide a step-up in cost basis at your death. In contrast to IRAs and annuities, this eliminates any income taxes due at death (but not any estate taxes). It is important to recognize that money management issues have to come before taxes—if they do poorly at making you money, taxes are the least of your concerns.

[6] PORTFOLIOS OF INDIVIDUAL STOCKS AND BONDS

One of the primary choices you have is to either manage this portfolio yourself or to hire professional managers to take care of this for you. You may read more about this in the chapter on portfolio management and investments. One of the most important decisions you make is to determine your asset allocation, so do not forget to be properly diversified.

[E] Planning Issues–Early Career

1. Maximize your retirement plan contributions now. This is the single most important step in having a comfortable retirement, since compounding on your money takes time to work. Remember, at 10%, your money doubles in value in around seven years, and the difference between a fair retirement and a great one may be the last "doubling" of your account.

2. Consider your other life goals in developing a savings and investment plan. You may need to pay off student loans, save for your children's college education, buy a home, or have start-up expenses in your practice. Generally, the shorter term your goal, the more conservative you should be in your investments. In addition, obtaining tax deferral may not be consistent with your goals, since most of these approaches have penalties for withdrawal before retirement.

3. Be sure to have three to six months' expenses set aside for emergencies. This can protect you from having to borrow money and from making large credit card interest payments.

If you need life insurance, and you can make a long-term commitment, consider a properly structured variable universal life insurance policy as a method of saving for long-term goals.

[F] Planning Issues–Mid-Career

1. If you have not done so yet, maximize your contributions to your retirement plan.

2. Assuming you have bought your home and have a relatively stable financial situation, now is the time to be saving additional money outside of your plan. First, determine if you qualify to fund an IRA, since these provide the lowest cost tax deferral available. You should consider contributing to a Roth IRA for your spouse and investing in growth-oriented securities. The tax-free income this provides in retirement can be a great complement to the taxable income from your qualified plan.

3. Remember to watch the tax-efficiency of your personal investments. This can really add to your retirement security.

[G] Planning Issues–Late Career

1. One of the most critical issues is to determine which accounts your income will be taken from in retirement. As a general rule, you want to maximize tax deferral when you can, spending your after-tax money first. There are many planning issues surrounding this, so you might want to get professional advice.

2. The larger your nest egg, the more critical the need for a tax-efficient investment approach. This should be one of the criteria you use in selecting an investment advisor or financial planner. What process do they use to maximize your after-tax returns?

Retirement Planning and Investment Style

Contrary to popular belief, your investment policy should be driven by your retirement planning, not only by your tolerance for risk. This approach ensures you will be comfortable in retirement, and gives you a context for decision making for both sides of the

Table 8-3 *IRA Plans at a Glance*

Contribution Limits		Contribution Limits If over 50	
2002–2004	$3,000	2002–2004	$3,500
2005–2007	$4,000	2005–2007	$4,500
2008+	$5,000	2008+	$6,000

Type of Plan	Contributions & Withdrawals	Adjusted Gross Income Limits for Tax Deduction	Required Minimum Distributions
Deductible IRA	See above chart for maximum contribution limits Each spouse can contribute Withdrawals subject to ordinary income taxes when received Withdrawals before age 59½ subject to 10% tax penalty	If participating in a company retirement plan: Single: Full deduction at $40,000 or less, phased out at $50,000 MAGI (Y-2003) Married filing jointly: If both are active participants, full deduction limited to $60,000 MAGI and phased out at $70,000 MAGI (Y-2003) If your spouse is covered by a plan but you are not, full deduction if your combined AGI is less than $150,000 and phased out at $160,000 MAGI.	Must begin by April 1 of the year following the year you turn 70½
Nondeductible IRA	See above chart for maximum contribution limits Each spouse can contribute Withdrawals are the same as above, except return of non-deductible contributions is tax free	None	Same as above
Conduit (Rollover) IRA	No maximum, since this is moving the balance from your company retirement plan into your own IRA account Withdrawals are the same as in the deductible IRA above	None	Same as above
Contributory Roth IRA	See above chart for maximum contribution limits Each spouse can contribute Withdrawals are tax free if they meet certain qualifications	$160,000 MAGI limit for married filing jointly. $110,000 MAGI limit for singles.	None
Roth Conversion IRA	No maximum, since this is moving the balance from your old IRA plan into a new type of IRA account Withdrawals are the same as the Contributory Roth	Not available if MAGI is over $100,000	None

equation—you can balance your retirement planning with the likely returns your tolerance for risk will provide.

[A] Planning Issues—Early Career

1. The focus at this point in your career might be on paying off student loans or buying a home with retirement planning being secondary. These shorter-term goals might be best served with a more conservative approach, and your retirement needs with a more aggressive approach. You might view these as different "buckets" of money, each with its own investment policy.

2. For retirement investing, recognize there's nothing inherently wrong with being a more conservative investor. The impact of lower returns, though, is a need to save more money each month.

3. Since you're likely to be saving money monthly and building up your nest egg, you need to realize the power of what's called *Dollar Cost Averaging*, where you invest a fixed amount each month regardless of what the market is doing. This approach makes you appreciate the occasional market drops.

[B] Planning Issues—Mid-Career

1. You may well be facing paying for college for your children, weddings, or other shorter term needs, while at the same time needing to prepare for retirement. You might want to consider having separate "buckets" of money, with more conservative investments for short-term needs and more aggressive ones for retirement.

2. The more money you accumulate for retirement, the less investment risk you may have to take in retirement. Many healthcare professionals find it comforting to take a conservative approach while they're retired, but this can only be achieved if you have adequate resources to provide for you and your family. Having an effective retirement plan can help you make this happen!

[C] Planning Issues—Late Career

1. While it's tempting to prefer a conservative investment approach, this might not be in your best interest. Remember, you're likely to live another 20 to 30 years or more in retirement, and your income will have to double or triple to keep up with inflation; and

2. The most effective way to know how conservative you can be is to do a retirement cash flow plan, as shown elsewhere in this chapter. Your future spending needs, savings to date, and many other factors will determine how hard your money must work for you!

Integrating Retirement with Estate Planning

Just like the two sides of a coin, your planning has two sides: retirement planning and estate planning. One of the major tasks in personal finance is balancing your own retirement income needs with your estate planning desires.

It is important to realize that many of the decisions you make to provide a comfortable retirement may diminish your heirs' inheritances. It is particularly problematic when your estate planner tells you to make gifts to your kids, while your retirement planner is concerned you may run out of money. Who should you listen to?

The most logical approach is to integrate both of these areas in your planning from the beginning, rather than one at a time.

The point here is to make decisions after evaluating them from both perspectives. This is an area where a competent Certified Financial Analyst, Certified Financial Planner, and/or Certified Medical Planner can add significant value. These professionals are often advisors versed in retirement and estate planning as well as insurance and investments. All these areas are intertwined in helping you make smarter decisions.

Let's examine some of the issues you might consider.

The first step in effective estate planning is a quality retirement cash flow plan, which should help you have a secure retirement. It also projects the likely value of your assets at different stages, which is invaluable in your estate planning.

Second, determine what part of your heirs' inheritance is likely to be from your qualified retirement plan. It is common today to see health care professionals with very significant balances in their 401(k) and pension plans, and the technical issues involved in passing this money on are among the most complex parts of the law today. We will be focusing on this for the balance of this section, since other estate planning issues are covered elsewhere.

Planning Note ■ The beneficiary designation you have specified to your plan sponsor determines who gets your money when you die—not your will, your living trust, or anything else. Be sure to get advice on this.

Here is a quick review of the rules covering estate planning for qualified retirement benefits. Retirement plan money passes outside of probate directly to your beneficiary, who receives both the money and the income tax liability on the money. In addition, there may be estate taxes due, depending on the size of your total estate including these balances.

With larger estates, it is not uncommon for income and estate taxes to take up to 75% of your retirement plan. Would you like to pass on only 25% of your money?

Therefore, proper retirement planning can also allow the healthcare professional's heirs to continue with tax deferral for their lifetime, which can add millions of dollars to the benefits they receive. This approach would provide minimum distributions to them over many years and might even allow the plan balances to pass on to their heirs.

Endnotes

1. Morningstar Principia, December 31, 2002.
2. Ibbotson & Associates.

Chapter 9

Estate Planning and Execution

Bequeathing Fruits of Labor . . . Avoiding Government Confiscation

Lawrence E. Howes
Joel B. Javer

When we hear about a colleagues' estate, we often conjure up images of rolling green countryside, horses, sprawling mansions and established family dynasties with more money than elderly Daddy Warbucks. These images of wealth have absolutely nothing to do with today's definition of an estate, and its importance in the life of most physicians. Most likely, you and your loved ones have estates that are worth protecting. Now, take the time to understand what your estate consists of, and why integrated financial, business and estate planning is such a valuable imperative for all medical professionals.

Dr. David Edward Marcinko, MBA, CFP, CMP

E state planning is an ongoing process for all physicians and should be part of your thinking every time you cogitate about the future. Your estate is the total value of everything you own. Specifically, it is your home and everything in it, the car, minivan, diamond brooch, wine collection, portfolio of mutual funds, other investments, retirement plans, medical practice, ownership in a family business, vacation homes, furniture, and clothing. It adds up very quickly, especially when you consider any positive effect that the stock market may have had on your investments and the escalation in the price of homes in many parts of the United States.

All too often, estate-planning decisions are routinely made for us, without our knowledge. For example:

1. When you buy a house, the realtor assumes that you want the house titled as joint tenants with your spouse;

2. Your investment account is opened, and it is titled in joint tenancy;

3. Your life insurance agent names your spouse as primary beneficiary and your minor children as contingent beneficiaries;

4. You do not take the time to draft a will, so by default, the state you live in has prepared one for you;

5. Your medical practice agreement does not address death or disability;

6. Your ex-spouse is still the beneficiary of your Individual Retirement Account (IRA) and 401(k) plan; and

7. Your parents are still the beneficiaries of your life insurance.

Regardless of the status of your current planning process, let someone know the whereabouts of your existing estate planning documents and the names of your advisors. Medical professionals keep these critically important wishes a secret, which adds a frustrating search process to an already sad and disruptive time in the lives of loved ones.

Estate planning is probably the last bastion for the sincere procrastinator. As a medical professional, you are likely so busy pursuing your career that you think you do not have time to plan. Perhaps the current state of flux in healthcare keeps you too unsettled to think about long-term planning. Maybe a fear of family conflicts, unresolved issues, or a belief that it will be too expensive to develop an estate plan keep you from acting.

There are three common impediments to estate planning that include:

1. Having to contemplate the consequences of one's own death;

2. A lack of understanding of the terms that advisors often use; and

3. Having to think through the allocation of money between providing a family legacy or funding a charitable cause.

This chapter will educate you on how to avoid common estate planning errors. Guidance is provided on what key elements should be part of your thinking and ultimately included in your estate plan.

There is no way that anyone can predict what future laws will look like. The best we can do is plan based upon current law. In 2001 for example, Congress passed the Economic Growth and Tax Relief Reconciliation Act (EGTRRA), the tax bill that reduced and may eliminate estate taxes, while the impact of Jobs and Growth Tax Relief Reconciliation Act (JGTRRA) 2003 is just now being appreciated. There are many intermediate steps phasing in over several years, which will be discussed in this chapter.

Estate Planning Overview

Planning for the disposition of worldly possessions begins with the wishes of the individual. Although estate planning is a team process, the individual must have a clear objective, or the final result will be confusion.

The four primary goals to consider are:

1. To maintain financial independence during your lifetime;
2. To reduce costs and not delay settling the estate;
3. To minimize estate taxes; and
4. To maximize the inheritance to chosen beneficiaries.

An entire estate planning team can consist of a lawyer, financial planner, accountant, trust officer, and insurance specialist. Each of the team members has a specific focus that is usually predicated on how they are compensated. The lawyer wants to draft your documents; the accountant wants to run the numbers; the life insurance agent wants to sell insurance; and the trust officer wants the money from your estate to fund the trusts. The financial planner should make sure that your estate planning goals and objectives are achieved by coordinating the efforts of the other team members.

The first step is to pull together all the information about yourself and your family. Create a balance sheet or a net worth statement. Make copies of all your existing wills, trusts, powers of attorney, durable power of attorney for health care, and business agreements. When were these documents last reviewed? Do they still name the correct people in the correct jobs? Is the guardian for your children still your first choice? Does the guardian know of his or her responsibilities and your wishes for the future of your children? Have your children grown up so that the guardians are unnecessary?

What about your life insurance? Has your agent checked the ownership or beneficiaries recently? Is the amount of insurance still correct? Are you able to keep any financial promises that you have made?

At this point, thoroughly review your current estate plan to see if it still adequately represents your goals and objectives. Remember that a good estate plan is an ongoing process with stages of implementation and careful review at least every five years.

[A] Meeting with Advisors

Make an appointment with a financial advisor to help you organize all your financial information and to work through your goals and objectives. Once you have a plan in mind, meet with an attorney to get documents drafted, talk with your life insurance agent, and meet with a trust officer if you are drafting a trust with a corporate trustee. Meet with all other relevant advisors.

If confusion sets in or decisions cannot be made in a timely fashion, advisors can develop their own type of paralysis and procrastination. This is usually evident when advisors:

- Move on to other clients;
- Appear to keep collecting unwarranted fees when there is no progress being made; and
- Push for a conclusion regardless of the wishes of the client donor.

[B] Finalizing the Estate Plan

Make sure all your assets are retitled appropriately and that your retirement plan and life insurance beneficiaries are coordinated with your new estate plan. The next step is to sign the documents.

Choosing a Personal Representative

Your personal representative is named in your will and is responsible for management of your estate including:

1. Gathering all estate assets;
2. Collecting all amounts owed the decedent;
3. Notifying creditors and paying all valid debts;
4. Filing claims for pension and profit-sharing benefits, social security, and veterans benefits;
5. Managing the estate's assets, including proper distributions and allocation of IRA accounts;
6. Selling assets as needed to pay expenses or as directed by the will;
7. Distributing assets to beneficiaries;
8. Filing decedents final federal income tax return;
9. Filing estate tax return; and
10. Filing state death tax return.

The position of personal representative entails much responsibility, involves many duties, and requires a considerable time commitment. The personal representative must petition the probate court for formal appointment.

Selection of your personal representative should not be made lightly or as a favor to a friend. This position requires a lot of work with very often little or no pay. Friends and family typically will not charge the estate for their time and work. Outside advisors like attorneys and accountants will not hesitate to bill for their work effort. Your selection criteria should include:

1. Longevity – the person should have a likelihood of being able to serve after your death;
2. Skill in managing legal and financial affairs;
3. Familiarity with your estate and wishes;
4. Integrity and loyalty; and
5. Impartiality and absence of conflicts of interest.

Alternatives to family or friends might be a corporate executor such as a bank, an attorney, or other advisor. Similar criteria should be used in the selection of a trustee.

Probate

The motivating issue and primary purpose of estate planning is to ensure the proper transfer of property to desired heirs with a minimum of expenses and taxation. The process of transferring property is called probate. Probate, meaning "to prove," is the legal process of a court-supervised property transfer whose disposition is guided by either your will, or if you do not have a will, by the state laws of intestacy. Other property or non-probate assets include property held in trust, in joint tenancy, most life insurance policies (because they have a named beneficiary), and most retirement plan assets (again because of a named beneficiary). All property is subject to estate taxation—whether or not it goes through probate. Avoiding probate does not mean you can also avoid estate taxes.

Probate avoidance is the subject of numerous seminars across the country. These programs rely mainly on people's fears of the unknown. In actuality, many states have adopted all or part of the Uniform Probate Code (UPC). The UPC provides for a streamlined probate process and, in most situations, residents of these states have little to fear when it comes to probate. However, the probate process is a public process. Anyone can go to the court and look up the will of a decedent and delve into his or her personal life and bequests.

An estate is usually probated, distributed, and taxed under the laws of the state in which you are domiciled. There are some states (e.g., California, Florida, and Nevada) that have no additional death taxes beyond the federal estate tax. Changing your residence to one of these states may avoid significant death taxes at the state level.

You can do several things to establish domicile in a particular state. Examples involve voter registration, automobile registration, driver's license, safe-deposit boxes, and having a principal residence there. Owning property in more than one state may cause multiple taxation by multiple states claiming jurisdiction if you are not careful. Determine the requirements for each state and take a definitive position on where you wish your property to be taxed and probated. This decision needs to be included specifically in your estate planning documents.

Non-Probate Assets

There are situations where avoiding probate is desirable, especially for those who want a lot of privacy for their finances after their death. There are relatively simple ways to avoid probate, but they all have consequences.

[A] Joint Tenancy

Joint tenancy is the most common way that property between spouses is titled. Each spouse maintains a 50% undivided interest in the property. This is the conventional way married couples own their property. It is simple, usually requiring only the check of a box on an application or loan form. Upon death, the property automatically, by operation of law, passes to the surviving spouse and avoids probate.

However, the automatic aspect means that a will does not control the disposition of the asset. Before you title anything, think about the consequences. There may be situations where you have an asset, for example, a brokerage account that you would like to leave to a charity. If you have titled the account as joint tenants with your spouse, the brokerage account will go automatically to your spouse and not to the charity as you intended. If a joint bank account is created between spouses, then each spouse owns one half of the account. If the account is established with a non-spouse, different rules apply. Be careful when establishing the ownership of all property.

[B] Community Property

Community property is another form of co-ownership limited to the interests held between husband and wife. Community property does not automatically pass to your spouse. When one spouse dies, the survivor continues to own only his or her half of the assets. The decedent's will determines the transfer of the other half. Only eight of the 50 states are community-property states, but it is estimated that 25% of the population resides in these states. The eight states are Arizona, California, Idaho, Louisiana, Nevada, New Mexico, Texas, and Washington. Wisconsin has a form of community property called marital partnership property. This form is similar but, as in all states, the specifics vary. The laws of the particular state must be examined to determine the effect on the married couple's property.

[C] Life Insurance

Life insurance is also property. The two aspects of the property are the face amount and, unless it is a term life insurance policy, the cash value. The critical item to remember is that, if you own the policy, then the face amount or death benefit is included in your estate and probably subject to estate taxes. The death benefit passes through the operation of a beneficiary designation. At the time of death, most cash value policies include the existing cash value in the death benefit. This is known as a type A policy. Type B excludes the cash value from the death benefit so it would be added to the face amount.

[D] Retirement Plans

Your retirement plans and IRAs are transferred by beneficiary designation. It is common to see a divorced physician client who is divorced with an ex-spouse as the named beneficiary on a retirement plan or life insurance policy. Making sure that all beneficiary designations are consistent with your current estate plan will avoid these unintended consequences.

[E] Revocable Living Trust

A revocable living trust is another legal arrangement that attracts much attention. Here your assets are voluntarily placed in a trust, thereby making you a *trustor*. The control of the assets in the trust is then transferred to a *trustee*. You can make yourself the trustee as well. The key word here is revocable, which means the terms of the trust can be changed, altered, amended, or terminated. Legal title to the property, however, is retained by the trust.

The trust document specifies what happens to the property upon death of the trustor, and hence property transfer occurs by operation of law. An interesting aspect of this trust is its ability to handle property upon disability or incompetence. Many single medical professionals who do not have relatives to manage their financial affairs or prefer not to use relatives could benefit from having a revocable living trust.

The trust can provide continuity of investment management, bill paying, collection of accounts receivable, and general financial stability until the medical professional is able to resume control of his or her financial affairs. In addition, if property is owned in more than one state, ownership of that property by a revocable living trust would eliminate the necessity of dealing with probate in several states.

[F] Buy-Sell Agreements

All your medical practice and other business agreements, which dictate what happens to your property, should be addressed in what is called a buy-sell agreement. This agreement stipulates what would happen to your practice should you die, become disabled, leave, or wish to retire. The agreement states that your partner or partners will buy your interest upon your death and stipulates that your estate will sell your interest. It is a binding agreement to both parties. The agreement will have a valuation method, which might be a stated fixed price or a formula. If a fixed price is selected, then a procedure should be in place to ensure at least an annual revaluation of the practice. Formulas provide a better ongoing representation of the value of the practice. However, the dynamic healthcare environment might warrant a review of the validity of your existing formula. If the practice is valued highly, then having sufficient cash to buy out a deceased partner might be difficult and possibly an overwhelming financial burden. Life insurance is commonly considered the best vehicle to provide the cash when needed the most, and a number of keys create a successful buy/sell agreement:

- It must be decided who will buy the practice from the disabled proprietor or partner or his or her heirs upon death. It may be the remaining partner(s), or the practice entity itself, or, in the case of a sole physician proprietor, a key physician employee.
- The buy/sell agreement must be stipulated as mandatory. According to the Internal Revenue Service (IRS), if the agreement is not mandatory, then the value of the practice is not considered fixed. As a result, the IRS might not consider the agreement binding in determining the value of the practice for estate tax purposes.

- Be specific regarding what specifically is to be purchased. This can include land, buildings, inventory, licenses, and even goodwill and other intangible (but valuable) assets.
- The most important key is determining the correct value for the practice or share in question. The IRS will rarely challenge a value for being set too high but will challenge those it deems as valued too low. Valuation should not be taken lightly and can be a fixed dollar amount or based on a formula. It is usually recommended to use a formula rather than a fixed dollar amount.

A number of different forms of buy/sell agreements are available. The following is a quick overview of four different variations.

[1] SOLE PROPRIETOR BUY/SELL AGREEMENT

Since a sole proprietor does not have a partner, other than a spouse, the sole proprietor usually must look elsewhere for a buyer. Therefore, the sole proprietor is likely to turn either to a valued physician employee or a competitor to continue the business. In this case, a life insurance policy is purchased on the life of the proprietor, and the agreement is signed between the current and the future owners providing the guidelines for the future practice transfer. In addition to being the owner of the policy, the future physician owner typically names him or herself as beneficiary as well.

[2] CROSS PURCHASE BUY/SELL AGREEMENT

This type of buy/sell is normally used for any practice with multiple owners, although it is best used for agreements with only two owners. In this arrangement, each owner purchases insurance on each of the other's lives. Again, the owner of each policy names himself or herself as beneficiary as well. Upon the death or disability of one partner, the remaining partner(s) are provided the funds to purchase a pro rata share of the deceased or disabled individual's practice interest.

[3] ENTITY PURCHASE BUY/SELL AGREEMENT

This form is used for multiple owners, and/or when the owner(s) of the practice wants to use the assets of the business to fund the insurance policies. In this arrangement, the practice owns the policies on each partner or shareholder and is also listed as the beneficiary of each policy. Upon the death or disability of the physician partner, the business would be able to purchase the shares from the disabled partner or the deceased's heirs.

[4] OPTIONAL PURCHASE/WAIT AND SEE BUY/SELL AGREEMENT

This type of agreement allows either the practice or the individual partner(s) the option of purchasing the deceased or disabled partner's interest in the practice. Normally, if the practice does not initially exercise its option to buy within a set period, the remaining partner(s) would then have a period in which to exercise their option. If they do not buy the outstanding interest, the practice would then be forced to purchase the shares.

Often, a trusteed agreement is advisable. It is not unusual to find situations in which the practice partners work together smoothly and efficiently. Their spouses, however, are not compatible. To remove personalities from the transfer of ownership interests for money, especially at a very stressful point in their lives, it is often a good idea to let a disinterested third party (a trustee) conduct the transfer.

Example

Dr. Samuel May has been the sole owner of The Family Physician Group, which includes six other physicians and 12 other employees, for over 10 years. He has often thought about who will continue this successful practice. In the past month, he has decided that Dr. Michelle Roy is the best candidate for the job. Dr. Roy has also expressed interest in becoming Dr. May's successor. As a result, they have decided to set up a trusteed sole proprietor buy/sell agreement that would provide for the smooth, mandatory transfer of the practice in the case of the death or disability of Dr. May. Once the practice is correctly valued, Dr. Roy plans to purchase a life insurance policy on the life of Dr. May, which will be owned by a third party trust, which will also be the beneficiary. Upon the death or disability of Dr. May, the agreement is executed by the trustee, and Dr. Roy becomes the sole owner of The Family Physician Group.

Documents of Property Transfer

[A] Wills

A will is a legally enforceable document that expresses directions for disposing of your probate property at death. In most states, any individual 18 years of age or older who is of sound mind may draw up a will.

One of the most important aspects of a will for those medical professionals who have minor children is the nomination of a guardian for your children and a trustee for your money in the event of your death. For a married couple, the surviving parent would become the guardian; however, in the case of a common accident, a guardian and trust would be beneficial. A divorced parent must consider that his or her ex-spouse would be the natural guardian. Special concerns should be addressed if there are reasons the ex-spouse would not be a suitable guardian. If you are a widowed parent, special considerations should be made when addressing the nomination of a guardian. The word nomination is important, because the selection of a guardian is only a recommendation to the court. Selection of a guardian is extremely important, since this person would be responsible for raising your children. The guardian is generally used when both parents are deceased. Prior to including this person or persons in your will, you should discuss your expectations and desires with the prospective guardian to make sure the person is willing to take on what could be a tremendous responsibility.

Divorced couples still retain their natural rights as parents independent of who was the custodial parent. If a divorced spouse is, in the other parent's estimation, not a suitable parent, then this issue must be addressed in the guardian section of the will.

A will is regularly contested if someone is unhappy with the will's contents. Normally a will contest occurs when an expectant heir believes he or she was not treated properly under the terms of the will. Many lawyers now draft a "no contest clause," which simply states, "I have only provided for the persons set forth in this will."

[B] Trusts

A very commonly used planning tool is a trust. Trusts come in numerous types with countless different purposes. There are three parties to a trust:

1. The trustor (the person putting the property into the trust);
2. The trustee (the person in charge of managing the trust according to its terms); and
3. The beneficiary (the person(s) entitled to the enjoyment or ultimate disposition of the trust property).

The beneficiary or beneficiaries might be entitled to receive money now or upon certain events like the attainment of a specific age. A trust usually contains two different legal types of property: *principal* and *income*. The principal of a trust is its invested wealth, and its size will fluctuate based upon the performance of the investments and any withdrawals made from it. Income on the other hand is money derived from the use of the principal, for example, dividends, rents, and interest.

Many trust documents are written to provide the beneficiary with income only during their lifetime. Hence, only income from the trust investments may be distributed to the beneficiary with the intent that the principal will remain intact and be available to the remainderman or ultimate beneficiary when the income beneficiary dies.

Modern investment theory takes a different approach. Instead of the trust investing for the separate components of principal and income, many trusts are invested to seek total return. This is portfolio appreciation without regard for the difference between principal and income. For example, a stock that appreciates 10% (additional principal) yet pays no dividend (no income) still provides a successful investment result to the trust in the form of additional capital. In this case, the trustee can sell some of the shares of the appreciated stock to provide income to the beneficiary. In this situation, a trust might provide a stated payout percentage like the greater of trust income or 4% of trust principal. Many lawyers recognize that states are enacting this newer concept, and the lawyers are adjusting the drafting of trusts.

[1] TESTAMENTARY TRUST

A testamentary trust can be established as part of your estate planning but does not become effective until you or your spouse dies. This vehicle is private and not subject to court supervision. It offers great flexibility, and the terms can be tailored to meet your individual needs.

Example

Dr. Charles Cheung is married and has a child who is a minor. He has established a testamentary trust to receive assets upon his or his spouse's death. The asset that is funding this trust is simply a beneficiary designation on a life insurance policy, which names the "Testamentary Trust created under the last will and testament of Dr. Cheung, dated." The trust provisions allow the trustee to spend money on behalf of the child for health, education, maintenance, and support (HEMS). Additional money will be spent on certain birthdays, such as 13, 18, and 21, and upon marriage. Ultimately, the balance in the trust funds will be distributed when the child reaches age 25.

[2] MARITAL TRUST

A marital trust is established to receive all property and assets that you intend to go to your surviving spouse. You may leave the property outright or in trust. If the portion of the estate that will go to the surviving spouse is large, it is best left in trust. The trust provides a container for all assets and simplifies the management of those assets for the surviving spouse. The spouse has total control over the assets and can remove the assets from the trust at any time. A variation on the marital trust, a qualified terminal interest property (QTIP) trust, allows assets to pass to a spouse only during the spouse's lifetime.

[3] INCENTIVE TRUSTS

These provisions in testamentary trusts are a way to transfer assets while trying to influence the behavior of the beneficiary(ies). They offer an incentive to the beneficiary to achieve some pre-determined goal, usually to seek achievements important to the decedent or other family members. For example: Each heir shall receive $100,000 upon graduation from medical, business, law, or dental school. Each heir shall receive an income distribution equal to three times the charitable contributions that the heir makes each year. The possibilities are endless, and these provisions can be a very powerful incentive to maintain and fulfill cherished family behavior and values.

[4] IRREVOCABLE LIFE INSURANCE TRUST

Life insurance has extreme leverage. By that, we mean that a relatively small premium can produce a large asset at death. Avoiding inclusion of this large asset in your estate can be achieved by using an irrevocable life insurance trust (ILIT). This trust uses life insurance as its primary asset. Upon death, the insurance proceeds are paid into the trust, and the money is then available to pay estate expenses and taxes; then the money is ultimately distributed to the beneficiaries of the trust. If a cash value life insurance policy is the asset, the buildup of equity may be accessible by the trust beneficiaries for limited use before death.

The important issue is to ensure that ownership of the trust never reverts to the insured, because this would defeat the whole purpose of an ILIT. Life insurance policies also require ongoing premium payments. Hence, the ILIT needs cash, assets, or periodic contributions to enable it (through the trustee) to pay the premiums. Because this is an irrevocable trust, any contribution is removed from the donor's estate, and the contribution cannot be taken back. The contribution does not qualify for the $11,000 annual gift tax exclusion, because the intent of the $11,000 exclusion is for a current gift, called a gift of a *present interest*, that is, money or property that can be used immediately by the recipient. Any gift, which is deemed to be a gift of a *future interest* or one that is accessible some time in the future, falls outside of the $11,000 annual exclusion. Therefore, when money is contributed to an ILIT, the beneficiaries would have to wait until death before they could receive the money. That defines a gift of a future interest. Hence, a gift tax return would have to be filed with each contribution, and a portion of your unified credit would be utilized.

Fortunately, this administrative nightmare was addressed by Mr. Crummey, who went to court to solve this problem. Under what is now termed the Crummey trust or Crummey provision, each time money is contributed to the trust, the trustee writes a letter to the beneficiaries stating that money has been placed in the ILIT and they have 30–45 days to request, in writing, their money. As the beneficiaries at that time have access to the money, the contribution is deemed to be a gift of a current interest and qualifies for the $11,000 exclusion.

Another way to remove a life insurance policy from your estate is to have another person own it. A life insurance policy is a piece of property with an owner, a beneficiary, and a premium payer. Ownership means inclusion in your estate. Hence, it is preferable to have the owner be the ILIT as described above, or, at least another individual. At first glance, naming a spouse as the owner seems simple and effective and avoids the expenses of setting up a trust. However, if your spouse is the owner and beneficiary of your policy, when you die the policy is not included in your estate, but the proceeds are included in your spouse's estate. So naming the spouse accomplishes only one half of the goal of removing a life insurance policy from your combined estates. In this situation, if your spouse pre-deceases you, then any cash value of your life insurance policy will be included in his or her estate. Naming adult children as owners solves the inclusion of the proceeds in the combined estate, but if they are the beneficiaries, they do not have an obligation to use the proceeds for estate settlement costs. The use of an ILIT is normally the best solution to removing life insurance proceeds from your estate even though there is a cost to establish and maintain ILITs.

You may have an existing life insurance policy that you would like to remove from your estate by transferring the ownership to your children or to an ILIT. If you die within three years of transferring ownership of a life insurance policy, the policy proceeds are brought back into your estate. It is normally best to apply for a new insurance policy when you are doing estate planning. This eliminates the concern over the three-year rule. If you have a health condition that makes you uninsurable or if life insurance underwriting establishes a premium that is not acceptable, then using a current policy may be the only alternative.

Disclaimers

In some situations, an inheritance might complicate an estate and add to the estate tax burden. If there are sufficient assets and income to accomplish financial goals, more assets are not needed. A disclaimer may be useful. This is an unqualified refusal to accept a gift or inheritance, that is, when you "just say no." You have decided not to accept a sizable gift made under a will, trust, or other document. When you disclaim the property, certain requirements must be met:

- The disclaimer must be irrevocable;
- The refusal must be in writing;
- The refusal must be received within nine months;
- You must not have accepted any interest in the property; and
- As a result of the refusal, the property will pass to someone else.

The property passes under the terms of the decedent's will, as if you had predeceased the decedent. If the filer of the disclaimer has control, the property will be included in the disclaimant's estate and can only be passed to another as a gift or as an inheritance. The intent of the disclaimer is to renounce and never take control of the property.

The use of disclaimers will likely become a more important tool in estate planning under EGTRRA. Many estate plans that were designed and drafted prior to EGTRRA may have unintended consequences when governed by the new law. Hence, disclaimers may be the only way to allocate estate assets according to personal desires compared with legal design.

Unified Estate and Gift Taxes

Extremely high tax rates are the motivation for estate owners to take advantage of every planning technique possible to reduce these taxes. The objective is ultimately to pass more wealth to family and heirs. Estate and gift taxes use the same tax table, commonly referred to as the unified rate schedule. (See Exhibit 9–1.) However, EGTRRA eliminates estate taxes in 2010, but not gift taxes. Hence, at that time, the gift tax rate will become the highest individual income tax rate. The law has a Sunset provision, which states if Congress does not permanently codify the law, the law will revert to the laws in place in the year 2002. At first glance, this would seem to make long-term planning difficult; however, prudence would indicate that keeping abreast of the law will eventually clarify planning needs. Until the law is resolved, a good relationship with a financial advisor and/or estate planning attorney is advisable. A taxable estate of just $100,000 is taxed at 30%, and amounts over $1,000,000 are taxed at 41% with the highest rate at 50%. The 50% rate is scheduled to decline by approximately 1% per year until 2007 when it will be lowered to 45%.

Exhibit 9–1 *Federal Unified Transfer-Tax Rates – Since 1977*

If the Amount is: Over (dollars)	But Not Over (dollars)	Base Amount (dollars)	Tentative Tax: Plus Percentage	On Excess Over (dollars)
$0	$10,000	$0	18%	$0
10,000	20,000	1,800	20%	10,000
20,000	40,000	3,800	22%	20,000
40,000	60,000	8,200	24%	40,000
60,000	80,000	13,000	26%	60,000
80,000	100,000	18,200	28%	80,000
100,000	150,000	23,800	30%	100,000
150,000	250,000	38,800	32%	150,000
250,000	500,000	70,800	34%	250,000
500,000	750,000	155,800	37%	500,000
750,000	1,000,000	248,300	39%	750,000
1,000,000	1,250,000	345,800	41%	1,000,000
1,250,000	1,500,000	448,300	43%	1,250,000
1,500,000	2,000,000	555,800	45%	1,500,000
2,000,000	2,500,000	780,800	49%	2,000,000
2,500,000		1,025,800	50%	2,500,000

In 2003:

If the Amount is: Over (dollars)	But Not Over (dollars)	Base Amount (dollars)	Tentative Tax: Plus Percentage	On Excess Over (dollars)
$2,000,000		$780,000	49%	$2,000,000
2004			48%	
2005			47%	
2006			46%	
2007–2009			45%	

2010 Estate tax repealed. (Caution is warranted, based upon the Sunset provision discussed above.) The maximum rate for gifts is 35% starting at $500,000.

[A] Calculations

Estate tax calculations are similar to income tax calculations in the methods used. First, we add up all your estate assets to determine your total gross estate. Items included in

ssets are cash, CDs, money market funds, life insurance proceeds, stocks, bonds,
nutual funds, retirement benefits and IRAs, personal property, real estate, vacation
omes, jewelry, art, coins, stamp collections, business interests, and all receivables.

Deductions are taken for estate administration, funeral expenses, debts, mortgages,
nd credit cards. The assets minus the deductions yield the adjusted gross estate.

Another set of deductions is taken for charitable gifts and transfers to your spouse.
he resulting figure is the *taxable estate* from which the final deduction is made for the
Jnified Credit. (See Exhibit 9–2.)

xhibit 9–2 *Federal Estate Tax Calculation Example*

Dr. Han Cheung decided to calculate the amount of his taxable estate in 2002, assuming he and
his wife might die in the same accident. He has a $500,000 life insurance policy on himself and a
$250,000 life insurance policy on his spouse. Here are his calculations:

Federal Estate Tax Calculation

Gross Estate			$2,830,000
Funeral and Adm*	$20,000		
Debts and Taxes*	$155,000		
Losses		$ _____	
Total Deductions		$175,000	
Adjusted Gross Estate			$2,655,000
Marital Deduction	$0		
Charitable Deduction	$0		
Total Deductions	$0		
Taxable Estate			$2,655,000
Adjusted Taxable Gifts			$0
Tentative Tax Base			$2,655,000
Tentative Tax	$856,750	Gift Taxes Payable	$0
Tax Payable Before Credits			$856,750
Tax Credits			
Unified Credit	345,800	State Death Tax*	$113,730
Credit Prior Tax	$0		
Total	$459,530		
Net Federal Estate Tax*		397,220	
Total Cash Required (Add All *)		$685,950	

Dr. Cheung made the following observations:

1. Because the estate is taxed in the 49% bracket, each additional dollar added to the estate would
   lose 49 cents to taxes. Or alternatively, a dollar reduction in the estate saves 49 cents. The graduated tax tables can make the savings lower than 49 cents.
2. Any gifts to charity can save significant estate taxes.

(*continued*)

Exhibit 9-2 *Federal Estate Tax Calculation Example (continued)*

3. The addition of the $750,000 in total life insurance proceeds included in the estate generated $118,700 in taxes. The heirs enjoyed only $631,300 of the policy proceeds.
4. Without the inclusion of the life insurance proceeds, the estate tax would have been reduced to the 45% bracket.
5. Due to the graduated tax tables, removing the life insurance from the estate would have saved $118,700 in estate taxes.
6. The Total Cash Required calculation indicates that more money than just estate taxes will be needed to settle the estate.
7. The new tax law reduced his estate taxes by $338,540.

Although the unified estate and gift tax rates are high, these taxes apply only after the unified credit is deducted. Everyone is entitled to the unified credit. A tax credit is a dollar for dollar offset, which in the year 2003 is set at $345,800. The credit applies only to property that is owned by the decedent at death. Hence, great attention must be paid to the correct titling and ownership of assets, especially within marriages.

[B] Exclusion Amounts

The exclusion amount is the amount of property that can be passed without taxation. In the year 2003, this amount was $1,000,000. In 2003, for a married couple, both spouses could pass $1,350,000 free of estate taxes. This action does require proper planning as described under the unified credit shelter trust. Under current law, the unified credit and exclusion amount will increase as follows:

Year	Unified Credit	Exclusion Amount
2002–2003	$345,800	1,000,000
2004–2005	555,800	1,500,000
2006–2008	780,800	2,000,000
2009	1,455,800	3,500,000
2010	Estate tax repealed	

The escalation of Unified Credits and Exclusion Amounts with the ultimate elimination of estate taxes has a potential wealth benefit for future generations of medical professionals. Skepticism is always a part of new tax legislation, and several pundits are predicting that estate taxes will not be eliminated, although many believe the exclusion amount will be permanently increased.

Estate Liquidity Planning

It has been said that you need credit to live but cash to die. Unfortunately, in many cases, cash may be needed quickly following a death to pay for a variety of obligations. These obligations can be subdivided into three general categories:

- Last expenses. These include federal estate and income along with state inheritance taxes, lawyers, accountants, appraisers, last illness, and funeral expenses;
- Funds to allow family members to readjust their lives. The amount is determined by the nature of the family; and
- Money for family needs. The money could be needed for upcoming college expenses or basic annual income requirements.

Determining the amount of cash needed for your estate requirements can be accomplished by a Certified Financial Planner, CPA, or life insurance agent.

The three major sources of cash for your estate are:

1. Cash in checking or money market accounts, assets in brokerage accounts, certificates of deposit, and mutual funds;
2. Life insurance proceeds; and
3. Loans.

You may not want your heirs to need to sell real estate or other assets, perhaps at reduced prices, because of the need to raise cash quickly. The sale of existing assets can provide some liquidity, but frequently there are insufficient saleable assets to satisfy the total cash requirements of your estate. When there are cash shortages, the least expensive way to provide for the shortage may be with a life insurance policy.

Life insurance premiums are relatively small when compared to the potential benefits. A properly structured life insurance policy will never have you paying more in premiums than the death benefit. Hence, life insurance provides tremendous leverage, and this is a small price to pay for a potentially large benefit when it is needed the most. With the phaseout of estate taxes, the need for life insurance on a long-term basis appears to be reduced. Estates that are subject to taxes through the phaseout period to 2010 should consider the purchase of term life insurance for liquidity purposes. With proper planning, the spouse with the lowest premium should be the one insured. If the law is amended and a more permanent need for life insurance arises, the term insurance may be converted.

Some medical professionals have been told that the beneficiary of a life insurance policy receives the proceeds tax free. That means *income* tax free, not *estate* tax free. Without proper planning your estate is automatically increased by the amount of insurance proceeds.

If you do not want to buy life insurance, then loans to pay the taxes may be an alternative. However, securing a loan for an estate may be difficult. Banks want to be repaid, and because estate liquidity is the issue, the banking community is frequently an unwilling partner. Estate loans may come from potential beneficiaries and other family members. This is a technique of last resort.

[A] IRC Section 303 Redemptions

A family business or medical practice may make up the majority of your estate. The business has a value, but very little cash. In recognition of the closely held business owner, the IRS allows stock in the company to be redeemed to pay federal and state death taxes, generation-skipping transfer taxes, and funeral and administration expenses. There are few tax-deductible ways of getting money out of a corporation, and salaries and business expenses head the list. The IRS maintains that, if a business is at least 35% of your adjusted gross estate, the business owner can redeem stock to pay for approved expenses. Since you get a step-up in basis at death, the shares redeemed should not generate a capital gain. The transaction is deemed a sale of a capital asset and not a dividend. (A dividend is not deductible, so it is taxable to the corporation as well as taxed to you personally upon receipt.)

The strategy of a § 303 redemption is prudent. However, there must be cash available to redeem the stock. Typically, a life insurance policy is purchased to provide the cash for the redemption.

[B] IRC Section 6161

The IRS has discretion under IRC Section 6161 to grant an extension to any estate for up to 10 years to pay estate tax upon a showing of "reasonable cause." The IRS charges interest, but if the estate does not have the money to pay all the estate taxes when initially due, then Section 6161 is a potential opportunity to reduce the immediate payment burden on the estate. Unfortunately, this extension does keep the estate open for the duration of the payment plan and incurs additional accounting and administrative costs.

[C] IRC Section 6166

Another benefit the IRS allows on the death of a qualifying small business owner is Section 6166. This provides for the extension of the payment of estate taxes over a period of 14 years. Recent legislation has made it more difficult to qualify; there are now three levels of qualification. The first is the same as for IRC Section 303. The second adds a strict definition of a closely held business. The third requires that the business must have been actually engaged in carrying on a trade or business *at the time of death*. The first four annual payments are interest only, and then the next ten annual payments are principal and interest. The interest rate on the first $484,000 of tax due is at 2%. Calculating the tax that qualifies for the extension requires applying the percentage of the adjusted gross estate attributed to the small business, multiplied by the total federal estate tax.

[D] IRC Section 2032A Special Use Valuation

Suppose you own a farm that for many years was located well outside the city limits of a growing community; however, now the farm is in the path of this growth. The dynamics of determining the fair market value of your farm have changed. You might be inclined to value it as a farm, and your estate would make the argument that it is a farm. The IRS would argue the property should be valued at its highest and best use. Unfortunately for your estate, the "highest and best use" might be as a mega mall, apartment buildings, or a high-rise office building. All of these are worth considerably more than the farm might be.

Valuation of a property at the highest and best use might force the survivors to sell the land to pay a large estate tax. On the other hand, valuation at its present use might enable the survivors to carry on in the farming business. Section 2032A permits qualifying estates to value at least a portion of the real property at its "qualified use." This sections applies to farms or other trades or businesses.

Five major requirements and conditions must be satisfied. Ultimately, the maximum amount by which the value of the special use real estate can be reduced is $800,000. This amount is indexed for inflation after 2000. While this is not an insignificant amount, if there is a large disparity between "highest and best use" and present use value, then planning to avoid the potential liquidity deficit is imperative.

[E] IRC Section 2057 Family Owned Business Interest Deduction

A qualified family business (the rules are quite complicated) is entitled to an additional $300,000 exclusion amount. (This amount is in addition to the current $1,000,000.) This benefit has been eliminated as of 2003.

Family Gifting and Loans

The annual gift tax exclusion allows you to give any individual $11,000 per year without paying or filing a gift tax return. There is no limit on the number of individuals who might benefit from your generosity. If you are married, then you and your spouse together may give to any number of individuals. The recipients do not owe any tax on the money. Gifts in excess of $11,000 are subject to current gift tax. A gift tax return must be filed by April 15 of the year following the gift. Gifts to qualified charities are subject to a different set of income tax rules discussed later.

Gifting assets to family members or others during your lifetime can be an effective estate planning technique. A gift of money or stock to your children automatically reduces your estate. If your *taxable estate* is in excess of $2 million, then you are in the 49% estate tax bracket. This means that each dollar you can remove from your estate and allow to appreciate in your children's estate can help reduce a significant potential estate tax liability. However, if the sole purpose of gifting is to reduce estate taxes, then EGTRRA's reduction and ultimate elimination of estate taxes will nullify this technique. Remember that tax laws are always subject to change, and EGTRRA has a Sunset provision, which in some form may not totally eliminate estate taxes. Gifting strategies may still be appropriate depending on your expectation of law changes, and when the estate is large, and life expectancy is limited. There are traps in these gifting situations, so consult proper counsel.

When you give stock, you also give the recipient your cost basis. If you have low basis stock that you are thinking about selling but are concerned about paying 20% in capital gains tax, you could gift portions of the stock to your children (or anyone in the 15% income tax bracket) and sell just enough to pay the 10% capital gains tax in their bracket. The gift value is the market price of the stock on date of gift. This is an outright gift, so before you make the gift, make sure you can afford to give up the cash or the asset forever.

Example

Dr. Jay Miller recently gave his son $500,000. He had an exemption equivalent amount of $1,000,000 in 2002. His gift reduced this by $500,000, leaving $500,000. (If you cannot remember, your gift tax returns will be a formal reminder.) In the year 2004 the exemption equivalent amount will increase to $1,500,000, so you will have recovered $500,000 and have $1,000,000 remaining to use in the future on gifts that exceed $11,000 per donee per year.

Example

Dr. Eva Gray has already given gifts in 2002 of $1,000,000, the maximum allowed under the exemption equivalent. She now wants to give an additional $100,000.

The tax table shows that the tax on this extra gift is $23,800 (30% marginal rate, but the graduated table levies a smaller total tax). Conventional tax wisdom has always been to delay paying taxes whenever possible. However, Dr. Gray has taken a closer look at what will happen if she gives $100,000 of property that is likely to rapidly appreciate to her adult daughter.

Dr. Gray is in poor health and believes her life expectancy to be less than seven years. If the property were to appreciate at 20% per year for the next seven years (until 2009), $100,000 would grow to approximately $360,000. All this appreciation is outside of Dr. Gray's estate if she makes the gift now.

If Dr. Gray kept the property, then the $360,000 would be included in the estate and taxed at 45%.

This example shows the leverage available with a gifting strategy. If appropriate in your estate planning, paying your taxes now could benefit your estate later. However, as mentioned above, this technique has limited applicability.

[A] The Uniform Transfer to Minors Act

The Uniform Transfer to Minors Act (UTMA) or Uniform Gift to Minors Act provide for an account to be established by checking a box on most mutual fund applications and/or brokerage accounts. No trust documents have to be prepared. A uniform trust has been adopted by each state. A custodian, normally a parent or grandparent, is named as the party responsible for making investment decisions and distributing assets for the benefit of the child. The account is primarily used as a tool for accumulating assets to pay for a child's college education; however, money may be used for almost any purpose that benefits the child—reading classes, computer camp, or ballet classes. Money gifted to the trust qualifies under the annual gift tax exclusion.

This money is a gift to the child, and, depending upon state law, the child has control of the gift at age 18 or 21. The assets are removed from the donor's estate, unless the giver dies while still the custodian of the account. In this case, the assets are taxed at the giver's bracket until the child reaches age 14; at that time the assets are taxed directly to the child's income. Investments can be selected to minimize or eliminate taxation. For example, individual stocks with no dividend might provide appreciation without generating a taxable event until the stock is sold after the child reaches age 14. Alternatively, low turnover, growth-oriented mutual funds, or tax-efficient mutual funds offer account growth with little or no taxable distributions.

[B] IRC Section 529 College Plans

IRC Section 529 Plans are for college education funding. These plans allow assets to grow tax-free if the money is used to pay for qualified higher education expenses. These costs include tuition, room and board, books, and some miscellaneous expenses. Penalties occur if the money is not used for qualified higher education expenses. Some states have what they call pre-paid tuition plans, and these plans vary dramatically from state to state. Contributions qualify for the $1000 annual exclusion, and the annual gift of $11,000 may be aggregated into one payment of $55,000. However, the right to use the $11,000 gift is eliminated for the subsequent four years. The maximum amount per beneficiary is $235,000. The account may be structured so that the proceeds will be part of the child's estate in contrast to the UTMA, where the account is included in the custodian's estate. Some states permit contributions to be income tax deductible.

[C] Medical Care and Tuition Payments

Medical care and tuition payments are either direct payments to a healthcare provider for the medical care of another person or direct payments of tuition to an educational institution for another person. These payments are not transfers for gift tax purposes. For instance, your parents may pay all the college tuition for their grandchildren free of gift tax. This is limited to tuition; room and board and other personal expenses are not included as free of gift tax.

[D] Intra-Family Loans

You may consider loaning money to your children or another family member. These loans are referred to as intra-family loans. These loans must respect the formality of any business arrangement, with a signed promissory note, a market interest rate, and term and amortization schedule. Without documentation, the loan will more than likely be judged to be a gift. If a gift is your intention, make the money a gift. The advantage of a loan is the ability to provide a favorable interest rate and repayment schedule. However, if you set the interest rate at zero or below the applicable federal rate, then you will be deemed to have made a gift. The forgone interest will be taxed to you as ordinary income. This consequence does not apply to loans of up to $10,000 for non-income producing property, or for loans of up to $100,000 if the borrower's net investment income is less than $1000.

Sometimes parents or grandparents will invest only in bank savings accounts or CDs. Some of these investments are yielding 2 to 5% percent. Loaning this money to a family member, who would be willing to pay 6 to 7%, would benefit everyone involved. In addition, if the lender is wealthy and does not necessarily need the interest income, this loan can be a good tax strategy. If a loan is placed for $50,000 at 6% interest, the interest cost is $3000 per year. The family member/lender may elect to waive the interest each year, which constitutes a gift. Since the gift amount is less than the $11,000 annual exclusion, no gift tax return needs to be filed.

Common Estate Planning Techniques

[A] By-Pass Trust

A Unified Credit Shelter Trust, called a Family Trust, By-Pass Trust, or an A-B Martial Trust, is established to receive property at death equal to the exclusion amount. Thus, the amount in the trust is carved out of your estate and does not go directly to your spouse but is still subject to estate taxes. However, the amount subject to taxes is offset by the unified credit, and hence no tax is due. Under EGTRRA, the increased exclusion amount, currently $1,000,000 and scheduled to increase to $3,500,000 in 2009, presents another planning issue. Smaller estates need to be careful, so that the majority of the estate does not end up in the credit shelter trust.

For example: Dr. Mary Garner, a medical practitioner with a $1.5 million estate, who died in 2003, would have $1,000,000 allocated to the credit shelter trusts, leaving only $500,000 outright to the surviving spouse. The surviving spouse might be surprised to find out that the majority of the estate is in trust and that the trust will be subject to withdrawal limitations. In 2004, when the exclusion amount increases to $1,500,000, the entire estate may go into trust, leaving nothing outright to the surviving spouse. These trusts need to contain provisions to allow the spouse access to the money under what is called an "ascertainable standard." This standard permits money to be paid out for HEMS.

This language has been approved by the IRS, and you should never tamper with it. If the trust document provides the spouse broader withdrawal power, the risk is that the assets in this trust could be included in Dr. Garner's estate, which defeats the purpose of carving out the trust assets in the first place. Upon your spouse's death, the assets in the trust are paid to your beneficiaries, commonly the children. If the beneficiaries are minors, provisions are included for their well-being until ultimate distribution, similar to the terms indicated previously under the testamentary trust.

A powerful effect of the trust is the potential for appreciation in trust value. If for example, the trust starts out at $1 million, and then seven years later the spouse dies, the trust might have appreciated to $2 million or more, and the appreciation is not subject to estate taxation. Drafting of trust language to allow for changing amounts and to accommodate different wording by Congress is important to avoid having to create new documents every time Congress decides to make changes. However, due to the far-reaching effects of EGTRRA, all estate plans and documents should be reviewed by estate planning lawyers.

[B] Unlimited Marital Deduction

Under the unlimited marital deduction, virtually all transfers to a spouse, whether made during lifetime or at death, are tax-free. However, there is a tax consequence for leaving your entire estate to your spouse. Leaving everything to your spouse does not utilize your exclusion amount, which is $1,000,000 in 2003. This has no effect after the first death, but when your spouse dies, the estate of the spouse will pay higher taxes. (See Exhibit 9–3.)

Exhibit 9–3 *Unlimited Marital Deduction Example*

Dr. Gary Welch died in 2003 and left his wife his entire estate, which amounted to $1,925,000. This approach qualifies for the unlimited marital deduction, so no estate tax is due.

However, if Mrs. Welch subsequently dies, her estate tax in the year 2003 would amount to $316,550. The simplified calculations are as follows:

Gross taxable estate	$1,925,000
Exclusion amount	(1,000,000)
Taxable estate	$925,000

From the tax tables, the tax on an estate of $925,000 is $316,550.

If Dr. Welch had created a credit shelter trust in his estate plan, calculations would look like this:

Gross taxable estate	$1,925,000
By-Pass Trust	(1,000,000)
Unlimited marital deduction	(925,000)
Taxable estate	$ 0

At Mrs. Welch's subsequent death, calculations would be as follows:

Gross taxable estate	$ 925,000
Exclusion amount	(925,000)
Taxable estate	$ 0

Mrs. Welch would include in her estate the amount she received by the unlimited marital deduction. While alive, she would have reasonable access to the $1,000,000 that was allocated to this trust in the husband's estate, but it will not be included in her estate.

At an estate amount of $925,000, the new estate tax due is $0 with the net savings of this approach calculated as follows:

First tax calculated	$316,550
New tax calculated	0
Savings with planning	$316,550

[C] The Qualified Terminal Interest Property Trust

A qualified terminal interest property (QTIP) trust was designed for those who have children from a prior marriage. The QTIP rules are complicated and deal with legal rights to assets and in whose estate the assets are titled. Congress has allowed a qualification on the normal terminal interest rules to provide for this situation. The result provides assets that qualify for the unlimited marital deduction, but a spouse does not control where the assets go upon the other spouse's death. The surviving spouse is entitled to the income generated from the trust for life and is also entitled to the use of tangible property such as the home and contents. In addition, QTIP trusts provide the surviving spouse a limited power to access principal for HEMS.

Advanced Estate Planning Concepts

All the following concepts provide family benefits in addition to potential estate tax savings. EGTRRA may eliminate the estate tax reasons for utilizing these concepts; however, giving to charity, transferring businesses to family members, and gifting large sums to children or grandchildren may still be part person financial planning desires.

[A] Charitable Giving

Charitable giving or transfers to charity, whether lifetime or at death, are supported by several provisions of the Internal Revenue Code that usually allows generous deductions on a contributors income tax, gift tax, and estate tax returns. Compelling as the tax benefits are, these contributions do not offset the loss of wealth to the family. Charitable giving must come from a sincere desire to support and provide for one or more charities with a true gift of the heart. Without this charitable intent, the best of strategies most likely will not have tax relief.

Selecting a specific asset to donate to a charity might provide additional value for you. Most medical professionals are familiar with the gift of cash. You write a check, the charity receives the money, and you receive an income tax deduction. However, the money gifted to the charity is out of your estate, and therefore this money will not grow and enhance the value of your estate. More importantly, the charity gets the current use of the cash.

In addition to cash, you may want to gift mutual fund shares or other assets that you deem appropriate. You could sell the stock or other assets, pay the capital gains, and give the charity the net cash. However, a better alternative is to gift the stock or other asset directly to the charity. You might actually deliver the stock certificate, or in today's electronic age, have the brokerage firm that holds the stock or fund deliver the shares directly to the charity's investment account. The value of your deduction is based upon the price of the stock the day it is delivered. There is no capital gains tax for the giver or the charity. Subsequently, the charity can sell the stock and receive the full value of the deductible gift.

Occasionally, we make investments that go down in value. In that case, it is best to sell the stock, realize the tax loss personally, and deliver cash to the charity.

[1] CHARITABLE REMAINDER TRUST

You may have a greatly appreciated asset with a low cost basis. If you sold the asset, you would have to pay capital gains on the difference between your cost basis and the selling price. Under current law, this amounts to a 20% tax liability. You may want to be free of the asset for various reasons such as the medical company stock is paying low dividends or the real estate is requiring extensive management and maintenance.

One common solution to this problem is a charitable remainder trust (CRT). Gifting low basis assets into a CRT accomplishes several goals.

- Capital gains are avoided on any subsequent sale;
- An income of 5 to 8% of the value of the asset can be generated. This percentage might be as high as 50%, but this high return requires special planning;
- A current income tax deduction is received for the gift. Because you are also receiving income back from the trust until you die, a complicated calculation is necessary to determine the value of the tax deduction. In general, the deduction will be worth 25 to 50% of the value of the asset; and
- After you and your spouse both die, you leave the value of the trust to your named charity or charities.

[2] NET INCOME CHARITABLE TRUST

A net income charitable trust is a variation on the CRT. Upon establishing the trust, you determine a percentage of the asset value that will be paid out each year, the same as you would do with a CRT. The trust may state that only income earned by the trust will be paid out. Trust expenses are deducted from the income before it is paid out. This technique allows you to contribute to a charitable trust and then have the trust invested in growth stocks (non-dividend paying stocks). If there is no income, there will be no payout. The contribution, which can be a one-time payment, or a series of payments over several years, will be partially tax-deductible. This creates a vehicle that can accumulate investments on a tax-deferred basis. Trading stock in the trust generates capital gains that pass through to you in the form of a K-1.

When you are ready to receive income, you change the investments to start generating an income. The trust owes you the percentage you originally chose for each year you did not receive income. Based upon trust accounting rules, part of your payout will be taxed at capital gains rates. Upon your retirement, the trust would likely owe a large payout, and if the trust earns the income, it can pay it to you.

If you are looking for a way to set aside additional money for retirement and have maximized your qualified plans, this approach has merit. The downside is that, when you die, the assets go to your favorite charity rather than to your family. If you begin making contributions and never get to the point of taking an income from the trust, the entire value of the charitable trust goes to the charitable beneficiary when you die.

[3] CHARITABLE LEAD TRUST

A charitable lead trust is a technique that allows you to provide a charity or charities current income (the lead), and at the end of a designated period, the money in the trust passes to designated family members. This is an excellent family wealth transfer technique, while providing an immediate benefit to designated charities. Any appreciation in trust assets passes to the family free of gift or estate taxes. As a result of the current low interest rate environment, this trust can be especially attractive because lower interest rates cause the gift or estate tax deduction to increase and cause the transfer tax value of the gift of the family interest to decrease.

[B] Intra-Family Sales

Family limited partnerships (FLPs) have become a popular planning tool for almost any business that is family owned and operated. This structure provides numerous advantages, including the following:

1. Parents can give away wealth and still retain control;
2. Transfers can be made at substantial discounts as compared to the value of underlying assets, thus saving unified credit and gift taxes;
3. Restrictions can be placed on transfers by children; and
4. There is some protection from creditors.

To establish an FLP, you must follow the requirements of your state's limited partnership act. The Uniform Limited Partnership Act requires that there is at least one general partner and one limited partner. The general partner retains all management control over the business or property, while the limited partner retains only an ownership interest. The limited partner has no voting power or authority over decision making. In addition, the limited partner cannot take assets from the partnership or otherwise force liquidation of the partnership before the term is up.

Example
Dr. Barrett Savely and his spouse have a medical office building valued at $5,000,000. He establishes an FLP with the limited partnership representing 95% of the total value of the building and the other 5% allocated to the general partnership interest. The limited partnership portion will be divided into 95 limited partnership units. Dr. Savely and his wife plan to transfer 20 units to each of their three children. Each unit represents 1% of the total building. At full value, 20% of $5,000,000 equals $1,000,000. Without the FLP, Dr. Savely would be giving a $1,000,000 gift to each child and paying the associated gift taxes. However, due to the structure of the FLP, the children are limited part-

ners, and therefore, they would not control the assets even though they own them. In addition, each child will have only a minority interest in the building. The IRS allows a valuation discount due to the minority ownership. That is, the children have an undivided interest in real property, which is neither easily partitioned nor readily marketable. Finally, their interest is non-controlling.

Giving up control over property is normally the biggest roadblock to an aggressive and substantial gifting strategy, but this lack of control is less of an issue with an FLP. The FLP is also advantageous in getting children involved in the business entity. Once they have a beneficial interest in the business, children probably will take a greater interest and role in how the entity works. Annual partnership meetings with all family members present should be established on a formal basis. Financial reports and a discussion about why the business performed well or poorly should be included. This meeting could be a good opportunity for a family retreat.

Income generated by the FLP must be distributed equally by partnership ownership. This can be a unique opportunity to shift income from the enterprise to your children's lower tax bracket. The adult might be in the 35% bracket while his or her children might be in the 15% bracket. Children under 14 will be subject to the "kiddie tax" for annual unearned income over $1500 (the 2002 amount), which is taxed at the adult's rate.

Additional concerns arise in today's society where divorce is commonplace. Language should be included in the FLP to identify a child's limited partnership interest as separate property and not subject to divorce negotiations. It would seem unlikely that the family would want to stay in business with one of the children's former spouse.

Gifts of partnership interests retain the cost basis. This is one of the disadvantages of gifting assets to your children. If the children were to sell an asset, then a potentially large capital gains tax would be incurred. Alternatively, if the children received the property at their parent's death, the children would receive a step-up in basis. Their cost basis would be the value of the property on the date they received it. Of course, if the children have no intention of ever selling the property, the low cost basis is a small price to pay to avoid a large estate tax payment.

FLPs also provide limited asset protection as long as the transfer was not a fraudulent transfer. By definition, this means that you did not transfer assets to an FLP to avoid a malpractice suit. It is also true that limited partnership units given several years before any financial difficulty should not be subject to attachment by creditors.

Costs to set up an FLP consist mainly of attorney's fees for drafting documents that establish the partnership. These fees range between $2000 to $10,000, depending on the nature of the business assets. The appraisal fees to establish the asset value and appropriate discounts may range from $5000 to $15,000. In addition, annual accounting fees will be charged for preparation of the partnership returns and K-1s that must be distributed to all partners. In most cases, a large gift is made when the FLP is established. Future gifting of limited partnership shares will require an updated appraisal to establish property value and applicable valuation discounts.

[C] The Donor Advised Funds

A variety of charitable organizations, mutual funds, and custodians like Charles Schwab and Fidelity offer donor advised funds. A gift to a donor advised fund is a gift for estate planning purposes that offers special opportunities for the donor to retain control over the money. The control is exercised by choosing which charity the funds are distributed to over time without any permanent commitments.

Example
Dr. Shela Brinker donates $50,000 to a donor advised fund. She takes a current year charitable income-tax deduction based upon the $50,000 gift in the year the gift is made. The donor advised fund invests the money aggressively to grow for the future, and Dr. Brinker selects a $50,000 gift every year to a different charity. Her one-time gift is spread to many worthy causes and gives her the opportunity to reevaluate her bequest every year. With good investment results, the original gift will ultimately supply much more money and be spread much further than the initial lump sum.

[D] Limited Liability Company

This device is more flexible than the S Corporation, which it replaces. A limited liability company (LLC) offers business owners the limited liability of a corporation with the pass-through tax advantages of a partnership. Each owner-investor is called a member, and an ownership share is called a member interest. Creating an LLC requires compliance with state statutes and avoidance of certain characteristics that the federal government looks for to try to tax the entity as a corporation. Proper legal advice will ensure pass-through taxation. LLCs also do not have the restrictions on stock ownership that S corporations have. S corporations are limited to one class of stock, whereas LLCs can have membership interests with different rights such as income, capital preferences, or voting. Trusts, foreign individuals, and other corporations can be members. Usually, LLCs are closely held. However, no restriction exists on the number of owners. Federal law limits the number of S Corporation shareholders to 75.

[E] Generation-Skipping Transfer Tax

When strategies are put in place that are deemed as tax avoidance, Congress acts to close the loopholes. One of these loopholes existed for more than 50 years. Prior to 1986 (laws were enacted in 1976, but repealed retroactively), it was possible to pass property to any generation without penalty. It was considered suitable to leave or give property to your grandchildren or great-grandchildren. Members of Congress finally realized that, with property passing down several generations, it could take 80 or even 100 years before that property would be subject to estate taxes. So, in 1986, the Generation-Skipping Transfer Tax (GSTT) was enacted to make up for the lost tax revenue when wealth is transferred and skips a generation.

The GSTT is assessed on amounts in excess of $1,120,000. The tax is in addition to normal taxes and is equal to the maximum federal estate tax rate in effect at the time of the gift. Currently, the maximum tax rate is 50%. Exhibit 9–4 is a simplistic representation of how the GSTT tax is calculated. This is a very complicated area, and the actual situation may greatly affect the actual calculation.

Exhibit 9–4 *Generation-Skipping Transfer Tax Example*

In 2003, Dr. Edwina Skye gave $1,600,000 to her grandchildren in a generation-skipping trust. The taxes were calculated as follows:

Gift	$1,600,000	Unified Credit	1,000,000
Taxable gift	600,000		

Taxes on 600,000 = $192,800 (37% tax bracket)

However, Dr. Skye exceeded the $1,120,000 GSTT limit by $480,000. This amount is taxed at 50% or an additional $240,000. The total tax owed would be $432,800.

Taxes were assessed at the marginal rate of 37%. The same asset at Dr. Syke's death would be taxed at 50%. Paying taxes in the 37% bracket is always preferable to paying taxes in the 50% bracket, assuming a taxable estate in excess of $2.5 million. In addition, the gift of $1,600,000 will grow for the benefit of the grandchildren. Seven years later, if it appreciated at 10% per year, the grandchildren would have in excess of $3 million dollars, and the appreciation would take place outside the estate. If this money were still in Dr. Skye's estate, $3 million would be taxed at 50%, for a total of $1.5 million.

Generation-skipping transfers do not always need to be along bloodlines. Congress created a methodology for those who may wish to gift or bequeath money to a younger person, who is not necessarily related. If the person or persons are more than 37.5 years younger than the giver, the GSTT applies.

[F] Private Annuities

Private annuities are an interesting version of the more familiar commercial annuities purchased from an insurance company. The difference is that in private annuities, the parties involved are usually family members. An asset is sold to a family member in exchange for an unsecured promise to provide a life annuity (income) to the seller. A life annuity is a predetermined annual income, which is paid for the lifetime of the recipient. Under a private annuity arrangement, the tax code has tables that determine the annual payment, which could be paid monthly. The giver's age and the current interest rate environment determine the payment. The federal government publishes various interest rates for calculations and planning purposes.

Example

Dr. Ian McCourt has shares in IBM worth $100,000 with a cost basis of $20,000. He plans to transfer the shares to his son, which will achieve an estate freeze on this asset. The payout is determined by the date Dr. McCourt enters into the private annuity arrangement. All future appreciation occurs in the son's estate. Dr. McCourt is 65 years old. Assuming that annuity interest rates are 6%, he will receive $10,600 for life, from his son. There is no gift taxation as long as, when the private annuity is established, Dr. McCourt has greater than 50% probability of living more than one year.

Use of a private annuity can be effective in transferring property when the seller is in poor health. There is no immediate income taxation upon creation of the annuity. However, recognition of the gain occurs as each payment is received. Taxation is under IRC Section 72, which deals with annuity payments.

At Dr. McCourt's age of 65, life expectancy using the tables is 20 years. The annual taxation would break out this way:

$1,000 is return of principle and income tax-free

$4,000 is capital gain

$5,600 is ordinary income

$10,600 Total annual income

If Dr. McCourt lives longer than 20 years, then all payments are ordinary income.

The annuity is for life-only, so upon the death of Dr. McCourt, no value of the IBM stock will be included in his estate. If he dies after two years, his estate would have received two $10,600 payments and his son would receive the balance tax-free.

Dr. McCourt's plan has three disadvantages:

1. There is no security, and this lack of security might increase the risk that the son will not pay the required amount;

2. No part of the annuity payment is tax deductible for the son; and

3. If Dr. McCourt lives a long time, his son has made a bad deal.

[G] Installment Sale

An installment sale is an alternative to the private annuity. Here you sell property to a family member (or outsider) for an installment note in which your family member agrees to pay principal and interest based on a fair market rate. Recognition of the gain can be in the year of sale or spread out over the term of the sale. The major differences between the installment sale and private annuity are:

1. The installment note has a security interest;

2. Upon your death, the remaining unpaid balance of the installment note (calculated on a present value basis) is an asset of the estate and subject to estate taxes; and

3. The sale of stocks and bonds does not qualify for installment reporting. Hence, the installment sale is used best for the sale of real estate or tangible personal property.

An estate freeze is accomplished, similar to that of the private annuity, as post-sale appreciation will benefit the new owner.

[H] Self-Canceling Installment Notes

Self-canceling installment notes (SCINs) are a provision that may be added to the installment note specifying that no further payments will be made after your death. Inclusion of this provision requires an adjustment to the structure of the installment note in the form of a higher annual payment. The benefit of the SCIN provision is that the value of the note is not included in the estate, which is the big financial problem with the installment note sale. However, the balance of the gain is reflected on the estate income tax return. This technique is aggressive and has only limited appeal.

[I] Grantor Retained Trusts

EGTRRA has virtually eliminated the need for this concept under the assumption that estate taxes will be repealed in 2010. The only benefit that could be derived from a grantor retained trust would be if the term of the trust ends before you die, and you die before 2010.

The primary motive for planning with grantor-retained trusts is to freeze the value of appreciating property without creating a gift. A variety of rules must be followed carefully, but with a properly drafted document, it can be an excellent planning technique.

Often the home is used in grantor retained trust planning because it has likely increased in value and might be a significant portion of an estate. In a qualified personal residence trust (QPRT), an owner removes a home from an estate, passes it and its future appreciation to the children, and the owner continues to live there. The trust agreement is drafted, and the house is deeded to the trust. At that point, a gift has been made to the children. This is a gift of a *future interest* and does not qualify for the $11,000 annual exclusion. In fact, the calculation of the amount of the gift is complicated, because the owner retains the right to live in the home, and the children will not receive full rights to the home until sometime in the future. In effect, the gifted value of the house is the remaining value after the grantor has used it for a period of years.

This situation should not to be confused with appraised value in the future. Several factors are used to determine the gifted value including:

- The grantor's life expectancy as determined by the mortality tables;
- The current interest rate environment as controlled by rates published by the IRS; and
- The number of years before the home is turned over to the children.

The last factor could have varied results. The grantor, who wants to live in the house for a long time, may pick 20 years. Unfortunately, if the grantor dies before the 20 years have elapsed, the house is brought back into the estate. This is not necessarily bad, but it defeats the purpose of removing the house from the estate. A common choice of term is 10 years. If the grantor is 75 years old, has a home valued at $500,000, and the current interest rate is 6%, the remainder interest of the home is $130,500. Gift taxes will be paid on this amount or the grantor can use the unified credit. In this case, the grantor has accomplished the following:

1. Your home is left out of the estate, as long as the grantor lives 10 more years;
2. The future appreciation of the home is left out of the estate;
3. The grantor may live in your house as long as he wishes; and
4. The grantor has used a small part of the unified credit or paid a small gift tax.

There is a minor catch to the QPRT. At the end of the term, the children own the home, and the grantor has to rent it back from them. However, this could be a useful way to help the children meet their financial needs.

New Implications of EGTRRA 2001

[A] Cost Basis

Under current law, when someone dies, the value of his or her property receives a stepped-up basis. That is, the new tax cost basis of all assets is equal to their date of death value. Upon repeal of estate taxes, in 2010, the stepped-up basis is replaced with what is called carryover basis. Basically, carryover basis means that assets inherited retain the cost basis of the decedent; or more simply stated, assets are no more stepped-up basis. Fortunately, there are two exceptions:

- Basis increase of $1.3 million per decedent may be allocated to any beneficiary, and
- $3 million additional basis allocation may be allocated to a surviving spouse.

Hence, a family can achieve the equivalent of the old stepped-up basis to the extent of $4.3 million. Although we are several years away from the introduction of this piece of legislation, maintaining good records on the cost basis of assets is becoming more important.

[B] Gift Tax

The exemption for gift taxes remains at $1,000,000 even thought the applicable exclusion amount increases to a maximum of $3.5 million. In 2010, when the estate tax is repealed, the maximum rate for gifting is set at 35%.

[C] Credit for State Death Taxes

Currently, most states allow their death tax to match the amount allowed by the federal government. Therefore, the state tax is a reduction from the federal estate tax, and no additional tax is required. However, EGTRRA has introduced a phaseout of the 100% state tax credit. Below is the new schedule:

Credit for State Death Taxes
    50% in 2003
    25% in 2004
2005 - credit repealed and replaced with full deduction

When to Review Your Estate Plan

Your personal and financial life is constantly changing. Significant changes always necessitate the need to review your life. However, a few key events trigger the need to review your estate plan. If any of the events below have occurred since you reviewed your estate plan, see a competent advisor to help you achieve your goals.

1. Birth of a child or grandchild;
2. Death of a spouse, beneficiary, guardian, trustee, or personal representative;
3. Your marriage or your children's marriage;
4. Divorce (Review beneficiary designations and asset titling);
5. A move out of state. An estate is settled under the laws of the state in which the decedent resided. Certain provisions of a will that are valid in one state may not be in another.
6. Change in estate value. A large increase or decrease in the size of an estate may greatly affect some of the strategies that were implemented;
7. Changes in business. Starting, buying, or selling a medical practice or other business has an impact on your estate. The addition or death of a business owner will cause a review; and
8. Tax law changes. EGTRRA 2001 and JGTRRA 2003 dramatically changed the way we plan for estate taxes. It is important to note that only planning for estate taxes has been affected. Estate planning involves much more than just the motivation to reduce or eliminate taxes.

Estate planning will ensure that:

- your family is taken care of financially;
- your children have the opportunity to go to college;
- your debts are paid;
- your charitable issues are achieved;
- you have made provisions for a needy child; and
- you have made proper selection of a guardian.

Please do not use the new law as an excuse to delay planning your estate.

Chapter 10

Selecting Financial Advisors Wisely

Choosing Consultants . . .
Realizing the Value
of Time

Daniel B. Moisand

Your representative owes you, not his industry only, but his judgment; and he betrays instead of serving you if he sacrifices it to your opinion.

Sir Edmund Burke

S ince a financial planning solution in one area can cause a new set of problems in another, most physicians realize the need for a financial team comprised of at least a financial planner, lawyer, management consultant, and accountant. Bankers, wealth managers, and real estate and life insurance agents are also important to include on your team. At different times, each member of the team will properly assume the role of "quarterback"; however, this discussion will emphasize the selection of financial planner.

Risky Ways to Select Advisors

While the merits of hiring the right advisor are obvious, the healthcare professional fears that hiring the wrong one can be devastating. However, this fear should not preclude getting the assistance necessary to manage your financial affairs. Take caution when following these sources of advice.

[A] Family and Friends

While family members and friends have a good handle on the essential elements of trust and rapport, the competence of the advice is most often the issue. The life and money handling experiences of those who are close to you certainly have value, but their experiences are not necessarily relevant to your unique goals and circumstances.

[B] The Media

A few years ago, the dominant media force in consumer-oriented financial matters was the print medium. Magazines and newsletters have continued to proliferate with the bear market. More recently, however, television has supplanted print. Nothing is wrong with watching television shows that cover the markets or with subscribing to a consumer finance magazine. However, be wary of the quality and applicability of information disseminated by the media.

[C] The Internet

One of the most terrifying sources of misinformation on the Internet is chat rooms because the entire interaction is clouded by anonymity. Some people enter chat rooms due to the comfort of anonymity when asking a question. However, there may be a danger in an anonymous answer. It is also essential to understand the level of accountability of your source of information.

[D] Discount and On-Line Brokerages

Many studies show that active trading garners inferior results when compared to a longer term buy and hold type of strategy. One of the most publicized studies was conducted recently by a University of California at Davis team led by Dr. Terrance Odean. The study examined the actual trading activity of thousands of self-directed accounts at a major discount brokerage over a six-year period. The results showed that regardless of trading level, most of the self-directed accounts underperformed the market and showed that the higher the number of trades, the worse the result.

Cost savings is the first reason that discounters appeal to investors. Second, discounters appeal to a person's ego and need to feel in control. Everyone wants to feel like a smart investor. Having a professional advisor should not result in insecure feelings, but should instead empower the investor. Advice to sell has a far greater impact on investment results than the cost of a purchase trade as long as the level of trading is kept at a prudent level.

A final reason people turn to discount and on-line brokerages is to avoid sales pressure. Unlike the stereotypical stockbroker, no one calls the investor to push a particular stock. Instead, sales pressure is created within the mind of the investor. By maintaining a steady flow of information about stocks and the markets to the account holders, on-line brokerages keep these issues in the forefront of the investor's mind. The probability that the investor will act on the information and execute a trade increases. Ironically, this focus on trading is one of the conflicts investors are trying to avoid by fleeing a traditional full-service broker.

[E] Traditional Full-Service Brokers

It used to be that the only way to get investments and investment information was through paying commissions to a traditional broker. Then in May 1975, the brokerage industry went through significant deregulation allowing for the discounting of commissions. Full-service brokerage businesses responded by emphasizing the scope of their services, such as research and advice, to compete with discounters. The demand for research and advice has continued to grow, even though research information is now readily available through many sources. The full-service brokerage firms continue to thrive despite their poor performance in analyzing tech stocks, as shown in the Enron, WorldCom, HealthSouth, InfoSpace, Lucent, and Global Grossing debacles.

Now, more obvious in hindsight, is the conflict between the investment banking department, the research department, and the retail brokerage operations in a firm. Even brokerage companies with no proprietary funds to sell may grapple with this issue. In this conflict, research is pressured to say favorable things about a particular company's stock by the investment bankers in the hope of obtaining more of that company's business. When a firm brings a company public, odds are great that a "strong buy" rating will come with the Initial Public Offering (IPO). Of course, the lesson remains—consider the source of the information.

Traditional brokers have a somewhat higher standard of accountability than on-line firms. If the healthcare professional buys the stock of a company that goes bankrupt through an on-line broker, he or she has little recourse. After all, buying the stock was your choice. If a full-service broker recommended the stock to you, the broker will have to defend the recommendation.

The Right Advisors

First, characteristics desired must be identified. Second, information must be gathered about prospective advisors and analyzed in that light. Then selection of an advisor must be made, and the results monitored relative to the original goals. Lots of little things make for a good working relationship with professionals in any field. They all seem to fall into three main categories:

[A] Competency

A hallmark of competence is good experience. At a minimum, five to ten years of relevant advising experience should be a requirement. The people most qualified to evaluate an advisor's competence are other advisors. Once a few names of advisors have been accumulated, the healthcare professional should ask these advisors whom they would recommend from outside their own firm. It is hoped that some of the same names will come up more than once.

There are several organizations that a healthcare professional can contact to assemble additional names and gather information regarding each candidate's abilities. Some are membership organizations, others grant professional designations and other credentials, and others organizations do both. The result is a ridiculous array of alphabet soup. Naturally, some credentials are more appropriate than others. The following is a brief list of the most significant organizations.

- **CFP Board of Standards.** This is a professional regulatory body that owns and licenses the Certified Financial Planner designation and the mark CFP. Licensing is a strictly voluntary activity. Telephone: (303) 830-7500; Web site: www.CFP-Board.org

- **FPA—Financial Planning Association.** This group, officially formed January 1, 2000, is the result of the merger between the Institute of Certified Financial Planners and the International Association of Financial Planning. This merger created a central organization for the financial planning professional. Telephone: (800) 322-4237; Web site: www.fpanet.org

- **iMBA—Institute of Medical Business Advisors.** The Institute of Medical Business Advisors, Inc, is the certifying body that establishes, monitors, and tests advisors for the corpus of knowledge it deems necessary for its charter-holders to perform integrated financial planning, business consulting, and healthcare practice management activities. iMBA confers the designation CMP on professionals who successfully complete four comprehensive written examinations and subscribe to iMBA continuing education and ethics attestation requirements. Since CMPs interface with the nation's medical, business, and financial communities, iMBA adheres to the *Health on the Net Foundation* "Code of Conduct" (HONcode) to address issues of Internet reliability and information credibility.

- **AIMR—The Association for Investment Management Research.** This group confers the title Charted Financial Analyst to those who have passed the three-part examination or the self-administered standards of professional practice examination. Telephone: (800) 247-8132; Web site: www. aimr.org

- **SFSP—Society of Financial Service Professionals.** This is the new name for the former American Society for CLU and ChFC, both popular designations in the insurance community. Accordingly, its membership is mainly insurance agents, and the organization is tied to The American College in Bryn Mawr, Pennsylvania, that grants these designations. Holding a designation is not a requirement for membership. Telephone: (610) 526-2500; Web site: www.financialpro.org

- **IMCA—The Investment Management Consultants Association.** Members must pass the Certified Investment Management Analyst course. Telephone: (800) 599-9462; Web site: www.imca.org

- **AICPA—American Institute of Certified Public Accountants.** The primary membership organization for CPAs. Telephone: (212) 596-6200; Web site: www.aicpa.org
- **NAPFA—National Association of Personal Financial Advisors.** A membership organization comprised entirely of fee-only financial advisors. Telephone: (888) 333-6659; Web site: www.napfa.org

[B] Credentials

Among these organizations the healthcare professional will find advisors with many different kinds of designations. A discussion of the merits of the most common and meaningful credentials follows along with their definitions:

- **CFP—Certified Financial Planner.** Currently, to become licensed to use this title, a financial advisor must complete an accredited educational course, subscribe to a code of ethics, show three years of full-time experience in addition to an undergraduate degree, and pass a comprehensive two-day, 10-hour examination. Maintaining the license requires adherence to the Code of Ethics and Practice Standards and fulfillment of the continuing education requirements. The continuing education requirement includes an ethics course once every two years.
- **CMP—**The Certified Medical Planner (CMP) title is a rigorous designation, first chartered in 1995 and awarded to advisors who have successfully completed all requirements put forth by the Institute of Medical Business Advisors, Inc. (www.MedicalBusinessAdvisors.com). It is an ideal compliment to the CFP designation for those financial planners interested in the burgeoning healthcare advisory space. To obtain the CMP certification, the following qualifications must be met.
- **Education.** An advisor must successfully complete a 24-course, 12-month long intensive curriculum of accredited didactic material to sit for *i*MBA's Board's Certification Examination. Medical practice management topics include healthcare economics, managed care reimbursement systems, setting up a medical office, physician unions, sexual harassment and workplace violence issues, insurance coding and billing, capitation econometrics, office expense models, marketing, advertising, sales and branding, cash flow analysis, Medicare and Medicaid, HMOs, PPMCs, MSAs, IPAs, HIPAA, OSHA, ASCs, APCs, activity based medical office costing, practice financial benchmarking, medical business decision making, fixed rate reimbursement, office compliance and medical credentialing, and others. Financial planning topics include estate planning, retirement planning, investment management, tax planning, employee benefits, risk management, insurance, medical practice valuation and sales, office succession planning, and others.
- **Examination.** An advisor must pass the *i*MBA Board Certification Examination, which tests the knowledge of a multitude of integrated medical practice management and financial planning topics. Thereafter, a CMP must obtain continuing

education credit every two years in the body of knowledge pertaining to core integrated principles.

- **Experience.** A CMP must acquire at least five years of management consulting and/or financial planning-related experience with physicians and medical professionals.

- **Ethics.** An advisor, who is a CFP, must voluntarily adhere to the *i*MBA Board's Code of Ethics and Confidentiality. This voluntary decision empowers the *i*MBA Board to take action if a CMP holder violates the code of ethics. Such violations could lead to disciplinary action, including the permanent revocation of the right to use the CMP marks. http://www.fpanet.org/journal/BetweenTheIssues/Links/UsefulLinks/pracmgtlinks.cfm

- **CFA—Chartered Financial Analyst.** Currently, to become licensed to use the marks, an advisor must pass three six-hour exams sequentially, have at least three years of full-time experience, and agree to adhere to a professional code of conduct. The CFA designation has been historically considered a highly specialized program focused on the principles of investment management and financial analysis. However, in recent years an increased number of CFAs have begun serving high net worth individuals.

- **ChFC—Chartered Financial Consultant.** This a broad educational credential granted by The American College in Bryn Mawr, Pennsylvania, which covers most aspects of financial planning. The majority of holders of the title are in the insurance business.

- **CLU—Chartered Life Underwriter.** This pre-eminent life insurance credential is also conferred by the American College.

- **CPA/PFSS—Personal Financial Specialist.** The PFS designation was obtained by CPAs, but the mark itself may soon be discontinued due to lack of interest in the title.

- **MBA—Masters of Business Administration.** An academic degree that might have some bearing on an advisor's ability to render sound personal financial advice. Typically, the MBA with a subspecialty in finance, insurance, securities, or accounting would add considerable value to the financial planning experience, particularly when coupled with the CFP designation. A concentration in marketing, technology, human resources, or project management would not add value. Certainly, the MBA with a specific medical practice management background, perhaps as a former physician, or in conjunction with financial subdisciplines, or with Masters in Healthcare Administration, would be very helpful in managing or consulting for a busy medical group, especially in the present environment of managed care. Similarly, the Master's of Science in Financial Services is an academic degree that integrates the financial planning disciplines.

- **RIA—Registered Investment Advisor.** This is not a designation but instead a registration with either a state securities office or the U.S. Securities and Exchange Commission. Obtaining this title requires advisor to file a form called an ADV and to submit a modest fee. There are no experience requirements or exams.

- **Fee-Only.** This term describes a method of compensation. It is supposed to be used to describe a service, an advisor, and/or a firm. In this form of compensation, no portion of the compensation is derived based upon the purchase or sale of a financial product either directly or indirectly. Essentially, advisors do not receive commissions. To establish a fee-only practice, an advisor needs only to register as an investment advisor as described above. Accordingly, fee-only compensation has no relevance to the competence of the advisor in question whatsoever.

The Certified Financial Planner

The financial planning world has no magic license that shows the world that a particular advisor is a good one. Beyond those qualifications already mentioned, there is a plethora of designations that are narrow in scope, irrelevant to most family's needs, or thin on quality content. These include Certified Employee Benefits Specialist, Registered Health Underwriter, Certified Investment Management Counselor, Certified Mutual Fund Consultant, Certified Insurance Counselor, and a host of others. However, by compiling enough information, the healthcare professional can get an adequate handle on an advisor's competence.

However, by far the most important designation, without medical practice management information, is Certified Financial Planner (CFP). A CFP licensee has demonstrated a reasonable level of competence as a generalist, in such diverse areas as personal and corporate income taxation; life, health, annuity, and property-casualty insurance needs analysis; investments, asset allocation, modern portfolio theory and risk-adjusted rates of return analysis; retirement needs with qualified and nonqualified plan types; and estate planning. Additional medical practice management specificity comes then with the CMP designation. Below, is a list of questions to ask a prospective advisor regarding competence and a discussion of what to do with the answers:

1. How long have you been rendering personal financial advice? (Minimum is five years.)

2. What is your educational and professional background? (A niche medical background might be best for physicians.)

3. What are your credentials? (No single credential will be the deciding factor but given the alignment behind CFP, finding the reasons that an advisor uses to defend not having the marks may be interesting. Some advisors do not have the title because of the considerable time involved in obtaining it, while others are hesitant to add another layer of regulation to their practices. The former may be a fine choice, but avoid the latter.)

4. Do you have any teaching or writing experience? (Ideally, the advisor will have taught some courses and have authored several articles published in the legitimate media.)

5. Do you have an area of specialization? (Obviously, the area of specialization should have some relevance to the situation at hand; medical professionals.)

6. What services do you provide? (Some advisors offer only financial planning, while others focus on investment management. Most, however, provide both services by delivering financial and investment management advice. To a degree, this makes sense. However, it makes even more sense to add medical practice management advice into the mix. A great plan poorly executed with a faulty portfolio will likely fail. Likewise, a well-managed portfolio or medical practice will not get far if other areas of the financial picture are flawed.)

7. When do you buy and when do you sell? (This investment question needs to be answered decisively and clearly. Initially, the answer may be vague but after some pressing, the advisor should be able to outline a clear investment approach, though in general terms. Lack of such an approach might indicate a lack of discipline.)

8. May I see a sample plan? (This should be provided with no reference to the real client. Lack of such confidentiality is impermissible. The work sample should give clues whether the advisor can communicate clearly in writings.)

9. Can I get client and professional references? (Again, confidentiality may yield a "No" to this question. Some advisors have lined up a few clients and allied professionals who have agreed to be used as references. Expect those individuals to rave about the advisor. How the advisor answers the question is the more useful information gleaned.)

10. Do you take possession of my funds? (The answer here should be no. Custody of stocks, bonds, funds, and cash should be with a brokerage firm. Never make a check out or sign over any asset to an individual—only a financial institution. The only exception to this should be the payment of fees.)

11. Will anyone else be working with me? (It is fine, even to be desired, that the advisor be more than a one-person operation. At the least, there should be one more staff member. What is important here is that the healthcare professional understands who will be responsible for what and that an understudy is not the prime source of advice.)

12. Do you personally research the products you recommend? (Yes is the correct answer to start with, but a better response is that the advisor uses several sources of research to complement his or her efforts.)

Investment Policy Statement

If investment management is one of the primary services desired by a medical professional, a shortcut question should be asked a financial advisor: "May I see an Investment Policy Statement?" If the advisor's answer is "What is that?" move on. An Investment Policy Statement (IPS) is simply a document that covers the policies, practices, and procedures for managing an investment portfolio. A well-written IPS helps ensure long-term adherence to an investment strategy. A healthcare professional should not retain an advisor who does not make the creation of a proper IPS a central component of the planning process. Specifically a physician should look for several items:

- Summary of client circumstances, resources, and obstacles;
- Objectives and time horizon;
- Risk tolerance and expected performance;
- Limitations on holdings and other restrictions;
- Recommended asset allocation;
- Monitoring and review process;
- A rebalancing discipline;
- Selection criteria for securities to be used; and
- Endorsement by advisor and client.

The physician should pay little attention to asset allocation recommendations or securities mentioned because they might apply only to this particular client. The language in the document should be specific to the client. For instance, "to maintain withdrawals of $6,000 per month after-tax, adjusted for inflation through 2025" is far superior to "maintain an adequate income."

The "Financial Advisors"

Most financial advisors are regulated by the National Association of Securities Dealers (NASD). The NASD is a self-regulatory agency comprised of the nation's brokerage firms. Upon completion of a required exam, the NASD will issue a variety of licenses. The most common are the Series 6, 7, and 24.

The Series 6 is essentially a license to sell packaged products, specifically mutual funds. This license is most commonly held by insurance agents and bank representatives. Series 6 is considered a relatively moderate test. Holding such a license allows the holder to collect commission income through his or her member firm.

The Series 7 exam is more robust and includes issues relating to individual securities such as stocks, bonds, and limited partnership interests. The pass rate is significantly lower than for the Series 6 license. The probable reason for this lower pass rate could be is the extensive questioning on margin and options—topics that most advisors are unfamiliar with prior to entering the securities business.

The Series 24 exam covers issues of compliance and supervision and is required of Branch Managers of brokerage firms. All registered representatives (the proper name for a broker) must be supervised by someone with a Series 24 license, also known as a principal's license.

Checking the background of a registered representative, a branch manager, or a member firm is done easily through NASD Regulation, Inc. (NASDR). NASDR maintains the central registration depository (CRD). The CRD can be checked for a description of disclosable events by phone or by Internet. The healthcare professional should request information on an advisor's firm as well as the individual advisor. The situation of a reputable advisor at a disreputable firm has its own set of potentially dangerous implications.

[A] Questions to Ask a Potential Advisor

Here are some important questions to ask to assess ethics.

1. HOW DO YOU GET PAID?

All compensation methods are flawed in some manner. Vague is bad. Specifically, in cases where two advisors are compared, one may properly disclose costs, and the other may not. To the unaware investor, the disclosing advisor may seem egregiously expensive. The advisor who fails to disclose may even encourage this line of thinking. In reality, the seemingly "more expensive" advisor is a better choice, and the advisor who fails to disclose should be avoided because of egregious compensation.

2. DO YOU RECEIVE COMPENSATION FOR REFERING ME TO OTHERS?

No is the desired answer. A good advisor hands the investor off to the team member best suited to serve the client. There is no reason to cloud the picture with referral fees. A higher degree of confidence results when no such payments are made.

3. WHAT IS YOUR PROFESSIONAL AND EDUCATIONAL BACKGROUND?

This question was also listed in the discussion regarding competence. For ethical purposes, the answer should be referenced to the written disclosure materials.

4. HAVE YOU EVER HAD COMPLAINTS FILED AGAINST YOU?

No is the best answer, but a yes might be acceptable. Sometimes things simply do not work the way they were designed. You want to hear the advisor's side of the story. Just because a client complained does not mean there really was a problem. Similarly, medical professionals frequently run across patients who do not necessarily repeat another medical professional's advice in a completely accurate manner. A bad medical outcome could result in a lawsuit about whether the physician acted improperly. Financial advisor clients sometimes act in the same way. Obviously, if the advisor says there have been no complaints, and the state securities office or CRD says something else, you should avoid a relationship with the advisor.

5. HOW HAVE THESE COMPLAINTS BEEN RESOLVED, AND WHAT HAS BEEN DONE TO PREVENT SUCH PROBLEMS IN THE FUTURE?

Even the best advisors can have a promising relationship go sour. Some clients say all the right things, but believe they are entitled to investments that only rise in value. Find out what lessons the advisor learned from the experience.

6. WHO DO I SEND MONEY TO, AND HOW WILL I KEEP TRACK OF MY INVESTMENTS?

An investor can send a check or stock certificate to an advisor's office, but you should never ever make a check payable or sign over a certificate to the advisor for anything other than fees. Checks for investments and certificates should be made out directly to the custodian, usually a brokerage firm. You should receive confirmations and statements directly from the custodian.

7. HOW DO I COMPLAIN OR SEEK RESTITUTION?

The answer depends on the nature of the complaint. Make the advisor walk you through the process for a simple issue and for a more serious matter. If a check did not get deposited in a timely manner, the advisor should take responsibility for assuring that the office procedures are more efficient. A serious dispute is typically sent to arbitration or mediation instead of to the courts.

8. HOW CAN I TERMINATE OUR RELATIONSHIP, AND WHAT COSTS ARE INVOLVED?

Ideally, an investor should be able to discontinue the relationship whenever deemed necessary without incurring more than nominal costs associated with transfering accounts to a new advisor. A truly excellent advisor is willing to be held accountable and earn his fees each year—year after year. The advisor should assume the risks of a bad relationship. If an investor is asked to agree to significant exit fees, the risk rests with the client. Most proprietary products will not transfer ownership, and therefore, they must be liquidated. The client would be responsible for any resulting tax liability and liquidation fees. This lack of transferability is another negative involved with proprietary products.

9. ARE YOU SUBJECT TO NO-COMPETE RESTRICTIONS IN YOUR CONTRACT WITH YOUR FIRM?

Most major full-service brokerage firms require a no-compete clause. By contract, the firm takes the position that they "own" the client. After all, the broker is a registered representative. If an advisor has to deal with such, he or she will probably be barred from contacting clients if he or she goes to another firm. Clearly, this interferes with the advisor/client relationship. It is a good idea that if an advisor does change firms, one does not merely give him a free pass. He or she should be able to communicate how it will benefit his clients.

10. WHO IS YOUR E&O CARRIER, AND HOW MUCH E&O COVERAGE DO YOU CARRY?

Errors and omissions (E&O) is an advisor's version of malpractice insurance. A smart independent advisor carries this coverage not only for protection but to somewhat level the playing field with the traditional brokerage firms. One of the drawing cards of the big firms is a perception of deep pockets if a problem arises. Adequate E&O protects all parties by ensuring that a mistake will not ruin either the advisor or the client.

11. WHAT HAPPENS WHEN YOU RETIRE, OR IF YOU DIE OR BECOME DISABLED WHEN WORKING WITH ME?

A plan should be in place for each of these circumstances.

[B] Compensation Issues

A raging debate is taking place within the financial planning industry regarding which type of compensation is best. Those who receive some level of commission income have taken offense at the assertion made by others that commission-based advisors are somehow less ethical than fee-only advisors. The fee-only crowd has been accused of being holier-than-thou zealots. All the while, both sides of the debate ignore that how an advisor gets paid is completely irrelevant to whether good advice is being rendered. It makes no more sense to pay a fee for bad advice than to pay a commission for bad advice.

[1] COMMISSIONS

Commission income has been a cornerstone of the financial advice business for decades. The primary advantage of paying on a commission basis is that this investor is paying on an as-needed basis. For instance, when a trade is executed, the commission is charged to facilitate the order. The rate paid will be higher than that charged strictly for execution, and a portion of that additional charge goes to the advisor for helping decide whether to execute that trade.

One of the significant disadvantages of this approach is the focus on transactions. The advisor, working in this capacity as a commissioned broker, has the financial incentive to either encourage a client to trade or to spend his time with a client who will. It is not uncommon for the best course of action to be no action at all. This compensation arrangement does not give the advisor financial incentive to render that advice.

In addition to the transactional bias, a common issue is the use of incentive commissions to generate sales of particular products. Traditionally, this occurs with the development of in-house or proprietary products. Rather than pressuring the broker directly through paychecks, the management team is given the incentive to push in-house products.

The discount brokerage firms are not immune to the proprietary product push. Instead of proactively pushing their products, these firms will put competing products at a disadvantage within their system. The in-house variety can be purchased without a transaction fee, while a competitor's version requires a purchase fee. Despite admonitions to review the prospectus before investing, the on-line firm is betting that the investor will elect the proprietary fund to save the transaction fee even though it typically carries a higher management fee.

[2] FEES

The three most common forms of fees are hourly, flat rate, and an annual percentage of assets or net worth. All eliminate the aforementioned problems but create their own potential conflicts of interest, though the conflicts inherent in a commissioned approach do not arise in a fee-only model.

[a] Hourly Rate

The hourly rate method has a similar advantage to a commissioned approach, namely you only pay when you want to. This is an appropriate way to address a project need or to get a second opinion or spot check of a particular situation. The obvious conflict arises from the incentive to take as much time as possible to do the work requested or to create work and the resulting billable hours. A more subtle issue is that this method of compensation may not promote good communication between planner and client. At times, a client may be hesitant to call with questions or requests for fear of a large bill. Conversely, the advisor may be hesitant to bill for time spent for fear of aggravating a client.

More problematic is the reliance on the client to determine when work is needed. Here, the client engages the advisor when the client perceives the need. The client may not be the best person to determine a need exists. Typically, the client will feel compelled to hire an advisor when there is a problem. This diminishes a significant benefit to hiring help—preventing problems from occurring in the first place.

[b] Flat Rate

The flat fee approach has many of the same advantages of the hourly method when applied to a project or second opinion situation. Again, however, ongoing attention is not available. Annual retainers can address this flaw to a degree, so that ongoing service can be obtained.

Two important downsides exist to this approach. First, in contrast to the hourly rate, with a flat fee, the incentive is to complete the work as quickly as possible and cut corners. The second downside comes into play with the delivery of investment management services. Performance has no bearing on the rewards to the advisor. This fact has led to payment of a percentage of assets as the most prevalent method of compensation.

[c] Annual Percentage of Assets

In theory, the percentage of assets method is the fairest when providing investment management services. Under this method, the advisor retains a percentage of the assets managed. With all the fee approaches, it makes no difference which particular securities are selected, and the compensation to the advisor is the same. The percentage method, however, changes this slightly since the result of the selection does impact compensation. If the investments appreciate, the advisor gets a raise; if the value declines, the advisor gets a pay cut. Share the gain, share the pain. Many believe this is a better alignment of advisor and client interests.

The most significant conflict arises from what to do with a particular sum of money. For instance, an advisor has an incentive to recommend that an inheritance be invested rather than applied to outstanding debts or to start a business. The advisor gets paid only if he or she manages the money.

[d] Percentage of Net Worth

Basing the fee on net worth instead of assets managed, the retirement of debt, for instance, does not alter the fee as much because the effect on net worth is substantially equal to putting the funds in an investment account. This method is not free of conflict and shares two issues with the percentage of assets.

Both methods work against the use of funds on a current basis. The more a household spends or gives to family or charity, the less there is to manage and the lower the net worth.

To a degree, the incentive to be more aggressive increases the value of an investment account or a household net worth. By being a bold investor, a good result can increase the assets managed, and the resulting fee income to the advisor. This potential problem is mitigated to a point by that being bold in the investment world does not always pay off. Stocks in particular do go down substantially from time to time, and this event translates to a pay cut.

[3] FEES AND COMMISSIONS (FEE-BASED)

Finally, a large percentage of practitioners use a combination of fees and commissions. Often the term fee-based is used for this practice. The varieties of fee-based arrangements are vast. Investment accounts may be managed on a fee-only basis, yet the planner may receive a commission for placing an insurance policy. Here we have a fee-only service (investment) but a fee-based planner. Confusing? It can be, but a good advisor will make clear disclosures to reduce your confusion. Another common version of this practice is to charge a fee for the preparation of a financial plan with the implementation of the plan resulting in commissions. Also, some states allow a fee-offset where a fee is determined and any implementation commissions are rebated to the client up to cost of the fee. Excess commissions are retained by the advisor.

The most common ethical abuse of the term fee-only, however, is manifested in investment management. A client pays an annual fee, but the brokerage firm does not inform him or her that some investments, usually mutual funds, will also pay 12b-1 fees (trail commissions) to the brokerage firm. Despite the commission, the arrangement is presented as fee-only. Anytime the advisor has an NASD license, the investor should ask and be told what role 12b-1s will play in the relationship.

[C] For Whom Does an Advisor Work?

According to securities regulations, a registered representative (stockbroker) owes his allegiance to his firm. This is true regardless of whether the broker is an employee or an independent contractor. This is also true of insurance agents.

A registered investment advisor, on the other hand, has a fiduciary responsibility to his clients. This is a high standard under the law. It is the same standard applied to trustees. A fee-only financial planner would be regulated as a registered investment advisor by his state or the Securities and Exchange Commission (SEC) depending on the amount of assets managed, would be acting in a fiduciary capacity, and would not fall under the auspices of the NASD. This situation sounds fairly simple and explains to a degree the growth of the fee-only approach. The problem, of course, is that for all the benefits of the fee-only approach both to the client and to the planner, fee-only still has no bearing on the quality of advice.

To complicate matters for the physician-consumer, a great number of advisors are dually registered as investment advisors and as representatives of an NASD member firm and fall under both regulatory structures. Therefore, it is possible for an advisor to deal with several regulatory bodies during the course of the day.

Advisor Rapport

Life is too short to do business with people you do not like. Accordingly, most people do business with people whom they like. A good rapport fosters a more pleasant experience. All things being equal, people want to enjoy themselves. However, there is more to rapport than having a good time together. This is after all a business relationship.

[A] Family Matters

There are many risks in the markets, but the most damaging risks to a family's security tend to arise from the family structure. As a result, a good advisor will inquire about a client's parents and how they have impacted or will impact the client financially. Are they healthy? Do they have the long-term means to care for themselves? Is an inheritance to be factored into the plan? Do the parents know the client is expecting an inheritance and that he or she is including it in his or her family's planning? Another source of interference, if you will, comes from children. Are they self-sufficient and likely to remain so? How does the client feel about his or her children's spouses? To what extent will the client need to help them financially for educational expenses? What about any grandchildren? To what extent does the client wish to benefit the children and grandchildren at his or her death or during the client's lifetime?

[B] Retirement

One of the major goals in life is retirement. Doctor clients are retiring earlier today because of managed care. If the client is not currently retired, when will that occur? To what will the client be retiring? How will the currently busy client cope with not having a job? For many the transition can be devastating if they are not prepared.

There is a fairly well known story about a physician (call him Dr. Smith), who several months after retiring was found dead. He had committed suicide. The note in effect said that a few months ago he was Dr. Smith but now he was merely Mr. Smith and not worth anything. Most retired medical professionals do not approach this extreme, of course, but most would also be well served to have some vision about what they will be doing after retirement.

[C] Form ADV—The Essential Document

By law, financial planners must provide you with a form ADV Part II or a brochure that covers the same information. Even if a brochure is provided, ask for the ADV. While it is acceptable, even desirable, for the brochure to be easier to read than the ADV, the ADV is filed with the appropriate state or the SEC. If the brochure reads more like a slick sales brochure or the information in the brochure glosses over the items on the ADV to a high degree, consider eliminating the advisor from consideration.

The ADV will describe the advisor's background and employment history, including any prior disciplinary issues. It will describe the ownership of the firm and outline how the firm and advisor are compensated. Any referral arrangements will be described. If an advisor has an interest in any of the investments to be recommended, it must be listed as well as the fee schedule. A description of the types of investments recommended and the types of research information that is used are included.

A review of the ADV should result in an alignment of the advisor's statements during the interview and the information filed with the regulators. If there is a clear discrepancy, choose another advisor. If the information is unclear, discuss the issue with the advisor.

Referrals

No financial planner can or should try to be all things to all people. In fact, a Certified Financial Planner has an ethical mandate to avoid areas in which he or she is not qualified to practice. Thus, at some point, a referral is in order. The most common referrals are to lawyers and accountants.

[A] Lawyers

Just about everyone in America knows a lawyer joke. However, an individual's legal needs are no laughing matter. Clients who retain outstanding legal counsel are amply rewarded. Those who hire an attorney without sufficient experience routinely pay dearly. Fortunately, the process for selecting an attorney is identical to selecting a financial advisor. The characteristics desired must be identified. Information must be gathered about prospective attorneys and an analysis performed on this information in light of what is wanted. Then a selection of an attorney must be made and the results monitored relative to the original goals. The sources of information and specific questions will differ somewhat. However, the same basic considerations—competence, ethics, and rapport apply.

[B] Accountants

Hiring an accountant for tax preparation, however, is only the tip of the iceberg. Today's accounting firms provide a number of valuable services to small business owners that range from bookkeeping to payroll to retirement plan administration and record-keeping to business consulting. Some firms have even entered the financial planning business.

Certified Public Accountants (CPAs) are not the only ones doing tax work these days. Enrolled agents and tax attorneys can handle returns and represent a client before the Internal Revenue Service. A medical professional in private practice is probably better off with a CPA firm. If the only service required is a 1040, an enrolled agent may serve. Ask the same questions as you would a potential financial planner or attorney.

The Role of Teamwork

The major players have been assembled. Will the team function together well enough to win the game? Getting all the players on your advisory team to function well together may seem like a daunting task. In reality, this should be the easiest part of the process, and you can take steps to help foster an appropriate level of teamwork.

1. Designate the quarterback. Only the Certified Financial Planner has the professional mandate to coordinate a client's financial affairs from the big picture perspective. The planner, however, must hand the ball off to the other players to get the job done properly. The Certified Medical Planner is ideal for medical managerial matters or as a second opinion or back-up mechanism for the CFP.

2. Make sure the players know about each other.

3. Define everyone's role and communicate your wishes to all the advisors.

4. Meet as a group on occasion.

5. Tolerate no arguments. The advisors should not debate the issues at hand in the client's presence for any personal matters.

6. Make the advisors clarify confusing issues. Sometimes a client, in a way that is not entirely accurate, may make a misrepresentation to a team member. If a clarification is desired, elicit the help of the remaining team members.

7. Always remember, and remind the advisory team if necessary, that the physician client is the boss.

[A] The Banker

Doctors carry notoriously heavy debt loads. Beyond the costs of a medical education are substantial costs for equipping and staffing a practice. Unfortunately, bankers are very conservative by nature. It may be increasingly difficult to borrow money, especially since modern bankers know that a medical degree is no longer the guarantee of a steady, high income that it was in the past. As more than one banker has often opined, "We don't usually loan money to doctors who really need it." Bankers also may not have a clue about what the practitioner can do to compete better in the managed care arena. Bankers have a good concept of local community politics, however, for those who are not familiar with a practice venue. They frequently can provide references to more focused advisors, and bankers generally do not charge a fee for their advice. The more business the healthcare professional does with a bank, the better the terms that can be obtained.

[B] The Real Estate Agent

Real estate agents come in all sorts of forms. A good one shortens the real estate sales cycle immensely. The choice of agent should consider both the size of the real estate agency and the experience of the agent. The agent desired is not a part-timer, nor someone with only a couple of year's experience. Further, the agent should be focused on the price range and type of property in question. A good agent asks lots of questions to try to keep buyers from looking at properties that do not match the client's needs.

When choosing a listing agent, the size and number of listings an agency maintains is an important consideration—the more the better. When interviewing an agent to sell a piece of property, ask about how the agent obtains and handles potential buyers. The essential question is would someone buy from this person?

[C] The Property and Casualty Agent

A good property and casualty (P&C) agent is needed to protect your home and business. The P&C agent should have an array of carriers with which the business can be placed. One should not hesitate to place different types of coverages with different insurers. Most insurance companies will offer a discount if you place multiple coverages with them. However, this plan may not be as beneficial as insuring each need with a specialist.

[D] The Life Insurance Agent

Nobody likes to pay life and disability insurance premiums. Inadequate coverage, however, can completely devastate a family by quickly wiping out a lifetime of asset accumulation. Buying and maintaining the right amount and type of coverage from solid insurance companies at a reasonable price eliminates these risks in a very efficient manner. Unfortunately, an essential and relatively simple concept like this risk transfer has evolved into an area that makes many people queasy. The saying goes "insurance is sold not bought." The easiest way to handle this issue is to get consensus agreement from the core team members to the amount and types of coverage. Proposals should include what is known as a ledger statement.

The Cost of Hiring an Advisor

Hourly rates vary widely. In less affluent areas of the country, rates will start at about $100/hour. In other circumstances, or for the complicated situations of some medical professionals, rates can go as high as several hundred dollars per hour. Flat rates for producing a plan for a family with relatively simple needs should be a few hundred dollars. Households with estates in excess of $2 million should expect to pay about $1500 at a minimum.

For investment management services provided on a percentage of assets basis, the fee structures also vary widely. To gain a perspective on these costs, the average annual expenses of a mutual fund in the United States is around 1.5%.

It is true that it does not necessarily take as much effort to manage $5,000,000 as it does $500,000—just add another zero to each transaction. Accordingly the fee should not be 10 times as great. It is also true that the tax consequences and the planner's liability exposure can be significantly greater with a larger portfolio, thus warranting a higher fee in terms of the actual dollars. As a result, the healthcare professional should expect that the percentage charged should decline as the amount of assets increases. For instance, one half percent of $5,000,000 results in a $25,000 fee. Whereas 1% of $500,000 yields a $5000 fee. The $5 million portfolio is 10 times as large but results in a fee only five times as large as the half-million dollar portfolio.

If individual securities are used, there will be no fund expenses. However, it takes a higher level of research and attention to effectively manage a portfolio of individual securities. Therefore, add one-quarter percent to the maximums listed above. Following these guidelines in conjunction with the other criteria for selecting a planner will result in a total cost that is no more than slightly above "average" for smaller portfolios, yet yield the ongoing receipt of high quality advice and service. For larger portfolios, the value increases to your benefit.

Acknowledgments

Rachel Pentin-Maki, RN, MHA, and Hope Rachel Hetico, RN, MHA, for the *i*MBA and CMP information in this chapter.

Index